TO STAND AND FIGHT

Martha Biondi

TO STAND AND FIGHT

The Struggle for Civil Rights in
Postwar New York City

HARVARD UNIVERSITY PRESS

Cambridge, Massachusetts, and London, England   2003

Library of Congress Cataloging-in-Publication Data

Biondi, Martha.
    To stand and fight : the struggle for civil rights in postwar New York City / Martha Biondi.
        p. cm.
    Includes bibliographical references (p.) and index.
    ISBN 0-674-01060-4 (alk. paper)
    1. African Americans—Civil rights—New York (State)—New York—History—20th century.
    2. Civil rights movements—New York (State)—New York—History—20th century.
    3. New York (N.Y.)—Race relations.   4. New York (N.Y.)—History—1898–1951.   I. Title.

F128.9.N4B56 2003
323'.09747'109045—dc21   2002191261

Contents

Note on Usage

In this book, "Black" is capitalized because it is used much as "Negro" or "African American" is used. As a proper noun, it reflects the self-naming and self-identification of a people whose national or ethnic origins have been obscured by a history of capture and enslavement. Similarly, "white" is not capitalized because historically it has been deployed as a signifier of social domination and privilege, rather than as an indicator of ethnic or national origin.

Prologue:
The Rise of the Struggle for Negro Rights

The *New York Age* announced in a January editorial that "1946 can be the most epoch making year in the history of our race. It can be the year when the Negro reaches first class citizenship in this country." The struggle that would eventually topple legal racial segregation in the United States began during World War II. The war sparked the largest internal migration in U.S. history, the emergence of a permanent international spotlight on Jim Crow, and perhaps most important, the biggest jump in Black earnings since emancipation. Coming after the utter destitution of the Depression, these changes created the conditions at war's end for a shift in Black consciousness and the rise of a grassroots equal rights struggle propelled by a determination never to return to prewar conditions. In 1945, New York City had the largest urban Black population in the world. Harlem—mecca of the New Negro, home of the 1920s cultural renaissance, and headquarters of the nation's largest Black mass movement, Marcus Garvey's Universal Negro Improvement Association—was also a launching pad for the U.S. civil rights movement. "The Negro people," Adam Clayton Powell Jr., the first Black Congressman from Harlem, insisted in 1945, "will be satisfied with nothing short of complete equality—political, economic, educational, religious and social."[1]

Powell's prediction came true: African Americans turned the war against fascism into a war against white supremacy at home. Over the next decade, Black New Yorkers fought for better jobs, an end to police brutality, access to new housing, representation in government, and college education for their children. Their battles against unexpectedly overt and lawful racial barriers pushed New York City and state to pass landmark antidiscrimination laws in employment, housing, public accommodations, and education—laws that inspired similar legislation in dozens of other states and became models

1

for national legislation. Their story reveals a striking degree of formalized racial discrimination and segregation in public accommodations, transportation, housing, employment, and schools that was doubtless not unique to
New York City. It reminds us that *Plessy v. Ferguson,* the 1896 U.S. Supreme
Court decision that gave federal sanction to state and local racial segregation, shaped public policy nationally, not just regionally.

By the time Rosa Parks sparked the Montgomery bus boycott in 1955, the
civil rights struggle in New York was already ten years old and had endured
a volatile rise and fall. African Americans in the North were less vulnerable
to racial violence than those in the South, and had greater resources and allies to wage a grassroots struggle against Jim Crow. But the dramatic differences in culture, political economy, demographics, and the nature of white
supremacy between New York and the deep South made the movement
in New York significantly different from the movement in the South. The
"struggle for Negro rights" in postwar New York should be seen less as a pre-
cursor to the southern civil rights movement than as a backdrop to the Black
Power era in the North. It forged the modern urban Black political agenda,
which included demands from criminal justice reform to affirmative action
that would shape Black advocacy for the rest of the century and beyond. But
the movement encountered powerful resistance that was, in turn, strengthened by the postwar anticommunist crusade.

The movement's defeats had profound consequences. In 1964, the year
that Congress passed the Civil Rights Act, a riot erupted in Harlem after a
white police officer shot an unarmed Black youth. The eruption of Black
frustration and anger in the North, while seemingly at odds with the tri-
umph of the southern civil rights movement, had a distinct historical backdrop. When Harlem leader Malcolm X declared in his 1964 speech "The Ballot or the Bullet" that "the government has failed the Negro," he reflected a
growing belief that liberal Democratic administrations in postwar New York,
and indeed across the nation, had failed to stem the spread of residential and
school segregation, had seemingly condoned police brutality, and had failed
to enforce state and local antidiscrimination laws. "There's more segregation
now," he asserted, "than there was in 1954." Yet the mass migration of
Black southerners to the North and West did not have to lead to greater racial segregation or culminate in riots. African American leaders in postwar
New York articulated an alternative vision—a plan of inclusive urbanization.
They advanced a range of proposals that force us to question the conventional wisdom that entrenched and institutionalized segregation was, or is,

impermeable to change. The story of Black New York's bold push to launch the "second Reconstruction" begins in World War II.[2]

World War II was a watershed for the northern civil rights movement. The migration of African Americans to the North and West in the 1940s far surpassed the Great Migration of the World War I era. The restrictive immigration laws of 1924 had disrupted the immigrant supply of factory labor, creating opportunities for groups of Americans previously excluded from industrial employment. "Strangely enough," observed a New York minister, "the chief gainers have been women and Negroes." In the 1940s, in a demographic transformation that created new opportunities and leverage for activism, African Americans went from being a mostly rural and agricultural population to a mostly urban and industrial one. Black and white southerners flocked to cities to fill jobs in the aircraft, shipbuilding, steel, munitions, explosives, and auto industries. Between 1940 and 1950 the Black population of New York rose 62 percent; Detroit, 100 percent; Chicago, 80 percent; Los Angeles, 116 percent; Cleveland, 76 percent; and Oakland, California, 292 percent. The Black population of New York City rose from 458,000 in 1940 to 700,000 in 1948. By 1950 the Black population in the New York metropolitan area was 1,012,883. During the same period the city's white population rose only 3 percent; unlike many other northern cities, New York did not experience a significant in-migration of southern whites.[3]

In New York, racial discrimination in employment was lawful and pervasive. According to the New York State War Council, 90 percent of defense plants in the state in 1940 refused to hire Blacks—only 142 of the 29,215 employees in ten war plants in the New York City region were Black. The three major aircraft companies in the region, Republic Aviation and Grumman Engineering, both in Long Island, and the Brewster Aeronautical Corporation in Queens, all refused to hire African American workers. The R. J. Hoy Company "in the heart of Harlem," which manufactured parts for anti-aircraft guns, refused to hire Black workers. Sperry Gyroscope, the recipient of $50 million in government contracts in 1941, refused to hire Black workers at its five plants in Brooklyn and Long Island.[4]

Despite the labor shortage, employers in war production industries resisted changing their hiring practices. Protests against discrimination in employment had begun in earnest during the Great Depression when African Americans in Harlem had organized boycotts and fought for the right to work in their own community. On the eve of World War II, Adam Clayton Powell and other activists were beginning to take the fight for Black jobs beyond Harlem, and the struggle grew rapidly as defense production commenced. African American leaders exerted pressure on state and federal government officials to compel the employment of Black workers. In March 1941, Governor Herbert Lehman appointed a Committee on Discrimination in Employment to investigate discrimination in war industries. Three months later, in the biggest civil rights victory of the war, President Franklin D. Roosevelt issued Executive Order 8802 banning racial discrimination in hiring by defense contractors and creating the Fair Employment Practices Committee (FEPC) to enforce it. Roosevelt signed the order on June 25, 1941, in order to prevent a mass march on Washington by Black workers called by A. Philip Randolph, leader of the Brotherhood of Sleeping Car Porters. In relying on collective Black power as much as on appeals to rights, the threatened March on Washington foreshadowed many protest strategies of the postwar era. The creation of the FEPC, too, launched a new era in the struggle for racial justice. The wartime FEPC made the federal government the enforcer of racial equality for the first time since Reconstruction; making the FEPC permanent became the single most important legislative goal of the postwar civil rights movement.[5]

The Communist left in New York City played a significant role in the burgeoning civil rights struggle, especially in the fight for jobs. In order to understand the nature of this role, as well as the subsequent effect of McCarthyism, it is vital to appreciate that the civil rights struggle began in an era when the left was a formidable force in reform circles. Communist parties were formed around the world after the Russian Revolution in 1917, including in the United States where a tiny Communist Party (CP) attracted working-class radicals, immigrants, and intellectuals. The CP tended to view white supremacy as a constitutive component of capitalist domination in the United States, and argued, in turn, that antiracism should be an explicit component of the anticapitalist struggle. This stance, among many others, distinguished the CP from the Socialist Party, which saw the race struggle as a divisive distraction from the primary task of unifying workers.

The CP's stance reflected Soviet leader V. I. Lenin's doctrine in support of national minorities in the Soviet Union, but it was also shaped by the ideas of Black radicals, such as the African Blood Brotherhood's fusion of socialism and Black Nationalism, and the early Pan-Africanism of W. E. B. Du Bois. In 1928 the U.S. Communist Party adopted the slogan "self-determination in the Black Belt" to signal its commitment to Black liberation alongside working-class organizing. Self-determination included support for a Black nation in the southern Black Belt, desegregation in the North and West, and full racial equality in the United States. This simultaneous embrace of Black nationalism and integrationism may appear contradictory, but it resonated with deeply rooted, and often interlocking, African American struggles for political sovereignty, cultural nationalism, and civil rights.[6]

Howard "Stretch" Johnson, a former Cotton Club dancer who was a CP organizer from 1938 to 1956 and later a sociology professor, was drawn to the party's thesis that Black Americans constituted a nation. The Communists, he said, "related it to imperialism on a world scale, so that I saw Black nationhood in the context of it being part of an entire world system, and there was an identification between Blacks in the U.S., Blacks in South America, Browns in South America, Chinese in China." Since the colonial era, African Americans had sought foreign allies in the struggle for freedom in the United States. They gained political aid, leverage, or sanctuary from Native American nations, Mexico, Japan, the Soviet Union, Cuba, France, England, China, and Ghana, among others. The Communist Party's internationalism attracted African American radicals seeking to become part of global anti-imperialist networks and struggles. In his 1932 trip to the Soviet Union, Langston Hughes judged it more as a person of color than as an American, appreciating Uzbekistan as "a *colored* land moving into an orbit hitherto reserved for whites."

During the Depression, the CP's influence grew as it led grassroots fights in many cities for relief, public works, and emergency housing. The party applied pressure on the New Deal, helping to win passage of unemployment compensation and Social Security laws, but the place of its greatest influence in the 1930s and 1940s was in the Congress of Industrial Organizations (CIO), a labor federation that it helped to organize. The party exerted influence in a broad range of "people's organizations," such as the American Youth Congress, Council on African Affairs, National Negro Congress, and dozens of others. Communists were the most influential leaders in these so-called front groups, but they did not necessarily constitute the majority of members nor solely determine the agenda. Along with a dozen or so left-led trade unions, these organizations constituted the heart of a dynamic political and cultural world in New York.

The CP was part of the Communist International (Comintern), which took political direction from Moscow. From 1935 until the Nazi-Soviet Pact in 1939, the Comintern followed a Popular Front strategy of collaborating with western democracies and forging reformist coalitions in order to stop the spread of fascism. When the Soviet Union became an ally in the war against Germany, U.S. Communists became major supporters of the Roosevelt administration, even dissolving the CP into the Communist Political Association. After the war, the CP reconstituted itself and resumed vigorous criticism of the U.S. government, particularly its foreign policy; but even after the rise of the Cold War, the Communist left continued to work within the U.S. political system for a variety of domestic reforms. The CP's antiracist organizing changed in accordance with these shifts between radicalism and reform, although the party never abandoned the 1928 Black Belt thesis: the idea that Black southerners historically constituted a nation. These shifts were alternately energizing and debilitating for the Communist movement, and inspired, among some, distrust about the reliability of the left. Nevertheless, many African American radicals continued to use the left's vast resources and infrastructure in the fight against white supremacy until the CP's demise during the McCarthy era.

While most histories of the left place its heyday in the 1930s and construct a postwar narrative of decline, the Communist left continued to play a significant role in racial justice struggles well into the 1950s. In the 1940s, the increase in Black unionization and urbanization gave the Black left a larger base. In many respects, the New York civil rights movement was a "Negro People's Front," or Black Popular Front, in that it brought together ideologically diverse groups—such as the Elks, fraternities, women's clubs, churches, and the Urban League, on the one hand, and left-wing Black activists, trade unionists, and politicians, on the other—around the goal of eradicating racial discrimination and segregation. The left's appeal to African Americans flowed not from its advocacy of a Soviet-style government, but from its rejection of gradualism and its willingness to engage in an uncompromising struggle for equal rights. Its most visible voice in Harlem was Benjamin Davis, a Georgia-born, Harvard-educated lawyer who joined the Communist Party during the Depression and rose to its national leadership body. When Adam Clayton Powell Jr. left the New York City Council in 1943 to run for Congress, Davis won his seat and held it until 1949.[7]

Most African American community leaders who worked with Communist-supported organizations did so to further an antiracist agenda. The CP was the only major American political party that formally opposed racial segregation; it devoted considerable resources to an array of anti-discrimination campaigns, and it created a rare space for Black leadership in a multiracial institution. As future Detroit mayor Coleman Young put it,

"The reality of the day was that anyone who took an active interest in the plight of Black people was naturally drawn to the Communist Party—not as a member necessarily, but at least as a friend and ally, owing to the fact that the Communists historically had been out front in the struggle for civil rights." Moreover, despite the CP's reputation for doctrinal rigidity, a range of nationalists, trade unionists, and cultural radicals passed through it. Audley "Queen Mother" Moore, who joined the party in the Depression and quit in 1950, remained a Garveyite the entire time, but she felt that nationalists "weren't so much about organizing as talking from a street corner," while "the Communists organized the mass struggles." As Adam Clayton Powell later put it somewhat defensively, but accurately enough, "We used the Communists more than they used us."[8]

Nonetheless, this portrait of the Communist Party and its orbit does not mean that every civil rights activist or Black worker found it appealing. On the contrary, many leading African American liberals, such as Walter White and Roy Wilkins of the NAACP national staff and the socialist A. Philip Randolph, opposed working with Communists for genuine ideological reasons that did not mirror the anticommunism of white supremacists or political conservatives. Similarly, while the Popular Front devoted considerable resources to the fight against racial inequality, many of its adherents likely found the degree of ideological discipline and conformity required for CP membership too onerous and constricting. For many leftists, being part of an international struggle embodied by a powerful nation was a major appeal, but for many other Americans, it was a major weakness.

The struggle for Black jobs in war production led to a potent convergence between the prowar and antidiscrimination stances of the left. In 1941 a coalition of labor, civil rights, and left-wing groups helped to desegregate the Sperry Gyroscope (now part of the Unisys Corporation) plant on Long Island. The left-wing National Negro Congress (NNC), along with members of the Brooklyn NAACP, Urban League, YMCA, Communist Party, and area churches, created the Brooklyn Joint Committee on Employment, picketed the plant, and appealed to Sperry management to hire Black workers. In addition, Local 1224 of the Communist-led United Electrical, Radio, and Machine Workers of America, CIO (UE) made fair employment practices an issue in its successful organizing drive. The company initially ignored the protest, but Roosevelt's executive order helped push the door open. As the NNC put it, "A nation preparing to fight fascism began to polish up its armor of democracy at home, to tighten the seams, to caulk the cracks." By 1944 hundreds of African Americans were working at Sperry, two-thirds were in skilled or semi-skilled jobs, three were engineers, one was a foreman, and of three hundred shop stewards, twenty-two were Black. Sperry's president became a wartime convert to racial brotherhood, even giving a speech at the NAACP's 1944 national convention in Chicago on the benefits of industrial integration. In line with the Popular Front effort to frame activism along prowar lines, the left's wartime rhetoric, like mainstream civil rights rhetoric, cast racial justice in the national interest. A National Negro Congress pamphlet declared that Sperry's fair employment policy "benefited itself, the community, and the nation."[9]

The National Maritime Union (NMU), a left-led CIO union, was associated with one of the most famous examples of integration during the war. Along with Eleanor Roosevelt and Paul Robeson, the NMU's Black vice-president, Ferdinand Smith, successfully lobbied the Merchant Marine to appoint its first Black captain, Hugh Mulzac. After Jackie Robinson, Mulzac was the most famous symbol of integration in the 1940s, but is today virtually forgotten. The Queens resident and Caribbean-born Mulzac had a skipper's license but racial discrimination had kept him in menial positions and denied him the opportunity to practice his craft. Mulzac sought opportunities in Marcus Garvey's Black Star Steamship line and then threw himself into the battle to organize the National Maritime Union during the Depression. During the war, Mulzac and his multiracial crew made twenty-two round trips, transported 18,000 troops, shot down two enemy aircraft, and did not sustain a single accident, loss of cargo, or human casualty. Mulzac's ship was often hailed by advocates of military desegregation to prove that mixed crews were capable of outstanding wartime performance. Mulzac became a civil rights activist, Popular Front idol, and Black war hero.[10]

Although A. Philip Randolph is the best known Black labor leader of this era, during the 1940s, many young Black trade unionists took up the fight against discrimination. Ferdinand Smith of the NMU, Ewart Guinier of the United Public Workers Union, Morris Doswell of Local 65 of the Wholesale and Warehouse Workers Union, and Charles Collins of Local 6 of the Hotel and Restaurant Employees Union organized the Negro Labor Victory Committee (NLVC), with the support of the Communist Party and many AFL and CIO unions, in order to press for more jobs for Blacks in defense employment. These men were, or would become, influential leaders of the labor movement and Black liberation struggles. The NLVC's goals—"to throw

Captain Hugh Mulzac at a rally in the 1940s, most likely a Negro Freedom Rally.

open the doors of industry to all Americans," to encourage Black workers to join unions, to end the exclusion of Black workers from trade unions with color bars, to win a permanent FEPC, and "to make the fight for complete equality for Negroes an integral part of the program of the organized labor movement"—reflect its ambition to make the labor movement an instrument of Black advancement. According to Charles Collins, the NLVC placed 15,000 African American men and women in war-related industries.[11]

Exemplifying the Black Popular Front was the collaboration between Adam Clayton Powell and the NLVC. Powell, the most influential political leader in Harlem, was pastor of Abyssinian Baptist Church and a city councilman until he won election to Congress from Harlem in 1944. He also copublished the left-wing Harlem weekly, the *People's Voice*. His political club, the People's Committee, along with the NLVC, organized the Negro Freedom Rallies, gala pageants at Madison Square Garden that were held in 1943, 1944, and 1945. The Negro Freedom Rallies, along with a Save FEPC Rally that A. Philip Randolph sponsored in 1946, were major political events in New York City that both marked, and helped to launch, a new stage in the African American struggle for equality. They brought the struggle downtown and put it on the city's broad cultural landscape. To the June 1943 rally, Powell declared, "This is our hour of opportunities. It will not come again in our lifetime."[12]

At the Negro Freedom Rally in June 1945, an audience of twenty thousand heard impassioned political speeches along with a Broadway salute and performances by Langston Hughes, Paul Robeson, and Josh White. The sponsoring committee exemplified the Black liberal-left alliance: Powell, Mary McLeod Bethune of the National Council of Negro Women, Edward Lewis of the Urban League of Greater New York, Republican City Council member Stanley Isaacs, Brooklyn left-wing community activist Ada B. Jackson, Herbert T. Miller of the all-Black Carlton YMCA in Brooklyn, Brooklyn Baptist minister Thomas Harten, left-wing labor leaders Ferdinand Smith and Charles Collins, Paul Robeson, City Councilman Ben Davis, and the actor Canada Lee. They called for an end to segregation "in all phases of American life." The Negro Freedom Rallies sponsored yearly contests for Miss Negro Victory Worker that paid "tribute to the important and patriotic role being played in the national war effort by Negro womanhood," and were intended to strengthen Black women's morale and support for the war effort. Miss Negro Victory Worker was to be "selected on the basis of her work record, plus other activities furthering the war effort." The 1945 winner was Ruth Hemmings, a machine winder at the United Transformer Company in Brooklyn and a member of UE Local 430.[13]

The stance of civil rights leaders toward the war encouraged the emergence of mass civil rights protest in the 1940s. African American leaders were determined not to repeat the experience of World War I, when W. E. B. Du Bois's famous call to close ranks and loyal Black military service were rewarded with postwar pogroms and no end to segregation. The federal government's own research confirmed high levels of Black frustration and anger over segregated conditions in addition to widespread admiration for the Japanese as people of color challenging arrogant Euro-American power. Nation of Islam leader Elijah Muhammad, for example, as well as James Lawson, an organizer of the student sit-ins in Nashville in 1960, both served time in jail rather than answer the draft. The slogan "Double V," signifying victory against fascism abroad and racism at home, was emblazoned on the masthead of the *Pittsburgh Courier* and symbolized a deeply felt grassroots Black sensibility toward the war. World heavyweight boxing champion Joe Louis, who had symbolized the United States in his defeat of the German Max Schmelling in 1938, headlined many NAACP rallies in the war years while serving in the army, illustrating the African American commitment to the "Double V" campaign. During the war, Black leaders had unprecedented radio airtime in New York, and they vigorously projected civil rights messages to the broad listening audience. "Today's struggle of the Negro has become part of the world-wide struggle against fascism," Paul Robeson declared in one broadcast, making the two fights one and the same. Robeson, one of the most famous and admired American performers in the world, was moving away from a primary identification as an artist toward a life as a full-time activist.[14]

Wartime racial violence forced northern authorities to address racial conditions. The August 1943 shooting of a Black soldier in uniform by a white police officer in Harlem set off a riot that left six dead, hundreds injured and arrested, and many stores looted and destroyed. In contrast to the white riot earlier that summer in Detroit, the Harlem riot, with Black people protesting police violence and looting white-owned retail stores, prefigured urban uprisings of the 1960s. The riot and the threat of future violence increased antidiscrimination organizing in the city and inspired a new public discourse around such themes as "group unity" and "race relations." Like they did after the 1935 riot in Harlem, activists seized on the outbreak of violence to press government leaders for reforms.

Two thousand labor, religious, fraternal, government, and civil rights leaders gathered at Hunter College a month after the riot for a Citizens' Emergency Conference for Interracial Unity. Dorothy Funn, a young African American schoolteacher, wartime activist, and Communist, organized the event. NAACP executive secretary Walter White gave the keynote address and Mayor Fiorello La Guardia also spoke. The group issued a call for "the systematic elimination of discrimination, segregation, and unequal opportunities in all forms." Their goal was to make civil rights an unofficial war aim. "United Nations are dedicated to the making of a democratic world," Funn wrote; "United Americans must dedicate themselves to the same objective on the home front, for this is an integral part of the whole war effort." The conference identified a range of goals that would be taken up by the postwar civil rights movement, including Black representation in the Board of Education and the Police Department; an end to discrimination by such huge private employers as insurance companies and department stores; Black consumer rights; the end of residential segregation; and the abolition of military segregation.[15]

In 1944 Mayor La Guardia created the Mayor's Committee on Unity (MCU)—the forerunner of the city's Human Rights Commission. Lacking autonomy, sufficient staff, and enforcement powers, the MCU would function as a go-between in civil rights battles, with an eye toward protecting the mayor. According to the American Council on Race Relations—which itself was created as a result of the wartime racial violence—by 1950 there were 1,350 groups in the United States concerned with improving "intergroup relations."[16]

By 1944 Black protest and the demand for workers had transformed the labor market. One and a half million Black men and women worked in war industries, making up 7.5 percent of defense workers. Despite the FEPC's fear of inflaming the politically powerful white South, and its preference for negotiation over regulation, it set an important precedent of state involvement in eradicating racial barriers. Black leaders hoped that it portended a new New Deal, one that would use governmental powers to promote racial justice. In five years, the FEPC settled nearly five thousand cases, including forty racially motivated strikes and threatened strikes. But racial disparities in income persisted. In early 1945, national per capita income for whites was $1,140, while for Blacks it was $779. In New York City in 1943, median Black income was $949.[17]

A Census Bureau survey prepared at the request of the Urban League of Greater New York in 1947 underscored how deeply the war had reconfigured the Black working class. Black New Yorkers were moving out of personal service occupations in "record numbers." There was a marked shift among employed Black women away from domestic labor and into clerical, sales, and semi-skilled jobs: 64 percent were domestics in 1940, while only 36 percent were so employed in 1947. There was also a sharp drop in service work for men, from 40 percent so employed in 1940 to 23 percent in 1947. From 1940 to 1944 the proportion of Black workers in skilled or semi-skilled positions had doubled. The biggest shift was out of personal service and into semi-skilled jobs. Breaking the glass ceiling of skilled jobs would be a major goal after the war.[18]

The mass Black migration to the North was strengthening Black voices in the Democratic Party's liberal wing. A civil rights legislative agenda crystallized in the war years that centered around winning passage of fair employment, anti–poll tax, and antilynching laws. African American activists also sought to expand New Deal programs to provide universal social and economic supports, such as national health insurance, that did not depend on one's employment or marital status. Black political leaders saw federal social welfare programs as powerful tools to reduce racial inequality. Reflecting their political roots in the New Deal era, they thought that government had the responsibility to bring about a just society. This outlook influenced efforts on the local and state levels as well. Postwar Black advocacy for public housing, public hospitals, public universities, public works, and public day care centers was propelled by both race and class considerations: to benefit poor and working-class communities *and* to ensure nondiscriminatory Black access to goods and services. Because the Fourteenth Amendment's antidiscrimination protections extended to state action rather than private action, civil rights activists fought to expand the role of the public sector as a bulwark from the pervasive exclusion of African Americans from the private sector.[19]

The experience of Black soldiers both in the United States and abroad also set the stage for a new era of militant Black protest. Three million Black men registered for military service, and the 500,000 stationed in Africa, the Pacific, and Europe witnessed the collapsing European empires firsthand. Racial segregation in the armed forces and white violence stateside produced anger, frustration, and a fierce determination by Black soldiers to demand their rights during the war and after.[20]

While racial harassment of Black soldiers is mostly associated with military bases in the South, it happened wherever the segregated military happened to be, including Fox Hills, an army camp on Staten Island. African Americans at Fox Hills raised issues that were flash points of racial tension in the military, including the race-based privileges enjoyed by European prisoners of war, segregation in transportation, and the refusal of local establishments to serve Black men in uniform. National Urban League president Lester Granger protested that "Negro troops are forced to hike to and from work each day, while Italian prisoners of war ride to the same jobs in trucks." Moreover, local taverns and "refreshment places" refused to serve the men. Granger hoped the public would

> understand why these servicemen who happen to be of the Negro race, and who are performing a valuable service in defense of their country, feel that they have been betrayed by the community in which they are assigned and have been badly let down by the government which they serve.[21]

A major wartime desegregation campaign was the struggle by Black nurses to gain entry into the Army Nurse Corps. Their battle, which helped to pave the way for A. Philip Randolph's campaign against Jim Crow in the armed forces, was led by Mabel K. Staupers, a Barbados-born immigrant and longtime advocate for more health care services in Harlem. Executive secretary of the National Association of Colored Graduate Nurses and a founder, with Mary McLeod Bethune, of the National Council of Negro Women, Staupers "adroitly seized the opportunity created by the war emergency and the increased demand for nurses to project the plight of black nurses into the national limelight." Before war's end, Staupers had mobilized a campaign that toppled the Army's quotas on Black nurses. She later led the fight to desegregate the American Nursing Association, and the National Association for the Advancement of Colored People (NAACP) awarded her the Spingarn Medal in 1951 in recognition of her efforts in behalf of Black women workers. Staupers, like the physicians Louis T. Wright, Godfrey Nurse, George D. Cannon, May Chinn, Charles Petioni, and Arthur Logan (as well as many other Black medical professionals), were key architects of Black civil society in Jim Crow New York, and unheralded leaders in the fight for equal rights.[22]

Black leaders in New York seized on international realignments hastened by the war—such as antifascism, anticolonialism, a decline of U.S. isolationism, and the emerging U.S. claim to postwar global leadership—in order to advance Black interests. Especially after the Harlem riot, local radio waves became filled with the message that America's future as a world leader depended upon domestic racial progress. Black state assemblyman William T. Andrews said the "majority of Americans" must make the war effort a means of domestic democratization, because "in extending democracy to the Negro at home, together we may carry our American democracy to other peoples of the world." On another broadcast, Helen M. Harris of the Urban League warned that "until equality of opportunity becomes a reality in our nation, we cannot properly assume our rightful place as leaders in this great struggle for a better world." As various forms of oppression came under attack across the globe, Black activists pushed U.S. leaders to champion freedom and democracy at home.[23]

It is no coincidence that the overthrow of Jim Crow coincided with the political independence of Asian and African states. The movement in New York was part of the global rise of people of color after World War II, a conflict that had weakened European colonial empires and eroded the credibility of doctrines of white superiority. Global forces functioned both as sources of inspiration and solidarity for African Americans and as sources of pressure on the U.S. government. The war against fascism, the challenges to empire, and the rise of the Cold War with its scramble to gain third world allegiances all nurtured global awareness and encouraged internationally conscious strategies among civil rights leaders. Many African American leaders linked their struggle for freedom with the colonial world. In a speech called "The Negro's Struggle for Power," A. Philip Randolph said, "The problem of color is not indigenous or peculiar to the South. It is but a phase of the world-wide problem of color and exploitation. This problem consists in the subjugation and oppression of the darker races in the undeveloped countries of the world by the great white power nations and the exploitation of their land and labor. Upon a black, yellow and brown pillow of flesh, the old colonialism and modern world imperialism have been built." Like so many other Black radicals of this era, Randolph emphasized that "racial, like national hatreds and prejudices, are not inherent in peoples; they are acquired." Randolph called it "a by-product of economic exploitation" and urged African Americans "to build organizations that can assemble, mobilize, and direct the Negro in great masses to struggle for economic, political and social power."[24]

The struggle for Negro rights in New York relied on Black communal organization and strength. Activists utilized the institutions and resources of Black New York as well as those in the city's broader progressive orbit. Black New Yorkers in the 1940s had high levels of membership in institutions that encouraged social consciousness and political activism: churches, women's clubs, the Elks club, fraternities and sororities, civil rights groups, trade unions, and neighborhood political clubs. Circulation rates of African American newspapers were high in the 1940s and Black New Yorkers subscribed in large numbers to the *Pittsburgh Courier* and *Chicago Defender* in addition to the *New York Amsterdam News*, the *New York Age* and the left-wing Harlem weekly *People's Voice*.

The war against fascism also sparked a fight against anti-Semitism in New York among Jewish Americans, which gave the African American struggle an ally in several significant legislative and legal battles in postwar New York. In 1946 the American Jewish Congress created the Commission on Law and Social Action, which was to draft many of the bills against racial and religious discrimination, and whose frequent collaborations with the NAACP constituted the basis of the Black-Jewish alliance in the civil rights movement. This alliance emerged in New York where the two separate struggles were occurring at the same time and providing aid to each other, rather than in the subsequent southern civil rights movement. Rabbi Stephen S. Wise, of the liberal-left American Jewish Congress, wrote that "our work is based on the premise that anti-Semitism, like all other forms of anti-minority bias and discrimination, is a product not primarily of ignorance and misunderstanding but of complex political, social and economic forces." Jewish workers filed 43 percent of the complaints to the FEPC office in New York. Nationally, 78 percent of the complaints were based on racial discrimination. The large numbers of Jewish complainants to the FEPC evidently surprised Jewish community leaders, who took up the cause for a permanent FEPC. The Black civil rights struggle impressed on them the benefits of a strong government antidiscrimination agency.[25]

The totality of ideological, demographic, economic, and social changes during the war years fostered a new rights consciousness among African Americans that permanently replaced a piecemeal or gradualist approach to racial equality with a new immediacy and sweeping vision. As the nation's oldest civil rights organization, the NAACP reaped the gains of wartime agitation. Under the dedicated leadership of Ella Baker, the director of branches, their membership skyrocketed from 54,000 to over 500,000, giving civil rights leaders a large organized base from which to bargain. According to NAACP executive secretary Walter White, "Negro militancy and implacable determination to wipe out segregation grew more proportionately during the years 1940 to 1945 than during any other period of the Negro's history in America."[26]

Civil rights, meaning the right to due process and equality before the law, was an important movement goal, but the struggle for Black rights did not begin in pursuit of civil rights alone. Nor was it a simple quest for integration; the movement aimed to change mainstream institutions and practices in order to increase opportunities for Black people. In a speech downtown, Lawrence D. Reddick, director of the Schomburg Library in Harlem, declared that "complete equality—economic, political, social and cultural, without equivocation is the goal of the Negro in New York." A declaration in 1945 reflects an optimism that would have been unimaginable either five years earlier or five years later. Doxey Wilkerson, a Howard professor who left the academy to become a Communist activist with the National Negro Congress, told the Brooklyn NAACP, "It is entirely possible within the next ten years to wipe the main features of Jim Crowism off the face of America."[27]

1 Jobs for All

The "struggle for Negro rights" in postwar New York began as a fight to keep jobs. While the movement's agenda grew rapidly to encompass the full measure of human freedom, economic mobility anchored its vision of African American individual and group progress. Black workers were determined not to lose ground during the economy's conversion to peacetime production. Civil rights activists pushed for a full employment law as well as an antidiscrimination law because both forms of state intervention had improved the position of Black workers during the war. They also strove to make organized labor an ally. Black support had been critical to building a stable CIO during the Great Depression; the labor movement was at the height of its political power, and Black workers looked for union support in the antidiscrimination struggle. Antiracist activists also conducted a multitude of direct action campaigns to open new job opportunities for Black workers: both with small employers in Black neighborhoods, as happened before the war, and increasingly in major plants and industries citywide, most famously at Ebbets Field.

Culminating in the 1940s, the shift in Black employment from personal service and agricultural labor to industrial and municipal employment altered class, gender, social, and political relations in Black communities. Black labor became a dynamic source of social struggle, race leadership, and democratic ideas. Both college graduates and unskilled laborers had a stake in shattering the occupational ghetto that consigned the majority of Black workers to personal service jobs, regardless of their level of education. The support of Harlem's middle-class leadership for social democratic, pro-union politics created a deeply enabling environment and a broad push for social change.

Full and Fair Employment

The movement's first goal was to pass a fair employment law. The federal FEPC, authorized by executive order to receive complaints of discrimination by government contractors during the war, was abolished at war's end, and efforts in Congress to create a permanent body failed. The white South had acquired wildly disproportionate representation in Washington as a result of the poll tax and other disfranchising devices, enabling southern Democrats to block civil rights legislation. As a result, civil rights forces expended considerable resources after the war on state and municipal campaigns for antidiscrimination laws. In 1945 state FEPC bills were introduced in almost every large northern industrial state. Will Maslow, a member of the FEPC and a leading civil rights attorney with the American Jewish Congress, noted that "not since the Civil War has there been so much local interest in preventing racial or religious discrimination in employment."[1]

The FEPC bill in New York state—the Law against Discrimination—was introduced in Albany in January 1945 by a Democratic assemblyman, Hugh Quinn, and a Republican state senator, Irving Ives.[2] Supporters of the bill organized an impressive grassroots mobilization, a strategy later credited as the key to its passage. The New York Metropolitan Council on Fair Employment Practices brought together fifty civic, religious, civil rights, political, and labor organizations to galvanize support from a range of constituencies. They stressed that many groups, Blacks, Jews, and Catholics, would benefit from an antidiscrimination law and repeatedly emphasized the theme of wartime sacrifice. Civil rights advocates skillfully appropriated the multicultural unity discourses generated by the war. In a radio speech, John H. Johnson, the Black minister of an Episcopal church in Harlem and member of the Mayor's Committee on Unity said,

> In battle, it doesn't make any difference if a soldier be Catholic, Protestant, Jew or Negro. They are united in their efforts to defend their country. We have the obligation to be united now to create that disposition and sense of justice that will make life better for all our citizens when this conflict is ended.

In another radio address, Algernon Black of the City-Wide Citizens' Committee on Harlem, an influential interracial group of civic leaders formed in 1941 to increase support for racial justice measures in city governance, criticized the opposition's call for education rather than legislation: "A man's right to a job should not have to wait until his neighbors get educated enough to be fair to him. The law must make his right to a job secure against discrimination. It must do so now while we are fighting a war for freedom." Community leaders discursively linked the antidiscrimination struggle to the government's wartime rhetoric, such as the Atlantic Charter's Four Freedoms. "One of the four freedoms," declared the Reverend Johnson, "is the freedom from want and the freedom from want means the right to work."[3]

The public hearings on the bill revealed the extent to which the war and Black mobilization had altered the political terrain in New York. Proponents of the measure, "one of the most influential delegations ever presented at a public hearing in Albany," one observer noted, outnumbered opponents eight to one. And "legislators were not insensitive to the fact that the proponents represented forces which could ruin a political career—state-wide representation of labor, the Jew, the Negro, and the Roman Catholic and Protestant churches." On the assembly floor, Harlem legislator Hulan Jack voiced the quintessential Double V link—between anti-Nazism and anti-racism at home—in urging his colleagues to "forsake the preposterous ideology of white supremacy and embrace the lofty spirit that our nation is only strong [if] it promotes the well-being of all its citizens."[4]

Opposition to the fair employment bill was led by the Chamber of Commerce, New York Board of Trade, real estate firms, manufacturers, railroad unions, and "one individual," Robert Moses, the powerful New York City Parks commissioner.[5] With representatives from the housing industry, all-white craft unions, and large employers, these groups represented the most powerful sources of opposition to racial change in the postwar North. Their arguments were similar to those used in later years by opponents of affirmative action, such as that an antidiscrimination law would lead to special preferences for African Americans. Robert Moses claimed that the bill "will make the life of every employer miserable. Business will be driven out of the state because employers will be at the mercy of every agitator, every tricky lawyer, every person who thinks he is aggrieved." The New York State Bar Association called the bill an unconstitutional infringement of freedom of contract, a wrongful attempt to legislate morality, and, echoing long-standing segregationist ideology, an enticement to racial hostility and riots.[6]

Despite this formidable opposition, the New York State assembly passed the Ives-Quinn Act on February 28, 109–32, and the senate did likewise 49–6. The negative votes were all cast by Republicans, but most Republicans, including Governor Thomas E. Dewey, found it hard to oppose the principle of fair employment in the midst of mounting victories in the war against fascism. The bill's passage testified to the success of Black wartime mobilization in linking racial fairness with winning the war, as well as to the effectiveness and breadth of the grassroots lobbying campaign. The Dewey administration, however, had succeeded in including an extra step of education and conciliation in the process of enforcement that may have made the bill more acceptable to many legislators. Signed by Governor Dewey in March 1945, it was the first law ever passed in the United States prohibiting racial and religious discrimination in private employment. The State Commission against Discrimination (SCAD) was established to enforce it.[7]

The mobilization for the Ives-Quinn Law was marked by relative unity among ideological rivals. Anticommunist liberal organizations and Popular Front groups both fought for the law rather than against each other—that the United States was still at war and allied with the Soviet Union likely encouraged them to suppress their antagonisms. In contrast, the efforts emanating from New York to pass a federal FEPC law previewed the ideological cleavages and conflicts that would escalate with the rise of the red scare. In one camp were groups who opposed working in alliance with the Communist left: A. Philip Randolph's March on Washington Movement, the International Ladies Garment Workers Union, B'nai B'rith, and others. Randolph's anticommunism had originated with his identification with the anticommunist Socialist Party in the World War I era, but he found common cause with many liberal leaders in the postwar era. The other pro-FEPC camp in New York included Communists, liberals, and independent radicals, and it garnered prominence by claiming the two members of Congress most associated with FEPC bills—East Harlem's Vito Marcantonio and Harlem's Adam Clayton Powell Jr.

Each side organized their own Washington lobbying teams, grassroots mobilizations, and star-studded rallies. Randolph's group organized an FEPC rally at Madison Square Garden in February 1946—dubbed "Save FEPC Day" by Mayor O'Dwyer—where twelve thousand people, the majority Black, heard national labor leaders and politicians, including both of New York's U.S. senators, vow to pass an FEPC bill. Randolph declared that "the whole world of color is in flames" and said the "long, dark centuries of exploitation and oppression . . . must and will come to an end." Neither Marcantonio, head of the House Steering Committee for FEPC, nor Representative Powell was invited, and Powell accused Randolph of "playing politics." These divisions, however, were overshadowed by the seventeen-day filibuster against the FEPC waged by southern Democrats and their allies in the Republican party. Dorothy Funn, a Capitol Hill lobbyist for the National Negro Congress, called the filibuster "the fascist fire brewing," while Randolph called it "a definite expression of totalitarian statism."[8]

African American leaders also lobbied vigorously in Washington for a strong governmental role in stimulating the postwar economy and providing "jobs for all." Black leaders in New York rallied behind President Roosevelt's 1944 idea of an "economic bill of rights." This encompassed support for full employment, housing and public works programs, price and rent controls, federal aid to education, national health insurance, progressive taxation, aid to small farmers, and the expansion of Social Security coverage to all Americans. Civil rights leaders argued that economic security was crucial to a peaceful reconversion process. As one civic leader explained in a radio address on why the Price Control Act was a means to overcome racial conflict, "You may ask what this has to do with racism . . . My answer is that both unemployment and inflation are two deadly enemies of good minority relations. We shall certainly have to develop a full employment plan too, for when sixty million scramble for thirty or forty million jobs there is bound to be race trouble."[9]

In 1945, the stage and screen actor Canada Lee gave the commencement address at Vassar College on the theme "What the Negro Wants and Hopes for in the Postwar World." "Equality is not enough," Lee said. "Our struggle must be for equality with meaning," and "with 'jobs for all' we can work . . . toward economic equality—an equality with significance." Although Congress failed to pass a full employment law after the war, the struggle for social democratic government policies would remain an important component of the northern Black rights struggle. In addition, African American elected officials and activists were major supporters of the effort to build a social democratic state in New York City. As a historian of New York has concluded, "Other cities built housing and operated transit systems, colleges, hospitals, and even radio stations. But no city offered services the scale and range of those in New York." In the postwar era, civil rights activists fought hard to make these services operate free of discrimination.[10]

Race and Gender during Reconversion

The conversion to peacetime production threatened the jobs of Black men and women and the economic gains of Black communities. Between mid-August and mid-September 1945, in one month alone, 44.7 percent of Black workers in twenty-five major war plants in the New York City area were laid off, as part of an overall 21 percent reduction of the workforce in these plants. While one-fifth of white workers lost their jobs during this month in the metropolitan area, two-fifths of Black workers did.[11]

Progressive Black labor leaders, especially those in the Communist orbit, spearheaded an effort to persuade trade unions to adopt affirmative action plans and modify seniority rules in order to forestall a return to segregated labor markets. Both before the war and after, protesters in New York and around the nation had advocated numerical goals to ensure more than tokenism in the integration of stores and other businesses located in Black neighborhoods. A proportional hiring plan was also part of a landmark 1941 accord to hire Black bus drivers on the Fifth Avenue bus line. Even the white dominated Uptown Chamber of Commerce had come to embrace the idea. A plank in its 1944 "tentative program for a New York Committee for the Improvement of Race Relations" read, "Educate employers throughout New York City to the wisdom of giving employment to a fair share of qualified Negro workers—now and during the postwar period—as their contribution to the solution of the Negro's economic problem." After the war, the proposal by some Black labor activists to modify seniority systems in unions sparked a debate over affirmative action whose main points still resonate half a century later.[12]

Affirmative action advocates argued that racial discrimination, like military service, should be taken into account in redesigning workplace seniority. The National Negro Congress asked:

> Will the unions, which have made such magnificent advances in tearing down the color barrier, allow unmodified and unadjusted seniority rules to become an instrument whereby pre-war discrimination may be frozen into postwar industry, the unions disrupted, the Negro and white workers alike weakened in organizational power?

In 1944 the CIO adopted a resolution in favor of a permanent FEPC as well as antidiscrimination clauses in every union contract, but it shrank from advocating seniority adjustments. It did, however, defeat an amendment that would have prevented unions from adjusting seniority for this purpose. CIO president Philip Murray reflected the position of the vast majority of (white) trade union officials in his opposition to "group adjusted" seniority for Black workers.[13]

The support for seniority adjustments was driven by a sense that Black progress depended on maintaining wartime occupational shifts. At an NNC-sponsored Conference on Postwar Employment in January 1945 with labor, religious, civil rights, and government leaders, Doxey Wilkerson, editor of the *People's Voice,* warned that not altering seniority systems might jeopardize the fragile racial peace forged by the CIO. "If we see great and disproportionate numbers of Negroes being kicked out of their jobs, there are plenty of people in our country who will exploit this situation to disrupt the alliance between Negroes and organized labor." In sharp contrast with the period after World War I, Wilkerson noted, Black workers were inside, not outside, organized labor. And it was precisely this interracial unity that made unions stronger than ever before.[14]

To be sure, not all Black labor leaders endorsed affirmative action during reconversion. George L. P. Weaver, the head of the CIO Committee to Abolish Discrimination, called seniority "a sovereign right of each international union" and affirmative action proposals "special privileges." Like most liberal leaders in the labor movement, Weaver opposed adjusting seniority on the grounds that it "would serve to drive a greater cleavage between white and Negro workers." He raised doubts as to the legality of altering seniority rules and stressed that the vast majority of union leaders considered it "suicidal to tamper with seniority provisions." At another conference on reconversion hosted by the NLVC, Charles Collins said, "We cannot accept the position of some labor leaders, including some Negro labor leaders, who have expressed the view that seniority is a sacred right—like the Ten Commandments—and cannot be touched or modified under any condition whatsoever."[15] Robert Weaver, an official in the Roosevelt administration who had successfully advocated racially proportionate hiring goals in the Public Works Administration, authored a 1945 tract called "Seniority and the Negro Worker" that endorsed seniority modifications. He was pessimistic, however, about the likelihood of unions to embark on such a bold course. And he was right. In industries that employed large numbers of Black workers, only one major union embraced this strategy in collective bargaining, the left-led United Electrical, Radio and Machine Workers of America (UE).[16]

The UE proposed a very limited affirmative action plan at Sperry Gyroscope. In the spring of 1945, Sperry employed 1,200 Black workers, but by the end of the year the number had shrunk to about 200 out of a total workforce of 4,600. Sperry Local 450 voted unanimously to press for a new seniority plan designed to prevent the number of skilled Black employees from going below the level employed as of November 15, 1945. Union organizer Sid Harris hoped the vote would "serve as a stimulus to all organized labor to bring about the closest unity possible between Negro and white workers." A drawing in the *People's Voice,* the left-wing Harlem weekly, pictured an interracial handshake over the statement: "Local 450 UE: The membership agrees that, if at all necessary, white workers will step aside on seniority to guarantee the jobs of their Negro brothers."[17]

Management proved a tougher sell. Sperry agreed to proposals on adjusted seniority for veterans but rejected it for African Americans. By June, only twenty-eight skilled Black workers were left, as Sperry continued to lay off workers on a strict seniority basis. In a few cases, Local 450 found jobs for laid-off workers in other departments, "and in at least one other instance," white workers in a department "unanimously agreed to allow a skilled Negro worker to stay instead of one of them." But the union's effort to impose even a limited affirmative-action-style plan had failed.[18]

The vulnerability of Black workers to disproportionate lay-offs was even more acute for women. During the war, the Household Division of the U.S. Employment Service referred applicants to war work, or other manufacturing such as the needle trades, instead of domestic service, contributing to an expansion of opportunities for African American women. A working-class Black feminism emerged at this historical juncture as Black women war workers were determined not to return to domestic labor. Jeannetta Welch Brown, the executive secretary of the National Council of Negro Women, called Black women "the most vulnerable group in America with regard to postwar lay-offs." Welch Brown emphasized that any full employment plan must "recognize the right of all women to work, irrespective of need, and without regard to color or religion." But she fused this equal-rights feminism with a consciousness of women's social realities and called for a broad agenda, including "flexible seniority rules," legislation guaranteeing equal pay for equal work, the right to advancement on the job, the right to keep the jobs "opened to us for the first time during the war period," child care centers, maternity leaves, mass transit, guaranteed medical care, hot meals on the job, and the extension of social security to domestic and agricultural workers. Welch Brown also asserted the right of African American mothers to be stay-at-home parents, and not only if they were unmarried and destitute, declaring that "provisions should also be made for wives who want to stay home and raise their children." Advocates for Black women workers sought to create a society granting women both equal rights in the workplace as well as security and rights as providers of child care.[19]

The Black left aimed to theoretically identify "the special oppressed status" of women of color alongside its program of action. The October 1945 Emergency Jobs Conference and Rally in Harlem, sponsored by the National Negro Congress, NLVC, New York State NAACP, ULGNY, and NCNW, was a prototypical Black Popular Front event. Its agenda sought to answer such questions as "Why do the job problems of Negro veterans, women and young people need special and particular attention?" and "What measures can be taken to prevent the Negro woman war worker from being forced to return to service and domestic positions?" The higher labor-force participation rates of Black women and the lack of private child care services open to them made publicly funded child care centers an important issue in Black New York. It was one example of the movement's effort to increase the size and role of the public sector. In light of the pervasive racism of the private sector, government was seen as an arena in which African American taxpayers could claim ownership and demand services.[20]

In 1946 Black women workers at the R. Gesell Company in lower Manhattan, manufacturer of Dorothy Gray Cosmetics, led a drive to bring in Local 121 of the United Gas, Coke and Chemical Workers Union, CIO. They saw the union as a weapon to end the company's egregious Jim Crow operation. The company assigned Black women workers to a building on Wooster Street and paid them $26 to $28 a week, while white women workers were placed at another building on Houston Street and paid $30 or more per week to do the same work. Workers at both plants reportedly signed union cards, but when the company refused to recognize the union, only the Black workers joined the strike. Led by shop steward Jennie Cox, the Black women workers stuck with the union through several weeks on strike. A newspaper photo entitled "Picket Line Girls" showed workers picketing the Fifth Avenue offices of Dorothy Gray Cosmetics and carrying signs attacking the anti-union, racially divisive policies of the Gesell Company. The white workers' embrace of race privilege over either class or gender solidarity doomed the CIO effort. Nevertheless, Black women seized this moment of postwar flux to permanently leave behind domestic labor, claim new opportunities and build new lives. After the war, many Black women would find work in the garment industry or in occupations such as telephone operator that were first opened to them during the war.[21]

The projection of African American women's issues in the progressive movement depended on Black women's voices, and there were relatively few Black women in formal leadership positions. Nevertheless, significant political contributions were made by many Black women, such as Victoria Garvin of the United Office and Professional Workers of America, Thelma Dale of the National Negro Congress, Claudia Jones of the Communist Party, and Ada B. Jackson of the Congress of American Women and the American Labor Party. Dale, a graduate of Howard who would later persuade the Progressive Party to nominate a Black woman as the vice-presidential candidate in 1952, wrote "The Status of the Negro Women in the United States" in 1947. She asserted that "approximately six million Negro women in the U.S. face the double oppression of both racial and sex discrimination," articulating the ideas of "double jeopardy" and intersectionality that would become hallmarks of Black feminist discourse. "Negro women," she wrote, "brought to this country as chattel-slaves, and used for three hundred years of slavery as breeders and hard-laborers, have found it even more difficult to attain a position of equality either with white women or even with Negro men."[22]

As the effort to win affirmative action guarantees during reconversion proved unsuccessful, many civil rights leaders argued that the best way of guaranteeing the security of Black workers in New York industry was through trade union membership.

The Black Labor Left

The desire to preserve the newly won piece of the industrial pie made the full and equal integration of Black workers in trade unions a major focus, and African American community leaders increasingly emphasized the importance to race progress of nondiscriminatory trade unions. In 1948 one million African Americans were members of trade unions. In this era when unionized blue- and white-collar employment was becoming a stepping stone to a middle-class lifestyle, autoworkers and meatpackers, nurses and postal workers, displaced the "talented tenth" as agents of Black community advancement.[23]

A pro-union attitude among Black community and civil rights leadership that took hold in the 1930s solidified in this period. Virtually every major leader embraced unions as a route to community economic development. Harlem leaders rallied in opposition to restrictive labor legislation proposed by President Harry Truman in response to a rail strike. In a "Message to the

President," the most prominent political, church, and civil rights leaders across the political spectrum declared: "The Negro people have learned that a strong and democratic labor movement is our best guarantee of security and progress. We will defend labor's rights as our own . . . We know we voice the will of the overwhelming masses of Negro people in urging you to withdraw your anti-labor legislative proposals."[24]

An editorial in the Republican *New York Age* illuminated the connection between unions and the prosperity of Black urban communities.

Unionization has brought greater security to all racial institutions and to all socio-economic groups in the community. Church collections are up, NAACP memberships are up, newspaper circulation is up, new businesses are up, and home ownership is up.[25]

This era produced a generation of Black trade unionists who became influential political and civil rights activists. They endeavored to broaden the intersection between the Black freedom struggle and the trade union movement, and to put the aspirations of Black workers at the center of both. In a 1945 report for Mayor William O'Dwyer on uptown political currents, Black journalist Earl Brown wrote, "In my opinion, the Negro leaders in the trade unions are the most genuine ones in Harlem." "In fact," he concluded, "Harlem voters listen to their shop stewards today more than to their preachers." In Brown's view, unions such as the Amalgamated Clothing Workers and the National Maritime Union "have done as much, if not more, to integrate Negroes into industry than any other organizations in the city."[26]

In March 1946 at the Communist-sponsored East Coast Conference of Negro Trade Unionists and Their Supporters in New York, Charles Collins delivered the keynote address to three hundred delegates.[27] A "new working class leadership," Collins said, is beginning to build "what must be built in America—a Negro liberation movement." Collins insisted that Black labor leaders had a responsibility to go beyond shopfloor issues and embrace a broader struggle. "A Negro trade union leader is but half a leader if he neglects his community and concerns himself only with wages and hours of his membership." This stance encouraged many left-wing Black labor leaders to get involved in community battles over politics, housing, and police brutality.[28]

Unions in New York most associated with antiracist activism were those with Black officials and organizers, and many of these were left-led—such as the United Electrical Workers, United Public Workers, National Maritime Union, and Hotel and Restaurant Workers of America—or had strong left ties for periods of time, like Local 65 of the Wholesale and Warehouse Workers Union or the Transport Workers Union. A scholar of the New York labor movement found that "nominal support for racial justice was wide-spread," but that "action in its pursuit tended to be most vigorous among black unionists and those within the communist orbit."[29] The International Ladies Garment Workers Union was less visible in community civil rights battles, although it had the largest Black membership of any union. To be sure, there were many unions that excluded or discriminated against Black workers, especially in the building trades and the railroad industry. New York was not home to a single predominant industry with a single powerful union—such as steel in Pittsburgh, autos in Detroit, or meatpacking in Chicago—in which Black workers' struggles took place. The labor struggle was more diffuse in New York, but it was just as significant.

Ewart Guinier returned from military service in the Pacific to become regional director and then secretary treasurer of the New York district of the United Public Workers of America, CIO. He rose in 1948 to become the international secretary treasurer, the highest ranking Black official in a majority white union. Born to Jamaican parents in 1910 in the Panama Canal Zone, Guinier learned about racism from the Jim Crow system the American authorities had imposed there, a system that his union would later lead the fight against. After emigrating to the United States, he graduated from the Boston English High School and gained admission to Harvard. But after learning that he was Black, the university denied him a scholarship and a dormitory room. Guinier was among a small but eminent group of Black students, including Ralph Bunche, William Hastie, and Robert Weaver, but the Depression forced him to leave for lack of funds.

He moved to New York City and completed his degree at tuition-free City College. Many Black activists in the New York civil rights struggle graduated from City, or if they were women, Hunter College, including Hope Stevens, Louis Burnham, Hubert Delany, Charles Collins, Victoria Garvin, and Pauli Murray. Brooklyn College produced Dorothy Burnham and Shirley Chisholm. Unlike their more famous white classmates, who became known as the "New York intellectuals" and who performed very public breaks from their college working-class ethnic radicalism, these City University graduates devoted their lives to struggles for social justice.[30]

Guinier joined the political ferment on the streets of Harlem and in the left-wing trade union movement. As chief examiner in the city's civil service commission, he began organizing municipal workers. The United Public Workers of America (UPWA) organized local, state, and federal workers and its locals in New York included teachers and welfare workers. Black workers constituted one-third of the 80,000 UPWA members. But despite the large number of Black employees in the public sector, "the U.S. government," wrote Guinier, "is the nation's biggest Jim Crow employer." A 1947 *New York Times* story identified fourteen federal departments that practiced racial discrimination, and overall, Black federal employees were assigned the most menial, lowest-paying jobs regardless of their education or qualifications. The UPWA used an antiracist unionizing strategy from its inception. It represented 17,000 federal employees in the Panama Canal Zone, winning them a wage increase, a forty-hour week, and paid holidays. The union also secured the removal of "gold" and "silver" signs—the two unequal forms of payment based on skin color that had become the signifiers of a system of apartheid in the Canal Zone.[31]

The UPWA also boasted the first African American woman to head a union in New York. Eleanor Goding was president of Local 1 of the State, County and Municipal Workers Union, which merged into the UPWA and represented workers in the Department of Welfare. Goding fought against the practice of referring African American welfare recipients to jobs as domestics or "menials" and she sought to develop solidarity between case workers and clients. Goding, who also served on the New York State Executive Board of the CIO, described her union as "the first place that I was ever accepted as a human being without discrimination because of my color." She was also a member of the Brooklyn Non-Partisan Committee for FEPC, Brooklyn NAACP, and National Negro Congress.[32]

The UPWA led a campaign in 1947 to save the jobs of two thousand Black female workers at an Internal Revenue Service office in the Bronx. This case reveals the setbacks that minority workers in a federal agency suffered after the demise of FEPC. Ninety percent of the 2,200 workers at the plant were Black women—the highest percentage of Black women employed in a government agency. Since the end of the war, workers had complained that the plant was forcing resignations to keep wages down. In 1946 and 1947 hundreds of workers, including sixty African American war veterans, were let go after their first six months in order to avoid upgrading them. And IRS administrator Ernest Campbell openly advocated a racial ceiling, saying that since only one in fifteen New Yorkers was Black, he could fire Black workers to achieve that ratio in the plant. United Federal Workers, Local 20 of the UPWA, which was trying to organize the plant, sought aid from the American Jewish Congress, NAACP, ULGNY, and National Negro Congress.

At the Hotel Theresa in February 1947, activists from two dozen organizations ranging from the Communist Party to the United Small Business Association came together in a typical Black Popular Front effort as the Citizens' Committee for the Job Security of Bronx Internal Revenue Service Employees. They called on Washington to ensure that all employees who passed civil service exams were given permanent status, and that there was no quota system to limit the number of Black employees. The Citizens' Committee also demanded an executive order creating an FEPC for government service. They lobbied government officials, held petition drives, sent telegrams to Washington, and sponsored outdoor neighborhood meetings. The City Council passed a resolution sponsored by its two American Labor Party and two Communist Party members calling on the Treasury Department and the president to "halt the anti-Negro employment policy" in the Bronx IRS office.[33]

In the spring the U.S. Civil Service Commissioner termed the proposed racial quota "illegal" and a Treasury Department official announced that the Bronx office would have to abide by "non-discrimination rules and regulations." But the government abruptly announced a decision to transfer the Bronx IRS office to Kansas City, Missouri, in June. Union official Florence Herzog called the plant relocation "the worst case of discrimination our union [has] ever met," and attributed it to "the Spoils System" and the "desire on the part of the Processing Division to eliminate 2,000 Negro employees from Government service." Adam Clayton Powell circulated a petition among the state's congressional delegation to block the move, but the administration (both Truman and the Treasury Secretary hailed from Missouri) quickly finalized plans to transfer the plant, citing Missouri's advantage as a "more central location."[34]

In the end, the south Bronx lost 2,200 jobs, but the struggles of these Bronx workers contributed to the development of a pro–civil rights platform in the Truman administration and the Democratic Party. While the Bronx protest was unfolding, the President's Committee on Civil Rights was holding hearings in Washington. The committee was appointed by Truman in response to a grassroots antilynching movement that had arisen after the war. Between January and September 1947, it heard twenty witnesses, including Thomas Richardson, an international vice-president of the UPWA, who referred to the Bronx case in his calls for an FEPC in government, preference for temporary wartime workers who pass civil service exams, and a central hiring register to bring fairness to labor practices: "It is our contention that the Government as an employer has the responsibility of setting an example for all other employers in carrying out those basic citizenship rights which are set forth in our Constitution."[35]

The United Electrical Workers was another union in which Black organizers found space to fight for racial justice. Along with hundreds of other Black women, Elaine Perry worked at the Brooklyn Navy Yard during the war. After being laid off she got a job at Teletone, a UE shop that made televisions, and became its first Black female district organizer. When Teletone announced plans to move to New Jersey, a plan Perry believed was intended to break the union, she organized buses to transport the largely Black female labor force in Manhattan across the river. "We fooled them," she recalled. The UE aired Negro History Week specials on its nationwide radio program, including one in 1948 to an audience of millions with Paul Robeson, Lena Horne, and W. E. B. Du Bois. In light of the repeated defeats of a national fair employment law, progressive labor leaders fought to gain antidiscrimination protections through collective bargaining. By 1952, the UE had successfully negotiated fair employment clauses in forty-seven contracts.[36]

Charles Collins, a Black trade unionist, became a prominent activist in the struggle for Negro rights in postwar New York. Born in Grenada in 1908, Collins moved as a child to Panama, where his schoolteacher father died building the Panama Canal. His mother took the family to New York City, where Charles graduated from City College and in 1936 became a labor organizer in the city's hotel industry. He rose to be vice president of Local 6 of the Hotel and Club Employees Union, AFL, and spearheaded the drive to bring thousands of workers of color into the union. Under liberal-left leadership that took over after a rout of organized crime elements in the union, the membership of Local 6 soared from 446 in 1938 to 20,881 in 1946, of whom approximately 3,500 were Black. Local 6 fought to get antidiscrimination clauses in collective bargaining agreements. In 1946, its contract with the Waldorf-Astoria Hotel led to the hiring of Black banquet waiters, and the 1945 contract between the AFL Hotel Trades Council and the New York Hotel Association opened the better-paying front service jobs to Black workers for the first time.[37]

Jamaican-born Ferdinand Smith, a vice president of the National Maritime Union (NMU), was the highest-ranking Black official in the CIO. After

A. Philip Randolph, Smith was the most prominent Black labor leader in the nation. The National Maritime Union made it a policy to send out mixed crews on ships. A resolution adopted at a 1947 New York NMU meeting is typical of left-wing unions of this era. It called for "the outlawing of Jim Crow in all walks of life" and demanded passage of anti–poll tax, anti-lynching, and FEPC legislation. In the 1944 presidential election, Smith campaigned heavily for President Roosevelt, as did fellow NMUer Captain Hugh Mulzac.[38]

The left-led United Office and Professional Workers of America, CIO (UOPWA) was one of the few unions to employ Black women on its staff. Victoria Garvin, a Harlemite from a Virginia family who worked in the garment industry as she went through Hunter College, later studied economics at Smith and became the research director of the UOPWA. "In time," she wrote years later, "we obtained contract clauses in many shops which provided for an adjustment of prevailing seniority rules to minimize the practice of last hired, first fired, as well as greater attention to hiring and promoting African-American workers."[39] In the early 1940s, the heads of the Urban League, City-Wide Citizens' Committee on Harlem, and the NAACP had prevailed on Chase Manhattan to hire Black bank tellers in its Harlem branch, but beyond Harlem, Jim Crow reigned. In 1948 the UOPWA's Financial Employees Guild won pledges by the Merchants Bank and the Royal Industrial Bank to hire Blacks as white-collar workers. In February 1949, social workers in a UOPWA local hosted a conference with the ULGNY that called for affirmative action to increase opportunities for African Americans in the field. Representatives from over fifty public and private agencies heard W. E. B. Du Bois give the keynote address. The conferees resolved to push agencies to "agree for a specified period of time, such as six-months to a year, to grant first hiring interviews to qualified Negro applicants" and to set up scholarship funds to finance social work school for Black college graduates. "Without a plan which grants first opportunity to Negroes for office and professional positions, the present ration of employment will naturally continue," they concluded.[40]

Breaking the Color Bar

Despite the disproportionate Black layoffs during the conversion to peacetime production, the antidiscrimination struggle and an expanding economy helped ease the transition and open new areas of employment to Black workers. The National Urban League reported that the Black employment level "has held remarkably well during the first year of peace." It attributed this to the policies of progressive unions, the effects of new fair employment laws, and the "general breakthrough in new employment opportunities" in the North in such jobs as light manufacturing, clerk, telephone operator, and cashier. In New York there were plenty of unskilled and low-paying jobs available, but far fewer of the higher-paying positions of the war years.[41]

After the war, African American activism unfolded all over the city. It was not a single struggle, coordinated by a single organization; rather, its breadth reflected a widely shared determination by Black New Yorkers to demand change. In addition to the legislative and trade union struggles, there were a multitude of community-based protests aimed at winning better jobs for Black workers. These efforts extended from 125th Street to the posh East Side—where an organization called the League of Women Shoppers worked with the department store union, District 65, to open up some sales jobs for Black workers in the major department stores. The most famous protest involved baseball, although the northern civil rights struggle is not generally credited with this achievement. Breaking the color line in major league baseball, was, alongside military desegregation and a permanent FEPC, among the top civil rights goals of the 1940s. On October 23, 1945, about four months after it had become illegal for professional baseball teams in New York State to bar Black players on the basis of race, the Brooklyn Dodgers hired the first openly Black player in organized baseball in the twentieth century. The desegregation of baseball occurred in the context of social struggle and amid intense pressure on the baseball team owners. It is inseparable from the larger Black rights movement in New York City, which had community leaders, trade unionists, and the new constituency of northern Black workers as its driving force.[42]

The upheaval of the war years, the financial success and popularity of the Negro Leagues during the 1940s, the new Law against Discrimination, and the growing attention to the racial contradiction in the "national pastime" generated a widespread sense of imminent change. Japan had even dropped leaflets in the South Pacific asking, "If Americans are fighting for the freedom and equality of all people, why aren't Negro Americans allowed to play big league baseball?" Black Communist City Council candidate Ben Davis sought to reappropriate their propaganda in a 1945 campaign pamphlet: "The Japanese propaganda leaflet told the truth! No Negro can play big league baseball!"[43]

Branch Rickey claimed to have been considering the idea of signing Black players since 1942, but an escalation of external pressure in 1945 precipitated his decision to act. After passage of the Ives-Quinn Law in March, sportswriters, politicians, and other activists turned up the pressure on New York clubs. Rickey vigorously tried to control the moment so that his signing of a Black player would not appear as "forced integration."[44] Vito Marcantonio introduced a resolution in Congress seeking an investigation of baseball labor practices. In May, the New York City Council unanimously passed a resolution introduced by Ben Davis condemning Black exclusion from organized baseball, and sent copies to the owners of the Dodgers, Yankees, and Giants. In July the state assemblyman whose district included Ebbets Field called on Rickey to integrate the Dodgers. Meanwhile, the left-wing Metropolitan Interfaith and Interracial Coordinating Council formed the Committee to End Jim Crow in Baseball and launched a grassroots campaign to increase public pressure on the teams. They declared August 18 "End Jim Crow in Baseball Day" and scheduled demonstrations at Ebbets Field and the Polo Grounds. In addition, the National Maritime Union organized a parade through Harlem. In August, with an election season about to begin, politics took over and ultimately forced Rickey's hand.[45]

The City Council passed another baseball resolution—one that requested an official investigation into baseball discrimination by the State Commission against Discrimination (SCAD). Indeed, illustrating what a potent issue all-white baseball had become in New York, the publicity shy, nonconfrontational Mayor's Committee on Unity initiated an investigation in the summer of 1945. Its chair, Dan Dodson, urged officials from all three teams to hire Black players. Yankee General Manager Larry MacPhail, who openly denigrated Black players, dismissed Dodson as "a professional do-gooder." Rickey however, informed him of his intention to hire a Black player in the near future and persuaded Dodson to put the proposed investigative committee under Rickey's control.[46]

Over the summer Rickey had recruited Robinson, but he wanted to delay signing the contract until perhaps after the New Year. Dodson played his part and Mayor Fiorello La Guardia appointed the Mayor's Committee on Baseball. Civil rights activists protested the selection of entertainer Bill "Bojangles" Robinson rather than an activist such as Councilman Davis to serve on the committee along with Larry MacPhail, Branch Rickey, and others. In a rare accommodation, however, they accepted La Guardia's promise of impending action and agreed to cancel the two large demonstrations scheduled for August 18. Controversy erupted in September after the release of a memorandum by MacPhail declaring his commitment to all-white baseball, questioning the ability of Black players, and underscoring that the

Good enough to DIE...
but not good enough to PITCH!

Cover of pamphlet used in Ben Davis's 1945 City Council campaign.

Yankees made $100,000 a year in rentals and concessions from the Negro Leagues. The End Jim Crow in Baseball Committee called for MacPhail's removal from the Mayor's Committee, and accused the committee of "doing nothing to remove this evil from our city." Both Rickey and MacPhail left the committee.[47]

In October SCAD demanded that the three area teams sign pledges not to discriminate in hiring. All three promptly refused and suffered no penalty. But it was also becoming apparent that breaking the color line in organized baseball made good politics in New York. La Guardia wanted to announce publicly that "baseball would shortly begin signing Negro players" as a result of his committee's work. Rickey, not wanting the signing of Robinson to appear coerced, prevailed on La Guardia to postpone the announcement for a week. He signed Robinson on October 23. According to Commissioner Happy Chandler, every other major league team owner voted to condemn the signing of Robinson. It took over fifteen years for all the teams to finally hire Black players and nearly thirty years before a major league team hired a Black manager. In this sense, baseball predicted the scope and pace of racial reform in the postwar era: intense struggle for small gains and gradual change.[48]

Ebbets Field was not the only arena of racial struggle in postwar Brooklyn. The campaign for jobs in Black neighborhoods that began in Harlem in the 1930s continued after the war and spread to Brooklyn. In the summer of 1947, the Brooklyn chapter of the United Negro and Allied Veterans of America (UNAVA), an interracial Communist-supported organization, launched a campaign against racial discrimination in employment in the Bedford-Stuyvesant area.[49] The first target of the campaign, led by the group's Committee for Equal Job Opportunities, was the White Tower restaurant chain. The UNAVA's Whitney Parker led a delegation of representatives from the Brooklyn Republican Party, NAACP, Tenants' Council, Communist Party, and the left-wing American Youth for Democracy to White Tower's Manhattan headquarters and demanded that they hire African Americans in all capacities in the company. A White Tower manager responded, "Negroes aren't capable of being good countermen." The ideology of Black inferiority was commonly used in this era to justify the virtual white monopoly on many jobs. Committee member Hattie Brisbane—a Brooklyn NAACP activist who later became active in the police brutality struggle after her son was assaulted by police officers, organized a picket line around the White Tower restaurant at Nostrand Avenue and Fulton Street. The boycott was extremely effective. The normally busy restaurant—with a 90 percent Black clientele—had only a handful of customers during the day and was forced to close in the evenings. After a week, the restaurant hired four Black counter workers.[50]

Shortly after the picketing at White Tower began, five other stores in the area hired Black workers for the first time. At a rally to celebrate the White

Tower victory, Republican political activist Maude Richardson echoed sentiments expressed in Harlem years before:

> We are negotiating with the Trunz Pork Store and the Kress people who must be made to know that we will only spend our money where we can work. These token jobs to Negroes must go. We must get a decent proportion of the jobs in these stores or we will spend our money where we do.

The Reverend Boise Dent declared that "Brooklyn has lagged far behind in this fight for jobs, but now we will take the lead."[51]

The committee—another example of liberal-left collaboration around civil rights—"shed its Provisional status" at a conference of over twenty community organizations in September 1947 and became the Bedford-Stuyvesant Council for Equal Opportunities, with Republican Maude Richardson as chair and Communist Whitney Parker as executive secretary. They arranged a meeting with members of the Fulton Street Merchants Association to discuss "large-scale employment of Negroes." Their next major target became the Brooklyn Union Gas Company, whose 3,400 workers included 250 Blacks who labored in "the murderous heat" of the coke ovens (which statistics showed drastically reduced their life expectancy) and as porters, cleaners, and messengers. Management denied bias, but the struggle continued for years.[52]

World War II had given African Americans some leverage to wage a war on racial inequality. Antifascist propaganda inspired and strengthened domestic antiracist mobilizations and rhetoric, from A. Philip Randolph's threatened March on Washington to the Negro Freedom Rallies. African American war workers and soldiers each emerged at war's end demanding equal opportunity in exchange for their wartime service and sacrifice. While Congress remained dominated by prosegregationist forces, New York City, with its large Black population, progressive race leadership, strong trade unions, and progressive print media, became a major battleground in the postwar push for racial equality. Activists hoped that the Ives-Quinn Law would be followed by a string of legislative victories against Jim Crow, and that New York's example would help lead the nation toward a second Reconstruction. For this, civil rights leaders believed that a political transformation was essential to ending white domination both in New York and in the nation. The world of politics quickly became another battleground, as activists sought to gain a voice in public policy and gain Black representation in government.

2 Black Mobilization and Civil Rights Politics

The wartime migration, and equal rights struggle that it spawned, set in motion a transformation of American liberalism. Scholarly explanations for the rise of civil rights in U.S. politics in the 1940s have emphasized the pressures of the international Cold War on domestic racial policy or the agency of northern white liberals. The role of the grassroots northern Black rights struggle, however, has been neglected. African American political mobilizations for racial equality in the workplace, courts, schools, neighborhoods, and military pushed civil rights into local, state, national, and even international political discourse. Black leaders forged a new urban agenda, putting issues such as police brutality and fair housing at the center of big-city politics. "Black politics" in postwar New York was insurgent, pro-labor, and with the rapidly growing Black electorate, driven by a new sense of power to wage a fight for racial equality.

In the postwar decade an unprecedented number of African American candidates ran for office in New York. Rather than a straightforward switch from the Republican to the Democratic Party, Black party affiliation in the mid-twentieth century was marked by fluidity and independence. An important vehicle for Black aspirants in electoral politics was the American Labor Party, a left-wing party created during the Depression and used after the war in the struggle for Black representation. African American candidates also waged insurgent struggles in other third parties and inside the two major parties in order to win greater Black representation. The emergence of the Democratic Party as the primary location of African American electoral struggle is a story of concessions, contingency, and finally, repression. A series of new rules and laws changed electoral procedures and tightened the control of Democratic Party leaders in their party, thus undercutting insurgency and reducing electoral choices.[1]

A Movement Politics Emerges

The election of African Americans to state and local government had proceeded at a snail's pace since the Great Migration. In 1917, Edward Austin Johnson, a North Carolina–born Republican, became the first African American elected to the New York State legislature, and he introduced a host of antidiscrimination bills. His election—three months after the NAACP's silent parade down Fifth Avenue to protest the murderous rampage by white mobs on African Americans in East St. Louis—symbolized the shift in Black leadership away from Booker T. Washington's approach of courting white patronage and spurning public protest toward a new era of social and political confrontation. The first African American Democrat was elected to the state assembly in 1923, and by 1945 there were three Black Democratic assemblymen from Harlem. But since the Democratic Party generally resisted nominating Black candidates for other offices, Black aspirants worked within and against the party machine, using both radical third parties and the Republican Party, especially during the liberal Republican/Fusion administration of Mayor La Guardia.

Since congressional district lines in northern Manhattan diluted Black voting strength, white Democrats represented Harlem in Congress until 1944. Black candidates challenged them on the Republican Party line. In 1930 twenty-eight-year-old Hubert Delany, a federal prosecutor and rising star in New York City who was originally from North Carolina, ran for the House on the Republican ticket. By 1934 Delany, who had worked his way through City College as a red cap at Pennsylvania Station, was the highest paid African American federal appointee in the nation, and had won 493 of the 500 cases he had argued in U.S. District Court. Mayor La Guardia named him tax commissioner and later a judge in the Court of Domestic Relations. The brother of Sadie and Bessie Delany, authors of a celebrated family memoir, Judge Delany sat on the NAACP board of directors and became a major civil rights leader in New York City. Ten years after Delany's run for Congress, Ira Kemp, a popular Black nationalist soap-box orator and organizer of "Don't Buy Where You Can't Work" campaigns, ran for Congress as a Republican and almost won. This near upset induced Albany elites to reassess uptown politics, and the next round of redistricting paved the way for the election of Adam Clayton Powell Jr., the first Black Congressman from New York State.[2]

In 1930 Democrats Charles E. Toney and James S. Watson were elected to the municipal court, becoming the first elected Black judges in the state. Watson, who became president of the Municipal Civil Service Commission in 1950, was the patriarch of a prominent Harlem family of Jamaican origin. His son James L. Watson would become a state senator and a judge; his daughter Barbara Watson became the first African American assistant secretary of state for security and consular affairs; and his nephew Colin Powell became chairman of the Joint Chiefs of Staff and secretary of state. In 1943 Francis E. Rivers was elected to the city court on the Republican and American Labor Party (ALP) tickets, showing that the ALP could provide the margin of victory to an African American candidate. The first African American to become a member of the New York City Bar Association, he later served as its president.[3]

La Guardia, the Republican/Fusion mayor until 1945, appointed Myles A. Paige to the Court of Special Sessions and Jane M. Bolin and Hubert Delany to the Court of Domestic Relations, now known as Family Court. Paige was the first Black judge of a criminal court in the State of New York. An officer in the 369th Infantry regiment known as "Harlem's Hellfighters," he was a founder of the Harlem Lawyers' Association. Jane Bolin, a Poughkeepsie native and daughter of an attorney, was the first Black woman judge in the United States. She was just thirty-one when appointed, and she served for forty years. When Bolin learned of southern lynchings as a child in an upper-middle-class family in the North, she decided to dedicate her life to the pursuit of justice. Her advisor at Wellesley College tried to dissuade her from taking up her father's career, telling her the law was no place for a Black woman. Outraged at the remark, her father said race should never stop her, but he also tried to dissuade her, saying it would be hard for a woman. Bolin persisted and became the first African American woman to graduate from Yale Law School.[4]

Two phenomena in the 1940s accelerated the struggle for Black electoral power: the massive northern and western migrations and *Smith v. Allwright*, a 1944 Supreme Court decision that ruled whites-only state primaries violated the Fifteenth Amendment. The migration "was a move, almost literally, from no voting to voting. The urban concentration, especially in the North, gave Blacks political muscle for the first time since Reconstruction." These developments vastly expanded the Black electorate and strengthened the mass consciousness and prolabor orientation of race leadership.[5]

The political agenda of the emerging New York civil rights movement was expansive and included support for antidiscrimination laws, colonial freedom abroad, international peace and cooperation, and, reflecting the needs of a working-class migrant base, social and economic rights. In 1944 twenty-five Black organizations issued a "Message to the Republican and Democratic Parties from the Negroes of America" urging support for military desegregation, "the right to vote in every state," "an unsegregated program of government-financed housing," and "an end to imperialism and colonial exploitation." It also stressed that Black migrants were new political citizens whose allegiance was up for grabs:

> Negroes no longer belong to any one political party. They will vote for men and measures. Negro voters played an important part in the election of a Negro Communist to the New York City Council, a Negro Republican as Judge in the same community, a Democratic Mayor in Cleveland, [and] a Republican Governor in Kentucky.[6]

An ideological cross-section of Black activists in New York supported the nomination of Henry Wallace, both as vice president over Harry Truman in 1944 and in 1945 as secretary of commerce. Their support reflected the predominant Black stance that progressive government social and economic planning—with which Wallace was most associated—was linked to the cause of racial justice. The membership of a February 1945 "We Want Wallace Committee of Harlem" suggests the degree of upheaval that the civil rights movement would face only three years later when President Harry Truman campaigned against his rival Wallace as an instrument of Communist subversion. The committee included Congressman Powell; assembly members Hulan Jack and William T. Andrews; Channing Tobias, a leader of the YMCA, Phelps Stokes Fund, and NAACP; Communist city councilman Ben Davis, trade unionist Charles Collins, and Dorothy Funn from the left-wing NLVC; Democratic district leader Guy Brewer; Republican editor of the *New York Age* Ludlow Werner; J. Raymond Jones, the future leader of Tammany Hall, the Manhattan Democratic Party machine; James Egert Allen, of the New York State NAACP; sorority leader Louise McDonald; the Reverend John H. Johnson of St. Martin's Church; Mabel K. Staupers, an advocate for Black nurses; Ada B. Jackson, a prominent left-wing Brooklyn community activist; and M. Moran Weston, a widely admired Harlemite whose career spanned from a leftist labor journalist to the rector at St. Philips's Episcopal Church in Harlem to the board of trustees at Columbia University.

The most visible national symbol of Black urban political power was the

Reverend Adam Clayton Powell Jr., the U.S. Representative from Harlem who became the voice in Washington for the northern civil rights movement. Powell exemplified the move to the left by many in the Black middle class during the Great Depression. The socialite son of the highly regarded pastor of Harlem's largest congregation, Powell was transformed into a committed radical activist, joining the fight for jobs and relief for Harlemites. He came of age in a volatile, competitive political cauldron, where nationalist street-corner orators attacked white domination of the local economy and Communist tenant activists physically halted evictions in the economically devastated community. Powell also embraced his father's social gospel and inherited the pastorship of Abyssinian Baptist Church. Progressive and ambitious, Powell's base was the Black church and a working-class Harlem constituency whose aspirations were bound up with the expansion of the public sector and the fight for racial equality. Rather than standing alone, Powell reflected the politics of his generation.[7]

Along with Vito Marcantonio, the leftist Italian-American U.S. Representative from East Harlem and Manhattan leader of the American Labor Party, Powell was an advocate for the Black labor left. The Negro Labor Victory Committee hosted an inaugural ball for Powell in 1945 in Harlem, with over three thousand activists, politicians, diplomats, and leaders from forty-five AFL and CIO unions. After his first six weeks in Congress, he vowed to launch "one of the most ambitious programs for people's rights since the days of Reconstruction." In Washington, Powell endeavored to speak for Harlem as well as the disfranchised Black south, and his career was followed by people of color across the country and the world. Powell brought Harlem radicalism to national politics, prefiguring the Black Power critique of racial liberalism. He demanded equality for African Americans not as junior partners, but from a position of power as voters, taxpayers, and workers, and he spurned the rhetoric of assimilation in favor of demands for rights and justice.[8]

Powell's 1946 All Harlem Legislative Conference reveals the range of issues that Black New Yorkers brought to the political table: police-community relations, food prices, segregated schools, African American History in public schools, desegregated and low-cost housing, discrimination in bank loans, higher relief payments, wage increases, and national causes such as Powell's antilynching and interstate travel bills and Marcantonio's anti–poll tax bill.[9]

When Adam Clayton Powell left the city council in 1943, another African

Adam Clayton Powell Jr. speaking at a rally in the 1940s, most likely a Negro
Freedom Rally.

American won his borough-wide seat. The grandson of a slave and the
son of a prominent Republican businessman, Benjamin Davis was a national leader of the U.S. Communist Party and an architect of Black Popular
Front politics in New York. Born in Georgia in 1903, Davis graduated from
Amherst College in 1923. He returned home after graduating from Harvard Law School, becoming only the second African American admitted to
the Georgia bar since Reconstruction. Davis was radicalized by the political

struggles of the Great Depression. He represented the Black Communist Angelo Herndon, who faced a death sentence for leafleting at an interracial political rally, an act the state of Georgia called inciting insurrection. He joined the CP, and at the height of the left's influence in American society and politics, Davis and his circle pushed hard to advance African American interests. He moved to New York and came to personify the cross-class nature of the Black Popular Front: a member of Alpha Phi Alpha, the Elks Club, and the Communist Party, Davis appealed to the masses and the middle class.[10]

Davis's first term exemplified the way African American activists, including the left, seized on the domestic political space created by the war against fascism. He introduced a range of antidiscrimination bills, including several successful resolutions urging New York's congressional delegation to support FEPC and anti–poll tax bills, and he cosponsored a successful law barring discrimination in urban redevelopment. He won resolutions in 1944 and 1945 proclaiming Negro History Week in New York City for the first time. He also won a resolution calling for the nondiscriminatory utilization of Black nurses, a struggle led by Mabel K. Staupers of the Association of Colored Graduate Nurses. The majority of his resolutions and bills did not pass, but they became important benchmarks in the evolution of urban antiracist politics. Davis also fought for a broad agenda of social and economic empowerment including affordable housing, veterans rights, and the maintenance of price and rent controls.[11]

While only a city council seat, it was an at-large rather than district-based vote, and Davis's 1945 reelection contest was widely seen as a bellwether of the postwar status of both the left and the antiracist struggle. Davis, whose political ideas would soon land him in the federal penitentiary, was immensely popular. The sponsors of the Ben Davis Ball at the Golden Gate Ballroom ranged from Lester Granger, the rather conservative executive secretary of the National Urban League, and Ludlow Werner, the publisher of the usually Republican *New York Age*, to celebrities like Lena Horne and leftists like Paul Robeson, Max Yergan, and Charles Collins. Harlem Republican and Democrat leaders doubted their ability to defeat him, and did not want to jeopardize the loss of a Black councilman. At the Ben Davis Ball, J. Raymond Jones, the legendary Harlem politico, delivered an endorsement by Tammany Hall, the Manhattan Democratic Party machine. "The new world is here," mused Adam Clayton Powell, in a reference to the recent book *New World A'Comin*, "when Tammany Hall nominates a Communist." Davis told his cheering supporters, "It is my wish that New York City become the first city in America free from Jim Crow racial discrimination and anti-Semitism, creating the most liberal city in America."[12]

This remarkable endorsement of a Communist by Tammany Hall occurred just as the Communist Political Association reconstituted itself as the Communist Party and the Popular Front came under internal party attack. As the wartime alliance between the United States and the Soviet Union came to an end, the party shifted gears and resumed its vigorous opposition to capitalism and western imperialism. Over the next year, Communists debated various approaches to the antiracist struggle and late in 1946 revived the nationalist "Black Belt thesis." Formulated in 1928, the Black Belt thesis identified Afro-American people as an exploited nation. An American version of the principle of self-determination for national minorities adopted by the Soviet Union, the thesis resonated with indigenous traditions of Afro-American nationalism.

Much Cold War historiography describes the party's shifting stance on the Negro question—from wartime pro-Americanism to the revival of the Black Belt thesis—as a sign of its crippling devotion to Moscow. But there were many African American Communists, including Edward Strong, Claudia Jones, and William Patterson, who welcomed the new Communist Party stance, seeing it as sanctioning an accelerated fight against white supremacy in a new period of layoffs and mounting racial violence. This racial backlash, they argued, necessitated a political shift. "The Negro question," according to party theoretician Claudia Jones, is "a *national* question." It was "the question of a nation oppressed by American imperialism, in the ultimate sense as India is oppressed by British imperialism and Indonesia by Dutch imperialism." The party debate over "the Negro question" suggests that moments of ideological revision, even though they were propelled by shifting geopolitics, became occasions to struggle over substantive differences. Many Communists opposed reviving the Black Belt thesis, on the grounds that wartime Black gains and demographic shifts merited a straightforward advocacy of integrationism. And indeed, the party would essentially adopt this stance by the 1954 *Brown v. Board of Education* Supreme Court decision. But others, such as Jones, argued that "integration cannot be considered a substitute for the right of self-determination," which had yet to be realized in the Black Belt.[13]

The 1946 resolution on "the right to Negro self-determination" combined calls for "the right to realize self-government in the Negro majority area in the South" with support for "full economic, social, and political equality for the Negro people." These ideas would emerge again in the 1960s, as many revolutionary Black Nationalists drew parallels with the third world and described Black American ghettos as colonies, and in some instances called for a separate state. Indeed, efforts authorized under the Voting Rights Act to create Black majority districts are part of a long tradition of seeking to gain Black political empowerment in a spatially segregated nation.[14]

The Communist Party's new line strengthened forces within the New York Democratic Party, such as Bronx leader Ed Flynn, who had been cool to the endorsement of Ben Davis. They rescinded the endorsement, and the major parties mounted serious efforts to unseat him. The Republican and Liberal parties nominated Benjamin McLaurin, an international field organizer for the Brotherhood of Sleeping Car Porters. While attending college in Jacksonville, Florida, McLaurin spent three summers picking tobacco in eastern Connecticut. When he was nine years old, his father, a successful businessman in Jacksonville, was lynched. Many other African Americans who rose to leadership positions in New York City—including Audley Moore, Ada B. Jackson, Harold Stevens, and Jane Bolin—either had direct experience with a lynching in the South or were drawn to public careers in order to stop racial violence in the South.[15]

The McLaurin campaign made Communism a major campaign issue. The iconoclastic Black writer George Schuyler produced material for McLaurin's campaign including a map of the South entitled "Map of Ben Davis' Ghetto for Negroes." Deploying the stock concepts of the anticommunist network— Davis "labored diligently to carry out the orders of his foreign masters to undermine and destroy the American government and way of life"—Schuyler simultaneously appealed to migrant Harlemites, calling the Black Belt thesis "a ploy for segregation." "Must we all go back to the Black Belt?" Schuyler asked, mocking the romantic incarnation of the South and conjuring images of a forced return. The Democrats nominated Ruth Whitehead Whaley, the first African American woman nominated to political office by a major party in New York State, and reportedly the first Black woman admitted to the bar in North Carolina. With Black representation available on many party lines, the election would test Earl Brown's prediction that "except for a handful of Socialists, and a few professional race leaders, red-baiting leaves Harlemites cold."[16]

Brown was right. The injection of anticommunism into the campaign failed to undo Davis's deep support in Harlem. The Soviet Union was a recent ally in the war against fascism, and the heyday of domestic anticommunism lay in the future. Many Democratic leaders still tacitly supported Davis. The left-wing *People's Voice,* published by Adam Clayton Powell and Charles Buchanan, the African American owner of the Savoy nightclub, was firmly in Davis's corner, and the Republican *New York Age,* which had given him a ringing endorsement in June—as "a brilliant and forceful councilman" who was "a credit to his country and his race"—refused to withdraw it under anticommunist pressure. On the eve of the election a *New York Age* editorial rebutted McLaurin's main point of attack, that Davis put the Soviet Union above all else: "In his every action in the city council, Mr. Davis has placed the interest of Negroes and labor above all other considerations. He deserves reelection." Even the *Amsterdam News,* which endorsed the entire Republican slate, didn't mention McLaurin by name. While McLaurin drew endorsements from anticommunist unions such as the International Ladies Garment Workers Union and from his most famous supporter, A. Philip Randolph, Davis also counted on considerable labor support, including the city's CIO Industrial Union Council, which represented 500,000 workers. Ferdinand Smith, an officer in the National Maritime Union and after A. Philip Randolph the most powerful Black labor leader in the United States, coordinated a voter registration campaign that canvassed Harlem door-to-door.[17]

In November Davis easily won reelection for a new expanded term of four years. In 1943 he won with 40,000 first-place votes; this time he received 63,000, the second highest vote of the twenty-one council members. It was estimated that Davis was the first choice of as many as 75 percent of Harlem voters. Council elections used the proportional representation system whereby voters ranked their choices to insure that their vote was never wasted. So if a voter's first choice had already secured the quota of ballots needed to win, her vote would go to the second choice. This alternative to the "winner take all" method gave citizens a range of political choices and produced a more representative council. One supporter hoped "that the strength of the Negro-Communist-Left-wing-Labor combination would set a new era in New York City politics." The first law passed in New York City in 1946 was a Davis-sponsored resolution proclaiming February 10–16 Negro History Week.[18]

Third Parties and Black Mobilization

After the war, a succession of third-party campaigns by Black candidates forced the Democratic Party to confront their constituents' desire for Black representation. In 1946 sixteen African Americans ran for local, state, and federal office, with ten on third-party tickets. In 1950, thirty-six Black candidates ran for office in New York State, many on third-party ballots. These campaigns foregrounded issues of importance to neglected working-class Black constituencies and shaped political discourse and consciousness in the city. Black radicals helped propel this strategy. At a conference of Black trade unionists sponsored by the Communist Party in March 1946, Charles Collins called for "independent political action of the Negro People led and organized by leaders in the trade union movement."[19]

Collins personally took up this challenge and organized a major effort to integrate the all-white New York state senate. There were three senate districts in Harlem—a gerrymandering that had prevented the election of an African American. In June 1946, a citizens' nonpartisan committee was formed to win the election of an African American from the twenty-first senate district, which had a slight majority of Black voters. The committee's membership signaled a continuation of the Black Popular Front, the coalition between liberals and radicals, despite the end of the war and the party's new line. It included George D. Cannon, a physician and loyal Davis supporter; John W. Saunders, pastor of Convent Avenue Baptist Church; Maude Gadsen of the New York State Beauty Culturists; Albert C. Gilbert of the Harlem Lawyers Association; Gertrude A. Robinson of the National Council of Negro Women; Thelma Dale of the National Negro Congress; Donellan Phillips of the Consolidated Tenants League; Frank Montero of the Urban League; Samuel Patterson of the International Workers Order; and James Robinson, minister of the Church of the Master.[20]

The American Labor Party nominated Collins, who quickly won the citizen committee's endorsement. He also attempted to enter the Democratic primary, but the Board of Elections ruled his nominating petitions irregular. Collins termed the action "anti-Negro bias," and after winning a flood of write-in votes, formed a new "People's Rights Party" for the general election. His platform included "decent low cost housing for the people of Harlem," rent control, price control, an end to all segregation and discrimination, more jobs for Black war veterans, and increased Black access to skilled jobs. Running in a diverse district, he appealed to voters across racial and ethnic lines, but stressed the need to win better jobs for African Americans.[21]

Collins won broad support—being an alleged Communist did not hurt him among most Harlemites in this pre–red scare era. Congressman Powell endorsed him in typical Popular Front rhetoric as "a man who follows in the

Democratic Party campaign rally, 1946. From left, state senate candidate Charles A. Collins, U.S. Senate candidate Herbert Lehman, and state assembly candidates William T. Andrews and Hulan Jack.

great political tradition of Franklin Delano Roosevelt—a man of the people." Canada Lee, a popular actor as well as the director of the Broadway play *On Whitman Avenue,* which explored the hostility encountered by a Black family moving into an otherwise all-white neighborhood, said Collins "represents everything that we are fighting for in *On Whitman Avenue* . . . the right of people, regardless of race or color, to live in peace and without fear." The Greater New York CIO Council and many CIO and AFL leaders also endorsed him. Collins lost his race to become the first Black state senator in New York, but he almost caused the defeat of the white incumbent. The Republican candidate was initially declared the winner, but after a recount the incumbent reclaimed his seat. Nonetheless, a message was sent to the Democratic Party. The campaign showed the power of social movement–style electoral efforts and the determination of Harlemites to end white political domination of Black communities.[22]

Insurgent Black candidates in the outer boroughs also used the American Labor Party as a vehicle to press for representation. In 1945 there were no Black elected officials in the city's four "outer" boroughs—the Bronx, Brooklyn, Queens, and Staten Island. In 1946 African American challengers vied for the state assembly in the seventh assembly district in the south Bronx, a largely Jewish area with a rapidly growing Black population. Chester Addison, a Virginia-born veteran who was active in the left-wing United Negro and Allied Veterans of America and National Negro Congress, sought the Republican nomination. After the Republicans nominated a white candidate who did not even live in the district to challenge the white Democratic incumbent, Addison ran on the ALP ticket. Another Black challenger, former Bronx NAACP president John N. Griggs, ran for the Liberal Party, which had been formed in 1944 by members of the ALP who objected to working with Communists.[23]

In 1946 the American Labor Party also nominated the Bronx's first Black candidate for U.S. Congress. Roy Soden was the comanager of the twenty-thousand-member Laundry Workers Joint Board of the Amalgamated Clothing and Textiles Workers Union, CIO, 60 percent of which was Black. The left-wing *People's Voice* praised Soden's charismatic speeches and said he was "destined to become the Adam Powell of the Bronx." A group of ministers organized Black church support for Soden and Addison. African American political activists of this era sought to collaborate with progressive Black clergy, and notwithstanding the importance of labor leaders to the early civil rights movement in New York, African American ministers were also a significant and visible source of antiracist leadership. Soden and Addison reflected the impatience for first-class citizenship by Black veterans and the hope and expectations generated by this highly organized and mobilized migrant generation. Neither man was elected in 1946, although for third-party efforts, both pulled in impressive numbers, which paved the way for future Black inroads in the Bronx Democratic Party. Soden polled over 24,000 votes, while Addison became the first African American to poll over 10,000 votes in a state assembly race. Moreover, both candidates beat their Republican opponents.[24]

In Brooklyn, with a Black population of a quarter million, a third-party challenge was also part of the historical background to the eventual election of a Black state legislator. The influx of Black workers to central Brooklyn war plants turned the seventeenth assembly district in Bedford-Stuyvesant into a majority Black area. Harlem already had three Black assemblymen and elected another in 1946, but no Black Brooklynite had ever been elected to the state assembly. In 1946, the Board of Elections added several predominantly white election districts to the seventeenth assembly district. "They don't want a Negro," one activist observed, but Black Brooklyn's desire for a political voice inspired a major effort to unseat the incumbent, John Walsh.

Ada B. Jackson, a health care, women's rights, and education activist, ran on the ALP ticket after losing the Republican primary to Maude Richardson, also African American. Born in Georgia, the daughter of a former slave, Jackson left the Republican Party in 1946 after a Senate filibuster defeated an FEPC bill. Explaining her decision to join the ALP, Jackson said: "More than 200 years of legal enslavement and another 70 odd years of illegal enslavement for the Negro is a long time to wait, watch, hope and pray for freedom through the Republicans or Democrats." Endorsed by the powerful Transit Workers Union Local 100, the *People's Voice* also urged a vote for Jackson, who had witnessed a lynching in Georgia and survived a lynch mob herself: "There is no better way for us to repudiate the lynch terror now rampant in the state of Talmadge than to send this daughter of Georgia, now our own Brooklyn leader, to the assembly of the greatest state in America."[25]

The two camps attempted to unite around a single candidate, but negotiations broke down, reportedly because the Republican Party rejected any collaboration with the ALP, although some felt the Republican Party had faint interest in a Black victory, even its own. The white incumbent won by only 77 votes. Walsh received 9,691 votes to Richardson's 9,614, while Jackson won about 4,000 votes. Since the neighborhood was solidly Democratic, Black Democratic leader Bertram Baker termed the outcome "a racial vote in protest" against the Democrats' failure to nominate an African American. Richardson and Jackson both lost, but their efforts encouraged the Democratic Party to nominate a Black candidate in the next election. In the short run, however, the Communist Party plunged into an intense, acrimonious debate over the correctness of the third-party strategy, because Jackson's votes could have put Richardson in Albany. In 1947 the chair of the New York State Communist Party announced that they had erred in not rallying their forces behind the Black Republican. This stemmed from their "basic under-estimation of the overriding necessity in this area of securing repre-

sentation for the Negro people through the election of a Negro to office."
This assessment pushed the left in future elections to emphasize Black representation, regardless of political party, so long as the candidate was popular
and progressive.[26]

The ALP's goal of Black representation could be seen in the Brooklyn City
Council race a year later, when a white ALP candidate withdrew in favor of
Ada B. Jackson. "As a war veteran and a Jewish-American," he announced,
"I am confident that the voters of Brooklyn, regardless of formal party affiliation, will recognize in the candidacy of Mrs. Jackson a signal opportunity to
elect a highly-qualified individual for vital public service and to strike a
blow at all discrimination." The City Council field in Brooklyn was otherwise all white. Jackson ran a strong campaign in the hopes of becoming the
first African American from Brooklyn on the City Council. Her platform
called for rent control on all dwellings; equal job opportunities; the nickel
subway fare; public day care centers; more libraries, schools, and parks; public housing without discrimination; the repeal of Taft Hartley; extended veterans benefits; federal antilynching and anti–poll tax laws; and a law against
a third world war. The *Brooklyn Eagle* dubbed Jackson "The Fighting Lady,"
a label that suggests that political activism could generate images of Black
women in stark contrast to the maids and mammies that dominated mainstream media. The Baptist Ministers Conference, Paul Robeson, Brooklyn's
own Lena Horne, Eleanor Gimbel, Susan B. Anthony III, and Dorothy
Parker campaigned for her. According to Horne, "We are not electioneering
for Mrs. Jackson, we are crusading." Jackson lost the boroughwide election,
but she won 135,967 votes, or 23 percent of the total, the highest that an
ALP candidate ever received in Brooklyn. She also won the majority of votes
in the predominantly Black seventeenth assembly district.[27]

Political elites moved swiftly to contain this explosion in insurgent electoral activism and assert control over grassroots self-activity. In 1947 conservative forces won two changes in electoral procedure that marginalized
third-party strength and minority voices in local and state government. The
Wilson-Pakula Law curtailed the influence of the ALP in state elections by
barring an individual from entering the primary of a party of which she
or he was not a member without the permission of the party's county committee. It transferred a significant role in the nominating process from the
party's members to the party's leaders.[28]

The second initiative changed the manner of electing City Council members from proportional representation to a district-based, winner-take-all

system. It was achieved through a ballot referendum, and fairly quickly transformed the council from a multiparty body to one under almost complete Democratic Party control. These changes paved the way for the Democratic Party's domination of city government and tighter control of internal party affairs by the "machine bosses." By removing the structural basis for political independence, these changes diminished the representation of minority groups in general, whether political or ethnic/racial.

Opponents of proportional representation, such as the Democratic Party and the Chamber of Commerce, claimed that it gave the Communist Party too much representation. But statistics indicate that proportional representation produced fairly accurate representation. For example, in 1945, 9 percent of the vote went to Communists, and two were elected—constituting 9 percent of the council. Democrats won 59 percent of the votes and had fourteen council members, or 61 percent of the body. The ALP won 10 percent of the votes and sent two members to the council, or 9 percent. Thirteen percent of the council was Republican, who had won 15 percent of the vote. Civil rights groups fought against both the Wilson-Pakula Law and repeal of proportional representation. The national office of the NAACP as well as city branches spoke out strongly in favor of retaining proportional representation, explicitly linking it to continued Black representation in the council.[29]

The Travia Law was a third measure that undercut insurgent organizing and electoral independence. Passed by the state in 1951, it required that people who circulated nominating petitions had to reside in the district and be enrolled members of the party. Finally, in 1948 the Democratic Party prohibited collaboration with the ALP. This was intended to force Adam Clayton Powell and other progressive Democrats to sever ties with the left. It aimed at unraveling an electoral Popular Front. Moreover, the anticommunist crusade further marginalized radical parties by making association with them potential grounds for deportation, loss of a job, or if one happened to reside in public housing, eviction.[30]

Despite this backlash and crackdown, the breakup of the activist electoral alliance and the demise of the ALP did not happen overnight. The explosion of postwar Black activism culminated in the 1948 election when nearly fifty Black candidates ran for office nationally on the Progressive Party ticket, and the Truman administration adopted a progressive civil rights platform. Although the attack on the ALP did undermine efforts in 1948 to elect an African American to the state senate from Harlem and to the assembly from the Bronx, the campaign to elect a Black state assemblyman in Brooklyn was victorious in 1948, with the election of Bertram Baker, born in Nevis, West Indies. Baker was able to suspend the Democrat's new rule against the ALP, and as Powell and Marcantonio had in the past, he received the nomination of both parties. He won by a landslide, defeating Republican Maude Richardson 21,086 to 1,528. Baker's victory showed how grassroots activism helped pressure the party machine to accommodate Black aspirations.[31]

Third-party Black candidates laid the foundation for many of the first Black electoral victories in New York City, a story that will be resumed in a later chapter. Even though ALP candidates rarely won, they forced the Democratic Party to recognize its growing Black constituency. The Wilson-Pakula law, repeal of proportional representation, and other measures, however, reduced populist pressures on mainstream politics. Thus, the emergence of African Americans as a majority Democratic voting bloc was the result of a paradoxical process of liberalization and repression.

Looking South

Harlem was a vital center of the civil rights and Black liberation movements in the postwar world. When Fannie Lou Hamer went North in the 1960s to raise money or gain allies, or when the North Carolina Black leader Robert F. Williams went to Harlem to procure support, and perhaps arms, or when Harry Belafonte gave benefit concerts in New York for the southern civil rights movement, they were calling on this antiracist support network. Black New Yorkers led lobbying campaigns in Washington, provided legal support, created solidarity networks, raised money, and gathered petitions aimed at overthrowing southern Jim Crow. For a city filled with folks born in the Carolinas, Georgia, Florida, and Virginia, there was a natural constituency for national (and international) antiracist political activism. According to a 1949 "Fact Sheet on Negro Americans in New York City," produced by the American Labor Party, "The one million Negroes in New York constitute the largest single urban concentration of Negroes anywhere in the world," making the city "both a national and international center for persons of African descent everywhere."[32]

In the first several years after the war, a flood of civil rights bills was introduced in Congress. From 1937 to 1950, there were 252 bills against discrimination introduced, 72 of them in the 1949–1950 session alone. But these bills failed to produce a single new law. Southern Democrats, elected in states without free elections for all citizens, joined antiregulatory Republicans to defeat them. But even moderate party leaders failed to fight for racial justice or give it high priority. Prosegregation forces in the Senate possessed the filibuster, a procedural rule that allows opponents of a measure to literally talk a bill to death unless two-thirds of the membership votes to stop debate. As a result, eliminating the filibuster became a major goal of African American rights groups and other liberal reform organizations.[33]

The first twentieth-century champion of civil rights laws in Congress was Vito Marcantonio, who, while not a member of the Communist Party, was its closest ally in Congress. An Italian American, he was for many years the chairman of the American Labor Party. "The People's Congressman" from East Harlem, Marcantonio fought for progressive labor, tax, social welfare, civil rights, foreign policy, and civil liberties bills in Congress from 1934 to 1936, and from 1938 until his defeat in 1950. An ideologue and a pragmatist, Marcantonio was a seasoned parliamentarian and an old-fashioned pol whose Italian, Puerto Rican, and Black constituency in East Harlem handed him easy victories until the state changed the election laws to help defeat him in 1950.

Marcantonio introduced the first Fair Employment Practices bill in 1941, and in 1945 he maneuvered to win continued funding for the wartime FEPC. In 1942, he introduced the first anti–poll tax bill to pass the House of Representatives, and in 1947 the House passed his bill again only to have it filibustered in the Senate. The poll tax was finally prohibited by a constitutional amendment in 1964. Beginning in 1942, Marcantonio attached what he called "Harlem riders"—nondiscrimination guarantees—to appropriations bills for armaments, housing, and education. After his election to Congress in 1944, Adam Clayton Powell joined Marcantonio as a militant proponent of FEPC and other civil rights bills, and after Marcantonio's defeat in 1950, he became the movement's primary advocate on the floor of Congress. Moreover, he continued the parliamentary practice of forcing politicians to confront the issue of civil rights by attaching "Powell Amendments" to social spending bills throughout the 1950s.[34]

Activist efforts in New York aimed at national or southern civil rights issues were numerous, and included A. Philip Randolph's campaign against military segregation, the National Committee to Abolish the Poll Tax, and antilynching mobilizations. One lesser-known example involved the 1946 struggle by Black Mississippians to block the seating of Mississippi senator Theodore Bilbo for using fraud, intimidation, and violence during his reelection campaign. Activists in New York, particularly the left-wing Civil Rights

Congress, provided support. Civil rights activists made Bilbo a symbol of the injustice of disfranchisement and the urgency of the anti–poll tax movement after he attacked the wartime performance of African American troops. In 1940, Bilbo was elected by 7 percent of the voting-age citizens of Mississippi. A product of white supremacist politics that relied on racial violence, Bilbo relished displaying his belief in white superiority. In response to an invitation to an anti-Bilbo rally at a Black church in Brooklyn, Bilbo said, "Please notify your whole mongrel congregation that I absolutely have no apology for anything I have said." The exchange was printed in the *People's Voice*, exemplifying the kinds of dramatic challenges and confrontations with aggressively racist politicians that were a hallmark of the New York civil rights struggle. Adam Clayton Powell's denunciations of segregation, for example, led to frequent verbal clashes with southern racist Congressmen.[35]

The *Smith v. Allwright* decision produced a jump in Black voter registration in the South, and war veterans, in particular, were determined to exercise their rights. In 1946 many southern incumbents openly endorsed night riding, cross burnings, and massive Klan demonstrations to prevent African Americans from coming to the polls. Two Black voters were killed. Bilbo, a self-identified Klan leader, exhorted his followers to violence: "I call on every red-blooded American who believes in the superiority and integrity of the white race to get out and see that no nigger votes . . . AND THE BEST TIME TO DO IT IS THE NIGHT BEFORE." In September, fifty Black Mississippians petitioned the Senate Committee on Campaign Expenditures to block the seating of Bilbo. Percy Green, the publisher and editor of the *Jackson Advocate* and a leader of the "Oust Bilbo" movement, came to New York to build national support. The Civil Rights Congress sent several investigators to Mississippi, challenged the election in court, and urged Truman to intervene. Canada Lee, a popular stage and screen actor, delivered a petition on the Senate floor signed by 25,000 New Yorkers urging the expulsion of Bilbo "for conduct unbecoming a member of Congress." The movement succeeded in securing federal hearings on voting rights in Mississippi—a development, declared the Civil Rights Congress, that was "history-making and unprecedented since the days of Reconstruction." At great personal risk, and foreshadowing the courage of Fannie Lou Hamer and her neighbors almost twenty years later, hundreds of African Americans came to Jackson from across the state to tell their stories of facing threats and acts of violence for attempting to vote. Bilbo, they argued, suppressed the votes that would have defeated him.[36]

New Yorkers pressured their own representatives to join the battle against Bilbo. Rallies were held across the city, including a "To Hell with Bilbo" rally at Abyssinian Baptist Church that called on Senators James Mead and Robert Wagner to denounce Bilbo's racist remarks against Black soldiers. City Council President Joseph Sharkey introduced a resolution urging the Senate to act against Bilbo, and both Mead and Wagner criticized Bilbo's remarks on the Senate floor. Former governor Herbert Lehman pledged to a group of upstate party leaders, "If I am elected as Democratic Senator from New York, I will do everything in my power to bring [Bilbo] before the bar of the Senate where his words and deeds can be judged." Lehman lashed out at Bilbo, Herman Talmadge of Georgia, and Mississippi's John E. Rankin as "fomenters of race hatred and leaders of an evil Fascist movement in America." The issue resonated with the city's large Jewish population, who also had an interest in reversing the enormous power in Washington wielded by undemocratically elected advocates of discrimination. The Senate held up Bilbo's seating, after allegations of bribes by war contractors arose, but fate intervened and this purveyor of hate speech died suddenly of throat cancer.[37]

Race and the United Nations

The obstacles to securing racial justice through domestic governmental channels, the filibuster and poll tax above all, prompted many African American leaders to pursue alternative avenues to protect African American lives and rights. Black leadership looked hopefully at the creation of the United Nations (UN) with its potential to promulgate and enforce international standards of human rights among its members. From 1946 to 1952 three different organizations submitted petitions to the UN seeking some form of assistance or intervention to aid the Black freedom struggle in the United States. This reflected an intensification of a long-standing strategy by African American political activists, beginning with the abolitionist movement, to seek international platforms or allies in their struggle against white supremacy within the United States.

Appeals to the UN were also fueled by a heightened Black American consciousness in the 1940s of being members of a global African diaspora. This sentiment peaked during World War II when even mainstream leaders, such as Walter White, championed third world independence, pressured the European allies not to rebuild their colonial empires after the war, and stressed the common links between Black Americans and the struggles of oppressed peoples of African descent around the world. Coverage of international events, especially in Africa, Asia, and the Caribbean, saturated the Black press in the 1930s and 1940s. UN petitions also sought to capitalize on the rising worldwide interest in U.S. racial practices, a product of African and Asian solidarity as well as Soviet anti-American propaganda as the Cold War intensified. The international press was similarly increasingly interested in covering U.S. racial segregation and violence, as well as the movement against it.[38]

The first petition to the United Nations was submitted by the National Negro Congress (NNC) in 1946. And it was not the only nongovernmental organization to submit one: by January 1946, the UN had received about a thousand petitions or appeals from such organizations around the world. A collection of scholarly articles, the petition described the social, economic, and political injustices faced by Black Americans and appealed for aid. Passed at the NNC's annual convention in Detroit, it was sent across town to UN Secretary General Trygve Lee, who happened to be in Detroit for the auto industry's Golden Jubilee. There was concern by some members of the NNC, particularly William L. Patterson, that the petition had been hastily created. Five years later, as executive secretary of the Civil Rights Congress, Patterson submitted *We Charge Genocide,* a petition that detailed the enormity of American racial violence and exposed the complicity of local, state, and federal officials.[39]

In 1947 W. E. B. Du Bois supervised *An Appeal to the World,* a petition submitted to the United Nations by the NAACP. In the introduction, he presented an overview of African American history stressing that slavery, disfranchisement, mob violence, and peonage had undermined democracy in the United States. "The disfranchisement of the American Negro makes the functioning of all democracy in the nation difficult," Du Bois maintained, because it allowed the conservative south to rule the nation—"and as democracy fails to function in the leading democracy in the world, it fails to function in the world." Du Bois warned that as the host nation for the diverse national representatives of the United Nations, (many of whom may be "mistaken for a Negro"), and as a world leader, the first obligation of the United States was to end the racial caste system. As the United States quickly moved into a position of control at the UN, however, it blocked any consideration of the domestic status of U.S. racial minorities.

Despite their failure to lead to UN scrutiny of American racial practices, these petitions stand as significant documents of postwar African American internationalism. They generated publicity in Europe and the developing world about Black discontent over American racial segregation and violence, creating and sustaining a global audience concerned about racial injustice in the United States that would play a strategic role in the ensuing decades of the civil rights movement. These efforts also contextualize Malcolm X's later refrain that the civil rights struggle was a human rights struggle. Indeed, when Malcolm X embarked on an internationalist strategy in the 1960s, and devoted himself to a United Nations petition drive in the period before his assassination, he was reviving, rather than creating, a long-standing Black radical tradition.[40]

To Secure These Rights, the 1947 report of President Truman's Committee on Civil Rights, reflects the influence of the New York civil rights movement. It called for the total abolition of racial and religious segregation and discrimination in the United States, and the withholding of federal aid to public education, housing, hospitals, and any other public services and facilities as a means to achieve it. It advocated passage of antilynching, anti–poll tax, and FEPC laws as well as the full enforcement of the Thirteenth, Fourteenth, and Fifteenth Amendments. In sum, it endorsed and legitimized the legislative agenda of the grassroots African American struggle for racial justice. Indeed, as the 1948 presidential election would demonstrate, civil rights activism and African American political mobilization in cities such as New York pushed issues of segregation and discrimination to the forefront of debates within the Democratic Party. While Black voters had been part of the New Deal coalition in the prewar years, civil rights issues had not. The northern civil rights movement was trying to put the Democratic Party in a position where it would have to embrace Black issues in exchange for getting Black votes.[41]

The convergence of Black migration, political mobilization, and shifting global politics increased the political saliency of civil rights and the political visibility of Black people in the 1940s. A multiparty system in New York City offered the African American electoral minority a way to mobilize a bloc vote and threaten to withhold it from the Democratic Party. The rapid moves to restrain this electoral independence underscored its power. In addition to the desire for economic security, a major motivation for Black political mobilization was the need to protect African Americans from postwar white violence. The Black rights movement moved rapidly after the war to demand governmental protection of the civil rights of African Americans.

3 Lynching, Northern Style

The murder of African Americans, especially of veterans in uniform, by police officers or white mobs escalated after World War II. The fight against lynching—the illegal execution of a person by a mob—became a major component of the New York civil rights movement. Southern migrants used their new political muscle in the North to demand federal protection of the right to due process of law for victims of racially motivated violence in the South. The antilynching struggle became a launching pad for the modern civil rights movement because it propelled the articulation of a national legislative agenda that shaped civil rights advocacy for the next two decades. But African Americans in New York quickly discovered that the upsurge of postwar racial violence was national in scope.

In New York City, there was an explosion of police violence against Black people, and activists moved to broaden the fight against racial violence to include police brutality as well as lynching. From 1947 to 1952 forty-six unarmed African Americans, and two whites, were killed by police officers in the state of New York. This correlated with a sharp jump in the city's Black population, rising Black income, and the beginnings of the civil rights movement. Between 1940 and 1950 the Black population of the city grew 62 percent, from less than half a million to over a million. As Black New Yorkers with high expectations, higher incomes, new clothes, pride, and determination demanded the right to live and work anywhere and to patronize downtown nightclubs and restaurants, complaints of police brutality "poured in" to the NAACP. African Americans were laying siege to old ideas and boundaries, and police officers moved to the front lines of defending white supremacy. Ordinary Black men and women publicly aired their stories of police abuse and made reform of police conduct and the criminal justice system part of their broader struggle for first-class citizenship.[1]

War at Home and Abroad

Several highly publicized cases of racial violence in 1946 sparked a mobilization for a federal antilynching law. In February 1946, on a bus from South
Carolina to New York City, Isaac Woodard, a recently discharged Black
army sergeant still in uniform, exchanged words with a racist white bus
driver, who summoned two police officers. The white officers gouged out
Woodard's eyes with their nightsticks, blinding him. The NAACP publicized
the assault, using the press, radio interviews, and celebrity support to attract
national attention. Some of the liberal media outlets that had rallied around
the campaign for "wartime unity" were still in place to mobilize popular
sentiment against "southern fascism." Ollie Harrington, the noted cartoonist
and public relations director for the NAACP, enlisted the aid of Orson Welles,
who performed a dramatic reenactment of the attack on Woodard over
his "Orson Welles Commentaries," broadcast nationally on ABC. Furious
white South Carolinians, however, denounced the network and demanded
Welles's dismissal. ABC canceled the show, bringing the actor's social activism to a halt. The blinding of Isaac Woodard became a cause célèbre that received international attention. Civil rights activists stressed the repercussions to the U.S. image abroad posed by such rampant and unpunished
racial violence inflicted by local authorities. One New York City Black newspaper said such brutality exposed the United States as "a farce and a fraud,"
and noted, "We have no title to world leadership so long as our own democracy is so counterfeit and bankrupt."[2]

Prefiguring southern crises over the next twenty years, most famously
in Little Rock, Arkansas, national and international attention to the Isaac
Woodard case helped prod federal intervention. A federal attorney prose-
cuted the white sheriff in U.S. District Court under the liberal judge J. Waties
Waring, a "scion of eight generations of Charleston aristocracy and son of a
Confederate veteran." But this outside exposure and mobilization was undercut by the FBI's cooperation with local white law enforcement. Federal
agents reportedly did little to produce witnesses or evidence to aid the prosecution, and the all-white jury acquitted the sheriff.[3]

The first major case of postwar racial violence actually happened in the
North. On the evening of February 5, in Freeport, Long Island, four brothers
from nearby Roosevelt were enjoying a reunion: Charles Ferguson, an army
soldier stationed in Greensboro, North Carolina, who had just reenlisted after an overseas tour; Joseph Ferguson, a navy sailor stationed on Long Is-

land; Richard Ferguson, an army combat veteran; and Alphonzo Ferguson, the lone civilian. The evening got off to a bad start when the white manager of a coffee shop refused to serve them coffee, saying there was none left. After vigorously protesting, the brothers left and the manager complained to the police about misbehaving Negroes. Later that night as the Ferguson brothers were heading back to the bus station, a rookie white police officer, Joseph Romeika, arrested them for disorderly conduct and ordered them, along with an inquiring passerby, also African American, to line up against a wall. When Charles and Joseph questioned the arrests, the officer kicked each man in the groin, and then abruptly fired his gun twice, killing Charles and Alphonzo and wounding Joseph. He later stated that Charles had said he had a gun. Eyewitnesses told a different story and all of the men were found to be unarmed. Immediately after the shootings police amassed in the area, readied with tear gas to prevent, according to the police chief, "a possible uprising of local Negroes."

Richard Ferguson was tried and convicted a few hours later. Judge Hilbert Johnson declared that "four fellows going out looking for trouble—they are going to get just what they are looking for. And I want to commend any Police Officer who can keep trouble away from this Village."[4] Charles, a married father of three, was buried in Long Island National Cemetery with full military honors. The day after the killings, Nassau County District Attorney James H. Gehrig called Romeika's conduct "unquestionably justified." On February 22, an all-white Nassau County grand jury (no African American had ever served on this body) announced its decision not to indict Romeika.[5]

The killing of the two Ferguson brothers sparked a five-month protest campaign in New York City and Long Island seeking the appointment of a special prosecutor, the indictment of the police officer, and, ultimately, federal intervention. Immediately after the shootings, relatives of the brothers contacted local activists, who organized support committees in New York City and on Long Island. Both were Popular Front formations, with left-wing activists in the forefront. On Long Island, Charles Ferguson's widow, Minnie Ferguson, and another Ferguson brother, Edward, joined with the United Veterans for Equality, the local NAACP branch, the American Labor Party, and the Nassau County Communist Party to form the Committee for Justice in the Ferguson Case. In New York City representatives from over sixty-three organizations formed the New York Committee for Justice in Freeport with Representative Adam Clayton Powell as honorary chair and

Dorothy Langston, formerly of the Communist-supported International Labor Defense, as executive secretary. Stanley Faulkner, a left-wing lawyer with a CIO union, represented the Ferguson family.[6]

There was considerable red-baiting by Long Island Republican elected officials from the beginning of the case. The district attorney blamed the public outcry over the killings on Communist subterfuge, and questioned grand jury witnesses about their political affiliations, attempting to impeach their credibility by associating them with radicalism.[7] The Freeport struggle highlighted the chasm between the NAACP national staff, which opposed Popular Front initiatives, and the civil rights movement in New York City, including NAACP branches, where they flourished. In Freeport, representatives of the Long Island NAACP branches were among the first to visit the mayor of Freeport after the shootings. James Egert Allen, president of the New York State Conference of Branches, and Lionel T. Barrow, president of the New York City branch, both served on the New York City Freeport Committee's executive committee, but NAACP executive secretary Walter White declined to join. NAACP attorneys monitored the Freeport case intensely, fearful that it would enhance the stature of the Communist Party within the civil rights movement. Roy Wilkins regretted that their lawyers had lagged in offering legal support. "If this case had occurred in Alabama," he guessed, "we would probably . . . go all out on it." Wilkins worried that in light of the Communist Party's "aggressive action on issues affecting Negroes, this might well be a case that they will build up to the greatest proportion possible." Publicly, however, the NAACP supported the Freeport campaign and endorsed the call for a special prosecutor.[8]

The NAACP also joined an amicus brief written by the nation's leading civil liberties and civil rights attorneys that was filed with the petition to Governor Dewey. It requested a special prosecutor for the Freeport case, which attorneys from the American Civil Liberties Union, American Jewish Congress, and NAACP put at the juncture of the war against fascism and the emerging civil rights movement:

> In an era that has seen a successful war to stamp out barbarism abroad, we cannot allow it to spring up at home; in a state that was first to legislate meaningfully against discrimination, we cannot stop the fight now.[9]

Believing that courts are swayed by public opinion and political pressure, a hallmark of Popular Front legal strategies was to develop a grassroots movement, or "mass action," alongside the court efforts. They organized rallies and petitions, and sent delegations to Albany to pressure Governor Dewey to intervene. Everywhere the meaning of World War II was stressed. "Freeport must be freed!" Powell declared at a "March on Times Square"—a name invoking the threatened March on Washington. "This issue," he predicted, "will determine whether we [have] won the war against fascism or lost it." Rhetoric in the New York civil rights movement frequently linked the domestic antiracist struggle, the labor movement, and anticolonialism. A leader with the Transport Workers Union shouted to the crowd, "Freeport, my TWU, the struggles in India, they are all the same fight."[10]

At a protest in Harlem, City Councilman Benjamin Davis said Romeika should join "the list of war criminals." The Jamaica branch of the NAACP sponsored a meeting at Amity Baptist church, with speeches by NAACP officials, clergy, and trade union leaders. And with Charles Ferguson's widow, Minnie, as a speaker, the Communist Party held a demonstration in Union Square on March 7 to protest the "lynch murders of Negro GIs in Freeport, Long Island and the terror against an entire Negro community in Columbia, Tennessee." The latter refers to a white mob attack met by armed Black self-defense that resulted in the vengeful police destruction of Black businesses, the arrests of dozens of African American residents, and the murder of two Black men in jail.[11]

A series of developments increased pressure on the politically ambitious Dewey, who would challenge Truman for the presidency in 1948: the Navy cleared Joseph Ferguson of misconduct; Richard Ferguson's disorderly conduct conviction was reversed; and the U.S. Army announced that Charles Ferguson was killed "in the line of duty," not as a result of his misconduct. Not only did this determination strengthen the family's claim that the shooting was unjustified; it also guaranteed a pension to his widow, Minnie Ferguson. A turning point in the case came when the Army issued a "Scroll of Honor" to Mrs. Ferguson signed by the president. It memorialized "Private First Class Charles R. Ferguson who died in the service of his country in the American Area, February 5, 1946." In addition, a five-star general issued a citation that portrayed Ferguson as a martyr.[12]

The *New York Age* said the presidential citation "raises still higher the temperature of what is already a pretty hot coal in the lap of New York's Governor Dewey." By June, there were eleven Freeport protest committees across the state and region and some fifty meetings and rallies had been held. Governor Dewey opted for a compromise, appointing Lawrence Greenbaum, the chair of the state's Board of Social Welfare, to review the case. Activists,

Protest in Harlem seeking a special prosecutor for the Freeport case, 1946.

however, were skeptical, since public hearings by Greenbaum did not include cross-examination of his witnesses. When the police officer testified that he had been told by the coffee shop proprietor that Charles Ferguson had had a gun and had threatened to kill him, a claim he had not previously made, the Ferguson family and their supporters protested the denial of a chance to challenge this new version.[13]

Greenbaum's report defended the district attorney, and the governor promptly dismissed the petition to appoint a special prosecutor. The widespread feeling that Governor Dewey had betrayed Black constitutional rights to protect the Republican machine in Nassau County likely hurt him among African American voters in the next election. In a radio speech during the presidential campaign in 1948, Adam Clayton Powell blasted Dewey, saying, "His hands still drip with the blood of the Ferguson brothers and the voters of this community will remember that next Tuesday." Efforts to secure a federal indictment of Romeika also failed. Tom Clark, the U.S. attorney general, contended that in light of a 1945 Supreme Court decision that promulgated a virtually unattainable definition of intent, he lacked proof that Officer Romeika had intentionally tried to deprive Charles Ferguson of his Fourteenth Amendment right to due process when he fired his weapon. This fueled demands for a federal antilynching law to enable such prosecutions—it was termed an antilynching law, even though it pertained to police killings as well.[14]

At the climax of the Freeport investigation, several cases of lynching in the South sparked protest across the nation, and pushed the issue further into the national spotlight. In July a white mob in Monroe, Georgia, ambushed a car with two African American couples, Mr. and Mrs. Roger Malcolm and Mr. and Mrs. George Dorsey. Roger Malcolm had just been released on bail; he had been jailed for stabbing the son of his boss, who reportedly had sexually molested Mrs. Malcolm. The four were pulled from the car, lined up, and shot more than sixty times. One of the women screamed out the identity of one of the killers right before she died. New York City Representatives Adam Clayton Powell and Vito Marcantonio protested on the floor of Congress, while Dixiecrats vigorously and openly defended vigilante violence under the rubric of states' rights.

The summer and fall of 1946 were bloody times in the South as white politicians fought to nullify the effect of *Smith v. Allwright,* the 1944 Supreme Court decision that declared the all-white primary unconstitutional. Eugene Talmadge had repeatedly threatened Black voters with violence in his ugly campaign for governor of Georgia. He even hung signs on Black churches warning, "The first Negro to vote will never vote again." On July 20, Maceo Snipes voted in the Georgia primary and was dragged from his home and killed by four white men. Channing Tobias, the director of the Phelps-Stokes Fund and future chairman of the NAACP, was almost lynched in Georgia during the campaign season. In Tennessee a Black man was shot for attempting to vote.[15]

African Americans in the north mobilized in defense of their southern kith and kin. Protests were held across the country. One of the largest was on 125th Street, sponsored by the Committee to Elect Charles Collins to the state senate. Collins's antilynching advocacy reveals the prominent place that fighting southern Jim Crow occupied in northern Black politics. Many Black people had migrated north to seek refuge from white southern violence, and they rallied to his cry. An "after church" rally of several thousand in Harlem was sponsored by a coalition of trade unionists and Harlem ministers, including Adam Clayton Powell, James Robinson, Charles Y. Trigg, and Shelton Hale Bishop. The protesters demanded federal intervention in the Georgia shootings, which the American Council on Race Relations called "the climax of a series of terror attacks on minority groups which threatens the internal peace of the nation."[16]

Many AME and AME Zion churches had long traditions of preaching the social gospel and developing politically active ministries. In August, nearly three thousand people attended a "Stop Lynch Terror Now" meeting at Mother Zion AME church on 137th Street, home of the Reverend Ben Robeson, brother of the acclaimed artist-activist. They passed a resolution demanding federal action, and endorsed the effort of W. E. B. Du Bois to petition the United Nations to address America's "domestic fascism." An antilynching rally of ten thousand at Madison Square Garden with Paul Robeson was the closing event of the AME Zion sesquicentennial celebration in September.[17]

A Theater vs. Intolerance Committee sponsored a benefit performance of *Anna Lucasta* starring Ruby Dee on behalf of the families of the Georgia lynching victims. A star-studded concert at Lewisohn Stadium in the Bronx raised $10,000 for the blinded veteran Isaac Woodard, who had moved to the Bronx and hoped to open a restaurant. Twenty-five thousand people came to hear Carol Brice, Canada Lee, W. C. Handy, Billie Holiday, Cootie Williams, Cab Calloway, Count Basie, Pearl Bailey, and Bill (Bojangles) Robinson. In the garment district, fifteen thousand New Yorkers heard world heavyweight champion Joe Louis, Paul Robeson, TWU president Michael Quill, and Mary McLeod Bethune denounce lynching and call for federal intervention. The New York City Council unanimously passed a resolution introduced by Ben Davis calling for a federal investigation of the Georgia lynchings. By November 1946, the Justice Department had received over thirty thousand pieces of mail urging federal action in Monroe. The federal government did impanel grand juries in both Tennessee and Georgia, but neither indicted anyone, intensifying the campaign for a federal antilynching law.[18]

In the fall two antilynching delegations—one led by the NAACP and the other a liberal-left group led by Paul Robeson—convened in Washington to pressure the government to protect African American civil rights. In his decades of civil rights leadership prior to the rise of a mass movement, Walter White, executive secretary of the NAACP, had developed a style that prized personal access to government leaders. He did not mobilize NAACP branches to participate in his delegation, even though branch membership was at an all-time high. In August, White and representatives from forty-two organizations formed the National Emergency Committee against Mob Violence. With representatives from all of the major American liberal groups, such as the American Jewish Congress, the AFL, and the YMCA, the committee's breadth testified to the NAACP's long years of publicizing the grisly details of southern lynching and forging alliances in the North. On September 19, they met with President Truman at the White House and pleaded with him to take action. The administration suggested a presidential committee to investigate lynching and mob violence and to make recommendations for federal action.[19]

Paul Robeson led the American Crusade to End Lynching to Washington a few days after the NAACP's visit. While their figure of 1,500 delegates is likely inflated, it had a diverse national Black leadership, including John Sengstacke, publisher of the *Chicago Defender*, and Harlem politicians and ministers such as William T. Andrews and Reverend Charles Y. Trigg. Mayor William O'Dwyer declared their date of departure "End Lynching Day" in New York City. The NAACP staff was irritated that W. E. B. Du Bois, a member of the NAACP executive board, and James Egert Allen, the president of the New York Conference of Branches, were among the sponsors of the Robeson group. Even though NAACP branches across the country had not been asked to join White's committee, their participation in the Robeson delegation sparked a sharp rebuke by headquarters and efforts to clamp down on "unauthorized" political action by branches. A Philadelphia branch leader protested that "there cannot be too much duplication on the part of progressive Americans to end lynching."[20]

President Truman also received the Robeson delegation in the Oval Office. Even though the Cold War would soon thoroughly demonize the left, in the mid-1940s Paul Robeson was at the height of his popularity and stature. In a dramatic encounter with the president, he sought to convey the feelings of Black veterans. "Negro war veterans who fought for freedom want to know that they can have freedom in their own country." African Americans, Robeson announced, were not afraid and would defend themselves. "The temper of the Negro is changed," he informed Truman, and unless the federal government stepped in to stop the violence, "Negroes would." Reportedly flustered, Truman denounced Robeson's warnings as a threat.

Just as controversial as Black self-defense was Robeson's suggestion that the United States was in no position to lead the prosecution of Nazi war criminals at Nuremberg while it permitted Black Americans to be lynched and shot. When Truman said the country should unify around Secretary of State James F. Byrnes, the avowedly segregationist South Carolinian, Robeson disagreed and asked, "How can Secretary Byrnes stand up in the Council of Nations as a representative of a land of freedom, when lynchings and discrimination are common occurrences in that land?" The president insisted that loyal Americans should never mix domestic and foreign policy, and asked Robeson if he were a Communist. Robeson proclaimed himself "violently anti-Fascist."[21]

Grassroots antiracist activism—the delegations, demonstrations, and petitions—as well as international coverage of U.S. race discrimination, were instrumental in Truman's decision to create the President's Committee on Civil Rights in December 1946. For the NAACP, which had fought for decades to rally American public opinion against lynching, this was a major victory. Although the peak era of lynch mobs had passed, the antilynching movement became the springboard for a broader postwar legislative agenda that embraced equality in education, housing, and employment under the rubric of "civil rights." Federal "civil rights" statutes during Reconstruction originated in the failure of local authorities to provide due process and protect citizens from violence; thus the phrase has a particular historical connection, in two different centuries, to the right to be free from violence.[22]

The committee, headed by the president of General Electric and marked by internal divisions, published in 1947, *To Secure These Rights,* a wide-ranging report that reflected the political influence of the struggle for Negro rights. Seven years before *Brown, To Secure These Rights* called for the elimination of racial segregation and discrimination in the United States. It was to shape civil rights advocacy for the next twenty years, although many of its proposals, such as its call for a federal law against police brutality, remain unfulfilled. While the filibuster and overrepresentation of whites in Congress thwarted legislative reform, executive action strengthened the grounds for the Justice Department to intervene in local jurisdictions. A Reconstruction-era statute, section 242 of title 18 of the U.S. Criminal Code, was revised, yet its prohibition against law enforcement officers' depriving persons of rights guaranteed by U.S. laws or by the U.S. Constitution has remained hampered by the requirement to prove intent.[23]

Police Brutality in New York City

An upsurge in questionable police killings, abuse, and misconduct in post-war New York galvanized protest campaigns that put the issue of police racism permanently on the urban political agenda. Activists discursively linked police brutality in New York to southern lynching and racist violence, but they offered a distinct analysis of urban police brutality. Attorneys and civil rights leaders sought justice in individual cases through local channels, but repeated setbacks eventually pushed them to appeal for federal intervention. Beginning in the 1940s, African Americans in New York sought intervention by the U.S. Department of Justice to halt police abuse, underscoring that in the civil rights era, African Americans in the North as well as the South appealed for federal protection of their civil rights. Activists developed a comprehensive agenda for criminal justice reform, including protection from unreasonable search and seizure, a halt to coerced confessions, the creation of an independent civilian complaint-review board, a law to end police immunity from criminal prosecution, greater accountability and disciplinary procedures within the department, more Black police officers, an end to the media stereotyping of Black men as criminals, a halt to the criminalization of poor, minority neighborhoods, and better, fairer policing of Black neighborhoods. The struggle aimed to extend the U.S. Constitution's Bill of Rights to state police procedure.

The social history of Black communities is replete with accounts of routine violations of individuals' rights and repressive policing. When Black Harlemites took to the streets in the Depression demanding to be employed in their own community, the city responded with intensified police surveillance. Police on horseback patrolled the area en masse, according to Langston Hughes, making Harlem the only neighborhood in the city with mounted police. Anger over the massive police presence, Hughes believed, fueled the riot in Harlem in 1943, which was sparked by a police officer's misconduct toward an African American woman. African Americans suffered disproportionately from a wide range of police abuse, including indiscriminate searches, station house beatings, and coerced "confessions"—"the third degree." In 1945 residents of Brownsville, Brooklyn, reported that it was "impossible for men to be walking the streets at night in parts of the Negro section without being stopped for questioning or being searched." Local police officers were said to "routinely" beat Black men with baseball bats and rubber hoses while they were in police custody.[24]

Civil rights attorneys became involved in police brutality cases in part because they often acted as public defenders. To gain immunity from prosecution when they used excessive force, police officers often charged their victim with a crime, usually resisting arrest or assaulting a police officer. Since the government was not required to provide counsel to an indigent defendant until the *Gideon v. Wainwright* U.S. Supreme Court decision in 1963, victims of police misconduct in this era, if they received any representation at all, typically turned to lawyers who were ideologically committed to fighting racism.[25]

The Communist left and their allies played a relatively prominent role in organizing an anti–police brutality movement after the war. This not only reflected the CP's postwar line of aggressively fighting white supremacy, but also illustrated a way in which radicals (including non-Communists) departed from the legal strategy of many liberals, including the national NAACP. Because the left believed that public opinion and political pressure ultimately mattered as much as precedent or evidence in affecting judicial outcomes, they endorsed the use of "mass action" tactics in legal cases. In December 1945, after a series of police shootings, including the shooting of a fourteen-year-old, Communist city councilmen Benjamin Davis and Peter Cacchione organized a Harlem / Bedford-Stuyvesant Citizens Committee against Police Brutality with trade unionists, veterans groups, and local NAACP leaders. They called for the prosecution of offending officers, a City Council investigation of police practices in Black communities, and a retraction of the mayor's alleged "shoot first" order to the police department. They demanded an end to the common police practices of "warning" whites to stay out of African American neighborhoods, and of questioning African Americans in white areas, which, they charged, reinforced neighborhood segregation. They argued that the media had criminalized Black people, or racialized crime, by reporting a "Negro crime wave" and racially identifying (only) Black crime suspects.[26]

Formed in 1946, the Civil Rights Congress (CRC) continued the antiracist and legal defense work of the National Negro Congress and the International Labor Defense (ILD), two Communist-supported organizations that had disbanded. The NNC, the most important antiracist Popular Front organization formed in the 1930s, had brought together Black intellectuals and workers to fight for racial equality. The ILD was a legal defense organization best known for defending the "Scottsboro boys," a group of young Black men in Alabama who were wrongfully convicted of raping a white woman.

Under the leadership of attorney William Patterson, the CRC aided the fight against police brutality and defended poor Black defendants facing life in jail or execution ("legal lynchings") after highly questionable trials. In the summer of 1946 the Civil Rights Congress publicized a series of cases that helped push the issue of police brutality onto the radar of City Hall. When a white cab driver refused to take Josie Stewart and two other women home to the Bronx, Stewart, a needle worker and union member, went to a police officer for aid, insisting on her right to equal service in a public accommodation. The officer hit her in the mouth, said "you people are always making trouble," and charged her with assault. At the precinct, he ordered Stewart to pull down her girdle, and kicked and punched her. A judge pronounced her guilty of assault, but Stewart refused to be thwarted by the city's attempt to make her the aggressor. She brought her case to Ben Davis and became part of the CRC's campaign. In another case, Carlton "Specs" Powell, the only Black musician employed by a network studio, was punished for protesting his difficulty hailing a taxi home from midtown Manhattan. On that early June morning, his request for police assistance resulted in deep cuts to his head and a charge of felonious assault.[27]

After these cases and several others, both Davis and Walter White called for a meeting with the mayor. Since 1943, fear of another riot in Harlem had made the city government more sensitive to police-community tensions. In August 1946, police officials met with civil rights and civic leaders, but Police Commissioner Arthur Wallander blasted the protests as "a concerted campaign of calumny against members of this department, without investigation, facts or justification." He resented comparisons made with southern racial violence, denouncing "these obvious attempts to associate the Police Department of this city in a similar category with deplorable incidents of lynching or racial prejudice that have transpired in other sections of the country."[28]

In October 1947, Councilman Davis's office published a pamphlet called *Lynching Northern Style: Police Brutality,* which presented the left's analysis of police violence. Pointing to the lack of disciplinary action in twenty-six cases brought to the police commissioner over the previous eighteen months, it concluded that "unpunished violence intensifies the severity of the brutality and increases the number of police brutality cases against Negro citizens." The causes of the recent escalation in police violence included a desire "to keep the Negroes 'in their place'" and to reverse their growing militancy since V-J Day; "to create the impression that Negroes are unworthy of the full citizenship which they rightfully demand; to divide Negro and white . . . [which] represents a direct threat to the trade unions, which are based on the public and private association of Negro and white"; and lastly, "to make the Negro and other minorities the scapegoat of repeated 'crime wave' slanders against Harlem and other Negro communities. This is the scapegoat technique of fascists the world over."[29]

That same month, five police officers entered the Harlem candy store of Samuel Symonette, arrested him for writing numbers, and allegedly beat him severely. Police Commissioner Wallander defended the officers, despite Symonette's long hospital stay and extensive injuries. The precinct captain defended the warrantless search, saying "we have our own law" in New York. Davis led a highly publicized protest campaign on Symonette's behalf and the Civil Rights Congress supplied Symonette with Joseph Tauber, one of the lawyers who handled the Scottsboro defense. Davis introduced a resolution in the City Council calling for public hearings on police brutality. At a conference he organized with over two hundred participants, including local NAACP and Democratic Party activists, Councilman Davis accused the city of operating a twin system of justice, "one for whites and another for Negroes." They formed a Citizens' Committee to End Police Brutality with Guy Brewer as chair. A Democratic district leader, Brewer was also an outspoken critic of police practices. He had been assaulted by a police officer on election day in Harlem in 1945, and then convicted of disorderly conduct. Brewer sent a letter to City Council members urging their support of the Davis resolution, with the proviso, "No, I am not a Communist nor fellow traveler. I was until July 31, 1947 a Tammany district leader."[30]

In November, a magistrate indicted four police officers for assaulting Symonette. But another judge, who also happened to be a former police lieutenant, quickly acquitted them in a courtroom filled with police brass. Despite this loss, pressure on the city to reform police practices continued to build. The police chaplain, John H. Johnson, the minister of a prominent Harlem Episcopal church, arranged a meeting between activists, including Davis and Brewer, and city officials at police headquarters on November 12, 1947. In an apparent concession, Wallander appointed a board of review, composed of five police officials and five community leaders (four of the community leaders were African American), to review the department's handling of recent cases. The board had no independently authorized powers, however, and Wallander reportedly undermined its efforts to conduct impartial reviews. Madison Jones, the NAACP's representative on the board, wanted to strengthen its mandate, but the board soon dissolved. Guy Brewer was bitter over the police department's obstructionism and blamed the police chaplain, Reverend Johnson, who he claimed had "sabotaged" their efforts because they would not "submit to his attempts to whitewash the police department." The substance of Brewer's allegations are unclear, but they signal what would become a pattern: a committee would be appointed in response to political pressure only to unravel under charges that its hands were tied. The failure of such in-house monitoring increased Black advocacy for independent civilian review boards.[31]

By 1948, the rise of the Cold War internationally and anticommunist sentiment at home provided a language for the police department to undermine its critics. Relations between the Soviet Union and United States broke down in the immediate postwar years—and as the United States pursued a strategy of aggressive opposition to the Soviet Union and American Communists pursued a strategy of aggressive opposition to U.S. foreign policy, domestic Popular Front politics suffered internal turmoil and external pressure. By 1948 the coalitions between radicals (both Communist and noncommunist) and liberals that had been so commonplace in the struggle for African American rights in New York were unraveling. The police department took advantage of the shifting politics in the nation to marginalize its critics, among whom were many leftists and open Communists, such as Ben Davis. Borrowing the common tropes of the anticommunist movement, the police department framed left-wing efforts as insincere—as part of a plan to sow internal discord in the United States and arouse racial enmity and strife. The Commerce and Industry Association said charges of police brutality "have provided a field day for subversive groups who thrive on smear attacks on the forces of law and order." In March 1948, Dan Dodson, the white southern-born chair of the Mayor's Committee on Unity, gave a controversial speech at Riverside Church that echoed the police charge that accusations of police brutality were stirred up by Communist agitators. "I have never been a red-baiter," Dodson began, but, he argued, "the repeated charges of police brutality" were being used by Communists to unfairly discredit the police department, a force of 18,000 in which "there are bound to be those who get out of line."[32]

Policing and the U.S. Constitution

In 1948 and 1949, as the left was increasingly preoccupied with defending itself against the anticommunist crusade, NAACP branches in Harlem and

Brooklyn moved to the forefront of the grassroots anti–police brutality movement. In March 1948, Jawn Sandifer, president of the Harlem branch, publicly criticized Dodson's analysis of police practices and announced a new branch campaign to end police brutality. The branch formed a committee for action against police brutality and sponsored rallies and picket lines in coalitions with unions and churches. Sandifer also articulated a new, two-pronged strategy: "We plan to go a few steps further and enter civil suits also. In criminal cases police enjoy almost complete immunity in the courts. By filing both civil and criminal suits at the same time, we have a much better chance of checking brutality." Over fifty years later, civil suits remain an important avenue for seeking redress, as American cities remain reluctant to impose criminal sanctions on the excessive use of force by on-duty police officers. Sandifer announced a plan to lobby the city to establish a committee outside the police department where citizens could bring complaints of misconduct, the beginning of a long struggle to create a wholly civilian complaint review board. Moreover, the state NAACP called on the governor to appoint a special investigator in order to get around the reluctance of district attorneys, who rely on close ties with police departments, to be aggressive.[33]

There was a major campaign by African American elected officials, progressive attorneys, and community activists to get the Fourth Amendment to the U.S. Constitution to apply to state criminal procedure. The police murder of George Waddell, a young father recently arrived in Brooklyn from North Carolina, galvanized a campaign to pass a law protecting New Yorkers against unreasonable search and seizure. Purportedly seeking out illicit gambling, the police had entered Waddell's home without a warrant, and beat and shot him in front of his wife. Assemblymen Hulan Jack and Elijah Crump introduced a bill barring the admissibility of evidence obtained from an unlawful search. Although such evidence was already barred in federal courts, the Supreme Court did not apply the exclusionary rule to state criminal courts until 1961. While the New York state constitution had prohibited unreasonable search and seizure since 1938, it refrained from excluding any evidence acquired through such a search. To many, this discrepancy, or contradiction, nullified the protections of the Bill of Rights and invited capricious police procedure. In testimony before the New York County Courts Bar Association, Mrs. Waddell's attorney Samuel Korb said it "creates an attitude, especially among juveniles, that they must fight back. It creates the feeling that the police are not the protectors of the home."[34]

After the police testified that they thought the unarmed Waddell had been armed, a grand jury concluded that they had acted within the line of duty. At this time, a "line of duty" defense protected police officers from prosecution. The Brooklyn NAACP petitioned Governor Dewey for a special prosecutor for this and other cases in the borough. The petition listed "grave and flagrant breaches of the law" committed by police officers: "unjustified physical assaults," illegal entries, searches and seizures, "third degree practices in police station houses," extortion, and perjuries. "These acts are not occasionally committed," the NAACP lawyers wrote. "They are practiced frequently and unremittingly." The petition analyzed why the worst police abuses fell overwhelmingly on Black residents: "Perhaps the facts are so because of racial prejudices, because of attitudes of white superiority, because of the assumptions that Negroes have little means to protest and resist and fight back, because of the knowledge that no law enforcement official or agency gives attention to the complaints of Negroes against police officers." Civil rights activists emphasized that the failure to hold police accountable to the public they served encouraged abuse.[35]

Civil rights activists challenged police immunity from prosecution. In 1949 the New York State NAACP Conference deplored the rampant "false arrests, unlawful entries, framings, and illegal convictions and the exoneration of guilty officers of the law," and demanded a state law removing police officer immunity.[36] The Brooklyn NAACP branch published several dramatic pamphlets, encouraging citizens to call their politicians, write letters, and sign petitions. With a cover reminiscent of pulp fiction, one flier screamed, "because his skin was BLACK!" and declared "O'Dwyer and DA McDonald— You are both responsible! YOU DON'T HAVE TO PULL THE TRIGGER TO COMMIT MURDER! You have whitewashed the murderers!" Another flier pictured Doretta Waddell with her five-month-old baby and asked her fellow New Yorkers: "Do detectives have a right to murder anybody in a private home?" Like many other antiracist struggles in postwar New York, this one was motivated by the desire to protect and strengthen migrant Black families.

On Memorial Day, 1949, white police officer Donald Mullen shot twenty-two-year-old unarmed Herman Newton in the back, killing him. Mullen was neither suspended, transferred, nor indicted. Lottie Newton, however, fought all the way to the state's highest court to clear her husband's name. She sued the city and an all-white jury in Brooklyn Supreme Court ruled in Newton's favor after the police presented no witnesses. The Court of Appeals upheld the decision in 1952 and awarded Lottie Newton $56,000—the first time, according to her attorney Samuel Korb, that the state's highest court had ruled in a case of police brutality committed against an African American.[37]

The struggle against police brutality pushed constitutional issues to the forefront of the northern civil rights movement. The Brooklyn NAACP sponsored a conference to "Save the Constitution" on June 27, 1949, at the First AME Zion Church. The culmination of the campaign to pass a search and seizure law, the conference was endorsed by many prominent civic and political leaders in the city, although the national NAACP privately fretted over the participation of alleged Communists. The NAACP director of branches recorded his concern that there are "a number of persons who have known Communist Party leanings" on the branch's executive board. The NAACP national officers had long opposed Communist ideology, but like many other large liberal organizations, their membership criteria was nonpartisan: it was open to all. Nonetheless, two trends in New York activism in 1949 were on a collision course: the rising political mobilization of Black New Yorkers and the rising perception of Communists or Communist sympathizers as disloyal Americans.[38]

In the summer of 1949 the Brooklyn branch sent a second petition to Governor Dewey accusing city officials of covering up police abuse of Black citizens. In August, Mayor O'Dwyer, who was up for reelection, appointed a three-person committee to investigate charges of police brutality in Brooklyn. Civil rights activists, however, criticized the committee's decision to only review police records and not hold public hearings. Arguing that the committee needed to hear testimony from the victims and fearing that O'Dwyer's response was simply political cover, NAACP branches demonstrated against it at City Hall in October. The committee disbanded a few months later.[39]

The postwar struggle against racial violence exposed southern Jim Crow regimes to national and international scrutiny, helping to weaken and isolate them on the eve of the southern civil rights movement. The anti-lynching movement increased the authority of the federal government to prosecute civil rights violations by local law enforcement, a recourse that has remained vital in the continuing struggle against urban police brutality. Activists in New York turned to state authorities when local authorities failed to provide equal justice to African Americans, but they also turned to the U.S. Department of Justice, illustrating that in the civil rights era, African Americans in both the North and the South appealed for federal protection of their civil rights. Struggles for police reform and defendants' rights are not usually associated with the civil rights movement, but they were a major component. Activists and attorneys sponsored bills to reform police procedure and protect the rights of defendants. They built a grass-roots movement that sought an expansion of rights for all Americans. In the early 1960s, several federal court rulings extended the Bill of Rights to state criminal proceedings, ensuring indigent defendants the right to counsel and barring the use of evidence from unlawful police searches. Like other judicial rulings of the era that expanded American liberalism, these were not isolated legal innovations, but outgrowths of a grassroots struggle for social justice.

4   Desegregating the Metropolis

On a February afternoon in 1947, Huddie Ledbetter, the African American folk singer known as Leadbelly, had three encounters with racial discrimination and harassment in public accommodations in New York. After performing at Sarah Lawrence College in suburban Bronxville, Ledbetter and three white professors were refused service at a tavern. The manager said he did not serve "niggers." Then a white conductor on the train to the city looked past Ledbetter and said to his companions, "Where is the nigger's ticket?" At Grand Central Station, a cab driver closed the door in his face and hurled the same racial slur, the third instance in only a couple of hours. Ledbetter brought this story to the NAACP.

Ledbetter's saga illustrates the extent of racial segregation in public services and establishments in New York, a portrait at odds with the popular image of liberal Manhattan. Indeed, the Black struggle for equal rights changed the landscape of New York and helped to give it a liberal image. After World War II, Black New Yorkers increasingly asserted their right to patronize public accommodations citywide without discrimination. They challenged exclusionary practices in restaurants, bars, nightclubs, hotels, swimming pools, trains, taxis, and the culture industries. Their efforts to desegregate the city's cultural life, nightlife, and transportation networks helped lay the groundwork for the rise of New York as a cosmopolitan global city. Like other antiracist struggles in postwar New York, attempts to desegregate the public sphere encountered resistance. Segregation in the home of the newly established United Nations was vulnerable, but in many realms, such as "high culture," or the swimming pool at Palisades Amusement Park, "white" space was zealously defended.[1]

"We Prefer Not to Serve Negroes"

A law barring racial discrimination and segregation in places of public accommodation was one of the few civil rights laws in New York State prior to World War II. Passed in 1872, and amended twice, it was enforceable by civil or criminal action. The law was not successfully utilized until the 1940s, however, when overtly discriminatory policies had become widespread, blurring any neat distinction between de facto and de jure discrimination. The first criminal conviction under the law happened during World War II. In 1943, William Bowman, an organizer with the United Auto Workers in Detroit, was denied a room at the Hotel Knickerbocker in Manhattan. He pressed criminal charges against the manager, who was fined $100. Bowman also filed a civil suit against the hotel and in 1945 was awarded $250.

Like Bowman's, other challenges to hotel discrimination were brought by leaders of national organizations. James Egert Allen, a grandson of a slave and an educator, frequently battled hotel discrimination in his capacity as president of the New York State Conference of NAACP branches, and as treasurer of the New York chapter of the Association for the Study of Negro Life and History. In 1945 he filed a protest against the Commodore Hotel at 42nd Street and Lexington Avenue after they refused him use of their banquet room. Two years later Allen accused four hotels in Hudson, New York of discriminating against delegates to the NAACP convention. The NAACP sued all four; attorney Cora T. Walker called it a test case that if successful would lead "to a change of policy on the part of many hotels throughout the state which now discriminate against Negroes." In 1948, Thurgood Marshall advised an Urban League official visiting from Cleveland who had suffered discrimination at the Lincoln Hotel to persevere, because the "the hotel situation does not seem to be getting better and we need to push cases like yours and some of the others we have."[2]

Langston Hughes wrote in 1946 that New York hotels were relatively open to Blacks, citing the Waldorf, Commodore, Roosevelt, Edison, and Taft hotels, if only to make a bleaker statement about the rest of the country. "Those of us who have traveled extensively in America know that very few cities welcome Negro guests in the first class hotels—so that is one more feather in New York's cap." Yet a year later, on a list of the "Types of Segregation and Jim-Crowism Which Are Most Irritating to the Negro Minority" compiled by the Mayor's Committee on Unity, number two was "the refusal of restaurants and hotels in the downtown sections to serve Negro patrons" and making them "feel unwelcome and uncomfortable when they appear." When Josephine Baker visited the city in 1948 with her French husband, she went to thirty-six hotels before getting a room. Black customers demanded equal service in restaurants and taverns—whether they were luncheonettes near the workplace or more upscale Manhattan eateries. An NAACP attorney sued the owners of a Bay Ridge, Brooklyn, luncheonette for ejecting three Black longshoremen with a threat of violence: "We don't serve n—— here. And if you coons don't get out, I'll take a knife and split your heads or call a cop." The proprietor evidently believed that police officers would aid him rather than the law-abiding customers.[3]

The many court victories against restaurants and other establishments by complainants ranging from ordinary citizens to celebrities suggests the broad push for change in postwar New York. A jury fined the owner of O'Gara's Bar and Grill on East 138th Street $300 because the bartender told Frank Wilson "we don't serve Africans here." The National Maritime Union provided a lawyer when one of its members, Linwood Carrington, was refused service by a Brooklyn barber. Carrington sued and won $110 in municipal court. The first Black judge elected to a New York City court, Francis E. Rivers, presided over a suit brought by Claude Marchant, a dancer with the Katherine Dunham Company, against the owners of an apartment building in Tudor City. Marchant had been denied access to the main elevator on two occasions. The jury awarded the dancer the maximum amount of damages, $1,000. The actor Canada Lee sued the Swiss Inn, a midtown restaurant, after he was denied service. His coworkers at CBS radio organized a picket line and boycott, which pushed the restaurant to settle. The owners apologized to Lee and "the colored race" and donated $250 to a charity of his choice. The "distinguished concert soprano" Ellabelle Davis donated $500 to the newly desegregated Sydenham Hospital after she won a civil suit against a west side restaurant.[4]

In 1949, in an indication of the success of African American activists in pushing the issue of race discrimination onto the agenda of white liberals, two dozen organizations formed the Committee on Civil Rights in East Manhattan. "Galvanized into action by the President's Report" *To Secure These Rights,* the group's goal was "interracial integration," especially in restaurants. Telford Taylor, who led the Allied legal team at Nuremberg, was its general counsel. It used 158 volunteers in interracial teams of testers to measure the extent of discrimination in the area of the United Nations, from the East River to Fifth Avenue and from 34th to 59th Street. It found that 42

percent gave Black customers inferior service, especially in terms of seat location, personal treatment, and length of wait.

Two years later the group returned to the east side and conducted a far
larger survey. They reported a sharp drop in the rate of discrimination,
down to 16 percent of the restaurants. In 1951, they also secured a pledge by
citywide restaurant unions and management associations to treat patrons
equally regardless of race. The protests and lawsuits were beginning to make
a dent: Black customers were beginning to experience the power to demand
better service, and restaurants faced penalties and sanctions for discriminatory practices.[5]

African Americans' challenge to segregated swimming pools was met with
considerably more resistance than they encountered in opening up restaurants and hotels. For many whites, integrated swimming pools fell into the
dreaded category of "social equality," raising the prospect of interracial inti-
macy, or they were associated with the racist idea of unclean Black bodies, a
notion that prompted whites in some communities to change the water in
pools that Blacks had swum in before using the pools themselves. From the
perspective of youthful civil rights activists, pools, beaches, and amusement
parks represented leisure, class mobility, and youth culture—aspects of the
so-called American Dream. The struggle to desegregate them was critical in
determining who could visibly participate in and claim these categories.

Directly across the Hudson River from Harlem, in the towns of Fort Lee
and Cliffside Park, New Jersey, Palisades Amusement Park was a summer-
time oasis for the white working class. Its owner, Irving Rosenthal, used a
typical exclusionary device of the era: he told African Americans that the
pool was a private club. In the summer of 1947, the Modern Trend Progressive Youth Group and the Congress of Racial Equality (CORE) launched direct action campaigns at the park. The Harlem-based Modern Trend organized an array of cultural and educational activities for youth. CORE, a local
branch of a national organization begun a few years earlier in Chicago, was
interracial but predominantly white. Seeking to go beyond "sympathetic lip
service," it engaged in "non-violent, direct action techniques so successfully
used in India and South Africa by the late Mahatma Gandhi." The Palisades
protest previewed the violence that nonviolent civil disobedience by CORE
would later generate in the South. James Peck, who joined the Freedom
Rides in 1961, was on the front lines in New Jersey in 1947.[6]

The youth conducted a "stand-in"—lining up near the pool's ticket booth
and chanting, "Don't Get Cool at Palisades Pool, Get Your Relaxation Where

There's No Discrimination." On the first Sunday in July they succeeded in closing the pool. Palisades security guards, many of whom were moonlighting police officers, used force to break up the picket line. They "manhandled" twenty-two-year-old Melba Valle, a "pretty Negro model," and two weeks later, they shoved and punched some of the protesters. Rosenthal called in the police, who physically ejected the protesters. Fort Lee Police Chief Fred Stengell told them, "Negroes are not allowed in this pool. They are allowed in the Park—if they behave themselves."

The protesters had no idea that they were dealing with a mafia-infested police force, a revelation that emerged four years later in congressional hearings on organized crime. When the group returned on August 3, seven were beaten and arrested by police officers and Palisades guards. As an officer pinned back James Peck's arms, a guard beat him, fracturing a rib and cutting up his face. Four others were seized for picketing at the park's gates. The activists were not easily defeated, however. They underwent training in nonviolence and came back every Sunday. On August 10, six CORE members were arrested as soon as they began picketing at the gates. At the end of the month, the police forcibly removed "the stand-inners" for the second time, but eighteen immediately returned and were arrested. A security guard reportedly told Peck, "I'd like to kill you," then beat him unconscious, breaking his jaw.[7]

African American leaders denounced the use of violence at the Palisades protest and called on federal authorities to halt "the Mississippi-style reign of terror." The *New York Age* deplored such violence in the North, "where we have a right to expect the natives to be semi-civilized." Activists in a variety of antiracist campaigns often invoked the rhetoric of sectional difference to undermine segregation in New York City. They drew parallels to southern Jim Crow in order to shame white New Yorkers into changing their practices. The youthful activists continued their picketing the next summer, taking the ferry across the Hudson to Palisades every Saturday and Sunday in June, July, and August. They again encountered resistance and hostility, although the violence by police and security guards appears to have abated.[8]

CORE filed state and federal civil rights suits against Palisades Park, which defended its right to discriminate on the basis of being a private business beyond the reach of federal regulation. But CORE won a significant legal victory in the U.S. Court of Appeals, which ruled that the sale of tickets constituted a contract, and that the right of Black citizens to enter into contracts on the same terms as whites was protected by federal law. In addition, partly as a consequence of the Palisades protest, New Jersey passed a civil rights law in 1949 that explicitly barred racial discrimination in swimming pools. The park's owner continued to resist change. He later claimed to fear that desegregation would scare away white business, but at the time, Rosenthal used the language and themes of anticommunism to oppose desegregation. His lawyers called the CORE effort "a Communist-inspired attempt to force admission of minority groups" into the swimming pool. Rosenthal even tried to bar the demonstrators from the pool by warning the Division against Discrimination, the agency created to enforce the state's new civil rights law, "I won't admit Communists." In 1953, Minnie France, the African American president of Modern Trends, was dancing with white Ellio Gasparetti of Friendship House in the poolside dance area. A manager asked France to leave, on the pretext that her pedal-pushers did not meet the amusement park's dress code. She protested that all the other dancers were dressed similarly, but police came and told them to leave. A bystander asked Gasparetti if the group were Communists. "No, I'm a Catholic," he replied. CORE urged the Division against Discrimination to enforce the law and developed a publicity campaign to encourage African Americans to use the pool. The long effort to bar Blacks, however, had created a hostile and unleisurely atmosphere that discouraged their attendance.[9]

Discrimination at Palisades undermines the notion that a clear-cut distinction between de jure segregation in the South and de facto segregation in the North characterized the pre–civil rights era. The story illustrates that antiracist activism changed the postwar North: the Palisades campaign helped generate a New Jersey civil rights law, making it part of the prehistory of federal civil rights legislation in the 1960s.

Freedom Riders

In the decade before Rosa Parks's refusal to relinquish her seat on a Montgomery bus launched the southern civil rights movement, many Black New Yorkers traveling on interstate trains refused to change seats when they crossed into the South. When they returned home, many filed lawsuits against the railroads, sparking a campaign to halt the complicity of New York's Pennsylvania Station in upholding racial segregation. These traveler-activists brought about the real-life implementation of the 1946 *Morgan v. Commonwealth of Virginia* Supreme Court decision, which held that segregation in interstate travel constituted an unconstitutional burden on interstate commerce. The plaintiff, Irene Morgan, like Ida B. Wells in the nineteenth century, is part of a long line of African American women who went to court to claim their right to sit wherever they wanted on public transportation. The continuing migration of African Americans out of the South increased the phenomena of return visits, and women, who have historically had the responsibility for sustaining kin contacts, played leading roles in the struggle to desegregate national transportation networks.[10]

On August 7, 1945, Nina Beltran and her five-year-old son boarded a southbound Seaboard Air Line train at Pennsylvania Station in New York. In Raleigh, North Carolina, a conductor directed all of the Black passengers to "retire" to the Jim Crow car at the front of the train. Encumbered by her baggage and small son, Beltran had a difficult time reaching the car, and by the time she did, there were no seats left. Desiring to sit down, and having bought the same ticket as everybody else on a long journey, she returned to her original seat and faced the conductor's wrath. At Hamburg, North Carolina, the conductor called in a police officer, who punched Nina Beltran in the back, shoved her son, and forced them into the overcrowded "colored car." Back in New York, Beltran enlisted the left-wing law firm of Neuberger, Shapiro and Rabinowitz, and in January 1947, Seaboard settled the case and awarded her $3,000.[11]

In July 1947 the NAACP filed suit against the Atlantic Coast Line Railroad and Florida East Coast Railway in behalf of Berta Mae Watkins of Harlem. In February 1946, Watkins had purchased a ticket in New York to occupy a specific reserved seat to Florida. In Jacksonville, agents of the two companies ordered her to move, and when she refused they called the police. The NAACP's Robert L. Carter filed suit for $25,000 in U.S. Court for the Southern District of New York, the same court on which he would later sit as a federal judge. Watkins saw her action as part of a larger struggle: "For my interest in this case is not only what can or may be gotton [sic] out of it financially, but to let the Southern Whites know that about thirteen million or more Negros men and women have gotton [sic] tired of being pushed around at their commands, as well as they told me they would teach a Nigger woman how to act in Florida." Watkins won her case and received a $1,000 settlement. Another African American woman in New York sued the Atlantic Railroad in 1947, and won a settlement over an incident that happened in 1942. A Brooklyn physician, Eulalie Mitchell Lee, was traveling with her young son to visit her husband in North Carolina. She refused to move from her seat when ordered to do so, and she was "almost thrown off the train" when it reached her stop. Lee was awarded a "very substantial" amount.[12]

As in the struggles against restaurant and swimming pool discrimination, this fight went from a series of individual legal attacks to a more coordinated effort, reflecting the growth of the New York civil rights movement in general. In 1948, Reverend J. C. Olden "launched an all-out drive to break down segregation in transportation." Olden, a visiting pastor at Salem Methodist Church in Harlem, whose pastor Charles Y. Trigg was also an activist, led a national campaign: he focused on the Jim Crow "change points" such as Washington, Cincinnati, St. Louis, and Kansas City. In New York, he mobilized a fight against the policy at Pennsylvania Station of assigning Black passengers to cars that would become Jim Crow cars in the South. As Olden said, "Perhaps we cannot do too much about conditions in Georgia, but there is no reason why anyone boarding a train in New York should be segregated." The "worst offender" was Seaboard Air Line's Silver Meteor, but all three major southern railways were involved. Pennsylvania Railroad booked southbound passengers for the entire trip, making their seat assignments a crucial point of either enforcing the *Morgan* decision or helping to flout it. Pennsylvania Railroad officials admitted that they racially segregated passengers in New York, claiming it was for their own convenience. It is not clear when the policy began, but it seems to have been intended to help southern railways avoid the confrontations and lawsuits and reentrench racial segregation in interstate transportation.[13]

Elmer Carter, an African American member of the State Commission against Discrimination (SCAD), began an inquiry. Railroad officials defended the policy as a "system matter" and said that if pressed to stop, they would refuse to sell through tickets and make everyone leave the train at Washington, D.C., and buy new tickets. "This, Mr. Carter took as a kind of threat," according to an official from the Mayor's Committee on Unity. In an unusually aggressive move, SCAD threatened to hold a public hearing and turn the matter over to the state attorney general unless the railroad changed its policy. Several months later, in October 1949, Pennsylvania Railroad stated that reserve seats on all trains from New York City to the South would be booked without discrimination. Yet railroads continued to violate the Supreme Court ruling in the South until at least the 1960s, and Black New Yorkers continued to bring, and to win, lawsuits in federal court.[14]

Even as it came under attack, segregated transportation reached new heights in the postwar era. In 1951 an American Airlines employee was fired for not cooperating with the airline's Jim Crow seating policy. With aid from the American Jewish Congress, Gabriel Gladstone filed a criminal complaint in Queens against the airline for "systematic discrimination against Negro passengers." Gladstone had been instructed to label passengers as Negro "by their southern accents or by the neighborhood in which they lived," and then segregate them. Such reservations were marked by the code symbol, "E 111." This system was used both to segregate passengers and to give whites preference on airline waiting lists. American Airlines was not simply tolerating a request for segregation made, for example, by a racist white passenger. This was a top-down, formal policy that employees were required to follow or face dismissal. American Airlines vigorously denied the charges, and released the statement, "Why, some of our best employees are Negroes and we are proud of them."

A paper trail caught them, however, and one week later, American changed their story. They admitted having a segregation policy that was, in fact, openly included in their training manual. "This is America," the Queens district attorney informed American Airlines, "and it is a time when Americans of every color, creed and national origin are spilling blood in far off shores to protect the American way of life." In a little-known chapter of movement history, civil rights activism thwarted the extension of segregation to air travel. The full story of airline discrimination that emerged from this case is quite remarkable, however, and underscores the power that segregationist ideology could wield in shaping national business practices. The case suggests the short walk from the supposedly sectional culture of Jim Crow to modern corporate racism. Several years earlier when regular commercial flights were first established, American Airlines segregated "Negro passengers on the right hand side of airplanes traveling in the South." The attorney claimed that the policy had been abandoned after *Morgan,* but as with the railroads, these practices persisted into the 1950s and only ceased when the civil rights movement mobilized against them.[15]

The YMCA was a segregated national institution whose Jim Crow branches in New York came under concerted attack after World War II. The YWCA desegregated in 1941, and in 1946 the National Council of the YMCA urged local branches to "work steadfastly toward the goal of eliminating all racial discriminations." Northern and western branches began a gradual process of integration that took well over a decade. Activists in Brooklyn fought to end the exclusion of African American men from the Bedford

YMCA, which was located in an area with a majority Black population. The general-secretary of the Brooklyn-Queens YMCA, Eugene Field Scott, a white southerner, dragged his feet in implementing the desegregation policy. Pushing him were the Civil Rights Congress, American Labor Party, the Brooklyn and Jamaica branches of the NAACP, the Mayor's Committee on Unity, CORE, Reverend Milton Galamison, and Herbert T. Miller, the popular leader of the all-Black Carlton Avenue YMCA in Bedford-Stuyvesant.[16]

In December 1951, after over a year of picketing by CORE and other groups and the resignation of the entire board of directors of the Carlton branch to protest Scott's firing of Herbert Miller, Scott promised to completely desegregate the Bedford branch. Black men, however, continued to complain about the especially lengthy application procedure and questions like, "Do you really want to join? Why not join Carlton?" Thus, the *Amsterdam News* perhaps exaggerated the extent of change when it announced that Brooklyn had become the first borough to "completely eradicate racial divisions" in its YMCA branches.[17]

In 1953 the YMCA continued to bar Black members from its branch at Pennsylvania Station on 34th Street in Manhattan. Helping to maintain segregation at the Y was the racism of the white railroad brotherhoods, whose members stayed there. "We have a lot of narrow minded fellows from the South in here," the branch director admitted, but he did not want to lose their patronage and become, as he put it, "a downtown branch of the Harlem YMCA." Consequently, Black redcaps and baggage men coming through Penn Station had to lodge up in Harlem, and they took the lead in challenging Y policy. As one Black railroad worker made clear, "When these southern railroad men are in Georgia, well that's their house, and we have to act accordingly. But this is my house, and they have to be made to understand that."

The redcaps found support from some prominent Black YMCA leaders, who were outraged to discover that the white unions had a contract with the Penn Station YMCA reserving beds for their members, while Black workers on the Pullmans and dining cars of the Atlantic Coast Line were assigned to the Harlem YMCA, as a result of a contract in effect between the company and that branch for many years. Their efforts helped to eventually overturn this practice. Judge Hubert Delany, a former member of the YMCA Board of Directors for twenty-two years, called the Penn Station contract a "direct violation of a policy of integration which we fought long and hard to win." "Railroads," Delany insisted, "have no right to determine the policy of any YMCA branch." Similarly, Channing Tobias, a member of the integrated International Executive Committee, stressed that restrictive practices were contrary to YMCA policy and "inexcusable in a city like New York."[18]

Black Consumer Rights

Just as Black New Yorkers fought to dismantle exclusionary barriers in places of public accommodation, they also fought to win greater recognition and respect as consumers in the vastly expanding postwar marketplace. Struggles against the racial discrimination produced by a racialized "free" market economy inexorably challenged laissez-faire: activists appealed to the government to ensure honest and fair business practices. As in other areas of the movement, African Americans looked to the state as a weapon against the entrenched racism of the private sector.

The predominantly white-owned shops on 125th Street and other thoroughfares in Harlem had been targets of Black consumer anger and protest since the Depression. Complaints included short-weights, spoiled foodstuffs, getting short-changed, unsanitary conditions, the sale of seconds at first-class prices, and rudeness from the shopkeepers. An episode of the landmark 1940s radio show *New World A'Coming* broadcast over WMCA in New York City featured a dramatic vignette on the plight of a harried and harassed Harlem shopper. After a butcher made an ill-tempered remark to the shopper, the narrator, Canada Lee, asked:

> How would you feel if a merchant spoke to you in that manner? You'd be pretty burned up wouldn't you? Yes of course you would. You'd probably never go in that shop again. But the Harlem Housewife has no other place to go. For Negroes are locked in a ghetto . . . Most of the merchants in Harlem are white. One merchant is pretty much like another—brusque, indifferent, hostile. In this setting merchants know they are not compelled to show the ordinary courtesies to shoppers. This is one condition that leads to tensions.[19]

Wartime price controls became a weapon to fight ghetto price gouging, and many activists, such as the United Harlem Tenants and Consumers Organization and the Harlem Committee for Price Control, led by Reverend Charles Y. Trigg of Salem Methodist Church, fought to extend the Office of Price Administration (OPA) into the postwar period. A 1946 OPA survey of 525 Harlem stores found that half were in direct violation of OPA price rules.

While the director's vow to bring every violator before his board in two weeks was probably not met, the OPA was an independent authority to which consumers could bring complaints. As such, it left an important legacy in Harlem. The establishment of cooperatives also became a way to avoid overpriced goods in Harlem markets. Congressman Powell's church, Abyssinian Baptist, established a food cooperative in its basement and sold a range of goods at cheaper prices.[20]

In 1947 the Consumers Protective Committee (CPC), "a group of housewives and homemakers" in Harlem chaired by Mrs. Walton Pryor, began a campaign against "unscrupulous" merchants on 125th Street that involved picketing, negotiations, and appeals to city officials. The *Amsterdam News* supported the protest, which also called on local businesses to advertise in the Black-owned press. The majority of businesses in Harlem at this time were white-owned. While there were reportedly more Black-owned businesses on other streets, just two of the 256 stores on 125th Street between Fifth and Eighth Avenues were operated by African Americans, according to a 1948 survey by the Mayor's Committee on Unity (MCU). The others were owned by whites, 90 percent of whom were Jewish. Harlem activists stressed the unfair practices of merchants, but many also complained about the white domination of business ownership in Harlem, and called for greater Black access to capital. Anti-Jewish rhetoric, which was more common in Harlem during the Great Depression, appeared less in this period.[21]

The CPC's appeal for mass picketing declared: "Harlem is nothing but a colony for the non-negro merchants to exploit." They implored ministers to "join us in this fight for a wealthier, healthier, happier Harlem home. Lead your membership to our meetings and lead them up and down 125th Street, until housewives, breadwinners, and our children are given a fair chance to survive." CPC letterhead used the honorific Mrs. for every female member, invoking the authority and status of a "wife" in the community. These wives, however, challenged the male establishment both in Harlem and downtown. The plan to conduct mass picketing on 125th Street sparked controversy in Harlem, because it threatened businesses—a local source of philanthropy, jobs, and services—and because the CPC's nationalist rhetoric and leadership polarized the Harlem political establishment. The Uptown Chamber of Commerce, some ministers, the Brotherhood of Sleeping Car Porters, the left-wing *People's Voice,* and the Republican *New York Age* expressed concern that mass picketing unfairly lumped all stores together. The city also voiced anxiety over the group's rhetoric. "There have been references on the sound truck to the fact that merchants on the street were all of a different race," noted Edith Alexander of the MCU.

Nevertheless, the CPC mobilized around an issue that resonated deeply in the community, and picketing began. Ironically, the group was able to turn the usually passive MCU into its ally, in part because ever since the 1935 and 1943 riots in Harlem, when anger had been directed at white-owned businesses, city leaders feared that community-merchant tensions could produce violent disturbances. This fear sometimes served as a catalyst to reform. Unwittingly propelling this idea, the white-led Uptown Chamber of Commerce wired the MCU, complaining of "rabble rousers" and warning that the picketers could spark "a serious disturbance." The MCU rushed to convene a series of hearings on the conflict. In a victory for the CPC, the MCU then released a report verifying the CPC's complaints and endorsing many of their proposed remedies.[22]

The CPC's organizing led to the creation of the Harlem Consumer-Merchant Arbitration Board. Chaired by the African American secretary of the MCU, Edith Alexander, the nongovernmental board was composed of merchants and community leaders, including Pryor. The CPC created a nine-point pledge of fair selling practices that hundreds of businesses adopted in return for bright red decals for their windows that read, "This store approved—Harlem Consumer-Merchant Arbitration Board." The CPC, which saw merchant corruption in Harlem as systematic, did not regard this remedy as optional. They vowed to picket every store that did not sign the nine-point pledge, and they established a dense network of supervisors to encourage merchant cooperation with the CPC. At a ceremony with Mayor O'Dwyer, the first decal was presented in September 1948 to Jack Blumstein, owner of Blumstein's, Harlem's biggest department store. In 1950, the CPC won an agreement by Harlem's largest furniture store to reduce its installment charge and to include it on the price tag. The store also agreed to hire a Black accountant recommended by the CPC. By January 1950, 90 percent of stores on 125th Street displayed the insignia.[23]

The CPC also lobbied for a government-supervised indoor marketplace in Harlem. The two dozen enclosed public markets in the metropolitan region, both wholesale and retail, made trading more sanitary and honest. This CPC campaign further illustrates the efforts of Black advocates in this era to expand the role of the public sector. The struggle began during the Depression, but was reinvigorated in the postwar years by the CPC and other organizations, including the People's Civic and Welfare Association, the *Amsterdam*

A Consumers Protective Committee picket line in Harlem. Their signs call for "A Fair Deal" for shoppers, echoing the slogan of President Truman's domestic platform.

News, the Urban League, and the City-Wide Citizens' Committee on Harlem. The Mayor's Committee on Unity supported the effort, viewing it as an antidote to future riots or racial conflict. A 1945 survey of food stores in upper Manhattan found that 45 percent of stores in Harlem were unsanitary, and that the meat sold there was of lower quality than in neighboring Washington Heights but marked at the same price. Mrs. Walton Pryor emphasized the salutary effect a public market would have on the whole community when she testified before the Board of Estimate in 1953: "We need this market to act as a barometer, a factor which will raise the standard of all community stores." For over a decade, promises for a public market in Harlem were repeatedly broken. But Mayor Robert F. Wagner Jr., who made it a campaign pledge in 1953, delivered. In September 1955 an enclosed public market with city inspectors opened on 143rd Street and Eighth Avenue—which was shortly renamed Frederick Douglass Boulevard.[24]

The Consumers Protective Committee and its allies succeeded in mobilizing Harlemites, articulating their grievances, and enlisting the city's support in their fight against exploitative merchant practices. In its quest to protect African American consumer rights, the CPC expanded its watchdog activities over a range of products, including auto loans and insurance. Nevertheless, complaints over rotten food and high prices in Harlem would continue, suggesting that the consumer arbitration board was ultimately not sufficient to correct the abuses of a ghetto market economy. The government's investigation of the causes of the violent urban unrest in the summer of 1967 revealed that this issue was not unique to New York. The Kerner Commission found that ghetto stores notorious for selling overpriced, inferior merchandise were common targets of violence.[25]

Self-Determination

In postwar New York there were a multitude of struggles by Black cultural workers for inclusion in the film, theater, television, and music industries as well as struggles over the content of cultural production. They were part and parcel of the desegregation of the public sphere, in New York City and beyond. In the 1940s, Black political activists increasingly linked Black representation in visual productions to the struggle for racial justice. Walter White and Lena Horne's efforts to combat racial stereotyping on the silver screen as well as Paul Robeson's effort to liberate his cinematic image were part of a broader push for Black cultural self-determination. In 1947 the cultural section of the National Negro Congress (NNC) held a conference in Manhattan with over a hundred workers in the culture industries "to survey the position of Negroes in the theater, radio, screen, music, and advertising." They generated reports on Black employment as well as the "characterization of the Negro people through the various cultural media." The findings revealed pervasive racial discrimination. The New York offices of the major motion picture companies, for example, employed seven African Americans out of three thousand white-collar workers.

There were a comparatively large number of employed Black musicians, but they were segregated and underpaid. Of the 10,000 Black musicians in the American Federation of Musicians, 2,500 lived in New York City. Discrimination prevented most from working full-time. There were no Black musicians in any symphony orchestra in the country. The only Black musicians in the pit of a musical were all working in the Broadway hit production of Duke Ellington's *Beggar's Holiday*. "No Negro side-man is ever employed at a catered hotel-room affair, commonly known as a club job. On rare occasions an outstanding Negro may be used, but most hotels and their management discourage this practice." In Hollywood none of the studios employed Black musicians, and when they did appear in a film, they were "depicted in a derogatory manner, drunk and vulgar." The report highlighted jazz clubs as the major exception to a whites-only musical universe. The NNC report advocated hiring Black writers, performers, producers, and white-collar service workers, and warned that excluding Black people from the culture and media of an affluent and powerful nation produced cultural stereotypes, distortions, and evasions.[26]

In 1949 the boxer-turned-actor Canada Lee delivered a speech, "Radio and the Negro People," that exemplified, in the cultural context, the radical voice of the struggle for Negro rights in New York. At a time when "the average listener spends some five hours" a day tuned in, radio's presentation of Black people in subordinate or criminal roles, Lee argued, abetted the postwar backlash. "With rare exceptions," he declared, "it is the lazy gambler, the shiftless-thieving, razor-wielding Negro that has come to represent the totality of Negro life." Media stereotypes were more insidious than mere slights or omissions; they were part of a dehumanization that went hand in hand with the denial of first-class citizenship. "To the people listening to the radio we do not exist. Our problems need no solution . . . Our people need not be respected, need not be given equal rights . . . , for we are not a people according to radio." Radio helped to create a picture of the postwar nation. "Negro life, its richness, its humor, its warmth and humanity, and its fighting spirit, is not felt to be a fit subject for depiction on the air." Instead, a white normative society is created and affirmed: "The news broadcast is that of the white world . . . ; the drama of radio is pure lily-white drama . . . almost never will a Negro enter into these stories except as a menial, or a loyal maid, who lives through and suffers the agonies of her white mistress." "On quiz programs you will find that, by and large, white people 'Stop the Music,' white people guess the answers; white people hit the jackpot."

Lee urged government regulation to compel change. "Radio is public property," he stated, turning Black people into owners as well as listeners and consumers. "No network or station broadcasts except with the express permission of the people, granted in a license with the Federal Communication Commission." For Lee, a democratic culture entailed the end of minstrelsy and its legacy, in all forms. In the next decade, market forces would induce white-owned stations to develop "Negro-appeal" programming. The desire to reach the vastly expanded Black urban market would cause a jump in Black-oriented shows, mostly music spun by Black deejays, from a handful in 1949 to over two hundred in 1952.[27]

The critique of media stereotypes found its greatest grassroots expression in various mobilizations to protest the screening of "the vicious anti-Negro hate film," *Birth of a Nation*. These efforts suggest that civil rights organizations have viewed questions of racial representation as deeply political and social rather than narrowly artistic and personal. The NAACP, and other civil rights activists, did not defend racist filmmaking as a constitutional right of the filmmaker. Despite having been banned in the city in 1915, *Birth of a Nation* was screened in postwar Manhattan, but boycotts and protests in at least three instances pushed the theaters to shorten its run. The Majestic Theater in 1946 withdrew the film after "severe criticism" and protests by the NAACP. A year later the Republic Theater withdrew it after another round of picketing and protests by various state NAACP branches cut the usual attendance in half. At this time there was a censorship board in New York State on which the Catholic Church wielded considerable authority. NAACP members urged Governor Dewey to appoint a Black member to the board, in an attempt to expand the focus of the censors from issues such as sexuality to issues such as race hatred. A range of groups from the MCU to the Communist-supported American Youth for Democracy lobbied city and state licensing commissioners to stop the film's authorization.

In 1950 *Birth of a Nation* was distributed with new sound features and shown at the Beverly Theater on Third Avenue and 50th Street. The Harlem NAACP branch organized picket lines and Roy Wilkins pressured Mayor O'Dwyer to ban the film in the city. The NAACP argued that the film should be seen as a form of violence, not speech, and reminded the mayor that it had been banned by numerous American cities when it was first released

Demonstrators protesting the screening of *Birth of a Nation* at the Republic Theater on Broadway and West 51st Street in 1947. The marquee calls it the "Greatest Picture of all Time."

more than twenty-five years earlier. The film "glorifies the Ku Klux Klan, preaches race hatred against Negroes and openly advocates mob violence against them." The picketing succeeded in keeping attendance minimal and in forcing the management to cut short a previously "indefinite" run. The effort to suppress *Birth of a Nation,* and the struggles against stereotypical Black characters and distorted depictions of the past and present, reflect assertions of Black pride and a desire for self-determination that were part of the pre-1960s northern civil rights movement. Yet the struggle against negative representation of Blacks was motivated as well by Black performers' desire for wider employment opportunities. Alongside other African American workers in the 1940s, they were engaged in a quest for broad social transformation in the United States.[28]

The massive northern and western shift of the African American population in the 1940s brought into greater public view that American apartheid was dynamic, national rather than regional, and capable of expansion. In New York, activists organized, picketed, sued, lobbied, and got arrested—all to halt the spread of racial segregation in public accommodations in the North. The campaign for equal access to public accommodations was accompanied by Black demands to be treated with dignity, whether as an individual customer or in cultural representations of the group. The mobilization of Black southerners, northerners, and Caribbean immigrants in New York City pushed the issue of racial discrimination into public view and forced the city government and judiciary to reevaluate the relationship between race and public policy.

The New York movement had a national effect. Many of the targets, whether airlines, trains, YMCAs, or the music industry, were national institutions, so the city's activists were on the forefront of defining the nature of rights and opportunities for a much larger group of people of color in the United States. These struggles were offensive as much as defensive. They reflected Black communities in transition and on the move, wanting more of the fruits of citizenship and access to the recreations and conveniences of modern urban living.

5 Dead Letter Legislation

After the passage of antidiscrimination laws in employment and education, a clash quickly developed between civil rights leaders and the Republican administration of Governor Thomas E. Dewey over the nature of their implementation. Civil rights organizations urged the state to vigorously enforce the laws by conducting industry-wide investigations and using race-conscious strategies and statistics to judge compliance. Reflecting their New Deal roots, civil rights leaders saw the law as an instrument of social change that made government into an active agent in the desegregation process, which they understood as beginning, rather than ending, with the passage of legislation.

The Dewey administration argued, in contrast, that integration equaled the absence of legal sanction for discrimination, rather than the promotion of African American advancement or a desegregated workplace. In 1948, for example, in response to criticism that racial patterns in employment had not changed significantly since the law was passed three years earlier, a commissioner with the State Commission against Discrimination (SCAD) argued that "a climate of equal opportunity and diversified recruitment is no guarantee of substantial minority group representation in the employment pattern." In its first decade, SCAD shunned vigorous law enforcement and adopted both the rhetoric of a "color-blind" state and a strategy of passivity—advertising with pride that it had not forced compliance in a single instance. The stakes of this struggle were high: Black workers stood on the eve of automation, plant relocation, and deindustrialization in a position of comparative vulnerability.[1]

A similar clash arose after the passage of the Fair Educational Practices Act in 1948, the first state law barring discrimination in private universities in the United States. Activists lobbied the Department of Education to use the law to actually open the doors of higher education for students of color. The emphasis by Black community leaders on access and advancement, as much as formal policies barring race discrimination, can be seen in their simultaneous efforts to create the State University of New York. Like fighting for full employment, a public market, and subsidized housing, expanding the scope of the public sector in higher education was a significant dimension of the New York civil rights movement.

The campaigns to pass antidiscrimination laws in postwar New York constituted an important piece, even the heart, of the much vaunted but often misunderstood Black-Jewish alliance in the civil rights movement. It was not primarily a phenomenon of one group aiding in another group's liberation struggle; rather, it was a collaboration between liberal organizations in fighting for laws that were sought by both groups. It was a coincident legislative and legal campaign against racial and religious discrimination. While an alliance of Black and Jewish organizations fought to pass antidiscrimination laws, the fact that each group faced different forms of discrimination gave rise to distinct advocacy regarding remedies and enforcement. The effects of the laws on each group similarly varied. The "color-blind" strategy embraced by the Dewey administration was better at rooting out anti-Semitism than anti-Black racism. In institutions of higher education, Jewish students faced quotas limiting their enrollment, while African Americans faced near total exclusion. Thus, while the removal of legal barriers was a helpful measure to combat anti-Semitism and to satisfy Jewish demands, some African American leaders tended to look to race-conscious remedies as an appropriate tool to increase Black hiring or enrollment. In addition, the law's prohibition on inquiries regarding religion on employment or university applications, as well as its prohibition of other devices designed to elicit Jewish identity, was helpful in reducing the number of complaints of religious discrimination to the state. The fact that Black people could not conceal the basis of their oppression, for example by "passing," meant that Black advancement in the United States would necessitate the acceptance of difference, rather than its suppression.[2]

A Policy of Limited Intervention

In 1945, people of color and religious minorities were watching SCAD with high hopes while conservative employers and segregationists were anticipating its actions with dread. Just as the passage of the Ives-Quinn Law—

which barred discrimination based on race, color, national origin, or religion in hiring or upgrading by private employers—took on national significance, the battle over its enforcement assumed heightened import. In a common refrain, the *New York Age* called SCAD "the most important body, not only in New York State, but also in the United States." Since New York was at the forefront of developing antidiscrimination remedies, SCAD's policies and practices would likely influence national civil rights policy and the lives of millions of workers. With the closing in 1945 of the federal FEPC office in New York, Algernon Black, head of the City-Wide Citizens' Committee on Harlem, urged Governor Dewey to pursue an aggressive course. New York, he declared, "can lead the way and set the pattern" of continuing integration for the nation. But a "failure to adopt an aggressive employment policy into the peace years will mean backsliding and inequality and disillusionment and bitterness and civil strife."[3]

Governor Dewey had appointed five commissioners to the State Commission against Discrimination, including an African American, Elmer Carter. SCAD had the authority to initiate investigations, issue subpoenas, hold public hearings, and issue court-enforceable orders. But as part of the compromise language inserted to win Republican support for the law, SCAD was also empowered to enforce the Law against Discrimination through the more gradualist means of "conference, conciliation, and persuasion." Soon after its creation, SCAD announced that it would avoid using sections of the law that authorized an activist enforcement strategy, or "forced" compliance, as a commissioner put it, and rely instead on "conference, conciliation and persuasion." SCAD's first major initiative revealed its basic approach to enforcing the law. In January 1947, the commission announced a settlement with thirty trade unions representing over 750,000 workers that had been operating under constitutions or bylaws that limited membership to white persons. The unions agreed to eliminate such clauses in New York State. Yet they continued to resist integration through other devices, such as seniority and apprenticeship systems, that proved just as effective as formal racial bars. As Black workers continued to bring complaints of discrimination, SCAD insisted that discriminatory seniority and apprenticeship systems were outside its purview—even though, as civil rights lawyers asserted, nothing in the law prevented such scrutiny of the racial effects of labor union practices. SCAD's stance reflected its policy of limited intervention.[4]

According to activists, the state's failure to publicize the law or penalize a single discriminating employer encouraged business as usual. A survey of employment agencies by the American Jewish Congress in 1947 found that 88 percent were willing to fill an order for a white, Protestant stenographer, and many even volunteered ways to skirt the law. During a six-month period in 1946, for example, a year after discrimination had become illegal, 348 openly discriminatory job orders such as "No Negroes" or "Christians Only" were submitted to the New York State Employment Service—a government agency.[5]

Civil rights leaders envisioned that SCAD would dedicate itself to opening up job opportunities for African Americans in major city industries. City Councilman Ben Davis called on SCAD to integrate the Metropolitan Life Insurance Company, "which collects fifty million dollars a year from Negroes and doesn't have a single Negro employed except as porters, janitors and the like." He also pointed to the whites-only policy of major league baseball teams in the state to prove that "there is nothing to investigate. We should require ball teams to hire qualified Negro players." NAACP executive secretary Walter White urged SCAD to "move in more vigorously in big industries" and "devote more time to attacking discrimination at its roots." Antidiscrimination advocates urged SCAD to allow organizations to file complaints; to hold public hearings and utilize the full sanctioning power of the law; to publicize the criteria used to determine compliance with the law as well as the outcome of complaints; and to focus more on providing justice to complainants, rather than negotiating privately with the employer.[6]

For their part, Black workers fought to make SCAD their ally. For decades Black workers in the railroad industry had been battling to keep their jobs and gain access to higher-paying positions reserved for whites. Railroad unions were among the most racially exclusionary in the nation and the last to remove formal racial bars to membership. In 1943 the FEPC ordered an end to the exclusion of Blacks as mechanics at the Pennsylvania Railroad in Manhattan and many longtime African American employees were promoted to mechanics. But after the war, the Black workers lost their jobs to less experienced white veterans. In May 1946, on behalf of six Black employees who had been demoted to coach cleaner, NAACP attorney Marian Wynn Perry filed a complaint with SCAD. Wynn charged that the railroad and the unions had wrongly implemented the "escalator of seniority" clause in the GI Bill of Rights. The U.S. Supreme Court had held that all returning veterans should reenter the workforce where they would have been had they not entered the armed forces, but the unions and management at Pennsylvania Railroad had manipulated the ruling to justify giving white veterans "superseniority."[7]

SCAD worked very slowly and provided no information to the complainants. From the perspective of civil rights lawyers, the wall of silence that surrounded SCAD's work and its snail-like progress in conducting investigations undermined faith in the agency and undercut its ability to deliver speedy justice. In January 1948 Perry wrote to SCAD, "We can think of no reason why it should take more than eighteen months to make a determination as to whether or not the complainants have probable cause for their charges of racial discrimination against the Pennsylvania Railroad." SCAD Commissioner Elmer Carter responded in the typically elusive SCAD style that their "ultimate objective" of eliminating overall discriminatory patterns presented "many complex problems."[8]

The NAACP persuaded SCAD to meet with the workers. Walter Sutherland "used very strong language" in pointing out that "almost two years ago they had come to the Commission for aid and that they now felt like fools and were regarded as fools by both the white and colored workers in their shops because they had thought they would get anywhere." Another worker, Thomas J. Byrd, said that "white men were being qualified daily and placed in jobs ahead of them and that their status was worse now than it was when they had filed the complaint." In July, Commissioner Carter rejected the workers' complaints on the grounds that he could find no probable cause to credit their allegations of discrimination by the railroad. These kinds of outcomes radicalized civil rights leaders, pushing them to challenge the Dewey administration's interpretation of the Law against Discrimination. Not until the fall of 1953 did Charles Morris of Harlem begin working for the Pennsylvania Railroad as the first Black brakeman—seven years after SCAD had declared the end of the color bar in New York labor unions.[9]

A case brought by workers building the Brooklyn Battery Tunnel further illustrates the high expectations workers had of SCAD, and it sheds light on the city's unwillingness to enforce its own law against discrimination on public works projects. Tunnel building in New York has historically been a multiracial occupation, but Black workers were given the most dangerous, dirtiest, and lowest-paying jobs.[10] In general, sandhogs—as tunnel builders are called—were assigned to segregated labor gangs. Black workers were blocked from the better-paying skilled positions regardless of seniority, according to Ed Cross, an African American worker-activist who fought to improve conditions in tunnel building and end racial discrimination. At a July 1948 meeting of their union, Local 147 of the International Hod Carriers Union, AFL, Cross, and several other sandhogs organized a Committee against Discrimination to investigate racial discrimination on union jobs. The Black workers, who constituted over one-third of the union, preferred to use the union, rather than the state, to fight discrimination, but they quickly ran into opposition from the union's leadership. According to Cross, many of the Irish immigrant rank and file supported the equal rights struggle, but the Irish union leaders did not. In August the committee was directed to resign by Local 147's executive board and told by the "openly hostile" president, Owen Kelly, "that there never was any discrimination and never had been." Ironically, the local's executive board urged the workers to turn to SCAD. But the workers wanted to "emphasize, as good union men who have stuck by our union through strikes and long periods of unemployment, that it was not our desire to call in a state agency."[11]

In 1948 ten Black sandhogs filed complaints with SCAD against three contracting companies and Local 147. One of the three projects was the Brooklyn Battery Tunnel, where the workers said they had been denied the upgrading and wage increases that their skills, experience, and union standing should have guaranteed them. One of the complainants, Walter Tannis, was physically threatened by his foreman and fired for protesting the treatment of Black workers. Another, Curtis Chaney, was demoted from valveman to assistant valveman after the contractor raised the pay of valvemen. The workers testified before SCAD that "the White worker with no experience in Tunnel work is considered so superior by the contractors and Unions that they receive the highest skilled and supervisory jobs." Chaney protested having to subsidize his discrimination: "Now the City of New York guaranteed the contractors on the tunnel project a fair profit. They are going to pay that profit with the taxpayer's money, all the taxpayers." The workers demanded "full back pay" since "it is against state law for an employer to discriminate on the Brooklyn Battery Tunnel." They also invoked their rights as union members, declaring that discrimination was also "a violation of the contract."[12]

SCAD was reluctant to intervene. The NAACP arranged a conference with all sides that degenerated into an attack on the sandhogs. Local 147 leaders supported the white contractor's denial of discrimination at the tunnel project, and SCAD reportedly subjected the workers to ridicule and harassment. NAACP attorney Marian Wynn Perry said the SCAD commissioner shouted her down, cut her off, or ignored her every time she tried to state the workers' case. The workers were questioned in a "vicious and antagonistic manner," and asked such questions as "You didn't want the job very much did you?" Perry also reported that further threats of violence had been made to other workers: "The reign of terror in the Brooklyn Battery Tunnel continues unabated and no effort is being made by the Commission to take any immediate action."[13]

Hoping that city officials would be more responsive to pressure, the NAACP and the workers turned to Mayor William O'Dwyer. Walter White argued that on public works projects in particular, "Negroes should be assured from the beginning of a fair chance for employment in all skills." But O'Dwyer shifted responsibility to Robert Moses, who as head of the Triborough Bridge and Tunnel Authority oversaw the project. Moses, according to his biographer, refused to enforce fair employment on his projects—a significant fact given that he created tens of thousands of jobs transforming the landscape of postwar New York City. "It's before SCAD," Moses curtly replied.[14]

The workers, however, refused to give up. They eventually won a symbolic victory that in retrospect seemed to have as much value for the U.S. government. Chaney was awarded $154 in back wages, and on the eve of a public hearing, Walter Tannis was promised $3,000 in lost wages as a result of a discriminatory dismissal. Critics had long urged SCAD to use its power to hold public hearings in order to encourage settlements. During the Cold War, the U.S. government wanted to project to the world a positive image of U.S. racial practices. The *Voice of America*, the U.S. radio program that played a key propaganda role in the Cold War, broadcast the story of Walter Tannis's victory around the world. The NAACP credited the victory to the activists in Local 147 who had brought critical evidence before SCAD. But this victory may have cost other workers tens of thousands of dollars in lost income. According to Ed Cross, several workers, including himself, were blacklisted for the next six years as punishment for testifying before SCAD.

But there were long-term gains. According to Cross, Black sandhogs worked under equal conditions for the first time during the construction of the Lincoln Tunnel in 1954. He credited the Port Authority for hiring African Americans in all positions and integrating all of the gangs for the first time. "It was the first big break we had," he recalled, and "it's been that way ever since." "I don't think the fellows really minded. Some of the officers may not have liked it, but they got used to it also."[15]

Affirmative Action?

Civil leaders mounted a campaign to transform the state's approach to enforcing the Law against Discrimination. In 1948 the Urban League of Greater New York, the American Jewish Congress, and the NAACP jointly established the Committee to Support the Ives-Quinn Law under the chairmanship of liberal Republican city councilman Newbold Morris. The committee recommended sweeping reforms, including speedier resolutions, more public education, and industry-wide investigations. Their emphasis on outreach, recruitment, and measuring change by statistical outcomes foreshadowed affirmative action strategies pursued nationally in the 1960s and beyond, and stemmed from the desire to translate legislative change into substantive results. At this juncture, affirmative action strategies, which had shaped grassroots job struggles during the Great Depression and the advocacy of left-wing trade unionists after the war, progressed to the level of the state.

The committee criticized SCAD's dedication to "the philosophy that it is more important to avoid antagonizing the business community than to give justice to the complainant." It stressed the aggrieved individual's right to redress, prefiguring the awarding of compensatory damages in employment discrimination law suits, both administrative and judicial. Reflecting the New Deal approach to planning that influenced many civil rights activists, Will Maslow thought SCAD should operate like the National Labor Relations Board and obtain consent decrees in order to make enforcement more effective. Maslow also urged that SCAD judge the extent of discrimination through regular reviews of overall racial employment patterns in the metropolitan economy. The committee's director Anne Mather concurred, arguing that "discrimination can rarely be proved against an individual because many pretexts are always available to reject an applicant." But "discrimination always shows up when a large number of hirings and rejections are examined statistically." According to these advocates, the commission had a mandate "to prevent and correct discrimination on a planned, systematic basis apart from a general exhortation to employers to comply with the law." They urged SCAD to intervene directly in large sectors of the local economy, including insurance, banking, transportation, public utilities, and department stores, in order to require the hiring of "qualified" minority applicants.[16]

SCAD rejected every proposal as "unrealistic and impractical," and refused to issue any clarification of what it considered compliance with the fair employment law. And it spurned industry-wide investigations, calling them "fishing expeditions," despite its own reports showing verified complaints in precisely these industries. The Committee to Support the Ives-Quinn Law concluded that the Law against Discrimination was fast becoming "dead letter legislation . . . for want of action under it."[17]

The committee appealed to Governor Dewey that "the process of democracy must be accelerated" and requested a comprehensive change in policy or the appointment of new members to SCAD. After learning of the impending release of the committee's highly critical report, Dewey agreed to meet with civil rights leaders in Albany. He refused to promise anything, pledging only to seek speedier investigations and to make more information about SCAD available to the public. The committee soon dissolved, and SCAD continued its policy of only using the "conference, conciliation and persuasion" component of the law without ever resorting to the sanctions, mass education, or large-scale investigations sought by African American workers and advocated by the early civil rights movement.[18]

The passage of a fair employment law in 1945 inspired efforts to win other antidiscrimination laws, including one covering private colleges and universities. The Committee on Law and Social Action (CLSA) was established by the American Jewish Congress in 1945 to "give new direction and strength to the struggle of the Jewish community for equality within the framework of American democracy," and "to fight every manifestation of racism and to promote the civil and political equality of all minorities in America." The CLSA released an influential study in 1945 verifying the widely held belief that Jewish admission rates to medical and other professional schools in New York State had declined sharply over the previous decade despite an increase in applications. In addition to uncovering the "quota system," the study verified the near total absence of African American students. Rabbi Stephen Wise of the American Jewish Congress sued Columbia University, arguing that it should lose its tax exemption because the state barred discrimination by tax-exempt institutions. He lost; the judge ruled that discrimination was not grounds to deny tax exempt status. Meanwhile City Councilman Ben Davis introduced a resolution denying tax-exemption to professional schools guilty of discrimination.[19]

In 1946 a similar report by the Mayor's Committee on Unity further publicized the issue and generated greater political support for action. City Council hearings into discrimination at five medical schools found "inescapable evidence" of discrimination against African Americans, Jews, and Italians, even though both Cornell and Columbia had burned the admission records of recent years. The studies revealed that in the previous twenty years, only nine African American students had been admitted to Columbia's College of Physicians and Surgeons, while the number of Jewish students had declined dramatically from 40 percent to 6 percent, despite rising numbers of African American and Jewish applicants. These studies also examined the admission rates of City College graduates to private institutions in the New York area as a means of uncovering racial and religious bias. Their findings that there were essentially no professional educational opportunities for graduates of public colleges pushed the legislature to appoint the Temporary Commission to Study the Need for a State University. New York lagged behind other states in establishing a unified public system of higher education.[20]

The City Council endorsed a CLSA-drafted bill in Albany barring discrimination as well as another bill to create state supported medical and dental schools. The movement had two goals that were widely seen as interlocking: opening private schools to minority students and creating a new public university system. This reflected the movement's overall emphasis on expanding opportunities and access for the large number of New Yorkers deprived of higher education in the state. A broad coalition of civil rights activists came together in an effort that was explicitly modeled on the strategy used to win the Ives-Quinn Law. They successfully lobbied the governor to appoint a temporary investigating commission, engaged in grassroots education and mobilization, marshaled studies, and won bipartisan support both upstate and downstate. The ULGNY, American Jewish Congress, NAACP, CIO, and Catholic and Protestant organizations formed the New York State Committee against Discrimination in Education (NYSCADE), and sponsored a major conference against discrimination in education in 1946. In an indication that opposition to religious and racial discrimination was becoming a significant feature of New York politics, both candidates for the U.S. Senate, Irving Ives and Herbert Lehman, addressed the audience of several hundred. "For a generation this state has driven through the most progressive legislation aiming at a democratization of our society," one activist said, expressing the vanguard feeling shared by many.[21]

Along with participating in this broad alliance, African American organizations formed a separate organization to push for a law that would remedy the specific needs of Black New Yorkers. At a meeting sponsored by Edward Lewis of the ULGNY, representatives of twenty groups formed the Harlem

Committee of the NYSCADE. The committee stressed that "Negroes experience the greatest discrimination of all minority groups in New York State universities," pointing out that Black medical students made up less than one half of 1 percent of all the medical students in the state. The Harlem Committee and the Urban League went on record "as strongly supporting the creation of a state university." But "these two organizations want it clearly understood that [this] does not in the least suggest that they will cease fighting for the complete elimination of discrimination in the existing professional schools of the state of New York which are tax free."[22]

Prior to *Baker v. Carr*, the 1962 Supreme Court ruling that mandated the "one person, one vote" rule of apportioning legislative districts, New York State was divided into districts that gave disproportionate political power to upstate, rural, white areas. In both 1946 and 1947 the legislature defeated bills barring discrimination in private, tax-exempt educational institutions. As legislation was being drafted for the 1948 session, activists were under considerable pressure to moderate their demands in order to overcome opposition, especially from the Catholic Church. This pressure undercut an effort to address the different Black and Jewish experiences with educational discrimination. City Councilman Stanley Isaacs and Judge Hubert Delany offered amendments allowing schools to consider race in order to "enrich the student body." In contrast to the language used to dismantle the exclusionary quota system, they proposed a plank to permit policies promoting "inclusion." Their proposals, however, were rejected by the larger committee. In a letter to Isaacs, Shad Polier of the American Jewish Congress wrote that although the amendment sanctioning "special favor for minority groups" had been rejected, he supported their goal and stated his belief that it could still be accomplished without amending the act. Isaacs complained to Judge Delany, "The major problem is still there, however, namely of validating procedures like those which we follow at Dalton [a private school in Manhattan]—deliberately designed to attract a varied student group, singling out people just because of their background."[23]

Civil rights leaders made many compromises in the final bill in order to win the Republican support needed for passage, including sacrificing harsher penalties. In April 1948 Governor Thomas E. Dewey signed the Fair Educational Practices Law, or the "Quinn-Olliffe Law," which barred racial and religious discrimination in nonsectarian, private institutions of higher education and created an office within the Department of Education to receive complaints. The law authorized the state to file complaints based on its own independent information. And even though the direct affirmative action clause did not make the final bill, the law empowered the administrator of the law to use enrollment statistics to judge compliance, revealing that there was an understanding that outcomes and results could be used to assess the law's effectiveness.

In addition, the legislature passed a bill to construct a massive statewide system of four-year colleges, community colleges, and medical, dental, and other professional schools. The Commission to Study the Need for a State University had released a report in January endorsing all the demands of the civil rights movement. It assailed the lack of affordable higher education in the state and called for a "vastly expanded" new system. As a "supplementary study" in the report, Black sociologist E. Franklin Frazier submitted an assessment of "the post-high school education of Negroes in New York State" that found growing demand for higher education by New York's expanding Black population, but a paucity of affordable and nondiscriminatory colleges and professional schools.[24]

Civil rights groups hailed the new laws as landmarks, but their enthusiasm diminished rapidly as the state proved reluctant to enforce the antidiscrimination law. Like SCAD, it urged voluntary, gradual change and refused to challenge directly the admissions policies of elite institutions. In his first meeting with civil rights leaders after the law passed, the education commissioner expressed concern over "irresponsible complaints being filed" and urged activists to screen them all first.[25] A year later, Rabbi Stephen Wise accused the board of regents of "undermining in its entirety the operation of the Fair Educational Practices Law" by its refusal to order institutions to refrain from making inquiries regarding race, religion, or national origin. Citing its desire not to "coerce" schools, the Department of Education instead disbursed pamphlets urging schools to drop "controversial questions" without specifying them. By 1950, civil rights activists had concluded that the department's record of enforcement was worse than SCAD's. In its first two years it had received only three complaints, and despite awareness of the systemic nature of the problem, it had resisted demands to initiate its own investigations. Moreover, activists found it difficult to assess the law's influence because the Department of Education refused to conduct statistical studies or analyze the applications of individuals rejected from the most notorious institutions.[26]

According to the CLSA, "the law so far has had an almost negligible effect because it has not been enforced." The first Fair Educational Practices administrator, Frederick W. Hoeing, said the state's role "should be limited only to a consideration of the admission policies of the institution" rather than the composition of the school. Despite his power to do so, Hoeing did not initiate investigations. Consequently, it was not until recruitment of Black student athletes in larger numbers in the 1960s, Black student protest on campus, and federal legislation in 1972 that significant numbers of Black students began to attend elite universities in New York State and around the nation.[27]

The Republican state government made an even bolder attempt to undermine the hope of civil rights activists while setting up the new state university. Republicans introduced a bill to transfer control over the new schools from the newly created and more representative board of trustees to the board of regents, a body that had done little to promote public higher education in recent years. Civil rights groups mobilized to prevent this move. The NAACP, ULGNY, and Harlem Committee against Discrimination led the effort to preserve the board of trustees. They accused the board of regents of wanting to set up "ghetto schools" and "destroy the original attempts of progressive education." George H. Haynes, an African American member of the board of trustees, said that to strip them of authority then was "to delay, if not to stop entirely, the development of such a real university system." The Harlem Committee accused the regents of condoning and abetting the system of quotas and minority exclusion from higher education in the state throughout its forty-five-year reign. It quoted Chancellor William Wallin's defense of the "right of discrimination" as "God-given." Signaling the importance of this struggle, the NAACP's executive secretary, Walter White, served as vice chair of the Committee to Save the University, and NAACP branches across the state sent telegrams and delegations to Albany to urge defeat of the bill. The bill was defeated, but civil rights leaders were put on notice. Edward Lewis announced that the Harlem Committee would rename itself Friends of the State University in order to fight for African American inclusion, both as students and workers, in all aspects of its development.[28]

Ironically, civil rights liberalism in New York was achieved and took shape during a Republican administration. Antidiscrimination legislation was, to a large extent, forced on lawmakers in Albany by a highly mobilized, popular, broad-based social movement that arose at an auspicious historical moment. The state reacted forcefully and immediately to curtail the transformative potential of racial reform. Alongside the African American rights struggle, and despite its successes, advocates of the racial status quo remained power-ful and influential in New York society. State government leaders charged with enforcing the new laws opposed the proactive use of affirmative action and other interventionist strategies that were designed to hasten racial equality and Black representation in mainstream institutions. They instead adopted a conservative strategy of gradual integrationism. Civil rights orga-nizations learned that victories were fragile and easily reversed. They found themselves compelled to function in a new role as watchdogs and critics of government agencies that they had hoped would be readier allies in the fight against discrimination. Yet they also sharpened their skills at making the political and legal case for affirmative action, which they would bring to the national stage in the 1960s.

6 An Unnatural Division of People

African Americans in search of housing outside overcrowded "Negro areas" in postwar New York City encountered staggering obstacles. A powerful industry composed of builders, realtors, and banks, in partnership with federal government agencies, was propelling the nation's peacetime expansion—and was devoted to a system of property valuation based on theories of racial difference. Demonizing Black people as buyers, renters, and neighbors was a central part of the profit strategy of the nation's biggest industry. As a result, and in contrast to trends in employment and public accommodations, the direction of the housing market in postwar New York was toward segregation. Civil rights workers, however, promoted a counternarrative to the resegregation of metropolitan America: a vision of inclusive urbanization that offered an alternative to a race-obsessed residential marketplace.

Civil rights and Black community leaders urged the government to build affordable, modern housing for the low-income population, a market that the private sector had found unprofitable to house in major cities. They fought for fair housing laws and an end to the many devices used to deny African Americans the right to engage in unfettered property transactions, including "red-lining"—bank policies that deprived Black home buyers and Black neighborhoods of loans. The goal of the fair housing struggle was access and fairness rather than integration as such. This was articulated most forcefully in struggles over the role and responsibility of the public sector: activists demanded that the government withhold legal protection or financial subsidy from any and all restricted housing.

The Price of Segregation

Harlem's population had more than doubled in the 1940s, without the slightest increase in the supply of housing. Discrimination in privately owned apartment buildings was lawful, open, and pervasive. "Whites Only" signs hung brazenly in buildings on Harlem's edge, restricting expansion and contributing to deteriorating living conditions for Black migrants. A muck-raking exposé found more than 3,800 people "jammed" in "one stifling square block in Upper Harlem." Harlemites were "underhoused, underprivileged and herded into three square miles of ghetto." The looming question that the writer impressed upon readers, whose memory of the 1943 riot was still strong, was, "How long before serious trouble will break out?"[1]

After the U.S. Supreme Court overturned a municipal ordinance from Kentucky in 1917 that barred Blacks from buying homes in areas designated as white, the engine of residential segregation moved away from government statutes and toward court-enforceable private contracts. Public racial zoning did continue in parts of the former Confederacy, but racially restrictive covenants in property deeds became a chief means of controlling Black spatial mobility and fostering segregation as Blacks migrated en masse to cities beginning in the World War I era. Robert Weaver called race restrictive covenants "the most dangerous" of segregationist devices because they "give legal sanction and consequently respectability to residential segregation." According to Weaver, this nonviolent form of neighborhood exclusion by the home-owning elite tacitly condoned and encouraged physical violence by the lower classes. "As long as the 'better people' in a community sign restrictions against certain groups and the courts enforce such agreements, other elements 'protect' their neighborhoods against minorities, too."[2]

Through both the courts and federal mortgage insurance programs, the state and federal governments legitimized and enabled private housing discrimination. In fact, the inclusion of racially restrictive covenants in deeds helped white home buyers receive federally guaranteed mortgages. Through the Federal Housing Administration (FHA), the United States encouraged segregated housing developments on the grounds, expressly stated in its *Underwriting Manual*, that homogeneous neighborhoods were better investments. Begun in the Depression, the FHA provided a huge stimulus to the housing industry—and its staff came from the thoroughly racist white real estate industry. The National Association of Real Estate Boards defined intentional race mixing as a violation of its code of ethics. It required the selling of homes on a strictly segregated basis. The FHA, in turn, endorsed the real estate industry's policy of "redlining," which ranked a buyer or property's credit worthiness based on the racial composition of the neighborhood. Mixed, or predominantly minority neighborhoods, were labeled as poor risks, and banks were discouraged from making loans both on property in such neighborhoods and to Black home buyers outside of minority areas. As one housing attorney later put it, "The manuals officially issued by the federal government during the very liberal Roosevelt administration read like pages out of the Nuremberg laws." Thus the federal government played a principal role in segregating metropolitan America, especially in luring whites to new suburbs, where business, jobs, and tax dollars would soon follow.[3]

Housing advocates conducted studies of the political economy of Black neighborhoods in order to counter the argument that Black residents were to blame for the declining state of the housing stock in racial ghettoes. They stressed, for example, that segregation created higher profits for landlords. While other Manhattan residents paid an estimated 20 percent of their income for rent, Harlemites paid almost 45 percent. Ghetto dwellers were a captive market forced to pay the landlord's price. "Yet ironically," an activist noted, "tax assessments were decreased, making way for the argument that property values deteriorate when Negroes move in—an argument wholly unfounded in fact." Landlords subdivided apartments into smaller units to create more rental income, creating a grid of social distress. "Plot any delinquency map, any infant mortality map, any disease map, and you will find that the areas of greatest infection are coincident with the minority group ghettoes in the community"—areas, he added, with the worst schools, poorest police protection, and fewest municipal services and recreational areas.[4]

The postwar building boom was rapidly expanding the segregated landscape just as the northern civil rights struggle was beginning and Black income rising. According to a 1948 survey, 85.1 percent of new, large subdivisions in Westchester, Nassau, and Queens contained restrictive covenants. New York was not unlike other northern cities: an estimated 80 percent of housing in Chicago was restricted to white Christians. Algernon Black noted that "the undemocratic principle of 'restricted' is a big selling point in certain suburban areas." Like many activists of this era, he believed that segregation stimulated racial prejudice and feelings of superiority among whites. "The very existence of such an idea," he said, "engenders color consciousness and race prejudice even in minds previously free of such bigotry." Black's organization, the New York State Committee against Discrimination in Housing, surveyed ten upstate cities in the late 1940s and found a pervasive, though unwritten, policy among bankers, real estate boards, and mortgagee companies to limit Black residential space. "The city was zoned, not officially by the government, but it was zoned for the separation of black people and white people."[5]

In 1945 public housing in New York City was the only housing in the entire state subject to an antidiscrimination law. In an era when private capital consistently ignored the Black market for decent and affordable housing, public housing was the only new, modern housing open to Black occupancy. Black community leaders and politicians thus supported public housing, although they would later oppose site selections that reinforced racial segregation. For many years in the mid-twentieth century, however, public housing signified an urban success story of modern, integrated communities, in stark contrast to its later representation as a zone of Black and Brown surplus labor awash in crime and under unrelenting political attack.

The overcrowded, "undemocratic" racial ghetto was a newly visible theme in citywide discourse in the 1940s. The radio program *New World A'Coming* dramatized Captain Hugh Mulzac's attempt to purchase a home in suburban Westchester County. Citing a racial covenant among the neighboring homeowners, the owner told Mulzac, "Don't blame me because you're colored." This broadcast, to a majority white audience, described the housing emergency in Harlem and the "well-organized" opposition to Black newcomers in white neighborhoods. "Public housing projects are the beginning" of "a new and democratic era," the narrator Canada Lee declared, reflecting the optimistic view that they would eliminate slums and remain interracial.

Civil rights leaders sought to counter the housing industry's claim—in manuals, textbooks, and regulations—that integration was a destabilizing force. To the contrary, they argued, segregation was the destabilizing force. Since 1943, activists had been warning city officials to expect another riot if they continued to ignore the mounting tensions above 110th Street in Manhattan. A survey by the Mayor's Committee on Unity on the types of segregation "most irritating to the Negro Minority" ranked residential segregation first. The head of the Harlem NAACP branch told a reporter, "Harlem will remain what you call a trouble spot so long as society persists in maintaining superior-inferior relationships between the people that comprise it.

It's the price of segregation." Segregation, warned Algernon Black, "breeds smoldering embers of hostility, rage, hatred and violence."[6]

A surprising development in August 1946 revealed how systematic and well organized the financial industry's promotion of segregation was. The U.S. attorney in Manhattan indicted the Mortgage Conference of Greater New York, a consortium of thirty-eight of the city's leading bank and trust companies formed in 1934, for violating federal antitrust laws by agreeing "to use their control of credit to cause the exclusion of certain minority, racial and national groups from certain areas." The U.S. government alleged in federal court that the defendants

> prepared, published, kept current and distributed maps of each section of New York City showing blocks on which Negroes and Spanish-speaking persons resided; refrained from making mortgage loans on properties in such blocks; and induced owners of real estate in certain sections of New York City to refuse to permit Negroes and Spanish-speaking persons to move into such sections.

Banks in the Mortgage Conference required the inclusion of racially restrictive covenants in property deeds as a condition for receiving a loan. The complaint charged that financial institutions confined African Americans and Puerto Ricans to overcrowded ghettoes where they were compelled to pay higher rents for property whose owners were denied the financing to maintain its habitability. Thus, the bank's lending practices both blocked Black access to new housing and neighborhoods and depressed the property in their neighborhoods. Such practices worked to prevent mixed race and mixed income neighborhoods, blocking, for example, the construction of 25,000 low-income dwelling units in "white" neighborhoods of Brooklyn. The remarkable irony in the Justice Department's prosecution of the Mortgage Conference is that the federal government's housing agencies openly endorsed all of its policies. As housing attorney Charles Abrams pointed out, "The prosecuting arm of the government was charging the banks with doing exactly what the administrative arm, through the FHA and Home Loan Bank System, was then sanctioning and encouraging."[7]

Civil rights groups urged the government to press forward with the suit as banks exerted widely publicized pressure to drop it. The NAACP denounced the business of ghetto maintenance: "These ghettos have grown up not alone from the bigotry and prejudice of their fellow-citizens, but as a result of a planned campaign which has confined them to small overcrowded areas

from the renting of which a greater profit can be reaped." "It is small wonder," wrote Ted Poston in the *New York Post*, "that between the formation of
the Mortgage Conference in 1934, and its court-ordered dissolution, Harlem
erupted with two major property-oriented riots."[8]

Twenty months later, the actor-activist Canada Lee joined a demonstration in front of the U.S. court in Foley Square with signs asking, "Are the Big
Banks and the Insurance Companies More Powerful than the U.S. Courts?"
In June 1948 the defendants, fearing the exposure of internal documents
that a trial would likely entail as well as the risk of financial penalties, agreed
to a consent decree enjoining them from denying mortgages to minority
groups in areas outside the ghetto. The decree, however, failed to establish
an effective means to monitor compliance or hold the banks accountable.
The Mortgage Conference case was an isolated prosecution of private-sector
discrimination at a time when the tide was going in the opposite direction.
It was a highly unusual Justice Department foray into the area of home
finance, a terrain that was vigilantly patrolled by the FHA and other housing
agencies.[9]

Leadership in the fair housing struggle came from across the ideological
spectrum—liberal advocates in organizations such as the American Jewish
Congress, Urban League, and City-Wide Citizens' Committee on Harlem;
Communists in grassroots tenant organizations and unions; independent
leftists; and Harlem community leaders. The movement's first goal was to
sever governmental support for racial discrimination in housing. There was
clearer constitutional prohibition of state-sanctioned racial discrimination
than of private acts of racial discrimination. Racially restrictive covenants in
property deeds were prime targets of the early civil rights movement because they depended on state judges to enforce them, making them vulnerable to a legal challenge under the Fourteenth Amendment. In addition to
the campaigns for a state Fair Employment Practices Committee and a law
barring discrimination in higher education, the fight against restrictive covenants was the third major example of Black-Jewish collaboration in the civil
rights movement in New York State. Since covenants in property deeds
commonly restricted sales to white Christians, Blacks and Jews each had
a strong group interest in abolishing them. In January 1945 Harlem Democratic assemblymen Hulan Jack and William T. Andrews introduced a bill
to ban covenants restricting the sale or lease of property based on race or
religion. Similar legislation was reintroduced in 1946 and 1947. In 1946,
members of the ULGNY, NAACP, City-Wide Citizens Committee on Harlem,

American Jewish Congress, and Citizens' Housing and Planning Council formed the Committee to Outlaw Racial Covenants to exert more pressure in Albany.[10]

The covenant issue made its Broadway debut at the Cort Theater in 1946 in *On Whitman Avenue*. Written by Maxine Wood, the play was produced by, and starred, Canada Lee. It addressed the racism encountered by a black family moving to Whitman Avenue, a street in "any pleasant, tree-shaded suburb in a northern state of this country." The play challenged white audiences to confront their fears and stereotypes, and ultimately their own complicity in racial segregation. "Into this peaceful, contented suburb comes suddenly The Situation," a promotional flier declared, "which hovers like a specter today over all American life—the specter of our unsolved race problem." African American journalist St. Clair T. Bourne predicted that the play would "stun whites with the realization that they are seeing demonstrated something which they themselves are doing everyday." The handbill asked, "As a white person, would you welcome Negro neighbors? Would you give them a month to get out? Or would you run them out forthwith? As a Negro, would you passively submit to being hounded out? Or would you demand a decent break? *You can't answer these questions until you've seen 'On Whitman Avenue!'*"[11]

The play validated a "situation all too well known to Negroes," not only in the current housing shortage, "but also when there were plenty of houses and apartments available 'for whites only.'" After one performance, American Labor Party state assemblyman Leo Isacson spoke about local housing segregation. The play inspired spirited debate in newspapers and over the radio about the limits to white liberals' devotion to liberty. Eleanor Roosevelt wrote about the play in her "My Day" newspaper column and had the cast over for dinner. After seeing the play, Rose Shapiro commented that many of her Jewish neighbors in upper Manhattan "worry about the movement of Negroes north from Harlem," and would move at the prospect of having Black neighbors, even though "if they tried to move to Westchester they in turn would find themselves unwelcome." Moreover, Shapiro added, "These same people are always the first to sign petitions against the poll tax and for the F.E.P.C."[12]

Fair housing advocates emphasized that education, planning, and new construction had to accompany desegregation, in order to overcome ignorance, prevent violence, and forestall what later came to be called "white flight." Naturally, this would depend on progressive elected and appointed

Eleanor Roosevelt and Canada Lee at a party she gave for the cast of *On Whit-man Avenue* at her home in Hyde Park, New York.

officials, but the state government in Albany was dominated by conservatives from overrepresented rural regions north of the city who vigorously opposed any legislation promoting unrestricted Black and Jewish access to housing. As a consequence, activists shifted their focus to the courts, hoping that New York's judiciary would be more enlightened than its elected officials. Despite the U.S. Supreme Court's approval of racial covenants in 1926, many attorneys saw them as vulnerable. Two judges in California had recently struck down racial covenants, including one in a Los Angeles case involving Black film stars Hattie McDaniels, Louise Beavers, Ethel Waters, and Noble Sissle.[13]

In June 1946 a street in St. Albans, Queens, "became Whitman Avenue" when a State Supreme Court judge ordered Sophie Rubin not to sell her home on 177th Street to Samuel Richardson, a Black merchant from Manhattan. The judge upheld Harold F. Kemp's claim that the sale would violate a 1939 agreement, signed by Rubin and several white property owners in the area, forbidding the sale, lease, or gift of property to "Negroes or persons of the Negro race or blood or descent" until 1975. Samuel Richardson was one of several African American home buyers across the country who were hoping to get the U.S. Supreme Court to strike a blow against racial covenants.

The neighborhood, the Addisleigh Park section of St. Albans, Queens, was home to forty-eight Black families out of a total of 325, including Lena Horne and William and Catherine Basie. But the affluent Black newcomers were extended a hostile and threatening welcome by some. Notes by the "Klu Klux Klan, District of St. Albans" [sic] stating "Warning to Negroes entering St. Albans. Beware . . ." were left in the mailboxes of Charles Collier, executive secretary of the CWCCH; John Singleton, a member of the NAACP Board of Directors; and William H. Pleasant. In 1952, a cross was burned in St. Albans not far from the homes of Jackie Robinson, his fellow Brooklyn Dodger Roy Campanella, and the jazz vocalist Ella Fitzgerald.[14]

Representing Samuel Richardson, the NAACP argued that racially restrictive covenants violated the Fourteenth Amendment. But because American courts had in large measure rejected constitutional arguments for African American rights since the overthrow of Reconstruction, the attorneys crafted arguments that covenants undermined public policy, and they even invoked the United Nations Charter. Many organizations, including the American Veterans Committee, American Jewish Congress, National Lawyers' Guild, New York State Industrial Union Council, and Committee of Catholics for Human Rights, submitted amicus curiae briefs elaborating the "social evils of segregation."

The NAACP also advanced an economic critique of the racial ghetto. "Aside from the legal unsoundness and the social viciousness of restrictive covenants," the brief argued, "one must consider the economic burden that it places upon the Negro by forcing him to pay higher rents and occupy inadequate accommodations." The racialized distribution of housing created pent-up demand and a constricted supply for African American home buyers that in turn shaped sellers' profit margins. The brief cited a 1945 real estate industry survey, which found that "Queens housing is sold to Negroes only when values have already begun to decline. Negroes, in search of housing, must take what they can get, so, at somewhat inflated prices, they buy these properties."[15]

In February 1947 the judge ruled in *Kemp v. Rubin* that in the absence of a state law prohibiting it, a racially discriminatory covenant was lawful. The Appellate Division upheld the decision, but on May 3, 1948, the Supreme Court ruled in *Shelley v. Kramer* that judicial enforcement of racially restrictive covenants constituted state action, and therefore violated the Fourteenth Amendment. As a result, the New York Court of Appeals reversed the decision in *Kemp v. Rubin* and Samuel Richardson was able to buy the home.[16]

Shelley v. Kramer did not end governmental support for racially exclusionary housing. The judiciary ceased enforcing racial discrimination, but the executive branch, through the FHA, continued to subsidize segregation. In 1950 the FHA ceased insuring mortgages on homes with newly written racial covenants, and removed from its manual the model covenant and language characterizing Blacks as undesirable home buyers. But racial discrimination in the sale or lease of a private home remained lawful and the FHA continued to provide financial backing to housing that excluded African Americans by means other than a written racial covenant. Under President Dwight D. Eisenhower, the FHA took the position that civil rights enforcement infringed on property rights. In 1952, FHA administrator Albert Cole bluntly stated that "it is not incumbent on the federal government to impose integration in federally insured and federally aided housing in violation of the attitudes, customs and practices of the local community."[17]

The Battle for Stuyvesant Town

In 1943 the City of New York and the Metropolitan Life Insurance Company signed a contract to create Stuyvesant Town, the largest urban redevelopment housing project in the United States. It would provide thousands of modern, spacious, low-rent apartments exclusively to young veterans and their families, in order to honor their service in the war against fascism. But Met Life practiced racism of its own when it openly denied Black veterans the right to live in Stuyvesant Town. This announcement, in the middle of the war, sparked a firestorm of controversy. The dollars of Black taxpayers and policyholders would be used to subsidize homes that Black people could not occupy: the struggle that ensued was less about integration than about justice, fairness, and democracy. The "battle for Stuyvesant Town" produced the first fair housing laws in the United States. And Met Life, in many respects standing in for the whole racialized housing industry, went all the way to the Supreme Court to defend its "right" to discriminate.[18]

Robert Moses and Met Life President Frederick Ecker loom large in this story. Moses, New York City's parks commissioner and behind-the-scenes power broker, engineered the passage of a new state law, the Urban Redevelopment Companies Act, specifically to ensure that Met Life would be free to bar Blacks from Stuyvesant Town. "If control of selection of tenants" is "to be supervised by public officials," he wrote, "it will be impossible to get insurance companies and banks to help us clear sub-standard, run-down, and cancerous areas in the heart of the city." Like other business advocates in the public sector, Moses often invoked capital flight as a weapon to make public officials fall in line. He derided his critics as "demagogues . . . who want to make a political, racial, religious, or sectional issue out of every progressive step which can be taken to improve local conditions."[19]

The law and contract authorized an unprecedented transfer of state resources to a for-profit private venture, including a twenty-five year tax exemption estimated at $53 million, the ceding of public streets, and the condemnation of private property, including the forced removal of ten thousand residents. The project was designed to be a walled "city within a city" of 8,759 families with no public streets, schools, or parks, in order to keep "undesirables" off the premises at all times. Stuyvesant Town set the pattern for postwar urban redevelopment: the transfer of prized urban space to the white professional class, under the reformist rubric of "slum clearance." Slum clearance in New York had been authorized in the new 1938 state constitution as a New Deal reform, and envisioned by many as government planning to ameliorate the misery produced by the profit-driven housing industry's neglect of the poor, but in the postwar era, private builders and their political allies succeeded in imposing their own race and class design on the metropolitan landscape. In the battle for Stuyvesant Town, this appropriation was instantly unmasked, deeply resented, and broadly challenged.[20]

Shortly before the Board of Estimate voted on the contract, Frederick Ecker publicly confirmed his intention to exclude Black tenants. "Negroes and whites don't mix," he said, and "if we brought them into the development it would be to the detriment of the city, too, because it would depress all the surrounding property." Moses strongly urged Ecker not to give in to Mayor LaGuardia's last-minute attempt to add language to the contract signaling nondiscriminatory tenant selection. The mayor signed the contract but made a statement that discrimination in tenant selection would, in his view, be a violation of state law, and that he would take this position in any litigation.[21]

"This is the first major effort," the CWCCH wrote to the Board of Estimate, which would vote on the contract, "to destroy the gains achieved in the contest for equal rights . . . If the city countenances a precedent under which discrimination is to be subsidized . . . It will open the door to further incursions on civil rights." City Council President Newbold Morris cast one of the two votes against the project. "I represent all the people," Morris began, rejecting Moses's privileging of private capital at all costs. "Huge as this project is, it dwindles down into insignificance as compared to the principle." Moreover, he disputed Ecker's underlying rationale: "Being 'desirable' doesn't hinge on racial origin." Moses and Ecker won this round, but the battle had just begun. In 1943 City Council members Adam Clayton Powell and Stanley Isaacs cosponsored a bill to bar discrimination in projects built under the Redevelopment Companies Law. But conservative forces engineered its defeat. A year later, Isaacs and Benjamin Davis succeeded in passing a law that barred discrimination, though only in future publicly assisted, privately owned housing projects. This still left Stuyvesant Town free to discriminate.[22]

As a defense to lawsuits, Moses urged Ecker to build projects in Black communities to show that he was also undertaking "model housing for colored folks." In 1944 Met Life announced the construction in Harlem of the Riverton Houses, an affordable, middle-income development "for Negroes." Housing advocates and civil rights activists debated the proper response to Riverton at a lively meeting in 1944. White attorney Charles Abrams declared that "the issue to be determined by the Negro community . . . is whether it is more interested in the few projects that may be built, or whether it is more interested in establishing an accepted principle of equality in housing." The national NAACP also opposed Riverton on the grounds that "as long as the Metropolitan maintains a closed-door policy to Negroes in its projects outside the Harlem area, the Riverton Project becomes a segregated, Jim Crow housing project." This was the minority view, however. In a neighborhood of extreme overcrowding, most residents welcomed the prospect of 1,200 new apartments. They shared the sentiment expressed by an Urban League official that "protesting Riverton to protest Stuyvesant Town is confusing the issue." Moreover, they argued, Riverton would be subject to the 1944 Davis-Isaacs Law, and would be legally open to whites.[23]

A year later, a CWCCH delegation asked Ecker: "Why is an interracial policy sound for one place, Riverton, which will be subject to the antidiscrimination law, and not sound for the other, Stuyvesant Town?" Ecker's response reveals the confidence that landlords had about their ability to violate the law with impunity. "What makes you think Riverton will be an interracial housing project?" he asked the group. "Metropolitan will own Riverton and be in complete control of tenancy selection." When it opened in 1947, Met Life judged the 50,000 applicants for the 1,232 units according to their "desirability," a category that African Americans allegedly could not fill—at least not downtown. The Riverton became a fashionable residence, a bedrock of the growing Black middle class shortly before it began to move out of Harlem to the more suburban-like outer boroughs. Like 409 and 555 Edgecombe Avenue in Sugar Hill, Riverton tenants were a veritable Harlem Who's Who, including future mayor David N. Dinkins and future Court of Appeals judge Fritz W. Alexander.[24]

On June 26, 1947, as occupancy of Stuyvesant Town was about to begin, three African American veterans sued Met Life for denial of housing based on race. The lead plaintiff, Joseph R. Dorsey, a former Army captain, social worker, father, and resident of a condemned tenement in Harlem, exemplified the African American veterans whose refusal to accept second-class status helped propel the civil rights struggle. The NAACP, American Jewish Congress, and American Civil Liberties Union sponsored the suit, which was argued by Will Maslow and Charles Abrams. Maslow, who was the nephew of David Ben-Gurion, Israel's first prime minister, headed the American Jewish Congress's Committee on Law and Social Action and drafted many of the antidiscrimination laws passed in New York State after the war. He argued that government assistance to Stuyvesant Town qualified as state action under the equal protection clauses of the U.S. and state constitutions. The tax exemption, use of eminent domain, and government-determined rent and profit ceilings all made possible under a public law that had deemed Stuyvesant Town a "superior public use" qualified, Maslow argued, as "state action."

Abrams challenged Stuyvesant Town from a different angle. The proj-

ect represented "a dangerous crossbreed"—government aid and no government control, enrichment of an elite at public expense. The Community
Service Society found that 75 percent of the thousands forced to relocate
did not qualify for public housing, and sounded an alarm that would be
sounded again and again during the era of "slum clearance": "Slums are
more than crumbling stones and rotting timber; they are the homes of thousands of people . . . If these people's homes are destroyed and they are scat-
tered abroad to seek other shelter, left to their own resources, they cannot
help but settle in other slums or substandard areas, thus aggravating and
perpetuating conditions in those areas."[25]

To counter the arguments of Robert Moses and others that lavish subsidies
to private enterprise were necessary to solve the affordable housing crisis,
urban planners, housing advocates, and civil rights organizations developed
alternative plans for "democratic," more affordable, and sustainable housing. The CWCCH, religious groups, and the Citizens' Housing Council put
forth a ten-year "re-housing" plan paid for by various revenue sources, including 1 percent of the sales tax. Mayor O'Dwyer pledged his support but
then abandoned the idea, evidently at the urging of Moses. Maxwell Tretter,
the head of the New York City Housing Authority, proposed that the city
could build its own self-supporting low-rent housing more cheaply than
Metropolitan Life. The Citizens' Housing Council criticized the state's rush to
grant tax exemptions to residential builders and proposed an alternative
plan of developing "self-sustaining public housing" at low cost. It argued
that "tax exemption . . . will not spur construction, or materially reduce
rents, and might impose a substantial and unnecessary loss upon the city."
Government leaders, however, did not pursue these proposals, preferring
instead to arrange more lucrative deals with private developers.[26]

In July 1947 State Supreme Court Justice Felix C. Benvenga ruled in favor of Stuyvesant Town. "Housing is not a civil right," he ruled, accepting
the defendant's definition of itself as private. And since there was no "established civil right where the question of private housing accommodations
were concerned," he refused to enjoin the openly discriminatory tenant-
selection process. The attorneys appealed the *Dorsey v. Stuyvesant Town* ruling
to the state's highest court. Meanwhile, the decision's implications for the
spread of legal segregation in New York City radicalized housing activists
and paved the way for the growth of new tactics in the desegregation movement.[27]

The *People's Voice*, Harlem's left-wing weekly, said the decision "gives a le-

Demonstrators protesting discrimination at Stuyvesant Town at the site of the St. Nicholas Houses in Harlem, 1950.

gal stamp of approval to segregation . . . and makes a mockery of democratic principles." It expressed incredulity that "a property which in effect is a township" could be deemed beyond state control. "With its money and power," the newspaper warned, "Metropolitan is crystallizing patterns of segregation and condemning thousands of Negroes to a secondary citizenship status for generations to come." Since the Urban Redevelopment Companies Law had already been copied in eleven other states, such foreboding was based on real and rapid social and economic changes. An editorial in the *New York Age* entitled "Hot Weather Thought" raised the specter of violence in its assessment of corporate segregation: "The Metropolitan Insurance Company is peddling a policy of hatred which will cost high in the premium of disunity and pay off the dividends of destruction." The contrasting opinions expressed by the mainstream press cast in sharp relief how radical were notions of racial equality in housing in 1947 New York. During the height of the Stuyvesant Town controversy, both the *New York Times* and the *New York Herald-Tribune* withheld editorial support for integration. The more liberal *New York Post* was the only major daily that consistently supported integration at Stuyvesant Town.[28]

While the case was fought in the courts, the New York Communist Party and its allies decided to wage a grassroots campaign around Stuyvesant Town. This was part of the CP's postwar stance on "the Negro question," which emphasized struggle against what they saw as the interlocking oppression of white supremacy and American capitalism. Black Communist attorney William Patterson wrote that "a major feature of the program in the North must be the struggle to destroy the ghetto." For the Communists, destroying the ghetto was part of the struggle for Black self-determination. Patterson noted that "a complete analysis of ghetto life and what it means, will help the Negro people see monopoly capital and its role more clearly." In a 1947 speech, a top New York State party leader declared that "there must not be a single apartment house anywhere in the city in which a Communist lives where a policy of officially or unofficially barring Negroes goes unchallenged." Over the next several years, many apartment buildings in the five boroughs became sites of direct action protest over the landlord's racial practices.[29]

The Communist Party's wide orbit of influence in several trade unions, publications, and "people's organizations," as well as the fact that several party members and sympathizers resided in Stuyvesant Town, made them well situated for this struggle. In 1948 a group of tenants formed the Town and Village Tenants' Committee to End Discrimination in Stuyvesant Town, which grew to 1,800 paid members. Composed of Democrats, Republicans, Liberals, Communists, and American Labor Party members, its chairman was ALP leader and former city official Paul Ross. According to Lee Lorch, a member of its executive committee, Communists, while not a majority of the tenants' committee, did most of the work. And, he recalled, relations on the committee were "very harmonious." Lorch believes that the Stuyvesant Town movement "wouldn't have happened without the CP" or the tireless work of women activists inside the housing project. The tenants' committee pursued two strategies—to ideologically undermine Ecker's claim that whites were opposed to interracial living and to begin the process of deseg-regation themselves, by subletting to African Americans. Their survey of tenants found that 66 percent of respondents opposed the exclusion of Afri-can Americans at Stuyvesant Town. The committee collected 3,100 signa-tures on a petition addressed to Met Life and the city. Mayor O'Dwyer claimed he was "powerless" to alter a contract signed by his predecessor, even though, as the tenants pointed out, he had changed it recently to raise rents.[30]

The literature produced by the tenants' committee was steeped in Popular Front Americanism—it called on America to live up to its lofty ideals and promise of democracy. The pamphlets had evocative illustrations and pho-tography that projected faith in democracy and optimism about the future. They situated happy images of family, home, and domesticity in a context that was urban, racially integrated, and harmonious. These scenes contrast sharply with the images later flooding mass media that put domesticity and family in a whitened suburban context, generally erased Black people, and portrayed cities as deviant and dangerous places. Leo Miller, who fought in the Battle of the Bulge, where "the courage and sharp shooting of a Negro machine-gunner saved my life with a dozen other white GIs," asked, "Can anyone of us who live in Stuyvesant Town say he may not be my neighbor? I can't." Another veteran and his wife said: "We don't want our children growing up as part of a privileged group and believing from their experi-ences that Negroes are a people apart. And we don't think our taxes should be used to support an unnatural division of people."[31]

Met Life quickly moved to discredit the tenant activists. With the Cold War building, it stoked fears of the Communist involvement. In its appellate brief, it tried to shift attention away from race and toward ideology, arguing that the lawsuit itself, indeed the whole struggle, was Communist inspired, and therefore illegitimate.[32]

In July 1949 in a 4–3 decision, the New York State Court of Appeals affirmed that there was no state role in the operation of Stuyvesant Town and so as private enterprise, it was free to engage in racial discrimination. Judge Bruce Bromley—whose opinion sparked an NAACP campaign for his defeat at the polls in November—wrote that the state legislature "deliberately and intentionally refrained from imposing any restriction upon a redevelopment company in its choice of tenants." The handiwork of Robert Moses succeeded. By denying the crucial role of the state, the decision helped to create the fiction that de facto housing segregation in the North originated outside the law and reflected market forces rather than purposeful, racially exclusionary acts of public policy.

Fair housing advocates expressed alarm. Congress had just passed the Housing Act of 1949, which authorized the expenditure of half a billion dollars for urban redevelopment. Shad Polier and Charles Abrams wrote in the *New York Times*, "There are ample indications that such projects unless open to all citizens equally will become another oppressive instrument for removing minorities from their homes and creating enforced ghettos." Harlem City Council candidate Earl Brown said the decision "implied that the slums are the places where the Negro shall dwell, though they are compelled to pay taxes to keep up modern housing developments constructed by private industry." Community activists and liberal politicians had long called for a greater government role in housing, but to their alarm, it was solidifying racial segregation, rather than destroying the ghetto. Attorneys appealed the case to the U.S. Supreme Court, understanding that a favorable decision would also help to desegregate public housing developments nationwide.[33]

The executive, judicial, and legislative branches of state and city government had now all sided with Met Life, and tenants began to integrate the project on their own. In the summer of 1949, Jesse Kessler, an organizer with Local 65, invited a Black family to stay in his apartment during his vacation. Hardine and Raefield Hendrix and their young son moved in, and Mrs. Hendrix, an organizer with the Domestic Workers Union, became very active in the Stuyvesant Town struggle and ultimately the citywide housing battle. A *New York Times* reporter found that twelve of fifteen of the Hendrixes' neighbors thought African Americans should be able to live in Stuyvesant Town, and 1,200 tenants signed a letter welcoming the Hendrix family. Upon Kessler's return, the Hendrix family moved into the apartment of Lee Lorch. A professor of mathematics and a leftist, Lorch was moving to Pennsylvania to begin a job at Penn State because his activism at Stuyvesant Town had cost him his position at City College.[34]

The left challenged the Metropolitan Life Insurance Company as a landlord, an employer, and an insurer. They pointed out that it was the largest absentee owner of plantations in the Mississippi Delta, "and the lives of the Negroes on those plantations is hardly removed from the chattel slavery of pre–Civil War days." Ewart Guinier contrasted the nondiscriminatory insurance policies of the left-wing International Workers Order with the Metropolitan, which "carries out a very discriminatory policy." He described his attempt to get a "so-called straight life policy" with Metropolitan, whose agent "told me I couldn't get it because I was a Negro." Yet the Metropolitan was "the largest holder of so-called industrial policies among the Negro people," whose weekly payments helped turn Met Life into the richest corporation in the United States in 1945. Met Life had the majority of Black insurance policies in the United States—thus, it was not only as taxpayers, but also as policyholders in a mutual corporation that Black dollars were being used to house whites in Stuyvesant Town.[35]

Mayor O'Dwyer's opponents in the 1949 municipal election sought to capitalize on his support for Stuyvesant Town. He was, after all, a Democrat, and by 1949, Black political mobilization had pushed the party both locally and nationally to support some civil rights positions. American Labor Party (ALP) candidates kept the issue at the forefront of the campaign. Paul Ross, leader of the Stuyvesant Town Tenants' Committee to End Discrimination, ran for state comptroller, and Ewart Guinier ran for Manhattan borough president. Guinier, the first Black nominee for the post by a major party, was a war veteran who had applied for an apartment in Stuyvesant Town. Vito Marcantonio, the congressional representative from East Harlem and mayoral challenger, continually attacked Mayor O'Dwyer for the city's support for Met Life in court. When Mayor O'Dwyer pledged to a gathering of Black Democrats to fight for integration at Stuyvesant Town, Marcantonio asked, "Why, Bill, why start now? How about the last four years?" Marcantonio reminded the mayor that "tomorrow your Board of Estimate is meeting. How about a resolution canceling the tax exemption to the Metropolitan unless they cancel their policy of discrimination?" The entire ALP slate did much better in Harlem in 1949 than they had done in 1948—Marcantonio won 39 percent of the vote in Central Harlem. Harlem voters sent a message to the

Democrats that they would give their votes to insurgents if Democrats supported segregation.[36]

The struggle to desegregate residential communities has rarely taken the form of a mass movement. Attorneys have litigated for the right, and Black individuals and families have usually had to bear the brunt of white hostility on their own. But Stuyvesant Town was such a raw display of government-sanctioned racial privilege in a supposedly liberal city that it registered broadly and deeply across Black New York. Father Divine, the charismatic leader of a large, interracial, celibate religious commune, warned Met Life that their deeds would "bring on such disasters as have claimed the lives of millions in recent years." (Indeed, Father Divine had personally claimed responsibility for a few recent natural disasters.) Jesse B. Semple, a.k.a. Simple, the beloved Harlem barfly created by Langston Hughes, gave voice to the resentment produced by segregation. White Harlem store owners, said Simple, "take my money over the counter, then go on downtown to Stuyvesant Town where I can't live, or out to them pretty suburbs, and leave me in Harlem holding the bag. I ain't no fool. When the riot broke out I went looking for justice." In a 1949 speech, Paul Robeson likened Met Life to Mississippi and blasted segregation at Stuyvesant Town.[37]

A new fair housing organization emerged from the struggles against racial covenants and discrimination at Stuyvesant Town. Launched in January 1949, the New York State Committee against Discrimination in Housing (NYSCDH) helped win passage in 1950 of the Wicks-Austin Law, which barred racial discrimination from any housing constructed under Title I of the Housing Act. The city was about to receive $35 million in federal funds to acquire and clear "slum" areas for resale to private developers. Algernon Black, a leader of the NYSCDH, warned that the massive new government role in housing could be "a vital weapon in the battle against housing discrimination." Or "we may find ourselves projecting into the North, the kind of Jim-Crow public housing which has been a betrayal of freedom and equality in the South."[38]

On June 5, 1950, the same day it announced favorable decisions in three cases that assailed the separate but equal doctrine in higher education and interstate transportation, the Supreme Court announced that it would not review the *Dorsey* case.[39] With legal hopes dashed, fair housing advocates redoubled their efforts to pass a city law. The American Jewish Congress drafted a bill for the NYSCDH barring discrimination in all publicly assisted housing, a bill that Earl Brown and Stanley Isaacs introduced in the City

Council in June 1950. Stuyvesant Town fought hard to defeat the bill. After Met Life announced that it would admit "some qualified Negroes" into its walled city of nearly 25,000 whites, Mayor O'Dwyer persuaded Brown to suspend the bill. But after three months of mayoral stalling, and pressure from churches, trade unions, his constituents, and all of the major progressive organizations in the city, Brown resumed his push for the legislation. This mobilization testified to the growth of the city's civil rights movement since the contract's signing in 1943.

Politically, it was getting more difficult for Met Life to offer a straightforward defense of segregation, such as they had done in 1943. The company continued to use anticommunism as a means to discredit and undermine the fair housing movement. Met Life sent a collection of clippings from the Communist and left-wing press regarding Stuyvesant Town to the *Daily News* and *Daily Mirror,* and each in turn wrote editorials against the bill on the grounds that it constituted a Communist conspiracy. In the City Council hearings, Communism dominated the debate on both sides, illuminating the extent to which foreign policy considerations came to dominate civil rights discourse during the Cold War. Earl Brown said the bill would "help our fighting men in Korea." Councilman Isaacs said "Stuyvesant Town has become a world-wide symbol of inequitable and undemocratic treatment of some Americans by other Americans. This bill will serve to . . . strengthen the concepts of democracy held by people throughout the world." From the other side, C. F. Reavis, the attorney for Met Life, accused the Communist Party of using the bill "to the hilt to create race hatred and race tensions." He emphasized that former Councilman Ben Davis, now incarcerated as a felon for being a leader of the U.S. Communist Party, had sponsored a similar bill.[40]

In March 1951, the City Council passed the Brown-Isaacs Law barring discrimination in all publicly assisted private housing. In the Board of Estimate, only Staten Island voted against it. "The people reversed the courts," declared the happy tenants' committee, crediting grassroots protest for the victory. For its part, Met Life did not give up easily. For decades, it resisted obeying the law and immediately set out to crush the disloyal whites in their midst. Stuyvesant Town began eviction proceedings against the Hendrixes and leaders of the tenants' committee, and mirroring the dynamics of McCarthyism, its list grew to encompass any tenant publicly associated with support for mixed occupancy. This crackdown sparked yet another citywide battle over Stuyvesant Town, as tenants turned the eviction threat into a test of their free speech rights as well as Met Life's commitment to desegregation. This crisis briefly reversed one aspect of the early red scare—the unwillingness of many leading liberals to defend Communists and Communist sympathizers. Liberal politicians and advocates were called on to use their clout with city leaders and help save the tenants, including Communists, from eviction.[41]

Stuyvesant Town announced that it would not renew the leases of thirty-five tenants. (At one juncture, a total of sixty-nine tenants faced eviction.) Thirteen were sponsors of the tenants' committee, including Paul Ross and Rabbi Daniel L. Davis, director of the New York Federation of Reform Synagogues; nine had invited African Americans as weekend guests; three had collected food and clothing for victims of a Harlem fire; and three had publicly welcomed the Hendrix family. Paul O'Dwyer, the brother of the mayor, represented the tenants in court. A crusading, Irish-born progressive attorney, O'Dwyer devoted his life to political, labor, and human rights activism in New York City. The Harlem NAACP branch condemned the evictions as well as "the Jim Crow policy of the Metropolitan Life Insurance Company."[42]

In November 1951 the New York Court of Appeals affirmed the trial court's ruling that Stuyvesant Town did not have to renew a lease. The deadline for evictions was set for January 17, 1952. Many of those targeted with eviction had moved out, but nineteen families vowed to stay until forcibly evicted, "in defense of this basic American principle." The stage was set for a dramatic, if not violent, confrontation. Civic and religious leaders rallied around the tenants. Despite the increasingly divisive anticommunist climate, the NYSCDH, representing sixteen organizations such as the NAACP, American Jewish Congress, Episcopal Church, and Citizens' Housing and Planning Council, issued an unusual plea for public support. "A crucial question of moral principle and public policy must be met by the citizens of New York City," it declared. Nineteen families "face the loss of their homes . . . for having committed the crime of working to end the project's undemocratic tenant selection policies." With every legal move exhausted, "their sole recourse is to the conscience and aroused public opinion of the people of our city." Algernon Black warned Frederick Ecker, "If you evict these people it will give the whole country a black eye. It will be news all over the world. It will be told even in tiny Asian villages." In a last-minute appeal, Frederick Ecker's son took his father out to dinner along with Frank Moore, the lieutenant governor of New York, and his son Earl Moore, who happened to be cochair of the Stuyvesant Town tenants' committee. The three men urged Ecker to let the tenants stay and to start renting to African Americans, but Ecker clung to his rationale that Black tenants would depreciate the value of his company's investment.[43]

As the day approached, the tenants stored food and barricaded their doors, while hundreds of supporters, many of them trade unionists, began a three-day round-the-clock picket of Met Life's headquarters in lower Manhattan. At one point, three thousand members of District 65 picketed Stuyvesant Town in a show of solidarity for six members of their union who were among the nineteen. Civic leaders scrambled to broker a compromise. On January 16, a Met Life executive announced that "after consultations with a number of civic leaders, the Metropolitan has decided to postpone action in the matter of evictions." City Council President Rudolph Halley and the NYSCDH negotiated a deal allowing all of the families to stay, with the understanding that Jesse Kessler, Paul Ross, and Lee Lorch would leave voluntarily at their convenience. Met Life agreed to officially admit the Hendrix family, and to speed the integration of the project, a pledge for which they provided no goal or timetable.[44]

The Communist activists and their sympathizers hailed the victory. They saw the liberal support for the tenants as a symbol of the power of "unity," in defiance of McCarthyism, to produce progressive change. Elected officials, however, portrayed the result as a vindication of American democracy. In City Councilman Earl Brown's view, "The fight for fair play and democracy at Stuyvesant Town was a fight against Communism. It took the Metropolitan officials a long time to see this point." The Communist tenants, he surmised, were "probably interested solely in helping the party along at the expense of the Negro." Brown even argued that the tenant leaders, who had negotiated with Met Life representatives to broker a deal, "would have liked nothing more" than an eviction because "it would have been a grand propaganda point for the Communists all the way from 1st Avenue and 14th Street to Siberia."[45]

Both the Popular Front and Cold War interpretations of the battle for Stuyvesant Town have some elements of truth. Organized protest played a major role in keeping the issue of Met Life's discrimination on the city's political radar. Yet the rise of the Cold War, which increased the U.S. government's concern over the world's perceptions of its racial policies, gave liberals at home a new weapon to dislodge Jim Crow. But whether it was a popular mobilization or shifting global politics that produced a fair housing law, neither was sufficiently strong to bring about the actual integration of Stuyvesant Town. The right of African Americans to live in Stuyvesant Town was won after it was fully occupied. The next phase of the Stuyvesant Town struggle followed the path that the education and jobs struggles took after their legislative victories: enforcement and access.

A year after the Brown-Isaacs Law, Met Life refused to accept applications from Blacks on the grounds that the waiting list was long enough. This generated calls for affirmative action. Mrs. Hendrix felt that "no more families should be housed until a certain number of Negro families are admitted." To Met Life's claim that this would be "unfair" to the whites already on the waiting list, Hendrix countered: "We insist that it is unfair, to say the least, that Negroes have never been allowed the opportunity to apply." Algernon Black of the NYSCDH also advocated a "compensatory procedure" to ensure quicker Black access to vacant apartments.[46]

Change at Stuyvesant Town came at a snail's pace. Moreover, the government did virtually nothing over the next two decades to enforce the Brown-Isaacs Law. In 1960, of a population of 22,405 tenants, Stuyvesant Town had forty-seven Black residents, or two-tenths of 1 percent of the total. In 1968 the city's Commission on Human Rights initiated a complaint against Met Life because the numbers of Black tenants in its three large housing projects—Stuyvesant Town, Peter Cooper Village, and the enormous Parkchester in the Bronx—were extremely low. In Parkchester, one-tenth of 1 percent of tenants were Black. And Peter Cooper housed ten Black families out of 2,495 apartments.[47]

The greatest significance of the Stuyvesant Town struggle was that it helped to launch the modern American fair housing movement. It led to the formation of the New York State Committee against Discrimination in Housing, which dissolved in 1963 after it realized its goal of winning a state law barring discrimination in private housing. It spawned the creation of the National Committee against Discrimination in Housing in 1950, which campaigned for fair housing laws across the country, culminating in the passage of the federal Fair Housing Act in the aftermath of the assassination of the Reverend Martin Luther King Jr. in 1968. This law was a direct legacy of the struggle by the early civil rights movement against the Metropolitan Life Insurance Company in New York City.

As the shift in rhetoric during the Stuyvesant Town struggle revealed, the

Cold War had begun to exert considerable force in all aspects of U.S. culture, including the struggle for African American rights. Just as the movement was gathering momentum and achieving small victories, the anticommunist crusade was emerging. It would profoundly alter the course of activism and reform.

7 Anticommunism and Civil Rights

The anticommunist crusade after World War II was the longest and most far-reaching period of political repression in U.S. history. The Cold War escalated in 1947 as the United States moved to assert global leadership, contain the influence of the Soviet Union, and halt the spread of Communism around the world. The anticommunist crusade was no less decisive. Begun during a liberal Democratic administration, it destroyed the legitimacy of the Communist Party, undermined the broader American left, unleashed fear and hysteria over the possibility of domestic subversion, and in the process, helped to generate mass support for the militarization of the economy and society.[1]

The anticommunist crusade clashed head on with the African American rights struggle in New York, which had a significant contingent of left-wing leaders. Virtually every leading activist suffered persecution, investigation, repression, or censorship. Yet there were countervailing domestic and international pressures that provided protection, even moral urgency, to the civil rights struggle during this difficult time. The rivalry with the Soviet Union generated enormous pressure on the U.S. government to jettison its support for Jim Crow in order to strengthen its claim to be the leader of "the free world." In addition, postwar Black political mobilization had established a beachhead within the Democratic Party that created a role for civil rights in postwar anticommunist liberalism.

The Rise of Anticommunism

Before the Cold War escalated and a liberal Democratic president embraced it, most civil rights leaders opposed organized anticommunism. They saw it as conservative opportunism, a vehicle to roll back the New Deal and stop the burgeoning civil rights movement. Empowering anticommunists in Congress meant empowering the most ardent supporters of segregation and racial violence. Thus, in 1946, New York City Councilman Stanley Isaacs cautioned his fellow liberals that "no matter how much we may disagree with communism, dislike Communists, or resent their activities, they are no real menace within this conservative country." He further cautioned: "The Rankins and the Bilbos, bitter enemies of democracy, have a large following."[2]

In 1945 the NAACP supported abolishing the House Committee on Un-American Activities, known as HUAC, on the grounds that it was "detrimental to Negroes." Civil rights leaders often pointed caustically to HUAC's exclusive focus on left-wing radicalism rather than right-wing extremism. "Like the Dies Committee, which spent most of its time looking for reds, while ignoring the KKK and other foreign and native fascist groups," this committee "has been used . . . to assail New Deal agencies and liberals in government that are doing their jobs well." They specifically charged it with harassing the wartime Fair Employment Practices Committee. HUAC was chaired by Mississippi white supremacist John E. Rankin, who publicly refused to sit beside his New York colleague Adam Clayton Powell. The *New York Age* called for HUAC's abolition: "We think Mr. Rankin has a confused idea of the difference between free speech and subversive action. He seems to believe that defenders of the rights of racial and religious minorities are un-American."

Even after the Cold War escalated, both African American radicals and liberals continued to insist that the real danger to democracy was racism. There was always a racial critique of McCarthyism that was grounded in the African American experience of unfreedom in the "land of the free." This view was shared by left-liberals such as Langston Hughes and Mary McLeod Bethune, ministers in the AME, AME Zion, Baptist, and Presbyterian churches, and even by some who had long been opposed to activist coalitions with Communists, such as A. Philip Randolph. They feared the institutionalization of a state apparatus that threatened civil liberties and they ceaselessly pointed to the contradiction of the federal government's persecution of leftists while violent white supremacists held state power in much of the South. In a statement to the Senate opposing the Nixon-Mundt bill, a measure that would have dramatically curtailed individual liberties, Black trade unionist Ewart Guinier called Jim Crow, Army segregation, and low wages the real "threats to our way of life." Moreover in 1954, Congressman Adam Clayton Powell proposed that the Smith Act, a sedition law used to prosecute Communists, be extended to cover those who violate the *Brown v. Board of Education* decision. Expressing a Black discursive strategy of the Cold War era, Powell was challenging the government to include segregationists in its definition of domestic subversion.[3]

In 1947 when the secretary of labor proposed outlawing the Communist Party, a group of Black leaders in New York, including leaders from NAACP and Urban League branches, ministers from large Harlem congregations, trade unionists, and prominent radicals Paul Robeson and W. E. B. Du Bois, protested to the president. "The Negro's historic goal of freedom from racial discrimination and oppression can be attained only in a society where the civil and political liberties of minorities are fully protected by government." They expressed concern that the crackdown would invite greater repression. "It is clear to us," they wrote President Truman, "that if the government in power can suppress the Communists, it can also suppress the American Labor Party, the Liberal Party, or any other to which it objects." They further warned that "even organizations of the Negro people fighting for Negro democratic rights, can be called 'Communist' and forced to disband." Wilfred E. Lewin, the head of the Harlem Elks Lodge, stressed that the CP's support for racial justice merited Black solidarity. "I can always hear the voice of the Communist Party loud above the common herd in demanding full democratic rights for Negro citizens." Now, he felt, African Americans "should swing out hard and rally the people against this effort."[4]

On March 25, 1947, as part of the recently announced Truman Doctrine and its policy of "containing" Communism at home and abroad, President Harry Truman issued Executive Order 9835, creating the Federal Employee Loyalty Program. The order authorized investigations into the beliefs and associations of every federal employee. The attorney general issued a list of seventy-eight "subversive" organizations, membership in which sparked an investigation that often led to dismissal. It included dozens of peace, labor, refugee, and antidiscrimination groups in which the CP had or had had influence from the Depression through World War II. Nine were primarily engaged in antiracist activism: the United Harlem Tenants and Consumers Organization, the National Negro Congress, the Civil Rights Congress, the Negro Labor Victory Committee, the United Negro and Allied Veterans of America, Veterans against Discrimination, the George Washington Carver School, the Southern Negro Youth Congress, and the Council on African Affairs. The order helped undermine the institutional infrastructure of the

Black Popular Front in New York. As state and private sector surveillance escalated into the next decade, other organizations that had been critical to civil rights organizing in New York came under attack or dissolved, such as the American Labor Party and the *People's Voice.*

The assumption that antiracism was evidence of sympathy for communism permeated loyalty investigations. Indeed, advocacy of racial equality was an official justification for heightened scrutiny of the employee. Witnesses were asked if they had friends of another race or owned Paul Robeson records. Dorothy Bailey, a Black Labor department employee whose firing as an alleged Communist led to a Supreme Court ruling upholding the program in 1951, was asked, "Did you ever write a letter to the Red Cross about the segregation of blood?" Evidently, "objection to blood segregation" was "a recognized 'party line' tactic." To gauge the influence of the loyalty program, it is necessary to appreciate the critical importance of government jobs to middle-class formation for African Americans. There were over 150,000 African American federal employees, a sharp increase from the prewar era. The largest single employer of African Americans in New York City in 1949 was the postal service. Its more than 4,500 Black workers, according to a Harlem journalist, "represent a stable part of the community and enjoy excellent community standing." Several owned valuable Harlem properties and apartment buildings, indeed "many of Harlem's most prominent citizens, judges, ministers, physicians and business men look back with pride to the days when they punched the Post Office time clock." Despite all the lurid allegations of Communist spies in the State Department, "the Post Office," according to a scholar of McCarthyism, "with its unskilled workforce and large numbers of minority-group employees, had the highest percentage of discharges. The more prestigious State Department had the lowest."[5]

The NAACP lobbied for the appointment of an African American to the Loyalty Board and offered to defend accused employees whose cases were based on race or membership in the NAACP or another "approved" organization. Walter White complained to Truman that workers active in the fight for an FEPC were being marked as disloyal—fighting for one executive order brought them under the scrutiny of another executive order. Black and Jewish federal employees mobilized against the loyalty program. The National Alliance of Postal Employees (NAPE), representing over 25,000 African American postal employees, called for its abolition. "We will oppose any professed loyalty program," NAPE announced, "the effect of which is to intimidate us in the lawful exercise of our constitutional rights in reaching our 35 year old objective—the total elimination of racial prejudice and discrimination." The United Public Workers of America helped win passage of a CIO resolution that called the loyalty order "a grave danger to the liberty of government workers" that threatens to establish "a thought police under which every form of political deviation on the part of government workers may become the occasion for their discharge."[6]

In 1948 the government accused postal employee Fred H. M. Turner, the former president of the Brooklyn branches of both the NAACP and NAPE, of "communistic leanings." He had been a member of the National Negro Congress, an organization launched by Black intellectuals and trade unionists during the New Deal that had come under Communist Party direction in the 1940s. Like many other victims of the red scare, Turner was indicted for belonging to an organization that was perfectly legal at the time. This twenty-five-year mail carrier received an outpouring of support from African American religious and civic leaders in Brooklyn. Turner was represented by Lewis S. Flagg Jr., a future judge, and two hundred lawyers, ministers, borough officials, merchants, and other supporters accompanied him to his hearing in Manhattan. The Loyalty Board eventually cleared Fred Turner of all charges, but his exoneration proved to be exceptional. A group of twenty-six mostly Black postal workers who protested their firings all the way to the U.S. Supreme Court was less fortunate. The workers argued that their dismissals were retaliation for their involvement in the struggle against religious and racial discrimination in the workplace. But in 1951 the Court upheld the Loyalty Board's action.[7]

Civil Rights Joins Anticommunism

The presidential election of 1948 marked the zenith of the postwar African American rights movement, yet the ideological polarization it caused ultimately undermined the movement. Former vice president Henry Wallace broke from the Democratic Party, primarily over the Cold War and red scare, and ran against President Truman as the nominee of the Progressive Party. Both the Progressives and Democrats intensely wooed Black voters. Indeed, the level of attention to race in this election would not be matched again until 1964.

African American activists in New York helped make antiracism a visible theme in the Wallace campaign. Paul Robeson, a co-chair of the Progressive

Party, campaigned extensively for Wallace, including in the South where violence, vandalism, and threats of violence were widespread. Charles Collins was on the party's executive committee; a fellow member, Yale Law School Professor Thomas Emerson, described him as "a militant, aggressive, intelligent person, very energetic and active," and "clearly in the most left position." Ewart Guinier managed Wallace's campaign in Harlem. Wallace stumped in Bedford-Stuyvesant for Ada B. Jackson, the first Black woman in New York nominated to the U.S. Congress; for Bertram Baker, the ALP and Democratic nominee for state assembly; and for City Court justice candidate Thomas R. Jones, "the first Negro ever to be nominated for the bench by a major party," who later became a judge. One hundred and fifty delegates at the Progressive Party convention were Black. Many NAACP branches endorsed Wallace, much to the displeasure of the pro-Truman national staff. Wallace embraced more vigorous civil rights positions than the Democrats, including a stronger federal civil rights act and the abolition of all segregation in government service and public housing. Wallace also endorsed the principle behind the Powell amendments—he pledged to deny federal aid to any state or city agency that practiced discrimination or segregation.[8]

In a speech over NBC radio, Wallace condemned "the lynchings and knifings of Negroes in the South" while acknowledging that they "have their counterparts in every part of our country." "While you cannot legislate love," he declared, "you can legislate against certain acts of hate." The "colonial peoples of the world," he said, must wonder about the meaning of American democracy. "Do we mean the democracy of Mississippi where three-tenths of one percent of the Negro citizens vote? Do we mean the democracy of Tom Dewey who would restore the Italian bankers to their former positions of empire as rulers of the colored people of Africa?" In this national network broadcast, Wallace closed by describing the shooting death the day before of a twenty-eight-year-old Black man in Georgia who had insisted on his right to vote. He vowed to see that his six children "shall vote and live as free Americans."[9]

During the presidential campaign, Harry Truman helped forge Cold War racial liberalism when he endorsed the legislative agenda of the civil rights movement, intensified the anticommunist crusade, and encouraged liberals to denounce the left. The African American rights struggle, expanding Black electorate, and Wallace's threat from the left strengthened pro–civil rights forces in Truman's campaign. The president's rhetorical claim to be the leader of the free world also put pressure on the administration to reject the Democratic Party's support for the segregationist doctrine of state rights. In an explicit rejection of that doctrine's rationalization of federal inaction on racial discrimination, Truman announced at the 1947 NAACP convention that the federal government must lead the way to racial justice. In February 1948, Truman addressed a joint session of Congress to endorse the recommendations of his Committee on Civil Rights. *Voice of America* broadcast the speech around the world, while WOR radio in New York aired a four-night reading of *To Secure These Rights*, reaching millions of homes. In April, after district leaders in Brooklyn and Harlem voiced concern about the possibility of a large Black vote for Wallace, a party official urged greater attention to civil rights to counter the Progressive threat. Truman was also being pressured to desegregate the military by A. Philip Randolph, who had threatened to advocate civil disobedience should a new conscription law pass without an antisegregation provision. "Negroes are in no mood to shoulder guns for democracy abroad, while they are denied democracy here at home," he told the president in March.[10]

At the Democratic Party convention, liberals defeated Truman's moderate civil rights plank, thwarting the administration's desire to prevent a walkout by the southern segregationist wing of the Party. A speech by Senator Hubert Humphrey reframing civil rights from an issue of states rights to one of human rights is widely credited with propelling the liberal victory. That Humphrey's views on a race were greatly influenced by African American political activists in Minnesota, especially Nellie Stone Johnson, is less well known, but in many respects perfectly illustrates the influence of Black mobilization on Democratic Party leaders. The Democrats produced the most progressive civil rights platform in their party's history, prompting a group of Deep South extremists to form the State's Rights Party and run Strom Thurmond for president. Truman, in turn, issued two executive orders to increase Black support—Executive Order 9980, which created a committee to study equality of opportunity in the armed forces, and Executive Order 9981, which created a fair employment board within the U.S. Civil Service Commission.[11]

African American politicos were key architects of Truman's fall campaign. In August the president conferred with several Harlem leaders, including restaurateur Sherman Hibbitt, the "Unofficial Mayor of Harlem." According to one historian, "Democratic strategists prepared for the greatest effort in the history of the party to attract the black vote." J. Raymond Jones, a Harlem district leader who nurtured a generation of politicians—including the city's first African American mayor, David N. Dinkins—sought to make the Truman campaign "a crusade" for civil rights. He organized the first-ever presidential campaign stop in Harlem. On October 29, at a rally of 65,000 people at 135th Street and Edgecombe Avenue, Truman spoke "like a cross between Jesse Jackson and Bill Clinton," Paul Robeson Jr. remembered. Still impressed fifty years later by Truman's promise to deliver the goods, Robeson remembered thinking, "It's over, Truman had the Black vote." Paul Robeson Sr. recalled the speech and the excitement it generated a year later. "I was right here in Harlem and heard him make those promises. And I heard thousands of people yelling their heads off for those promises." Anna Arnold Hedgeman, a New Yorker who ran the March on Washington Movement's Washington office, was appointed executive director of the National Citizens' Committee for the Reelection of President Truman. Hedgeman was one of many activists who linked the 1940s and 1960s civil rights struggles. She helped organize the 1963 March on Washington and lobbied the all-male "big five" civil rights leaders to include Black women on the speakers list and stage.[12]

During the campaign, Progressives attacked the Democrats for courting war with the Soviet Union and betraying civil liberties at home, while Democrats attacked the Progressive Party as Moscow controlled and Wallace and his supporters as unwitting dupes. In November 1947, White House staffer Clark Clifford advised the president that "every effort must be made to identify [Wallace] in the public mind with the Communists." Clifford even urged that the United States cause friction with the Soviets to help win the election. In July 1948 eleven national leaders of the Communist Party, including New York City Councilman Ben Davis, were arrested under the Smith Act for allegedly conspiring to advocate the violent overthrow of the federal government. Henceforth in U.S. politics, any political link to Communists would have the taint of criminal subversion.[13]

According to the Progressive Party, the Truman administration was provoking conflict with the Soviet Union, shoring up European empires through the Marshall Plan, and abandoning Roosevelt's supposed vision of free trade, peace, and power sharing in the United Nations. Progressives feared the military aims of the Americans, who possessed a monopoly on nuclear weapons, more than the Soviets, despite increasing moves by the Soviets to control the political affairs of Eastern European nations. This campaign marked the twilight of a mainstream left challenge to U.S. foreign pol-

President Harry S. Truman's campaign rally in Harlem, 1948; 135th Street at the intersection of St. Nicholas and Edgecombe Avenues, looking north.

icy before Communist successes and aggression in Eastern Europe, Korea, and China intensified bipolar conflict and made sympathy for the Soviet Union and criticism of the U.S. appear disloyal. While strongly influenced by Communist Party members, most of the leaders and supporters of the Progressive Party, including Henry Wallace and Paul Robeson, were not Communists. Yet Progressives staunchly defended the right of Americans to be Communists. Wallace assailed "the highly emotional attacks on Communists, which provoke violence and lead to the suppression of civil liberties." In testimony before the Senate Judiciary Committee on an anticommunist bill, Paul Robeson vigorously defended the civil liberties of Communists, particularly as supporters of the "complete equality of the Negro people." He stressed the latter point both to explain the appeal of the CP to many African Americans, such as himself, and to challenge, if not provoke, Congressional leadership. In response to the charge that Soviet support sustained the CP, Robeson asserted that unjust social conditions did, and he answered the charge of Soviet totalitarianism with stories of death threats in white supremacist America. His matter-of-fact praise for Communists and Progressives who embraced "the suffering and needs of millions" galled the committee, with one senator glibly remarking afterward that "Robeson seems to want to be made a martyr. Maybe we ought to make him one."[14]

As a novice successor to the most popular president ever and the incumbent during a time of high inflation and labor unrest, Truman won an "upset" victory in the four-way presidential race. Wallace lost badly, winning slightly over a million votes, finishing fourth after the segregationist Strom Thurmond. Nationwide, Truman won two-thirds of the Black vote. According to one assessment, in California, Illinois, and Ohio the Black vote was crucial to his election; had that vote gone to either Dewey or Wallace, Dewey would have won. In Harlem, Truman won 69 percent of the Black vote, more than Roosevelt had four years earlier. Wallace won a much higher percentage of the Black vote than the white vote in New York State: he polled 17 percent in Harlem, while only 8 percent of the statewide total. His percentage of Harlem votes was more than Dewey, the signer of the Ives-Quinn Law, received. Dewey had courted white southern votes and, unlike Truman, had played down his support for civil rights. Wallace voters cost Truman victories in New York, Michigan, and Maryland. Yet the Wallace defeat revealed the limitations of the Popular Front in the Cold War era. An alliance with pro-Soviet forces could be very costly.[15]

Democrats gained majorities in both houses of Congress, giving them an opportunity to make good on their campaign promises. But a Democratic majority also meant the problematic rise to power of Dixiecrats with seniority. Walter A. Pinn, president of the two-hundred-member Baptist Ministers Conference in New York, led an "Anti-Dixiecrat and Civil Rights Cavalcade" on the steps of the Capitol building on January 2–3, 1949, the eve of the new session. The conference members had conducted a petition drive in New York to "oust the Dixiecrats," reduce southern representation in Congress, "stop the filibuster," and expel Representative John E. Rankin on the grounds of "disorderly behavior" under Article I, section 5 of the U.S. Constitution. The way forward for a deeply divided Democratic Party was unclear and hotly contested.[16]

Purging the Labor Left

The most intense immediate fallout of the Democratic Party's fracturing, however, was felt on the left rather than the right. The defection of the party's left wing sparked rancor and recriminations after the election—effects that, alongside the deepening international Cold War and domestic anticommunism, poisoned the political environment that had nurtured the struggle for African American rights. The election bitterly divided the labor movement and precipitated the ouster of the left from the CIO. While Communist Party members made up less than 1 percent of the CIO, they held significant leadership posts. In 1949, the CIO banned Communists from holding positions of leadership in member unions. And in 1949 and 1950 it expelled eleven Communist-led or influenced unions, representing over one million workers, and established rival unions to raid their membership. This was a major turning point for the Communist Party, which had prized its influence in organized labor. The CIO's national officers had supported President Truman for reelection, and they subsequently came to define a union's support for Wallace as a sign of fealty to Moscow rather than loyalty to the CIO and good trade unionism. CIO leaders also felt pushed by the 1947 Taft-Hartley Act, which required union leaders to sign noncommunist affidavits in order to use the National Labor Relations Board.[17]

The anticommunist purge in the New York labor movement undermined the dynamic Black-labor-left nexus at the heart of the city's civil rights movement. The Hotel and Club Employees Union, AFL was dominated by mobsters until the Depression when a progressive slate had taken over, but in 1946 the death of a progressive official triggered a shift in the balance of power. Union leaders tried to fire Charles Collins, the leftist vice president of Local 6, on the grounds that he had spoken at Communist-endorsed events using his union title. Collins, a major antiracism activist in the city, did not identify himself as a Communist, but his opponents considered him a Communist or "a fellow traveler"—someone who followed the party line—for participating in initiatives that had Communist support, such as the protest over the police killings of the Ferguson brothers and the "Trade Union Committee for the Re-election of Ben Davis." But the union's constitution guaranteed freedom of political belief; noncommunist leaders of Local 6 defended Collins and urged the international leaders to investigate racketeering instead. The attempted dismissal of Collins, which seems to have been motivated by a factional fight for union leadership, illustrates that while allegations of Communism may have been grounded in reality, they could be deployed for a variety of reasons, including to oust a rival. Soviet, or other external, influence in Local 6 was never alleged, nor shown, and does not seem to have motivated Collins's critics.[18]

By 1950 the balance of power had shifted further within the Hotel and Club Employees Union, and Collins and twelve others were dismissed. The U.S. government, in turn, began denaturalization proceedings against Collins, who was born in the Caribbean island of Grenada, then a colony of Great Britain. It accused him of being a Communist and of having concealed this when he became a U.S. citizen in 1939. Collins fought his deportation with the legal counsel of Vito Marcantonio. Favorable rulings in two cases that reached the U.S. Supreme Court in 1958 set precedents that helped end many pending cases against foreign-born radicals, including Collins. In a judicial season during which the red scare was set back in several cases, the Court ruled that mere membership in the Communist Party did not constitute the "clear, unequivocal and convincing evidence" of subversion required in denaturalization proceedings.[19]

Many other deportation efforts in the McCarthy era, however, did succeed, including one against Ferdinand Smith, who, like Collins, was a Caribbean-born labor leader who had helped to create and give shape to the northern Black rights struggle. As a vice president, Smith was the highest-ranking Black labor official in the CIO until 1947, when he and other pro-Communist leftists were ousted from the National Maritime Union. His firing turned the CIO's executive committee into an all-white group. The FBI arrested Smith in 1949 and he was deported in 1951 to his native Jamaica, where he continued his activism in Caribbean labor and anti-imperialist movements. But between his arrest and deportation, he joined with Ewart Guinier in founding the Harlem Trade Union Council to continue the struggle to upgrade Black workers in the metropolitan economy.[20]

The United Public Workers of America (UPWA) was purged from the CIO for following the Communist Party line. In 1974 its president, Abram Flaxer, reportedly acknowledged having been a member of the Communist Party. The ouster of the UPWA, a union with a long record of opposition to discrimination in government employment, illustrated how the red scare undercut the struggle for racial equality. The UPWA was one of the most integrated unions by race and sex in the CIO and played a major role in lobbying for a federal FEPC and fighting against a racialized payment system in the Panama Canal Zone. The international secretary-treasurer, the second-highest officer, was Ewart Guinier, a leading activist in the struggle for racial equality in New York City. Since Communism was being defined as criminal subversion, accused Communists did not have the option of defending their views by citing the First Amendment. One strategy they used to both defend themselves and maintain a moral high ground was to stress their antiracist activism. At a "trial" of the local industrial CIO councils that had supported Wallace, Ewart Guinier reminded CIO officials that they had tolerated racist practices by southern CIO leaders in defiance of CIO policy, including segregated meetings. "Those are the people," he insisted, "that should be here on charges and removed for violation of CIO policies."[21]

After its expulsion from the CIO, New York City refused to recognize the UPWA as the collective bargaining agent in the Department of Welfare. The UPWA had encouraged solidarity between its members and welfare recipients and begun to build an incipient welfare rights movement. After the purge, the city imposed new rules—such as surprise night visits—that alienated welfare workers from their clients. Not satisfied with the union's defeat, the department launched a red scare of its own against the rank and file. In 1950, Welfare Commissioner Raymond Hilliard fired Eleanor Goding, president of Local 1, UPWA and the only Black female local leader in the country. The Brooklyn and Manhattan branches of the NAACP protested Goding's dismissal, but a review board upheld it, citing her latenesses and an alleged plan to "sabotage" the department. Of 175 staff and union members penalized, suspended, or dismissed at that point in the Hilliard administration, 172 were Black or Jewish. This illuminates the racial and ethnic backlash facilitated by anticommunist purges as well as a labor Black-Jewish alliance. Hilliard himself admitted to the use of dirty tricks to remove union activists;

he hired undercover police officers to spy on workers, to follow them after work, and to harass and intimidate them.[22]

After the purge, Negro History Week programs in welfare centers throughout the city were canceled. Negro History Week events had featured such luminaries as Kenneth Clark, Hubert Delany, and Thurgood Marshall, exemplifying the identification by the Black middle class with the Black working class and poor that was a hallmark of 1940s activism. The program's passing was one of the many fatalities in civil rights as a result of the red scare. Clearly, the anticommunist purge was a useful weapon in the hands of rival labor factions and of management seeking to weaken union strength. It was also a weapon to be used against women and Blacks.[23]

The United Electrical Workers (UE), one of the local labor movement's most vigorous champions of the FEPC, was also purged from the CIO. At one-third of the total, the UE had the largest number of women in the organized labor movement. Indeed, feminist writer Betty Friedan got her start writing for the *UE News* from 1946 to 1952. Elaine Perry, the first Black woman district organizer for the UE, was red-baited by an anticommunist rival union—it accused her of stomping on an American flag that had fallen off a machine during a rally. Perry revered the UE; she said it empowered women and truly involved the rank and file. The Communists in the union, she recalled, were discreet: no one ever tried to force her to adopt a particular position or point of view. They stressed a broad political education, diverse leadership, and community involvement, in stark contrast to her subsequent experience with the UAW at a Bendix plant in New Jersey, where she later worked for twenty years.[24]

The two unions with the highest percentage of Black women officials were the Food and Tobacco Workers Union and the United Office and Professional Workers of America. Both were ousted from the CIO, but subsequently merged with District 65, the warehouse and department store workers union in New York City that had pulled out of the CIO rather than submit to the purging requirements of the Taft-Hartley Act. "We don't trust the organizers of the anticommunist movement," District 65 concluded. The merger gave the union a total of 18,000 Black members. A quarter of stewards and organizers were Black. In 1951, however, the union acceded to the requirements of the Taft-Hartley Act, dismissed some alleged Communists, including Victoria Garvin, and gained access to the National Labor Relations Board. But District 65 retained progressive Black organizers like Morris

Doswell and Cleveland Robinson, who continued to advocate close ties with civil rights organizations and campaigns.[25]

The anticommunist purge had a major influence on maritime workers, and hit Black workers particularly hard because so many had joined the National Maritime Union (NMU) during the Depression to improve working conditions, eradicate racial barriers to promotion, and raise wages in the industry. Communist labor organizers had helped secure victory for the National Maritime Union, as they had in many other large CIO unions with multiracial workforces, and they had won leadership posts in the new union. Captain Hugh T. Mulzac, the only Black officer in the merchant marine during World War I, was denied the right to be ship's captain after the war. The brutal labor conditions and racism in the shipping industry radicalized the young sailor. Mulzac supported the antidiscrimination struggles in his home port of New York City and held the National Negro Congress and Negro Labor Victory Committee memberships that would later be used against this generation of leftists, labor radicals, and civil rights pioneers.[26]

The 1950 Port Security Act and an executive order authorizing the Coast Guard to dismiss maritime workers whose loyalty it questioned bolstered the conservative faction of the NMU, which had come to power in 1947. Denied the right to due process and to face their accuser, a generation of labor activists was blacklisted from the waterfront. At a Harlem labor conference in 1952, a shipyard worker estimated that a staggering 80 percent of those labeled "security risks" were Black. A historian concluded that 50 to 70 percent of sailors and longshoremen dismissed were either Black or foreign-born. These racially disproportionate figures reveal the broad net of the red scare—on the one hand, it was aimed at and ousted actual Communists, some of whom were Black, but on the other hand, it was used against a range of "militants," some of whom may have been so labeled due to their involvement in struggles against the mafia or for racial equality. Hugh Mulzac was banned from ever sailing again. A man in his sixties who had risen to the top of his field, he was forced to work as a short-order cook, elevator operator, and delivery "boy." As he had done all his life, Mulzac fought back. A group of seamen sued the government and in 1955 the Ninth Circuit threw out the Coast Guard's blacklist. Fearing an unfavorable Supreme Court decision, the government transferred the screening job from the Coast Guard to the ship owners and the union. But the workers, including Mulzac, sued them as well. Finally, in April 1960 a federal court ruled that the blacklisting of over two thousand seamen on the grounds of "doubtful loyalty" was a form of illegal discrimination.[27]

As a veteran of both world wars, Mulzac vehemently protested when the *Amsterdam News* pictured him in a 1951 article by Ray Welles entitled "Communists Woo Harlem." "I have always tried to fight for the rights of all the people and especially my race," Mulzac wrote the editor. "I know that by doing this I will be called a Communist, for that is the smear word today, but I will keep on fighting this great fight until I die, or until we get our every right—no matter what unscrupulous people may call me." Implying that the article may have been written at the government's behest, Mulzac asked, "Who is this Ray Welles? Who knows him? What has he done for his people, his race? Let him tell us." Mulzac reframed the question of loyalty that was at the center of political discourse during the Cold War. "Can Ray Welles find nothing more fitting to 'expose' than this? What about the Cicero riot, the wholesale appearance of the Ku Klux Klan flag, the Amos and Andy show, the relentless persecution of Negroes everywhere? Why doesn't he fight that?"[28]

With the purges, the abandonment of Operation Dixie (the southern unionization drive), and the merger of the AFL and CIO in 1955, the labor movement jettisoned the progressive role on race that it had been developing since the formation of the CIO in 1935. Although representatives of organized labor would remain important participants in the civil rights movement, the labor movement as a whole became an occasional ally, not an essential source of leadership. And many large CIO unions in the 1950s, 1960s, and 1970s, most notably the United Steel Workers and the United Auto Workers, resisted the aspirations of their Black members to full equality in the workplace. In a period when unionization was a critical stepping stone to the middle class, organized labor's retreat from the integration of industry was a major setback for workers of color. To be sure, not all unions moved away from civil rights advocacy during the Cold War. Unions in New York that maintained more progressive profiles over the next three decades usually had significant memberships of people of color, as well as close-to-left pasts—such as Hospital Workers Union, Local 1199; the Transport Workers Union; and District 65 of the United Retail, Wholesale and Department Store Worker's Union. District 65 was to become a key supporter of the southern civil rights movement—its secretary-treasurer Cleveland Robinson, an activist in Black left-labor initiatives in the postwar years, helped organize the 1963 March on Washington and the U.S. anti-apartheid movement.[29]

The Persecution of Black Radicals

Beginning in 1948, three towering figures of the American left, W. E. B. Du Bois, Ben Davis, and Paul Robeson, came under attack. African American activists—both Communists and noncommunists—became particular targets of "McCarthyism" for several reasons: the Communist Party's emphasis on fighting racism, FBI director J. Edgar Hoover's well-documented personal racism, and the fact that the anticommunist crusade also targeted the broader Popular Front, which had undertaken myriad antiracist campaigns. State persecution of Black radicals, including surveillance, jailings, deportations, and later, killings, began its twentieth-century phase during the post–World War I red scare, and in the 1960s it continued under the FBI's counterintelligence programs.[30]

In July 1948, Ben Davis and ten other Communist Party leaders were charged with violating the Smith Act, for "unlawfully, willfully and knowingly conspiring to organize the Communist Party . . . a group . . . [that] teach[es] and advocate[s] the overthrow and destruction of the Government of the U.S. by force and violence." The nine-month trial focused entirely on ideas rather than any alleged acts, and relied on testimony by informants about Communist philosophy and the contents of books by Soviet leaders V. I. Lenin and Joseph Stalin. Federal judges accepted the government's contention that membership in the Communist Party equaled a willingness to engage in and advocate revolutionary violence. The defense, however, won some support when it uncovered systematic racial discrimination in federal jury selection in New York City. The jury clerk marked the papers of prospective Black jurors with a "c" to signify colored, but the judge ruled that he saw nothing "criminal" about it. The clerk also used professional, university alumni, and special neighborhood directories that would generate an elite pool of jurors. The Communist Party's call for democratic jury selection was considered radical. As the *New York Times* put it, "It is the defense contention that all jurors should be selected from voting lists indiscriminately and none should be taken from special directories."[31]

Ben Davis and his codefendants were convicted on October 14, 1949. Despite his conviction, Councilman Davis ran for reelection a couple of weeks later. W. E. B. Du Bois chaired his reelection committee, which included Hope Stevens—a founder of two Harlem businesses, Carver Federal Savings and United Mutual Life Insurance Company; the writer and activist Shirley Graham; future judge Thomas R. Jones; Amy Mallard, an antilynching activist; and Captain Hugh Mulzac. Davis, a felon running on the line of an "enemy" party, faced a political newcomer, Earl Brown. Born in Virginia in 1902, Brown graduated from Harvard in 1924, and was an editor at the *Amsterdam News* and a writer for *Life* magazine when he accepted Tammany's call to unseat Davis. Careful not to risk an upset, the Liberal and Republican parties gave Brown their nominations as well.

Tammany Hall and Black nationalists found common cause in anticommunism and denounced white Davis supporters who campaigned in the district, which was 60 percent Black. According to journalist Ted Poston, Tammany leaders called this "invasion of outsiders" proof that a Communist was being foisted upon Black constituents. Meanwhile, street corner meetings by Marcantonio and Davis in central Harlem were sometimes "violently" disrupted by members of the United African Nationalist Movement (UANM). The UANM was led by James Lawson, who would be a prominent nationalist leader in Harlem for years. Lawson denounced white women working in the campaign, playing on the anxiety over sexual relationships between Black men and Euro-American women, which were widely associated with the Communist Party. According to Poston, a "whispering campaign—disclaimed by Tammany—is spreading in Harlem urging Negro women to strike back at the 'white invaders' at the polls."[32]

In a remarkable radio broadcast, Davis and Ewart Guinier, the ALP's candidate for Manhattan borough president, sought to counter the notion that Davis's politics were not indigenous to Harlem. The left, they insisted, stood for Black representation. The ALP had ten Black candidates on its slate, Guinier noted, while "the *only* Negro candidate on the Democratic ticket is Earl Brown." Guinier explained why the ALP endorsed a Communist: "The ALP had endorsed Ben Davis *for what he has done* and for what he stands for," Guinier declared, citing Davis's record of fighting against a higher sales tax, anti-Semitism, police brutality, "the Jim Crow Metropolitan Housing Project," and for child care centers, free milk, slum clearance, and rent control.[33]

Brown beat Davis 63,000 to 21,000. Ted Poston wrote that Davis was "still a powerful vote getter" at "the height of U.S. anti-communist hysteria." A month before the end of his term, the City Council expelled Davis, by a vote of 15–0, with two abstentions. Davis called it "a legislative lynching." Davis's City Council record included sponsoring or cosponsoring fifteen successful pieces of legislation. He brought the civil rights struggle downtown and championed a range of issues vital to his working-class, ethnically diverse constituents—child care centers, low rent housing, a public market, police brutality, and more schools. Earl Brown, ridiculed by his critics as "look down Brown" owing to his alleged tendency to avoid looking white people in the eye, served two terms on the council before accepting Tammany's request to run against Adam Clayton Powell in 1958. In this second attempt at trying to oust a popular Harlem politician, however, he lost badly.[34]

In 1951 the Supreme Court upheld the convictions of the Communist Party leaders under the Smith Act. But, as Justice William O. Douglass reminded in his stinging dissent, "not a single seditious act is charged in the indictment. To make lawful speech unlawful because two men conceive it is to raise the law of conspiracy to appalling proportions." Davis served four years in Terre Haute, Indiana, where he filed a lawsuit to desegregate federal prisons. Claudia Jones, a Communist Party leader also facing federal indictment, invoked the history of kidnapping, rape, and enslavement in a pamphlet for Davis's case and asked, "Do not our people have a *right* to have *radicals?*" In posing this question, Jones not only adopted a frontal challenge to the red scare—one that most people avoided—but also drew attention to a Black radical tradition that predated the Comintern. Davis's conviction silenced a Black leader who combined a global analysis of race and class with a local militancy, removing from Harlem an alternative to either the chastened stance of anticommunist liberals or the more insular Buy Black agenda of Harlem nationalists during the 1950s.[35]

At the end of World War II, the singer, actor, and activist Paul Robeson was one of the most famous and admired Americans in the world. As an officer in the Council on African Affairs, he was also a link between the emerging Black liberation movement in the United States and a global community of socialists and anticolonialists. Robeson claimed never to have joined the Communist Party, but he was proudly procommunist. As his opinions increasingly clashed with U.S. global ambitions, he suffered greater censorship and repression. After the 1947 indictment of the Hollywood Ten precipitated the blacklisting of Communist sympathizers by Hollywood moguls, Robeson lost many bookings. As the Cold War escalated, this backlash increased, leading FBI director J. Edgar Hoover to order a new report on him in January 1949 "in view of the tense international situation."[36]

During the Cold War, Paul Robeson ignored censorship, show trials, and other injustices in the Soviet Union and emphasized, instead, the role of the Soviet Union as a counterweight to the expanding American military presence across the globe. From Robeson's perspective, the U.S. government and multinational corporations were bringing military bases, white supremacy, and neocolonialism to the developing world. At the World Congress of Partisans of Peace in Paris in April 1949, after declaring that America was built on the backs of immigrants and enslaved Africans, Robeson said, "We shall not put up with any hysterical raving that urges us to make war on anyone. Our will to make peace is strong. We shall not make war on anyone. We shall not make war on the Soviet Union." The Associated Press misquoted Robeson, setting off a firestorm of controversy that proved to be a decisive episode in the anti-Black red scare, and a turning point in Robeson's life. The AP reported that he said, "It is unthinkable that American Negroes would go to war on behalf of those who have oppressed us for generations against a country which in one generation has raised our people to the full dignity of mankind."

The government seized on the statement as an opportunity to sideline Robeson. In this period of incipient decolonization, the United States was coming to regard images of American "race relations" as an explosive area of foreign policy. The State Department suspended the passports of not only suspected Communists in the McCarthy era, but also African American activists who criticized U.S. racial practices abroad. At the same time, in order to promote an image of Black American freedom, it funded international tours of African American musicians and athletes. In July the State Department revoked Robeson's passport, on the grounds that he was an alleged Communist, and held it until a federal court ordered it returned eight years later. A government official stated, however, that it was revoked in order to prevent him from condemning American racism abroad. Robeson was blacklisted and found himself unable to get stage, concert, or film work.[37]

The anti-Robeson crusade was joined by several prominent African American leaders, who were likely motivated by genuine ideological differences, red scare pressures, and personal rivalries. Black leaders used this occasion to distance the civil rights struggle from the increasingly unpopular Communist orbit and to firmly cast Black aspirations in the language of American nationalism. After a meeting initiated by Roy Wilkins, A. Philip Randolph, Adam Clayton Powell, Mary McLeod Bethune, Channing Tobias, AME Zion bishop William J. Walls, and others criticized Robeson and stressed that he did not speak for African Americans, who were patriotic Americans. In the *Crisis,* Roy Wilkins expressed a prominent anti-Robeson theme—that he had abandoned his people for a foreign cause. Robeson, he claimed, "has none but sentimental roots among American Negroes."[38]

Max Yergan, a former official in the Council on African Affairs (CAA) and the National Negro Congress who had close ties to the CP, penned a scathing critique of Robeson in the *New York Herald-Tribune.* Evidently, audits showing missing CAA funds and the discovery of a letter from Yergan blackmailing his former lover—the wife of CAA funder Frederick Field, a Vanderbilt heir and Communist—contributed to Yergan's departure from the CAA and decision to cooperate with the FBI. The Justice Department subsequently dropped its investigation of the alleged blackmailing. As evidence of the inapplicability of Communist ideas to American conditions, Yergan focused on what would become a staple of anticommunist writing on race—the Black Belt thesis. He argued that the left was un-American because it advocated Black self-determination, a form of nationalism. He called the phrase, routinely used by Robeson and other leftists, "the Negro people" part of "the ridiculous and futile effort of Communists to persuade American Negroes to think of themselves as a 'nation.'" Despite his personal motives for turning against the Communist left, Yergan articulated the emerging emphasis on progress, integrationism, and Americanism that would increasingly mark Black leadership outlooks in the 1950s. "Any objective examination of the facts makes it clear," Yergan argued, in a repudiation of internationalist solidarities, "that this country is moving forward in all fronts and in all geographical areas in bringing about social well-being, democracy and a realization of constitutional guarantees for all its citizens, including American Negroes."[39]

The most famous Black anti-Robeson performance was the testimony before HUAC in July 1949 by Jackie Robinson, a second baseman with the Brooklyn Dodgers. The committee, under the chairmanship of Georgia segregationist John S. Wood, called hearings in response to Robeson's statement, and later published them under the title *Communist Infiltration of Minority Groups.* Robinson was in many ways the embodiment of the postwar civil rights movement and, ironically, Paul Robeson had contributed to the campaign to desegregate the white baseball leagues—at a meeting with team owners during World War II, Robeson had urged desegregation of the national pastime and helped to make it a national political issue. In a statement he cowrote with the Urban League's Lester Granger, the slugger declared his loyalty to the United States, criticized Robeson's statement, and is-sued a vigorous attack on discrimination and segregation. In a highly visible articulation of the emerging paradigm of Cold War racial liberalism, Jackie Robinson aimed to separate the struggle against racism from Communism: "Just because Communists kick up a big fuss over racial discrimination when it suits their purposes, a lot of people try to pretend that the whole is-sue is a creation of Communist imagination." White newspapers and veter-ans' organizations hailed Robinson's testimony and lavished him with praise. Many years later, filled with doubt, Robinson explained that he had testified because "I had much more faith in the ultimate justice of the white man than I have today."[40]

The anti-Robeson stampede turned violent in August at an outdoor con-cert in Peekskill, New York, to raise funds for the Civil Rights Congress. A white mob attacked early arrivals with rocks, brass knuckles, and clubs; set fires; and burned a cross, all while police reportedly failed to act. Robeson and thousands of New Yorkers returned a month later and again faced a mob of rock-throwing whites hurling racist and anti-Semitic slurs. Robeson and two dozen others unsuccessfully sued the county for failing to provide police protection. A grand jury investigation instead blamed Robeson and the concertgoers for instigating the violence. Communists, rather than the marauding white mobs, were guilty of fomenting "racial and religious ha-tred." This reflected a view of the CP that was widely disseminated in anti-communist trials and congressional hearings: that its objective was to create discord as part of its plan to overthrow the U.S. government; and that its op-position to racial inequality was a pretense that obscured its desire to foment racial division.[41]

The State Department directed an international campaign to discredit Robeson. The U.S. Consulate's Public Affairs Officer at Accra, Ghana, engi-neered the publication of an anti-Robeson article in the NAACP's *Crisis* mag-azine that was distributed across Africa. In "Paul Robeson: The Lost Shep-herd" by Robert Alan, Robeson was transformed into a wayward, pitiful victim.[42] Walter White continued the assault in "The Strange Case of Paul Robeson" printed in *Ebony* in February 1951. White was in many ways the most significant nongovernmental architect of Cold War racial liberalism. As part of his effort to encourage a partnership between African Americans and the federal government, White increasingly came to regard Black radicals or dissidents as obstacles in this quest. Robeson, "this wonderfully talented man," he wrote, "was detoured and derailed somewhere in his great career and went careening into the Communist camp." Russia, he surmised, became "an escape" into a "dream world" where racism did not exist. White's pen transformed Robeson, a forceful, brilliant and widely respected figure, into a "bewildered man . . . more to be pitied than damned."[43]

The effort to marginalize Robeson was, however, contested and resisted. Robeson was still widely admired, and many Black leaders defended his right to political and artistic freedom. In 1950 Eleanor Roosevelt, the host of a television show on NBC, invited Adam Clayton Powell to speak for the Democrats, Robeson to speak for the Progressive Party, and a Black Mississippian to speak for Republicans on the theme "The Position of the Negro in American life." This network program not only illustrates the impact of Black political mobilization, but also shows Paul Robeson's continuing status as a spokesperson on Black issues. The right-wing *New York Journal American* reportedly encouraged a flurry of phone calls to protest Robeson's appearance, and NBC caved quickly. An executive said his appearance "would only lead to misunderstanding and confusion and no good purpose would be served in having him speak on the issue of the Negro in politics." Fellow radicals, but even some liberals, rallied to defend his free speech rights. The Harlem Trade Union Council picketed Radio City, and both the NAACP and ACLU criticized the network. Powell defended Robeson's right to speak. As an elected U.S. official during the Cold War, Congressman Powell would mute his criticism of the nation's racial oppression while traveling abroad, but he always critiqued domestic anticommunism as a distraction from the real "un-American" problem of white supremacy. "Until we change our laws and ban free speech neither Paul Robeson nor any individual should be singled out as a 'whipping boy,'" he declared.[44]

For his part, Robeson refused to remain silent or change his views. "I am a radical. I am going to stay one until my people are free to walk the earth," he declared in June 1949. On several subsequent occasions he repeated his opinion that Black Americans had nothing to gain from waging war on Communist nations. At a Civil Rights Congress rally at Madison Square Garden on June 28, 1950, he called on President Truman not to send American troops to Korea. "I have said it before and I say it again," Robeson resolutely declared, "that the place for the Negro people to fight for their freedom is here at home." Nevertheless, Paul Robeson's vigorous critique of American militarism, and his commitment to the Communist left at a time when its usefulness to the African American struggle for equality appeared to be in sharp decline, would increasingly estrange him from mainstream civil rights circles.[45]

The NAACP dismissed W. E. B. Du Bois as director of special research projects in September 1948. Du Bois, a supporter of Henry Wallace, opposed what he saw as the self-serving new NAACP policy of supporting Cold War foreign policy in exchange for promises of civil rights gains. Du Bois supported a more vigorous challenge to American support for European colonizers in Africa and to the growing penetration of Africa by American corporations. For Walter White, the rivalry between the United States and the Soviet Union presented an opportunity to win significant domestic concessions. Increasingly worried about the appeal of communism in the colonial world as independence loomed, the United States became willing to distance itself from white supremacy in order to buttress its claim to be the free world's leader. The NAACP, and civil rights leaders generally during the Cold War, sought to turn this development to their advantage. The clash between Du Bois and White signified the widening chasm and tense relations between Black leftists and liberals during the Cold War. When a memo by Du Bois criticizing White's leadership was leaked to the *New York Times*, White pushed through a resolution dismissing Du Bois.[46]

After his dismissal, Du Bois moved closer to the left. In 1950 he agreed to be the American Labor Party nominee to the U.S. Senate from New York, making him the "first Negro in the state's history to be nominated for high state office." He called for an end to U.S. intervention in Korea and assailed what he saw as the American desire to dominate the globe. "There are in this nation today," Du Bois stated at a press conference in Harlem announcing his candidacy, "powerful interests which are determined on war." Citing the blacklisting of Paul Robeson, Du Bois accused the government of "suppressing the Bill of Rights so as to stop discussion, distort the facts, and stampede the nation through the hysteria of groundless fear."

Ewart Guinier managed the campaign, whose chair, Bishop W. J. Walls of the AME Zion Church, said a vote for Du Bois would "strengthen the cause of justice and freedom for our people," and "the cause of peace in our land and throughout the world." Du Bois polled a "remarkable" 13 percent of the vote despite "the deepening freeze of the Cold War." The scholar-activist was arrested three months later, however, for being an "unregistered foreign agent" of an unnamed country. Being arrested and handcuffed by federal marshals was, Du Bois wrote, "the worst thing that ever happened in my life." He and four others were indicted under the Foreign Agents Registration Act for failing to register the organization they led, the Peace Information Center, as an agent of "a foreign principle." The center was helping to circulate the Stockholm Peace Pledge, which Secretary of State Dean Acheson had deemed Communist propaganda.[47]

In court, Du Bois outlined his lifelong internationalism, beginning with the Pan African congresses early in the century. He called the indictments "a shameful proclamation to the world that our Government considers peace alien, and its advocacy criminal." The trial took place during the Korean War, when polls showed low public support for a faraway conflict that seemed unrelated to national security. Yet at the same time, North Korea's invasion of the South exposed Communists to be aggressors, and served to further marginalize the American left. In November, after a short trial in which the government never even identified the "foreign principle" that Du Bois was alleged to be working for, the judge ordered a directed verdict of acquittal. Still, Du Bois did not get his passport back until 1958, when the Supreme Court overturned the State Department's policy of barring suspected Communists from traveling abroad.[48]

Du Bois's supporters included Albert Einstein and Reverdy Ransom, the ninety-one-year-old bishop of the AME Church who was a socialist, founder of the NAACP, and committed fighter for civil rights during the long age of Jim Crow. The board of directors of the NAACP opposed the indictment of its esteemed founder: "This action against one of the great champions of civil rights lends color to the charge that efforts are being made to silence spokesmen for full equality for Negroes." In the *Chicago Defender* Langston Hughes wrote, "If W. E. B. Du Bois goes to jail, a wave of wonder will sweep around the world." Judge Hubert T. Delany, who had voted against the NAACP's firing of Du Bois, believed that the indictment was meant to silence civil rights leaders. "Our so-called leaders," he wrote Du Bois, "have folded their tents, closed their mouths and become apologists for all of the injustices our government permits against the Negro today."[49]

By 1950, the FBI was investigating a broad range of Black intellectuals, activists, and politicians, including Mary McLeod Bethune, Adam Clayton Powell, E. Franklin Frazier, William Patterson, George Crockett, Alpheus Hunton and Langston Hughes. So many Black leaders came under scrutiny in part because of J. Edgar Hoover's professed fears of strong Black leadership and his opposition to racial equality—which permeated the entire Washington national security establishment—and in part because not just the Communist Party came under attack, but also the broader Popular Front, which had attracted many noncommunists.

Mary McLeod Bethune, for example, was investigated for her participation in the American Committee for the Protection of the Foreign Born and the American League for Peace and Democracy. Howard University scholar E. Franklin Frazier was investigated for his membership in the Negro People's Committee to Aid Spanish Democracy. And two informants paid by the Justice Department, but later determined to be perjurers, swore that Ralph Bunche was a Communist. A top-ranking UN official who had won the Nobel Peace Prize in 1950, Bunche was quizzed in a twelve-hour Loyalty Board hearing about his relationship with the CP in the 1930s when he had helped to found the National Negro Congress. As one historian has written of the FBI, "Its purpose was not to deter subversion but to discredit Blacks deemed too independent, unconventional or influential."[50]

The Cold War and domestic anticommunist crusade caused a split between African American liberals and leftists in their attitudes toward the federal government and their stance toward U.S. foreign policy. A symposium in the winter 1949–1950 issue of the short-lived *Harlem Quarterly* on "Are Negroes Winning Their Fight for Civil Rights?" reflected the new political terrain changed by both *To Secure These Rights* and the Cold War. The answers to the question articulated the main thrusts of modern African American liberalism, with its emphasis on progress and attachment to the Democratic Party, and left-radicalism with its emphasis on grassroots agency, criticism of the ruling elite, and emphasis on the plight of workers and unemployed.

Mary McLeod Bethune responded strongly in the affirmative, praising Truman and pointing to court victories that were widening opportunities for African Americans. A. Philip Randolph said civil rights bills were "the most important legislation before the American people." An FEPC law, he argued, "would do more in the fight against communism than all of the millions of dollars for the arms program, the Marshall Plan and the Atlantic Pact." William Patterson, of the left-wing Civil Rights Congress, credited the movement rather than the government for recent civil rights gains. "The victories of the Negro people are being won despite an atmosphere of *official* government terror by Federal, State and City government bodies." Ben Davis stressed the strength of white supremacy and the "the big war-mongering, fascist-minded monopolies of Wall Street." Of all the writers, Davis accentuated the negative: "Lynch terror, police brutality, discrimination and jim-crow unemployment against the Negro workers and their families have reached alarming proportions."[51]

The political turmoil in the wake of 1948 election, together with international developments, paved the way for the demise of the Black Popular Front and the rise of Cold War liberalism. Communists increasingly came to be seen as ruthless agents for the Soviet Union; and as China went Communist and the USSR exploded an atomic weapon, fear and alarm increasingly defined the American people's reaction to allegations of Communists in their midst. The Cold War and red scare encouraged liberal civil rights leaders to regroup and project the movement as thoroughly wedded to anticommunist Americanism. Still, African American political identification with the federal government, and the disproportionate Black reliance on public sector employment, would create a whole series of contradictions as the Cold War escalated and the national security apparatus expanded.

8 The Paradoxical Effects of the Cold War

The Cold War had two opposing effects on the struggle for African American rights: it cracked down on domestic dissent and opened up domestic policies to a global audience critical of American segregation and racial inequality. The repression had far-reaching consequences. Most significantly, it dramatically slowed Black mobilization in New York City. It undermined the civil rights–trade union alliance, reduced civil rights leaders' calls for economic reform, and muted these leaders' criticism of U.S. foreign policy; it discouraged street protest and grassroots insurgency in favor of elite negotiations and lawsuits; it punished the most militant leaders, and imposed greater controls on more mainstream leaders; and above all else, the anticommunist crusade spread fear across American society.

Yet at the same time, international events provided new leverage for African American leaders in the fight against domestic segregation. The international spotlight of the Cold War and the rising challenges to colonial rule in Asia and Africa made the U.S. government acutely conscious of a global audience critical of American racial oppression. As this sensitivity became clear, many civil rights leaders tried to turn the Cold War to their advantage. In a shift that would come to pervade mainstream discourse, civil rights leaders began to cast desegregation as a weapon against Communism. Civil rights for Blacks, liberal leaders argued, would aid the foreign policy goals of the United States. This strategy was most pronounced in the later struggle against de jure segregation in the South, in part because the height of the southern civil rights struggle coincided with the independence of African nations in the early 1960s. Would the Cold War be useful in creating moral and diplomatic leverage to dislodge the white power and privilege of the urban North? In the 1950s, Cold War liberalism eclipsed the prominence of left-progressivism in Black political discourse and activism. The repression and fear of the red scare, the seeming benefit of Cold War rhetoric to racial progress, the concessions won in the postwar civil rights struggle, and the rise in Black education levels and income due to northern migration and World War II generated a new, controversial discourse of integrationism.

The Red Scare in the NAACP

President Truman won Black votes after a historic endorsement of civil rights, but critics charged that the new administration failed to go to bat for civil rights on Capitol Hill. Seventy-two civil rights bills were introduced in the 1949–1950 session. None passed, and prospects worsened when Congress made it more difficult to stop a filibuster, increasing to two-thirds the votes needed to close debate. Insurgents in the NAACP wanted to increase popular pressure on the government. Guy Brewer, a leader of the branch in Jamaica, Queens, complained that the "national office objects to branches cooperating with other organizations sponsoring militant action upon Washington, yet sits by like a bump on a log and takes no affirmative action of its own. *Let them beware less these chickens come home to roost.*" "We live in a new era," Brewer declared. The days when the NAACP could singlehandedly carry the movement "have long since passed."[1]

A resolution introduced by a member of the left-led United Public Workers of America and approved at the NAACP's 1949 convention called for "the greatest outpouring of Negroes and their allies" to gather in Washington to bring to Congress "the demands of the people for the speedy enactment of a comprehensive civil rights program." The National Emergency FEPC Mobilization in January 1950 was intended to be the culmination of efforts to pass a fair employment law. Unlike the CIO, the NAACP permitted Communists to be members of its branches. But the CIO worked with Roy Wilkins in sponsoring the mobilization, and fearing that Communists and their allies would introduce other issues or tactics, they let it be known that Communists were not welcome. In response, Lindsay White, president of the Harlem branch of the NAACP, stressed to his membership that divisive issues such as foreign policy were off-limits in Washington. Many New York organizations sent delegations, ranging from the National Association of Negro Beauticians and Professional Women to the Committee to End Discrimination at Levittown. On the eve of departure, a rally in Harlem called on Truman to "keep the promises that he made during the 1948 campaign at 135th Street and St. Nicholas Avenue." The anticommunism of the mobilization's organizers, however, was at odds with the eclectic Black Popular Front nature of the participating groups, setting the stage for a showdown in Washington.[2]

On January 15, nearly five thousand delegates from NAACP branches, CIO and AFL unions, and Christian and Jewish groups from thirty-three states converged on the nation's capital. According to FBI informants, 90 percent of the delegates were Black, "of a high type, being from the professional classes, ministers, teachers, and white collar workers." Controversy erupted when the CIO-controlled credentials committee denied admission to hundreds of delegates on the grounds that they had not undergone the required preclearance procedure. Many accounts of this clash describe it in racial terms, as an episode of behind-the-scenes, but aggressive, white control of the civil rights movement. According to Ewart Guinier, who may well have been among those denied entry, "at the door of the conference was stationed a white liberal whose job was to indicate to NAACP officials who he thought was a Communist and they would be barred." About 410 delegates were denied entrance for alleged Communist Party membership or association. "On this man's say," Guinier said, "Black people, delegates from local chapters of the NAACP, were barred from participating on the grounds that they were Communists." The committee refused to honor letters that Harlem branch president Lindsay White had mimeographed for his delegation. White called it "utter disrespect"; Guy Brewer decried the committee's "Hitler-like tactics and Rankin rules." He called the ejections "the most despicable thing I have ever seen," and blamed "the stupidity and lack of morality of top officials of the NAACP."[3]

Lindsay White also reported that racial frictions were created by white CIO representatives barring Black NAACP delegates: "To many Negro members of the NAACP the denial by a white person of their right to participate in a mobilization initiated by their own organization was ludicrous." Moreover, it created "wide dissension and indignation within the ranks of the NAACP membership." White strongly objected to the treatment meted out to his delegation and demanded an apology. In a letter to Roy Wilkins, he asked if "the widely publicized presentation of a check for $5,000 to the NAACP by the CIO was the reason, or the price, for the abandonment of the policy laid down by the 40th annual convention." An offended and furious Roy Wilkins demanded an apology of his own, and searched in vain for evidence to link White, one of only a few Black firefighters in New York City, to the Communist Party. The two men engaged in a bitter exchange, but Roy

Wilkins ultimately survived a vote of confidence by a divided board of directors. The city's Black newspaper, the Washington *Afro-American,* echoed the left's criticism of the NAACP. "The so-called civil rights mobilization was in fact a mechanism to demobilize the NAACP, weaken its leftist support and remove it from its position as the only powerful spokesman for the colored peoples. Mr. Wilkins fell right into the trap baited no doubt by the promise that if he repudiated the leftists he would get fatter checks and more support from the conservatives."[4]

Jane Bolin, the only Black woman judge in New York, resigned from the NAACP Board of Directors, complaining that the NAACP "had blown the Communists up to such fantastic proportions that we give them more of our attention and time than we do the American Negro." Calling the association's program "sterile and barren," Bolin applauded the legal department, but said the national staff yelled "'Communist' and 'fellow-traveler' about every Board member and branch which is opposed to its inaction and wants to see come out of the NAACP less talk and more action on a vital civil rights program."[5]

At the June 1950 annual convention in Boston, the NAACP passed an anticommunist resolution. Roy Wilkins wrote to Walter White that there would be "no more 'wrangling over what is liberal' or 'hesitating to identify ourselves with a kind of McCarthyism.' We do not want a witch hunt, but we want to clean out our organization." While the resolution claimed that "there is a well organized, nation-wide conspiracy by Communists either to capture or split and wreck the NAACP," Wilkins and others seemed motivated by the desire to create a liberal consensus within the organization. NAACP president Arthur Spingarn acknowledged that of 1,497 branches and chapters, only eight were actually considered targets of Communist "infiltration." Nevertheless, the resolution called for an investigation of the "ideological composition and trends of the membership," and it instructed the board "to take the necessary action to suspend and reorganize, or lift the charter and expel any branch . . . coming under Communist . . . domination." A "vocal minority" vigorously opposed the resolution during a stormy two-hour debate, but it passed. According to Stuyvesant Town tenant leader Lee Lorch, Rosa Parks voted against it. Reportedly, many of the delegates who voted in favor of the resolution were government employees who felt pressured to support anticommunism because of their vulnerability under the Loyalty Program.[6]

The political transformation of this era entailed more than purges and firings: it was also ideological in nature. A component of the repression of the left—by both government and nongovernmental sources—was an assault on the image and motives of American leftists. For two decades, the Communist left had been widely associated with the fight for racial equality, even as the CP's "party line" or approach to the race question alternated between a more Black nationalist stance and a more integrationist stance. During the McCarthy era, this commonplace view of the CP would be almost entirely reversed. The NAACP engaged in such an effort to undermine the CP's image in the midst of its purge. Board member Alfred Baker Lewis, a white socialist and insurance executive from Greenwich, Connecticut, sought out A. Philip Randolph in an effort to "see a committee set up to combat the growth of Communism among Negroes similar to the committee which has been set up to combat the growth of Communism among Jews." Lewis's goal was to "put out a leaflet" for NAACP branches "explaining how the Communists damaged the fight for Civil Rights in this country," and to provide articles "from time to time" in Black newspapers. His idea appears to have been realized in a pamphlet published by the NAACP in 1951. In *The Communist Party—Enemy of Negro Equality,* Herbert Hill, another NAACP leader deeply committed to anticommunism, wrote, "If Communists gained influence among Negroes they would not hesitate for a moment to foment racial strife and dissension, and all in the interests of the Soviet Union." In the introduction, Roy Wilkins wrote, "Far from being sincere about doing something for Negro rights, the Communists use the Negro merely as a pawn in the Soviet campaign against the United States and the western world."[7]

Alfred Baker Lewis also spearheaded an effort to charter a new NAACP branch in Harlem, complaining that the current branch was circulating copies of Jane Bolin's "vicious and untruthful" statement. The effort fumbled. They failed to produce evidence that any of the thirty-three board members of the Harlem branch were Communists. The Brooklyn branch, however, went through "a thorough reorganization and all left-wing elements seemed to have been cleared off the board." Purges of alleged Communists also took place in the Flushing, Corona, Jamaica, Great Neck, and Freeport branches, among others in the region.[8]

In the 1950s, New York City NAACP branches disappeared as a leading source of civil rights leadership in grassroots struggles. Internal turmoil and repression demoralized members and led many to leave—an exodus that worsened when dues were doubled in 1949. Membership figures declined sharply across the country. The membership of the Harlem branch, for example, dropped from 7,129 in 1946 to 907 in 1949, and total branch membership declined 60 percent—from 420,000 in 1946 to 248,000 in 1949. The 1951 membership campaign by the New York branch was termed "a failure" because of "the general cynicism prevalent with regard to the NAACP." A report on the 1952 membership drive stated under the heading "Union" that "this source of memberships and revenue was not widely exploited." A suggestion to contact business agents was rejected "with the explanation that there were too many Communist unions in the area," a reference to the continuing presence of left-led unions as well as their legacy in Harlem trade union culture. Ella Baker had resigned as branch secretary in 1946 because she felt that the NAACP condescended to local people and refused to incorporate the energy and insights of grassroots members, a sentiment that Jane Bolin also emphasized in her letter of resignation. This demobilization of the NAACP shaped the future direction of both the northern and southern civil rights movements.[9]

In part because the actual number of Communist Party members was never very large, many NAACP rank and file saw the purges and investigations as a means to impose tighter control on branches. In the Jamaica branch, Guy Brewer, an activist who never shied from challenging authority, launched an effort to create an autonomous branch communication network in order to strengthen the collective voice of branches within the association. After the national office denied his request for the addresses of branches, Brewer and Lawrence R. Bailey, chair of the Legal Redress Committee in the Jamaica branch, sued the NAACP, arguing that it violated incorporation laws by improperly withholding material from members of the organization. In court, Wilkins claimed that attorney Bailey and future Democratic Party leader Brewer must either be Communists or "Communist sympathizers"—a doubtful assertion, although the latter category is, of course, vague.[10]

The court ruled in Brewer and Bailey's favor; the NAACP appealed, and the courts finally leaned on the attorneys to settle the dispute. In the end, Brewer and Bailey's effort to increase branch autonomy did not succeed, but their critique of top-down leadership and belief that anticommunism exacted a high price for racial justice movements reveal that there was no anticommunist "consensus" in liberal organizations. On the contrary, this was a period of considerable conflict and dissent.[11]

Progressive branch leaders sometimes tried to soften the internal anticommunist crusade. Indeed, some of them had participated in the same Popular Front organizations that the NAACP, following the U.S. government, now deemed subversive. In 1957 the Harlem branch had a Special Committee on Subversion whose task was to screen candidates for branch office. Two members, Ella Baker and the Reverend James Robinson—whose experience as a victim of the red scare doubtless sensitized him—suggested to Roy Wilkins that the committee discontinue using the attorney general's list of subversive organizations as its blacklist. They wanted to make membership in the Communist Party alone, rather than in the broader Popular Front groups, the criteria for disqualification. Their effort appears to have failed.[12]

The demobilization of many NAACP branches came at a critical juncture when Roy Wilkins was beginning a ten-year reign as executive secretary and southern Jim Crow was beginning to crack. According to one historian, "Because Wilkins shared with [J. Edgar] Hoover an obsession with Communism and a hatred for Martin Luther King Jr., Hoover was able to use this NAACP leader in his campaign to damage if not destroy the larger movement to which both Wilkins and King belonged and gave so much." For two decades Wilkins and other NAACP leaders, including Thurgood Marshall, shared information about alleged Communists with the FBI. Like many liberals in this era, they acted out of a belief that they were shielding the NAACP from suspicion.[13]

The interracial anticommunism and top-down leadership style of the FEPC mobilization were institutionalized in a new organization. Beginning in 1950, activists connected to labor, Jewish groups, and the Americans for Democratic Action put together a permanent organization to lobby for antidiscrimination legislation. Named the Leadership Conference on Civil Rights (LCCR), it became a prominent presence on Capitol Hill for decades, and marked the consolidation of a civil rights establishment in Washington, D.C., with substantial white leadership. Jewish antidiscrimination organizations had also undergone ideological purges during the red scare, which pushed the American Jewish Congress, for example, to the right. Cold War liberalism tended to eschew mass mobilization strategies because anticommunists had defined them as too susceptible to Communist influence. This put LCCR supporter A. Philip Randolph, a proponent of both mass protest and anticommunism, in an awkward position—one accentuated by Randolph's being a socialist in an anticommunist environment that was being pushed rightward by national political pressures. The issue of white leadership also added to the dilemma for Randolph, whose wartime March on

Washington Movement was avowedly all Black. One of his assistants, Theodore Brown, confided his belief to Randolph that the new organization was more committed to a vision of "waging a fight against the Communists" than it was to Black advancement. "The American Negro should assume the leadership of this fight for FEPC," he argued, but he feared that "the present set-up as I see it, has relegated the Negro to an ineffective role." In the context of Cold War America, Randolph was never able to fully resolve these dilemmas. By contrast, Ella Baker and Conrad Lynn, two other prominent African American radicals with roots in the anticommunist left, came to see a right-wing agenda in the postwar anticommunist crusade, and opposed it.[14]

Some left-wing activists felt that McCarthyism, by creating categories of legitimate and illegitimate resistance, imposing patterns of surveillance, and making those with Popular Front biographies ineligible for leadership, strengthened elite, and therefore white, stewardship of the civil rights movement. Ewart Guinier observed years later that interracial work through the Urban League and NAACP "tended to be on the basis of what whites would not find objectionable." He said that "rifts entered into the NAACP and the Urban League by those Blacks who felt that the control of them, the direction of them, was taken over by whites, whites who were afraid of Blacks that they considered radical."[15]

Red and Black: Unblending Colors

As part of the effort to sever ties between African Americans and the left, a portrait of Communists as insincere civil rights advocates, even racists, was widely disseminated in the 1950s. Various forms of media, public discourse, and intellectual production promoted the idea that Communists were false allies who "used the Negro" to foment racial strife and conflict in the United States. The left social movement was subtly whitened in the public imaginary, and Black leftists were either erased or made into pawns of the Communist International. Public anticommunist testimony was the most dramatic means used to convey this idea, but various kinds of published work as well as government propaganda played important parts in transforming the image of Communists from ardent proponents of racial equality to fanatical hypocrites.

Two studies published in 1951, Wilson Record's *The Negro and the Communist Party* and William Nolan's *Communism versus the Negro* traced the shifts in the official Communist Party stance on the Negro question since the forma-

tion of the Communist Party. The shifts, they argued, illustrated the duplici-
tous and foreign nature of Communist ideology, especially the Black Belt
thesis. Record's work, part of a prestigious series by liberal intellectuals,
took the Communists seriously as influential radicals, but stressed their manipulation of Black grievances and empty posturing. His message was that
"the Communists have engaged in a lot of fuss about race equality in the
post-war period, but have done little about it." A sociologist, Record was
a former organizer with the anticommunist International Ladies Garment
Workers Union. William Nolan framed Communists as devious and unbal-
anced. Since the CP was said to be engaged in sabotage, Nolan characterized their lobbying efforts for an FEPC as a purposeful failure. Their "trick"
to sabotage passage was to send "neurotic and irresponsible youth to visit
members of Congress" and thereby "antagonize people who might be dis-
posed to listen to a more normal presentation."[16]

The government borrowed Wilson Record's book for its propaganda productions aimed at Africa and Asia, discussing it in three broadcasts of *Voice of
America*. Record, a white Texan, was presented as Black in an effort to
whiten and delegitimize foreign "isms." "This is the real American Negro as
he is described by the distinguished Negro sociologist, Wilson Record," the
announcer intoned. "He bears not the slightest resemblance to the Phantom
Negro conjured up by Communist propagandists." The broadcasts described
the Herculean efforts by the Communist Party to woo Black Americans, and
their ultimate failure, saddled as they were by "the absurd albatross of Black
Belt self-determination tied around its neck by the inflexible oligarchs of the
Comintern." The broadcasts urged "leaders of the under-developed countries" to study "the strange pattern of failure and betrayal that is the history
of the Communist effort to win the American Negro."[17]

A 1955 study by scholar Daniel Wynn called *The NAACP versus Negro Revolutionary Protest* helped to accelerate the erasure of the Black left from the
civil rights movement. It lauded the NAACP and disparaged the left, denying
it credit for any achievement or contribution in the African American struggle. Robeson and Du Bois "made no direct efforts at the attainment of civil
rights for Negroes." Interestingly, Wynn sees the main Black leadership rivalry at that time between "Negro protest actionists" who sought "unrestricted inclusion in the system as is," and "Negro protest revolutionists,"
who, he argued, aimed to transform it. Black nationalism is notably absent,
but the repression of the left produced a political void that paved the way for
the reemergence of Black nationalism in the 1960s.[18]

The public testimony of former Communists and paid infiltrators was an

integral part of the ideological campaign against the left as well as the atmosphere of fear and intimidation that pervaded the country at the height of
McCarthyism. There were reportedly many Black people among the one
thousand FBI informants in the Communist Party and "front" groups in
the late 1940s and 1950s. Manning Johnson was a star Black ex-red who
testified in the Smith Act trial, in Congress, and even in southern state legis-
latures in later years on behalf of segregationists who were using the anticommunist apparatus to thwart the civil rights struggle. Johnson later admitted that he had lied at trials. In the 1949 HUAC hearings about Paul
Robeson, Johnson testified that Robeson aspired to be "the Black Stalin"
among African Americans. In a classic of its genre, *Color, Communism, and
Common Sense* published by Alliance, Inc. in 1958, Johnson penned a novel
attack on Du Bois, finding the origins of his left turn in his break from
Booker T. Washington. Other passages prefigure interpretations of the Black
left advanced by cultural nationalist writer Harold Cruse, whose 1967 *Crisis
of the Negro Intellectual* is regarded by many as an authoritative history of
Harlem radicalism. Johnson wrote that the "betrayal of the Negro people
may well come through Communist corruption of the Negro intellectual,"
who, he wrote, "went after Communist inter-racialism like a hog going after
slop." The Black left was, in Johnson's hands, a potent brew of racial
inauthenticity and neurosis. "Deep in the swamp of inferiority, lack of ability, muddled thought, the Negro intelligentsia looks to the phony white liberals, politicians, and progressive hypocrites for leadership, guidance and
money."[19]

The anticommunist network struck gold when it discovered that a Black
activist in the wartime left was a teacher currently employed by the Board
of Education. The New York City public school system had become an epi-
center of local McCarthyism. Sol Moskoff, an assistant corporation counsel
for New York City, was assigned full-time for almost a decade to ferret out
alleged Communists and unrepentant former Communists. Fifty teachers
were dismissed and nearly four hundred resigned rather than face the prospect of naming names—which the board had made a condition of job retention—until the state commissioner of education eventually overruled the
practice. The board's anticommunist crusade was also used by management
to crush a militant union. Superintendent of Schools William Jansen openly
acknowledged this: "If we found that they dropped their membership in the
Teachers' Union which was Communist dominated, we gave them the benefit of the doubt."[20]

Most of the teachers dismissed by the Board of Education were active in the union. Indeed, in 1950 the Teachers' Union was removed as the collective bargaining agent of teachers. The union had supported the CP's opposition to U.S. foreign policy and expressed admiration for the Soviet Union, but it also represented important positions in the indigenous American left. It promoted a brand of teacher unionism—supporting desegregation and "intercultural education" and stressing solidarity with the community—that was lacking in its successor, the United Federation of Teachers, which would position itself against the aspirations of Black communities in the community control movement of the late 1960s.[21]

Virtually all of the former Communists who submitted to Moskoff's interrogations dutifully rejected leftism, but none corroborated his anticommunist narrative. Despite relentless efforts by Moskoff to locate evidence of supposed party plans to indoctrinate children, none was found. On the contrary, over and over again witnesses discussed their radical past with unmistakable nostalgia—describing how as underpaid, idealistic teachers during the Depression they had built a union to acquire clothes and shoes for poor children, smaller classes, better conditions, and job security. Apart from the union, anti-Nazism was the most important struggle of their lives. Even after she decided to protect her job and name names, Dorothy Funn testified before Congress with similar conviction and principle in explaining that she had joined the Communist Party to fight for racial justice during World War II. Until 1947 Funn worked for the National Negro Congress (NNC) and for a time was their lobbyist in Washington, where she pushed for FEPC, anti–poll tax and antilynching legislation, as well as a host of prolabor bills. "It is with deep regret that I leave the staff of the Congress," she wrote in her letter of resignation, but she vowed to remain a member and help strengthen the Brooklyn council of the NNC. She stayed in the left orbit at least through the 1948 presidential election, when she was active in the Bedford-Stuyvesant Wallace for President Committee.[22]

In May 1953 the House Committee on Un-American Activities came to New York City and Dorothy Funn publicly named dozens of teachers and former comrades in the NNC as having been members of the Communist Party.[23] Her testimony was a highly publicized performance designed to further discredit the radical left in the area of civil rights. HUAC even requested that the light-skinned Funn racially self-identify, so the racial message would not be lost on the public. Thelma Dale, another Black woman activist in the NNC and someone Funn named as a red, nevertheless felt many years later that Funn had been "used," and called her testimony "sad." But conservative Black columnist George Schuyler gushed in the *Pittsburgh Courier* that "Mrs. Funn deserves great credit for telling what went on behind the fronts, many of which professed to be out to save the Negro while working like Trojans to spread racial ill-will."[24]

Funn provided a picture of an insincere Communist Party and a self-portrait of a sincere Communist motivated by noble goals. After stating that "we were really a puppet of the Communist party, and that there was truly no interest in furthering Negro rights," she testified that Communist lobbyists in Washington, including herself, worked strenuously for passage of FEPC, as well as anti–poll tax and antilynching bills. In a move that southern anticommunists would try frequently in the coming decade, a committee member tried to get her to call those bills Communist inspired, but she threw the question back on the committee, urging HUAC to pass an FEPC bill as a true example of its Americanism. Despite Funn's cooperation with HUAC, she did not share its hostility to racial equality.[25]

The Red Scare and Black Culture

The red scare hurt cultural workers active in the racial justice movement. The theater and pageantry of the Negro Freedom Rallies, benefit dances at the Savoy, the play *On Whitman Avenue*, and concerts by Paul Robeson were all integral to forging social consciousness and bands of solidarity in the movement. Along with labor leaders, community activists, and politicians, Black artists, actors, poets, and painters were pressured during the 1950s to move away from radical affiliations, discourses, and worldviews. This pressure was not abstract; it was enacted in blacklisting, death threats, and congressional subpoenas.

Because of the comparatively small numbers of African Americans in film and television in the 1940s and 1950s, the blacklist is not typically associated with Black performers. A generation of Black screen and stage stars, however, felt its force. Hazel Scott, star of the first Black television show, the *Hazel Scott Show*, was blacklisted. Scott, the glamorous pianist and wife of Congressman Adam Clayton Powell, was listed in *Red Channels*, a 213-page exposé of alleged "Communist Influence in Radio and Television" published by Counterattack, an organization staffed by ex-FBI agents and funded by antiunion corporate sources. Among its evidence of suspicious affiliations was membership in the left-led Committee to End Jim Crow in Baseball. Scott was also listed for being on the Ben Davis Reelection Committee, and for having entertained Soviet troops alongside American ones during the war. Thinking she could personally beat the charges, Scott requested to appear before HUAC. But her public appearance resulted in the cancellation of her network television show and the disappearance of other broadcasting jobs.[26]

Canada Lee and Langston Hughes, two major artists active in civil rights struggles in New York, came under attack for their ideas and associations. Neither was a Communist Party member, but both were willing to work with Communists. Lee was a violinist, jockey, and boxer who discovered his acting talent in the Federal Theater Project with Orson Welles during the Depression and became a major screen and stage star in the 1940s. He starred in *Native Son, Lifeboat, Othello, Body and Soul,* and *The Duchess of Malfi,* in which he became the first Black actor cast in a white role on the American stage. Lee broadened the portrayal of Black men on the stage and screen in the 1940s, resisting the narrow and demeaning depiction of Black people in white-controlled visual productions. He was also deeply involved in the effort to turn World War II into a war against racism on the home front. He spoke at rallies, joined delegations to Congress, and did extensive radio work to promote desegregation, tolerance, and social justice, most famously in *New World A'Coming* over WMCA in New York. In 1949, Lee was named as a "fellow traveler"—someone who follows the Communist Party line—in the espionage trial of state department employee Judith Coplon, and he was subsequently put on the entertainment industry's blacklist. At the height of his career, CBS canceled his radio contract and stage and screen jobs vanished.

Lee struggled to clear his name. At a press conference in Harlem, he denied being a Communist and professed his loyalty to America. "But this does not mean that because America has extended to me a bit of fame and fortune, that I am to close my eyes to the plight of my people. If I protest a lynching does that make me a subversive?" Lee identified what he saw as the racism bound up with the red scare, and highlighted the stakes of political repression for a racially oppressed people. "Call me a Communist and you call all Negroes Communists," he said. "It is very difficult under the circumstances for a Negro to be a good American and a Negro at the same time." Lee's appeals fell on deaf ears, and like some other blacklist victims, he found work abroad. A British producer cast him in the antiapartheid film *Cry the Beloved Country* in 1950. Ironically he was invited to do *Voice of America* broadcasts in Europe, where Black Americans were sought to represent

America to the rest of the world during the Cold War. Lee's return home brought continued rejection. He was never able to get off the blacklist, and he suffered a heart attack and died in 1952 at age forty-five. Ten thousand mourners came to his funeral at Salem Methodist Church in Harlem. "They said he was a Communist," Adam Clayton Powell said. "They felt a man couldn't fight for dignity, for everybody's rights as a man, without being a Communist. They knew really he wasn't a Communist, but they broke his heart."[27]

The African American writer Langston Hughes devoted most of his literary life to the struggle for social justice. He published in Communist-sponsored publications and appeared at Communist-supported rallies and benefits, and on an extended visit to the Soviet Union in 1932–1933, Hughes praised the Soviet commitment to eradicating second-class citizenship for people of color and to abolishing forms of segregation that had existed under the old regime. When he returned, he felt misunderstood. "I have never been a Communist, but I soon learned that anyone visiting the Soviet Union and speaking in favor of it upon returning is liable to be so labeled."

In 1953, he was subpoenaed to testify before Joseph McCarthy's Senate Permanent Subcommittee on Investigations, as part of its investigation of the State Department. State Department libraries contained sixteen books by Hughes that McCarthy claimed "largely follow the Communist line." Many of Hughes's writings from the 1930s and 1940s praised the left and questioned the direction of American society, but ironically, his poetry likely served the State Department's interest in projecting Black American success to overseas audiences. Hughes testified that he once believed in the Soviet form of government, but had experienced "a complete reorientation" of his thinking about four or five years earlier, prompted by "the very great increase in the acceleration of improvement in race relations" during the war and since.[28]

The repression of left-leaning Black artists did not stop Black activism in the cultural sphere. Ossie Davis, Dick Campbell, and Frederick O'Neal—three New York actors as well as committed activists, were blacklisted, yet all persevered and remained committed to antiracist work. "We didn't know how thoroughly we were being watched," Davis recalled. But he said that he and his wife, Ruby Dee, "figured we would go crazy if we tried to figure out if we were blacklisted because we were Black or blacklisted because we were red." Winning Black jobs and representation in radio, television, and film was a major goal of the New York civil rights struggle. A Mississippi native, Frederick O'Neal founded the American Negro Theater, became the first Black president of Actor's Equity, and was named the cultural affairs commissioner of New York City in 1975. In 1952 O'Neal cofounded the Coordinating Council for Negro Performers in Harlem (CCNP), to fight for more Black employment in the entertainment business. The council's fliers asked, "Did you see a NEGRO on television last night?" Ten percent of the nation, Blacks constituted one-half of 1 percent of television actors. Mirroring the direction of employment struggles in the 1950s, the CCNP stressed the importance of Blacks as consumers. "Negroes comprise a large part of the *consumer* market, and *the consumer* makes commercial telecasting possible." NAACP protests had led studios to move away from casting Black actors as servants or in comic roles, but the CCNP warned that this "well-in-tentioned but ill-directed sensitivity to this problem has worked inadvertent harm to the Negro artist" because no new roles were in the offing. "We must correct this situation, not by eliminating the Negro artist, but by enlarging his scope and participation in all types of roles and in all forms of American entertainment—just as in American life, the Negro citizen's role now extends from the kitchen to the United Nations."[29]

Dick Campbell was another blacklisted artist who led the CCNP. He arranged for a series in the *Amsterdam News* called "Jim Crow in Radio and TV" that surveyed every metropolitan area radio and TV station. An important theme was the power of the $15 billion Black consumer market: "This extremely lucrative market has been completely ignored." Campbell and O'Neal knew that advertisers cited a fear of alienating the white southern market to justify their censorship of Black images, so their strategy was to prove that the Black market mattered too. Campbell organized a Saturday night television "black-out," and a few jobs were won as a result. The group expanded its advocacy to include films, radio, and the theater, as well as technical, backstage jobs.[30]

Guilt by Association

Targets of the anticommunist crusade went well beyond the relatively small numbers of Communists and former Communists in the United States. The search for reds ensnared many others, from liberals to radicals, who had associated with a left-wing group or cause. Because of the close history of the left and the antiracist struggle in New York, significant numbers of African American leaders felt the sting of McCarthyism. Their stories reveal how the red scare intimidated and imposed hardship on this generation of civil rights radicals.

The red scare destroyed the judicial career of one of the most respected African American judges and civil rights leaders in the nation. Hubert T. Delany, a former U.S. attorney, city tax commissioner, and since 1945, a justice in the Court of Domestic Relations, hailed from a prominent North Carolina family and was a member of the NAACP Board of Directors. But like many Black professionals of his generation, he embraced cosmopolitan, prolabor, anticolonial politics. Judge Delany was also a vocal critic of the red scare, particularly for the chilling effect it was having on the African American rights movement and the damage being done to civil liberties. "I'm sick of hearing about the rights Russians don't have—I'm concerned about the rights we don't have right here in this country," Judge Delany said in 1952 speech. In 1955 Democratic mayor Robert Wagner declined to reappoint Judge Delany. "I feel I do not agree with some of the positions that he has taken," the mayor stated, without ever identifying them. The American Bar Association had labeled Delany "outstandingly qualified," its highest ranking. Delany felt that he was being punished for vigorous civil rights advocacy, and declared that "if a Negro cannot speak out in defense of Civil Rights and justice for his people, then this is a sad day for America."[31]

Wagner's decision sparked an outcry from the city's liberal civic and religious leadership. There was speculation that the Catholic archdiocese had exerted pressure on the mayor, since Delany had participated in Black-Jewish advocacy for secular liberalism and the separation of church and state. But he had also joined Popular Front organizations. And the Federal Bureau of Investigation had compiled a file on Delany as a result of his membership in the New York City chapter of the National Lawyers' Guild, a group cited by the attorney general as a subversive organization. His file was composed of newspaper articles from 1937–1953 chronicling his support for various antiracist causes as well as his critique of the red scare at the height of the Cold War.[32]

Algernon Black, the son of Ukrainian immigrants and leader of the Ethical Culture Society, was a major figure in the New York antiracist movement who, like Judge Delany, symbolized integrity and a broad commitment to social and economic justice. Best known for his efforts to combat housing discrimination, Black was a noncommunist progressive who participated in Popular Front activism. He too wound up on various government blacklists. In 1954 he applied for a visa for an educational trip to the Soviet Union, but to his surprise the State Department requested his passport, on the grounds that he might "travel abroad to foment and promote international communism." To get it back, and protect his job, Black signed a noncommunist affidavit.[33] The fear that his "subversive" past might harm the civil rights movement shaped all of Black's subsequent political decisions. In 1955, when the Mayor's Committee on Unity was strengthened and renamed the Commission on Intergroup Relations, Black was offered a position. He declined because he felt that "the work that it might do on race relations was more important and constructive than possibly weakening public faith in it because of my 'leftist associations.'"[34]

The country's move to the right in the 1950s strengthened Cold War liberalism among African American leaders, even though it did not entirely eclipse left progressivism. As the Council on African Affairs and its leaders came under attack, left-wing anticolonial activism declined in the United States, but it would forcefully reemerge in the 1960s, especially after the victory of Fidel Castro in Cuba and the murder of Congolese prime minister Patrice Lumumba. The career of James Robinson, a minister and civil rights leader in New York, offers a view of the trajectory of Black anticolonialism in a bipolar world as well as the shift from left progressivism to Cold War liberalism in antiracist advocacy. A victim and an opponent of McCarthyism, James Robinson nevertheless enlisted in the international Cold War in an effort to bring Black American Christian liberalism to Africa. His desire to fuse a pro-U.S., anti-Soviet stance with a race-conscious anticolonialism posed an interesting challenge.[35]

Born in 1907 in Knoxville Tennessee, Robinson was educated at Lincoln University in Pennsylvania and Union Theological Seminary in Manhattan, where he began a decade-long involvement in Popular Front activism. Robinson became pastor of the Presbyterian Church of the Master in Harlem; founded the Morningside Community Center, which served four thousand children in Harlem; ran a summer camp in New Hampshire; and later served on the board of the National Urban League. In 1951–1952 Robinson traveled to India, Egypt, and the Middle East as a goodwill ambassador for the National Council of Churches. "I was on a mission to address students and young people, the future leaders of Asia for whose souls and minds Communism is making a supreme bid," he wrote in his book *Tomorrow Is Today*. While overseas, he expressed mild criticism of racial conditions in the United States and endorsed the liberation struggles in Africa and Asia. But Robinson's goal was to convert anti-American third world critics. He even volunteered his services to State Department personnel in India, Germany, and Hong Kong. The State Department praised his work, and the incoming secretary of state, John Foster Dulles, attended his welcome home dinner. Nevertheless, the anticommunist network, always alert to Negroes abroad, went into action. A "vigilante" group in Indiana that disliked the portrait of Robinson presented in *Presbyterian Life* magazine informed the government that his name had appeared in the *Daily Worker*. The government launched an investigation and requested his passport. They found many Popular Front connections, including American Youth for Democracy, an organization on the attorney general's list that Robinson had addressed in his capacity as NAACP youth director (at the White House in 1941 with President Roosevelt in attendance).[36]

As a highly regarded clergyman and noncommunist, Robinson received an outpouring of support. Walter White wired Secretary of State Dean Acheson to remind him that "the State Department itself has praised the work of Mr. Robinson in his round-the-world tour last year in which he, as an American Negro, told the truth about racial relations in the U.S., both good and bad." While Paul Robeson's *Freedom* newspaper had criticized the minister's becoming a goodwill ambassador in 1951, during the crisis Ewart Guinier praised Robinson for his "general New Deal outlook." Powell called the "ridiculous and stupid" move "an effort to keep liberal Negroes in the U.S. from talking abroad." Two months later the State Department canceled its request for Robinson's passport.[37]

Robinson helped create Cold War racial liberalism. In 1954 he founded Operation Crossroads, a private program that brought American students to Africa and that later inspired the U.S. Peace Corps. Throughout the 1950s he labored to convince the United States that it should support colonial liberation in order to defeat Communism. "We talk long and loudly about being against Communism," Robinson wrote, "but we talk so little about what we are *for*. That is the reason people in Asia and Africa are losing faith in us." Nevertheless, he conceded that Asian and African skepticism about U.S. motives was understandable based on U.S. support for the colonial powers, on the one hand, and American promotion of arms deals and extraction of natural resources, on the other. He also acknowledged that many Africans and Asians found the Soviets more culturally sensitive and their promises of economic development more appealing. But Robinson argued passionately that distrust of the United States was unmerited. He related stories of African American freedom struggles, portraying them as representing America, and simultaneously warned against "the sinister aims of Soviet imperialists."[38]

Robinson believed that American anticommunist liberalism held promise for the developing world. He, and other Black leaders, sensed real progress being made for African Americans in employment, civil rights, and educational opportunities. This new mood was epitomized in the popular Black-owned national magazine *Ebony*, published by Johnson Publications in Chicago, and in the hastened dissolution of the Popular Front, which had already been weakened by anticommunist persecution. In 1956 Robinson volunteered to put together a book of essays called *Love of This Land: Progress of the Negro in the United States* to educate State Department personnel in Asia.[39] "While we have not achieved perfect democracy," he wrote, citing various indices of Black progress since World War II, "we are moving rapidly in the right direction." Ironically, the book celebrated achievements of the northern civil rights movement, many of whose leaders were now under government investigation. The book was intended as government propaganda, but it also reflected a genuine development in the outlook and expectations of an influential segment of African American leadership.[40]

This assessment differed sharply from the social and economic forecast of the left, which highlighted the fragile gains of the Black working class, the threat of plant relocation, and the vulnerability of Africa to American business and military interests. According to a 1953 Communist Party pamphlet *Next Steps in the Struggle for Negro Freedom*, "The bourgeoisie, conscious of the new influence the Negro question has on international affairs, is engaged in a far-reaching intervention in the Negro liberation movement." The pamphlet identified a flurry of recent articles in mainstream publications that celebrated Negro progress and undercut calls for continued activism, including a 1953 *Time* magazine article "The U.S. Negro," which asserted that "a decade of progress has wrought a revolution in his life, brought him more prosperity and freedom." The African American, according to *Time*, was "the nation's new Babbit." The problem was that "there are not enough qualified Negroes" to satisfy all the eager employers. Underscoring the Americanness of Black aspirations, this major newsweekly concluded, "The majority of U.S. Negroes feel no more kinship to the Kikuyu than to the man on the moon."

The left was in crisis throughout the 1950s, devoting most of its energy to self-defense. But as the antiracist struggle was being redefined ideologically during the Cold War, some Communists castigated the new integrationist orthodoxy as capitalist assimilationism. "The stated goal of the Negro movement, as outlined by a majority of its leaders," the CP argued, "is that of total integration, without discrimination or segregation, into every sphere of American society, *as it is presently organized and functioning*." The Communist pamphlet called this solution "one-sided and inadequate," and emphasized that integrationism "all but excludes the class position of Negro workers in industry."

Ben Davis put it more bluntly, arguing that a new race discourse of individual success stories was displacing attention from the more urgent problem of group retrogression. "Judge Hastie has a $15,000 job. But Negro workers cannot get jobs to drive milk wagons. Dr. Ralph Bunche has a $20,000 a year job. But the airplane factories in Long Island will not hire Negro workers. Channing Tobias is the first Negro director of a Wall Street bank. But the brewery corporations, General Electric and other giant monopolies will not employ Negroes. There is a $28,000-a-year General Sessions Negro Judge in New York. But the Negro Black Belt sharecroppers do not make enough to live on, and never get out of debt." "These relatively high paying jobs," he argued, "come to individual Negroes in an attempt of the ruling class to head off and undermine the militant struggles of the Negro workers for jobs and freedom." Ultimately, the CP would be divided in its reaction to domestic racial reform. Vastly curtailed in size and influence, the party would embrace the *Brown v. Board of Education* Supreme Court decision and support the integrationist goals of the southern civil rights movement, but some African American comrades would lament that the focus on Black workers had been abandoned.[41]

To be sure, there was noncommunist skepticism of this new discourse of Negro progress. E. Franklin Frazier organized a conference at Howard University in 1951 on the "Integration of the Negro into American Life," which aimed to reclaim control over representations of race. Frazier stated frankly that his intent was to critique the way the U.S. government had appropriated and exaggerated recent gains in Black American status. He noted that the "government of the United States has been especially eager to publicize the gains which have been made on integrating the Negro into American society." He commissioned a series of papers to investigate such claims, and argued that they "dissipate the exaggerated notions concerning the extent of the integration of the Negro." The papers also stressed that integration did not or should not require assimilation into white American culture. As the poet Sterling Brown wrote, "By integration, I mean . . . complete acceptance . . . first class citizenship." "Integration," he wrote, "should mean fundamental respect for genuine quality, whatever its source, and acceptance of it in its wholeness."[42]

Uses of the Cold War

The repressive aspects of the Cold War clearly damaged the New York civil rights movement. In trying to account for the precarious financial status of the New York State Committee against Discrimination in Housing, its director cited "fear. A great many people are shying away from all activity on the civil liberties and civil rights fronts. We are so eminently respectable a group that this is probably less of a tangible factor than others, but it undeniably hurts us." Barnard College president Millicent Macintosh also felt that McCarthyism was making whites retreat from racial equality. "Reform has become associated with Communism. On college campuses, someone who believes in interracial equality becomes suspect because the Communists say they believe in it."[43]

Yet at the same time, the Cold War opened up U.S. racial practices to an unprecedented degree of international exposure and scrutiny, giving African Americans many potential new allies. The competition with the Soviet Union for the allegiance of new Asian states, and the independence of African states on the horizon, gave the federal government an interest in moderating white supremacy and projecting a global image of American racial harmony and progress. Civil rights attorneys and leaders sought to use the U.S. government's new sensitivity over its image abroad to the advantage of the domestic struggle against racism. Thus, ironically, as civil liberties were being violated at home, racial oppression was being framed as an international human rights issue. This approach was a staple in federal briefs before the Supreme Court, and sometimes appeared as rationales in the justices' rulings themselves. Cold War pressures, however, did not accelerate the passage of civil rights legislation. In Truman's second term, the willingness of Dixiecrats to filibuster any antidiscrimination bill and the administration's desire to build broad congressional support for controversial foreign-policy initiatives combined to crush prospects for civil rights reform.[44]

A study by the American Jewish Congress and the NAACP confirmed the lack of symmetry between the Cold War abroad and efforts against discrimination at home. "The year 1950 revealed a marked change from the encouraging trend we had noted in 1948 and 1949. The country has been concerned with repelling international aggression and internal subversion. It has been far less concerned, unfortunately, with maintaining and expanding those democratic freedoms and rights which alone make that defense meaningful and worthwhile." In 1951 Adam Clayton Powell expressed his "disgust" over the abandonment of civil rights, and threatened to bolt from the Democratic Party before the next presidential election unless "the party took immediate steps to insure the integration of Negroes and other minorities now." In 1952, Democratic presidential nominee Adlai Stevenson opposed a "compulsory" FEPC, a move that not only reflected the strength of segregationists within the party, but also suggested the weakness of northern Democrats' commitment to redistributionary civil rights policies—or as they put it at the time, those "with teeth."[45]

As political currents shifted, liberal activists and politicians began to characterize racial discrimination as detrimental to U.S. foreign policy. "What a field day the Russians had when Dr. Percy Julian's home was bombed in Chicago," Walter White declared. "And what ammunition they got when racists in Birmingham tried to blow up the house of a Negro woman! What a comfort to communists, indeed, is a character like Levitt of Levittown and the directors of the Metropolitan Life Insurance Company which own Stuyvesant Town." At a pro-FEPC dinner at the Waldorf Astoria, A. Philip Randolph said, "The most powerful political propaganda weapon Russian Communism now holds in its hands is discrimination against Negroes." "Is there any wonder," he asked, that "the people of the world have no faith in the pompous and ponderous declarations about our democratic principles in Europe, when we cannot make them function below the Mason-Dixon line in our own country?" A year later, frustrated at another round of legislative failure, he wrote that even "if the Russian hordes were at the gates of America," Dixiecrats would not stop their filibuster "because they are determined to keep Negroes enslaved."[46]

At the dedication of Frederick Douglass Circle in Harlem, with ten descendants of the abolitionist, writer, and diplomat in attendance, Manhattan borough president Robert Wagner announced that "the United States must keep its own house clean if it is to sell democracy abroad." If the image of racial harmony helped the United States fight the Cold War, the Cold War gave racial equality moral and strategic urgency. "It is particularly vital to make democracy work at home," Wagner declared, "when the world is split in a struggle for men's hearts and minds and when Americans are dying in Korea in defense of human rights."[47]

Earl Brown, Ben Davis's successor on the City Council, emphasized that it was impossible "to separate the fight for racial and religious rights from the fight against Communism." He declared that "one way to encourage the Indians, the Chinese and other colored peoples to fight on the side of democracy and against communism would be for the U.S. Negroes to redouble their battle against racial oppression at home." But rather than reinvigorating the movement, anticommunism seemed to be demobilizing it. Brown simultaneously issued anticommunist appeals and disparaged civil rights leaders for their fear of being labeled Communists. He called it a "national disgrace" that groups such as the NAACP were shying away "from national civil rights cases because the Communists had become interested." Councilman Brown actively participated in demonizing the left and then chastised liberals for the paralysis and inaction that this demonization had helped to create. His position illustrates the tension between liberal anticommunism and the grassroots mobilization so necessary to the civil rights struggle.[48]

"The Negro Fights to Save America" was a conference called by Adam Clayton Powell in 1952. The title reflects a significant discursive shift of the 1950s. Rather than fighting for Negro rights or to save the Constitution, the fight became one for American nationalism. Powell's political career began by leading the Harlem masses in demanding racial justice and moved in the 1950s to persuading the government that its foreign policy demanded racial equality at home. His most famous Cold War performance was in 1955 at a conference of Asian and African states in Bandung, Indonesia. There Powell told the global media that "racism in the United States is on the way out." In a statement that stunned many back home, he said, "A few years ago Washington was an open cesspool of United States democracy. . . . Today it is a place of complete equality. Every hotel, restaurant, amusement place, school and golf course is completely integrated."[49]

On October 16, 1951, when the Cold War was at its height and struggle for Negro rights in New York was under siege, the Stork Club, a fashionable Manhattan eatery that had a reputation for snubbing nonwhite patrons, mistreated the glamorous superstar Josephine Baker. The rhetoric in this story reflects the supercharged environment of the Cold War. "How can America preach democracy to the world," Baker asked, "and not be concerned with the practice of democracy in New York City, supposedly the most liberal city in the country?" Baker was dining with actor Roger Rico, a fellow fighter in the French resistance during World War II, his wife Solange, and Bessie Buchanan, reportedly Baker's ex-lover. Like Baker, Buchanan bridged the entertainment and political worlds. She had danced at the Cotton Club, appeared in the legendary Broadway musical *Shuffle Along,* and was later elected to the New York state legislature.[50]

Baker ordered a bottle of wine and a steak, which an hour later had yet to arrive. A waiter later revealed that Stork Club owner Sherman Billingsley had entered the room, seen Baker, and said, "Who the fuck let her in?" What ensued became the subject of rancorous dispute. Feeling mistreated, Baker plunged into action. Anticipating a legal challenge, she phoned Walter White from the restaurant. Baker tried ordering something else, which did arrive as she and her friends were about to leave, but it was too late. Over the next twenty-four hours, Baker and the NAACP launched a media and political campaign against white privilege at the Stork Club that reverberated around the city and the world.[51]

Josephine Baker and Bessie Buchanan may have had the flush of a recent victory on their minds. Three months earlier in Los Angeles, the two women had visited the plush Biltmore Hotel for a midnight snack. When an intoxicated white man made "loud disparaging remarks" about their presence, Baker made a citizen's arrest. A judge later fined the man, a corset salesman from Dallas Texas, $100 for disturbing the peace. "I was not acting for myself," Baker told the press. "I insisted on the arrest for the benefit of all people everywhere." Entertainers are unsung heroes of the early civil rights movement. As Black travelers, they daily confronted, and frequently challenged, segregation in transportation, restaurants, and hotels. As affluent African Americans they were often on the front lines of integrating more upscale residential neighborhoods. Baker and Buchanan broke racial barriers in the elite spaces of two major American cities.[52]

The Stork Club battle was fought, in part, in the media. Nightclubs were popular sets for radio and television shows in this era—there was a Stork Club TV show—and Walter Winchell, a powerful network radio commentator and Hearst newspaper columnist, was a Stork regular who was also present that October evening. Winchell, whose power to smear celebrities was considerable, had praised the military service of African American soldiers and saw himself as a "friend of the Negro." But he was close to both Billingsley and J. Edgar Hoover, and had become a virulent anticommunist.

NAACP official Walter White, actress Mary Martin, and others picketing the Stork Club, 1951.

Winchell was angry when Walter White tried to enlist him on their side, and he used his media outlets to ridicule the protest and, increasingly, to call Baker a Communist.[53]

Baker aired her side of the story through Ted Poston, a reporter for the *New York Post*. The first African American reporter on a major New York daily, Poston wrote evocative, powerful narratives on the postwar Black freedom struggle. Walter White appeared live on the *Barry Gray* show on WMCA, at Chandler's restaurant on the east side. "I am frightened for my country," he told the crowd of several hundred, "because an incident like this in a phony place like the Stork Club . . . smears and lowers the prestige of America all over the face of the world."[54]

The "Stork Club incident" reenergized the civil rights struggle. Baker and the NAACP filed a complaint with the Mayor's Committee on Unity, and Democrats on the City Council launched an inquiry. "I have no intention of suffering deliberate humiliation without striking back," Baker declared, as the NAACP launched a picket line in front of the club that put a dent in Billingsley's business, even inducing Mayor Vincent Impellitteri to boycott his regular haunt. Prominent New Yorkers joined the picket line, including Walter White and Thurgood Marshall, politicians Earl Brown and Herbert Bruce, and trade unionists and Broadway stars. World heavyweight champion Joe Louis pledged financial help. As the *Amsterdam News* wrote, "This thing is bigger than Josephine Baker."[55]

A behind-the-scenes controversy within the NAACP, however, was a reminder that fear of association with the left plagued reform organizations during the McCarthy era. The national staff wanted to halt picketing after three days, in order to "prevent persons from left-wing affiliations from participating," while Lindsay White, leader of the New York branch, wanted to continue. Walter White had been policing the picket line and complained that it had taken "the combined efforts of Messrs. [Thurgood] Marshall, [Henry Lee] Moon and myself as well as several other members of the staff to keep the line 'pure.'" White urged Stork regular J. Edgar Hoover to condemn racial discrimination there because it "plays directly into the hands of Communists." Hoover, who was ever suspicious of Communist involvement in African American protest, and who was searching for negative publicity to use against Josephine Baker, wrote back, "I don't consider this to be any of my business."[56]

The city wanted Billingsley to issue a pledge of nondiscrimination, but he refused. The mayor reportedly "suppressed" an MCU report criticizing Billingsley, and a furor erupted when the MCU subsequently released a statement clearing him. The NAACP called it a whitewash and continued the battle on the airwaves. In a remarkable example of how civil rights issues had penetrated public discourse in New York, Barry Gray held a three night "radio trial" with Baker, Walter White, Arthur Garfield Hays, a leading civil libertarian, and Major Jacques Abtey, Baker's commanding officer in the French Resistance.[57]

The Stork Club case left a trail of casualties. Federal authorities, with the media assistance of Winchell, pressured employers in the United States and abroad not to hire Baker. Winchell also helped destroy Barry Gray's career. He relentlessly attacked him, calling on sponsors and audience members to boycott his show, and Gray was physically assaulted twice. In this case, what went around came around; the incident precipitated downturns in the careers of both Billingsley and Winchell. But the case also left a positive legacy. In 1952, as a result of the mobilization around the Stork Club, the state passed a law that shifted the manner of combating discrimination in public accommodations from a criminal infraction to a civil rights violation handled by the State Commission against Discrimination. The case also generated international publicity, highlighting the global saliency of American racial practices in the postwar era.[58]

McCarthyism and the Cold War had a dramatic and disruptive effect on the postwar northern civil rights movement. Detroit's future mayor Coleman Young, an African American radical who suffered during the red scare, perhaps overstated his claim that the "government was unable to make a distinction between civil rights and communism." But his memory that "it was all but impossible for a black person to avoid the Communist label as long as he or she advocated civil rights with any degree of vigor" captures the chilling effect of the red scare on antiracist advocacy. While anticommunism did not create opposition to the civil rights movement, it strengthened white institutional resistance to Black demands for social change. The Cold War heightened the government's interest in projecting an image of itself as racially harmonious, and imbued the struggle for Black rights with a more America-centered rhetoric and a narrower—though for the United States, still transformative—equal rights agenda. The suppression of the left set the stage for a new Black protest paradigm in the 1960s in which the dominant polarity was defined as integrationist versus separatist or Black Nationalist. This polarity ignored those activists who embraced ideas that U.S. politics would not admit, including anti-imperialism and socialism. Leftists remained influential activists during the Black Liberation movement, although they were discouraged from identifying themselves as such. To a striking degree, activists who had been purged, harassed, or were under siege endeavored to reinvent themselves and continue in the movement.[59]

9   Racial Violence in the Free World

        Grassroots mobilizations in the 1950s against police brutality and southern racial violence were constrained by anticommunist pressures yet emboldened by the era's ubiquitous rhetoric of American freedom. Activists recognized that racially motivated bombings, beatings, murders, and lynchings posed a public relations problem for the "leader of the free world." In an effort to encourage federal action, the NAACP stressed to government authorities that unpunished racial violence hurt American credibility and undermined the fight against Communism. Leftists put the issue on a world stage. They brought charges to the United Nations that the United States was criminally culpable for systematic racial violence against African Americans, provoking outrage by U.S. authorities who feared that such an allegation tarnished their image and gave credence to Soviet propaganda.

"There was a time when racist violence had its center in the South," the Civil Rights Congress stated to the United Nations. "Now there is not a great American city . . . that is not disgraced by the wanton killing of innocent Negroes. It is no longer a sectional phenomenon." Yet would the killing of Black people by police officers in the urban North inspire the same degree of government anxiety or international condemnation as did the murder of Blacks by southern Klansmen? The answer was unclear, but African American activists in New York continued to make criminal justice reform a major component of the urban civil rights struggle. In 1953 they won the first civilian complaint review board in the nation in the wake of revelations about the New York Police Department's efforts to block federal investigations of its officers.[1]

A Very Explosive Situation

Harlem came close to a riot in December 1950 after two white police officers, Louis Palumbo and Basil Minnakotis, shot and killed an unarmed Black Korean War veteran on 119th Street and Eighth Avenue. Wounded in action, twenty-four-year-old John Derrick had been discharged twelve hours before his murder, and was still in uniform when he died. The disappearance of $3,000 in discharge pay as he lay bleeding on the sidewalk intensified community anger. The next day, a witness to the killing told a crowd of three thousand at the Golden Gate Ballroom that "John never even had a gun. He was murdered."

Derrick's death sparked a rapid mobilization of protest in Harlem. Many observers noted the irony of Derrick being wounded in Korea on behalf of his country, only to be gunned down by fellow Americans within twenty-four hours of his release. Adding to the fire was considerable discontent over the treatment of Black soldiers in Korea, who remained segregated in the Army despite Truman's 1948 executive order, and who experienced court martials and other disciplinary action dramatically out of proportion to their percentage in the military. The *Amsterdam News,* which paid for Derrick's body to be shipped home, declared in an editorial: "While there is an ounce of ink in our presses, we will pursue this case until justice is done."[2]

Ironically, City Councilman Earl Brown, the African American Democrat who had defeated Benjamin Davis a year before, was thrust into a struggle that Davis had championed. And Brown rejected any cooperation with the left.[3] Some Harlem leaders worried about Communist involvement in the fight against police brutality and endeavored to sideline radicals from the protests. As a result, ideological divisions shaped the protest, but internal tensions were somewhat offset by the widespread outrage at the city's reaction to John Derrick's death.

Republican mayor Vincent Impellitteri did not condemn the killing, offer sympathy, or display remorse. Nor did he take any action against the officers. Only the suggestion of violence induced the mayor to reassign Palumbo and Minnakotis. Reverend James Robinson, head of the John Derrick Citizens Committee, warned that "a very serious disturbance in Harlem" might result if the two police officers weren't transferred.[4] "The general lack of confidence which most of the citizens of our community have in the Police Department," Robinson said, has "resulted in the existence of a very explosive situation in Harlem." After Congressman Adam Clayton

Powell demanded that they be out of Harlem within twenty-four hours, the officers were moved. Every elected official in Harlem attended a rally at Bishop R. C. Lawson's Refuge Temple, where the bishop declared, "We want to be saved, not from sin, but from police brutality." Walter White predicted that the United States would reap "a crop of grisly bitterness from the colored people of the world" if such flagrant government racism continued. Derrick's father came up from Augusta, Georgia, to recover his son's body and plead with authorities to hasten their investigation. A photo of the victim in his casket was used to publicize the case in the mass media, as was the story of the loving son who had reliably sent money home, and who was planning to buy his family a home and car with his discharge pay.[5]

After hearing forty-five eyewitnesses, an all-white grand jury refused to indict the two officers. Earl Brown called the decision "a serious miscarriage of justice," and National Urban League President Lester Granger called the city's handling of the shooting "one of the most effective cover-up operations in local history." NAACP lawyers filed a $100,000 civil suit against the city on behalf of the Derrick family. Adam Clayton Powell requested federal prosecution of Palumbo and Minnakotis for violating John Derrick's constitutional rights. "We don't call them that, but we do have lynchings right here in the north," Powell said. "If a lynch mob can be investigated in Georgia, the murder of a Negro by two police officers in New York should be investigated." Given the great difficulty of convincing most whites to punish police officers for killing African Americans, however, a federal grand jury also declined to indict the officers, effectively ending the case. But from this point forward, the NAACP decided to appeal to federal authorities in cases of police murder and brutality in New York.[6]

Racially motivated police violence was a contradiction in the official discourse of Negro progress. It exposed the routine policing of Black physical mobility and the precarious advantage of education or affluence. After William Delany, crippled from polio, was beaten unconscious and kicked in the face on the sidewalk in front of his home on Bradhurst Avenue by white police officers in 1951, his uncle Justice Hubert Delany released a long, despairing statement about the widespread tolerance for police mistreatment of African Americans. The "police in Harlem," wrote Delany, "consider that they have the God-given right . . . to keep the peace with the night stick and blackjack whenever a Negro attempts to question their right to restrict the individual's freedom of movement." "Police brutality," he insisted, "has been the mode in Harlem for years. The nurses and staff at Harlem Hospital see the bloody results daily. No policeman in Harlem has been convicted for police brutality or murder in over thirty years of many unnecessary killings, and hundreds of cases of brutality." At the Derrick rally in his church, Bishop Lawson recounted his own family's experience with police abuse. His son, who had just come out of the Army, had been looking in the window of a jewelry store on 125th Street along with two young ministers when an officer came over and accused them of "casing" the store. As the officer was ordering the group into a taxi, he reached for his gun. The young men calmed him down and successfully defused the situation, but they all ended up in jail.[7]

In 1951, the tenth police killing of a Black male in a four-month period sparked a major protest campaign. On May 26, white police officer Sam Applebaum shot and killed Henry Fields, an African American laborer and father of four, at a busy intersection in the racially mixed Brownsville section of Brooklyn. Applebaum "rammed into" Field's car to stop him for a traffic infraction, and claimed that Fields refused an order to halt when he got out of his car—an unusual defense for firing a fatal shot. Eyewitnesses stated that Fields got out of his car with his hands raised, was unarmed, was never told to stop, and never posed a threat to the officer who nonetheless fired his gun twice on a crowded street. A large, angry crowd coalesced and police poured into the area. They enlisted the aid of the Reverend Boise Dent of the Tabernacle Baptist Church, who implored the crowd to disperse.[8]

Meanwhile, another minister, the Reverend A. A. Reeves, led a group of residents to the local precinct and demanded the arrest of Applebaum. Reeves told the police captain, "If an ordinary person shot another man, you'd arrest him in two minutes. And if a Black man did it you'd lynch him in two minutes." The first arrest in the case, however, was of a concerned citizen. The police "raided" a community meeting at a church that evening and demanded the names of the three white men present, presumably suspecting them as Communists. Police harassment and surveillance continued throughout the year-long struggle for justice in the shooting of Henry Fields.[9]

Fields's widow, Alberta, and father, Henry Fields Sr., joined local activists in forming the Brownsville Committee for Justice in the Case of Henry Fields to mobilize pressure on the district attorney, but they quickly encountered resistance. According to the July 1951 issue of *Jewish Life* magazine, some citywide leaders from liberal anticommunist Jewish groups were pressuring Brownsville Jewish leaders on the committee to withdraw because of the alleged left-wing ties of some of its members. The Fields case brought forth a surprising degree of visibility by radicals at the height of the red scare, but also an expression of fear by mainstream liberal groups of engaging in grassroots activism that they did not fully control. The Brooklyn NAACP, which had led the borough's 1949 police reform campaign, followed a new policy against joining coalitions open to left-wing activists. It announced that it would avoid "engaging in hysteria and meaningless agitation." This new approach was rewarded with effusive editorial support and greater access to government leaders. The Reverend Boise Dent and the NAACP urged the community to have faith in the criminal justice system. The *Amsterdam News* called this "a step forward for the Negro of Brooklyn," and suggested it could bring political dividends—"for without the blood and gore of red propaganda, indications are to the effect that more will be gained by the democratic approach."[10]

But the *Amsterdam News* also understood the risk that such a strategy posed, and urged the branch to be "on their collective toes so that the final conclusion will be acceptable by all people involved." Indeed, such a warning was prescient at a time when Black communities' sense of disfranchisement remained acute. In the very same issue of the *Amsterdam News,* a reader recalled the fiery leadership of Ben Davis and complained that "most of the lousy leaders we've got are so busy eating dinner with the same men who give orders for head busting in Harlem that they can't do nothing about what's really wrong here."[11]

In June an all-white Kings County grand jury heard a parade of witnesses, all African American, testify that Applebaum made no attempt to stop Fields prior to firing his weapon. Nonetheless, it refused to indict, prompting even the assistant district attorney to call it a "gross miscarriage of justice." He persuaded the judge to allow an unprecedented second grand jury presentment. But a week later the second grand jury also recommended no criminal action against the police officer. As in the Derrick case, white grand jurors evidently granted Black eyewitness testimony very little weight.[12]

NAACP activists consulted with representatives from Jewish civil rights groups from Brooklyn and Manhattan to devise a response. NAACP Labor Secretary Herbert Hill opened the meeting with a report on "the operations of the Communist Party and its affiliates in the matter, and how the NAACP successfully took the case away from the Stalinist organizations." He presented possible actions: demanding a departmental trial for the police officer, filing a civil suit, holding a public meeting to update the community, and forming a Brooklyn Citizens' Committee composed of "legitimate" groups. Hill reported with dismay, however, that "the general consensus of the Jewish organizations was that legal action should be conducted but that no future organizational activity in the Brownsville community was advisable." Hill "strongly objected" and stated his group's "obligation to report back to the community." He said this approach would leave the Communists as the "sole organizers of opinion in the Brownsville area" and he acknowledged that "this had happened too many times in the past." Hill worried about "the weaknesses of many liberal organizations functioning in the civil rights field," an ironic concern since the NAACP's own recent purge had contributed to this crisis. The Jewish groups finally agreed to participate in a Citizens' Committee, but they refused to join the proposed mass meeting. Their belief that "responsible leaders" needed to avoid activism that appeared open to leftist participation spread among mainstream civil rights leaders in the 1950s, and tended to make them move away from grassroots mobilization as a social change strategy.[13]

Meanwhile, the Brownsville Committee for Justice in the Case of Henry Fields held a "community public trial." Bishop Reginald Barrows declared that "this time the case will be presented not to a hand-picked lily white grand jury, but directly to the citizens of Brownsville, who will serve as a jury." The police harassed and intimidated the group, interrogating Bishop Barrows about the political affiliations of its members. Two whites on the committee, Terry Rosenbaum and Max Gilgoff, lifelong residents of Brooklyn and public school teachers, were threatened with dismissal by the Board of Education for alleged membership in the Communist Party. Schools Superintendent William Jansen questioned the two about their activism in the case, and demanded to know if either had ever been a member of the Communist Party. Both teachers answered no. After Judge Hubert T. Delany made "a stirring appeal" for action, a group of citizens formed the Committee to Retain Gilgoff and Rosenbaum, chaired by a Brooklyn rabbi. Gilgoff died one year later, and Rosenbaum was dismissed by the Board of Education after pleading the Fifth Amendment before a Senate Committee.[14]

The city's response to the upheaval in the summer of 1951 was to appoint an African American, William L. Rowe, to the newly created post of seventh deputy police commissioner, to act as a liaison between Black community groups and the police. The hiring of Blacks in the police department at all levels had long been a demand, but African American leaders were critical of the selection of Rowe, a syndicated theatrical reporter, over "a half-hundred Negroes who could meet all the necessary qualifications." This view reflected a broad effort to reconfigure racial politics in the city, including ending the appointment to politically sensitive posts of Blacks perceived to be accommodationist. Nevertheless, Rowe served for the remainder of the Impellitteri administration and is credited with introducing classes on "human relations" at the Police Academy.[15]

A year after the shooting, the Brownsville Committee continued to call for the dismissal of Applebaum, financial support for Fields's widow and their four children, and legislation to combat police brutality. It did succeed in getting Applebaum transferred again after he had been reassigned back to the local precinct. Alberta Fields lost a civil suit for the wrongful death of her husband in 1953; but she persisted, and in 1961, ten years after his death, she was awarded $130,000. Confronted with the intransigence of police, criminal courts, and elected officials, attorneys increasingly filed civil lawsuits against the city. According to the city's counsel, ten lawsuits against New York City for police brutality went to court in the 1951–1952 fiscal year: five were won by the city, four by the plaintiffs, while one was settled. The city paid over $200,000 in damages, but all of the accused police officers remained on the city payroll and were never charged with crimes nor subjected to internal discipline. In 1951, Earl Brown introduced a City Council bill calling for the dismissal of the police officers in civil cases that had cost the taxpayers money. "These officers must be made to learn that all Negroes are not criminals," declared Brown, expressing a concern that racial stereotyping ensnared the innocent. The bill was defeated and civil liabilities against a police officer still have no formal connection to his or her employment status.[16]

We Charge Genocide

Alberta Fields's political activism was emblematic of other African American women in her position in these years. Many female relatives of victims of police brutality or lynching traveled the country on behalf of the NAACP or Civil Rights Congress, giving speeches and raising money. Their witness was an important way of forging national networks and keeping alive stories of resistance in an era of increasing conservatism and repression. Amy Mallard witnessed the ambush-murder of her husband in Georgia in 1948, and became a national advocate for federal antilynching legislation. Rosalee

McGee toured the country on behalf of her husband, Willie McGee, who was on Mississippi's death row after being wrongfully convicted for the rape of a white woman. His case became a cause célèbre and protests from around the world flooded the governor's desk, but McGee was executed in May 1951. In the fall of 1951, a national delegation "of the wives, mothers and victims of race hatred" convened in Washington, D.C., and became part of a new Communist-supported group, the Sojourners for Truth and Justice. Reflecting the left's desire during the red scare years to project the view that the fate of civil rights and civil liberties were linked, the Sojourners advocated in behalf of Black victims of racial violence as well as Black victims of the anticommunist crusade.[17]

The Civil Rights Congress (CRC) handled McGee's case, as well as other "legal lynchings," including the Martinsville Seven case in Virginia, in which seven Black men were executed for alleged rape. Capital punishment, or "legal lynchings," had supplanted "illegal lynchings," according to the CRC's analysis of shifts in racial violence. Charles Collins led a delegation to the White House seeking a stay in the Wille McGee case. Two ministers in the group told the president's assistant, "The President should know that the church people of Harlem are aroused by the legal lynching which is about to take place in Mississippi unless the President intervenes."[18]

Rosa Lee Ingram, a Georgia sharecropper, widow, and mother of twelve, was given a death sentence after she shot her landlord in self-defense against sexual violence. The resistance by Black women to rape and sexual assaults by white men seldom received national attention. Ingram's problems started when "he told me I would not live hard any more if I would do like he said, but I did not do what he wanted me to do." One day as he was physically assaulting her, her young son hit him, and Mrs. Ingram grabbed the violator's gun and shot him. Her resistance to an attempted rape inspired an outpouring of support from African American women leaders, who established the National Committee to Free the Ingram Family, led by veteran activist Mary Church Terrell and Brooklyn activist Ada B. Jackson. Ingram's mother and sister became part of the national campaign to free her. A "Save Mrs. Ingram Committee" in New York City, headed by Audley Moore, went to Washington to appeal to the president and attorney general to save her life. Their goal was to get the case before the General Assembly of the United Nations. In the end, the mobilization helped saved Ingram's life, but she still served a long prison term.[19]

Since 1946, the CRC had been involved in legal defense work for Black

Howard "Stretch" Johnson, a former Cotton Club dancer who became a Communist Party activist, at a 1949 rally organized by the Harlem Civil Rights Congress to protest a lynching in Georgia.

victims of racially motivated prosecutions as well as the struggle against police brutality. Its encounters with institutional racism in courtrooms across
the country, and its belief that lynchings, mob violence, and police killings
met the United Nations definition of genocide (as defined in the UN Charter
as well as the Convention on the Prevention and Punishment of the Crime
of Genocide), led it to petition the United Nations in December 1951. Cold
War liberals sought to use international pressure to shame the U.S. government into self-reform. They deployed this criticism at home and generally
praised the progress in American race relations when they traveled abroad.
The left, however, used international, as well as domestic, forums to expose
what it saw as U.S. hypocrisy on the issues of democracy and freedom.

William Patterson, executive director of the CRC, defied government efforts to stop him, and presented *We Charge Genocide: The Crime of Government against The Negro People* to the UN Secretariat in Paris in December 1951.
Paul Robeson presented it simultaneously to UN officials in New York City.
The 225-page petition exhaustively documented the litany of postwar racial
abuse around the country—including 153 killings of African Americans—
and presented a legal argument that identified systematic violence and terrorism as a component of a governmental policy of subordinating a national
minority. The goal of this violence, the petition asserted, "is the splitting and
emasculation of mass movements for peace and democracy, so that a reaction may perpetuate its control and continue receiving the highest profits
in the entire history of man." The petition was covered in the African American and European presses, but ignored in mainstream U.S. media. As the
third petition to the United Nations appealing for intervention on the
grounds that U.S. racial practices violated human rights protocols, *We Charge
Genocide* was part of a broad international turn in Black protest strategies.
The "racist theory of government of the U.S.A. is not the private affair of
Americans," the CRC insisted, "but the concern of mankind everywhere."[20]

The U.S. government sought to silence this criticism and prevent leftists from traveling abroad—after Patterson deposited *We Charge Genocide* in
Paris, the State Department immediately suspended his passport. The United
States succeeded in tabling *We Charge Genocide* at the United Nations, but its
effort to persuade several Black American leaders to publicly oppose the petition produced mixed results. The State Department, according to a historian of this episode, "called on prominent African Americans to denounce
the petition as so much communist propaganda." The United States wanted
to counter this troubling narrative of American society. It saw the petition as

calculated anti-Americanism that disrupted the government's efforts to project an image of racial harmony. Howard University scholar Rayford Logan, who was in Paris representing the NAACP, resisted the government's pressure. Though he favored the NAACP's style to the more confrontational and ideological approach of the CRC, Logan believed that *We Charge Genocide* revealed the truth about racial violence in the United States. The two Black Americans in the U.S. delegation to the UN, Channing Tobias and Edith Sampson, also reportedly resented the pressure to denounce *We Charge Genocide*, although each finally spoke out against it "as an American, rather than as a Negro."

As the executive secretary of the NAACP, Walter White not only had a history of rivalry with left-led antiracist organizations, including the Civil Rights Congress, but he also was pursuing a very different strategy of racial reform. According to one historian, White "agreed unhesitatingly to denounce the petition." But his choice met with opposition from some members of the NAACP Board of Directors. Judge Hubert Delany felt that White was sacrificing the independence and integrity of the NAACP by rushing to the defense of the U.S. government against charges of abetting and tolerating racial violence. White composed an attack on *We Charge Genocide* that stressed Black progress and American democracy, and the State Department urged him to publish it in book form for distribution overseas.[21]

In Mims, Florida, on December 25, 1951, a bomb exploded beneath the bed of NAACP leader Harry T. Moore and his wife, Harriette, killing them both. With U.S. forces embroiled in a war against Communism in Korea, racial terrorism in Florida sparked a national outcry. A tireless grassroots activist, Harry Moore had led the Florida state conference of NAACP branches and had organized a Progressive Voters League that made itself a major factor in local politics. His registration of tens of thousands of Black Florida voters in the aftermath of *Smith v. Allwright* had helped destabilize white supremacist politics in Florida, and had unleashed a torrent of Klan violence. His assassination sparked protest across the country and the world, reportedly causing the FBI to embark on what was at that time its most ambitious investigation of a racially motivated murder.

The governor of Florida was deluged with telegrams and letters of protest and delegations from the North, where there were many rallies and protests demanding the arrest and prosecution of the Moore assassins. At an NAACP rally at Madison Square Garden, Langston Hughes recited a poem in honor of the slain couple. At a rally in Harlem, the generally cautious Walter

White called for a national work stoppage by the nation's 15 million African American workers to prod federal intervention.[22] At a rally in Queens, Guy Brewer of the Jamaica NAACP called for a boycott of Florida's multimillion dollar citrus industry: "We're not forced to buy Florida oranges and I do not see why we should continue doing so." At Concord Baptist Church in Brooklyn, Judge Delany denounced the FBI's obsession with rooting out "reds" while murderous bigots ran riot in the land. All of these rallies sent resolutions to the president signed by Black and Jewish civil rights groups, churches, and lawyers' organizations. Bertram Baker, the first Black state assemblyman in Brooklyn, urged Congress to see that the killers "be brought to justice and be punished." The bombings violate "every human right guaranteed by the Constitution of the United States," Baker argued.[23]

The Harlem American Labor Party held a rally at the Golden Gate Ballroom with Black United Auto Workers leader William Hood, former Congressman Vito Marcantonio, the white radical journalist I. F. Stone, Harlem attorney and political activist Jacques Isler, Rabbi Max Felshin, and the Reverend Thomas Kilgore of Friendship Baptist Church in Harlem. The Civil Rights Congress organized a delegation that reportedly became the first interracial group to confer with the governor of Florida. Charlotta Bass, publisher of the Black newspaper the *California Eagle* and the 1952 Progressive Party's vice presidential candidate, told Governor Fuller Warren that "this mounting terror against the Negro people . . . shames and discredits our beloved nation in the eyes of the world." No one was ever convicted of the murders.[24]

Up South

In the early 1950s, the city was reportedly swept by a "crime wave." In response to "a sex-crime deluge in the New York press," civil rights leaders criticized the role of the media in promoting racist law enforcement practices. In October 1952, a diverse group of civil rights, religious, labor, and civic leaders came together as the Committee against Racial Bigotry in the Press, and published a statement debunking the media-hyped "crime wave." Pointing out that statistics actually showed a decrease in the crime rate, "it is time that men and women of good will and rational minds speak out calmly and firmly against a rising crime wave hysteria which contains all the explosive sparks of racist provocation and racial tension." The long statement bears quoting at length: "We are disturbed greatly by what we feel to be a pattern of singling out of the Negro and Puerto Rican people and stigmatizing them as criminals." It accused the New York press of "using the language of the racist press of the South" and creating "a highly inflammatory atmosphere" with such terms as "a tall, powerfully built Negro" and "a Black man with ape-like arms." They declared, "We Americans of all faiths and colors . . . reject the overtones of wholesale libel against the Negro community," and, recalling how the Nazis had "incited and justified" violence against Jews by labeling them "sex-perverts," the signers expressed their fears that this current "provocation may mount to a crescendo of hate and violence" in New York.[25]

The 1952 shooting death of Enus L. Christianii, an African American graduate student at New York University, by a security guard who claimed that Christianii went "berserk," showed the urgency of this warning. Christianii got into a scuffle with a white student after he had protested a white fraternity's dart board with a racist caricature of a Black woman as the target. A married veteran attending NYU on the GI bill, Christianii was active in the NAACP and the Community Fair Employment Practices Committee, which fought both racism and anti-Semitism. He helped get Confederate flags as well as "stereotyped Jewish hooked-nose masks" removed form local stores, and joined efforts to win new jobs for Black workers. A group of students at NYU and local activists organized a campaign to pressure the district attorney to prosecute the security guard, but they do not appear to have succeeded.[26]

The postwar campaign against police brutality culminated in the early 1950s after an attempt by the New York City Police Department to evade a federal law designed to protect the constitutional rights of African Americans. In an explosive exposé, a journalist revealed that top police officials had made a "secret" agreement with officials in the U.S. Justice Department to keep the FBI from investigating charges of civil rights violations by New York City police officers. This evidently had come about because New York police officers had not liked being interrogated by the FBI for the killing of John Derrick.[27]

At a meeting with Assistant Attorney General James A. McInerny and U.S. Attorney Myles J. Lane in Foley Square in Manhattan in July 1952, First Deputy Commissioner Frank Fristensky and Chief Inspector Conrad H. Rothengast of the NYPD requested that all allegations of civil rights violations made to the Justice Department concerning the New York police be turned over to the NYPD instead, for an internal investigation. McInerny, a former police officer in a small town in upstate New York, agreed to the request. According to NAACP attorney Thurgood Marshall, McInerny "had a very bad—not a normally bad—record on civil rights in the ten years that I've had anything to do with him. He has been thoroughly uncooperative along every step of the road and has allowed the Federal Fugitive Warrant statute to be used to return Negro prisoners to southern chain gangs even after northern governors have refused extradition."[28]

A month later the police beat a thirty-one-year-old Black truck driver named Jacob Jackson. Jackson, along with his wife, Geneva Jackson, and a friend, Samuel Crawford, said they had been arrested on the west side of Manhattan because "they didn't move along fast enough." Jacob Jackson and Crawford were severely beaten in the station house: Jackson needed two operations on his skull, and metal plates were inserted in his head. All three were charged with assaulting a police officer. Edward W. Jacko, attorney with the New York branch of the NAACP, pressed the case at every turn despite repeated roadblocks and vigorous police resistance. His efforts to have the officer indicted were unsuccessful, prompting a $100,000 civil suit and a complaint to federal authorities.[29]

Reportedly, the agreement between NYPD officials and McInerny and Lane was not known by many officials in the Justice Department. After the police refused to submit to questioning in the Jackson case, Police Commissioner George M. Monaghan informed the FBI's New York chief Leland Boardman that civil rights laws only applied "south of the Mason Dixon line." Assistant Attorney General Daniel Greenberg was angered by a report on the case by Chief Inspector Rothengast that omitted the allegations of physical abuse and Jackson's hospitalization. After getting a complaint from Boardman, J. Edgar Hoover informed Attorney General James McGranery about the existence of the agreement, and on January 14, 1953, McGranery reportedly terminated it.[30]

McGranery ordered U.S. Attorney Lane to proceed with a federal grand jury investigation of the two police officers accused of violating Jacob Jackson's civil rights. Monaghan, however, persisted in refusing to allow the interrogation of his men and traveled to Washington to try to convince the new deputy attorney general, William P. Rogers, to renew the agreement. Rogers refused. Frederick Woltman reported the already widely leaked story in the *World Telegram and Sun* just as the federal grand jury in Foley Square began hearing testimony in the Jackson case. The NAACP was outraged. Ella Baker of the New York branch announced that they might seek federal action in over one hundred cases from the past thirty months. The national NAACP demanded a federal review of all cases of police brutality in the city. And Lane announced that he had turned over to the FBI twenty new allegations of civil rights violations by the New York City police.[31]

Civil rights leaders called for the dismissal of all the officials involved, especially Commissioner Monaghan. "Everyday that he's in office is a disgrace," pronounced a disgusted Adam Clayton Powell. Roy Wilkins wrote the mayor that "there are no exceptions to the enforcement of civil rights. A violation in New York is just as heinous as one in Georgia or Mississippi and New Yorkers have no right to ask exemption from general procedure under federal law." Mayor Impellitteri, however, never removed Monaghan, who denied under oath that there was ever a pact, despite written evidence to the contrary.[32] In response, a broad group of civil rights, religious, and labor leaders called for a series of reforms, including the creation of a board "independent of the police department" to review all charges of police brutality, indictments and speedy trials in pending cases, and a city investigation of the police department. Activists also called on the police department to spell out its mysterious disciplinary procedures and issue explanations of how it handled cases of police misconduct.[33]

At Congressman Powell's urging, New York Republican Kenneth Keating of the House Judiciary Committee held hearings on the alleged agreement. Assistant Attorney General Daniel Greenberg testified that he had allowed Monaghan to conduct his own investigation in the Jackson case after Monaghan personally informed him of the "agreement" and complained of the low morale of his officers. But Greenberg termed the NYPD report "a complete whitewash." McInerny told the Keating Committee that the arrangement was an "experiment" that he did not regard as an "agreement." Police Commissioner George Monaghan denied making the agreement, calling it "a lie, an outright lie." And the Policemen's Benevolent Association testified before Congress that "Communists used violations of human rights charges to drive a wedge between the police and the FBI."[34]

In his testimony, Walter White told Congress that "the most consistent fight against police brutality has been made by the NAACP and other non-Communist groups," and to suggest otherwise "gives undeserved credit to the Communists." But Ella Baker countered the tactic of the Policemen's Benevolent Association more directly: "No communist plot can explain away the fact that Jacob Jackson had to undergo two brain operations . . . , nor does it explain how other able-bodied persons have walked into police precincts, but had to be carried out as hospital cases." As this drama unfolded in New York and on Capitol Hill, the fate of Jacob Jackson became a powerful reminder of how entrenched police power remained. Despite eyewitness testimony and Jackson's severe physical injuries, a federal grand jury refused to indict officer William J. Brennan. Moreover, it refused to undertake a review of other allegations of police brutality in New York City. Finally, the Jacksons themselves had to face assault charges. After deliberating for ten minutes, a three-judge panel found them both guilty. The NAACP called the outcome "unthinkable" and filed a $100,000 civil suit.[35]

In July 1954 the Keating Committee released its report. While the headlines declared "Monaghan Denounced for Improper FBI Deal," the report characterized the whole affair as a case of poor judgment by an overzealous police commissioner that did little damage and apparently violated no one's civil rights. "The truth about this matter is not as distressing as the initial charges," it determined, and "little practical harm seems to have flowed from the episode." City leaders endeavored to limit the fallout from the scandal and created an all-police Civilian Complaint Review Board in 1953. In a signal of the department's intentions, Monaghan appointed to the board First Deputy Commissioner Frank Fristensky, one of the two police officials who had made the secret agreement with the Justice Department. He was now put in charge of precisely the type of investigation that he had sought to block.[36]

The problem of the police attempting to police themselves was immediately criticized. Saying there was "nothing civilian about it," Councilman Earl Brown called the board "the same old system with a new coat of whitewash." The struggle to staff it with civilians remained a demand for the next forty years, was achieved briefly in 1966 (only to be repealed by referendum), and won again during the administration of David N. Dinkins, New York City's first African American mayor. The early civil rights movement made aggressive efforts to have police officers subject to the same criminal law as other citizens, but they encountered intransigent opposition.[37]

During the 1950s, public discourse in the United States was saturated with celebrations of American freedom and moral courage in opposing totalitarian tyranny. Civil rights leaders understood the power of this propaganda to raise the expectations of American and international audiences. Their appropriation of Cold War rhetoric put pressure on government leaders (and the public) to confront the contradiction between American claims and the violent reality of white supremacy. Northern civil rights activism in the first decade after World War II stimulated a national awareness of racial violence and a willingness to protest that was to become especially manifest after the 1955 murder of Emmett Till, a fourteen-year-old Chicagoan, in Money, Mississippi. The interest in the Till case by northern Black politicians and major media outlets, and the agency of Till's mother and uncle in seeking justice, built on, and reflected, strategies in earlier struggles.

The grassroots struggle for police reform stands as an important historical backdrop to the landmark U.S. Supreme Court rulings of the 1960s that restrained police behavior and expanded the rights of an accused person in state criminal proceedings. Expanding the rights of the accused was a major goal of the northern civil rights movement. Finally, securing federal intervention in cases of police brutality was also a hard-fought victory of the civil rights movement. As Walter White emphasized to the Keating Committee, "The experience with the New York Police Department demonstrates the need for strong and vigorous enforcement of federal civil rights laws in the north as well as the south." But while winning broader authority for federal action has been important, new rules have not by themselves sparked federal action. Urban uprisings, grassroots protest, and political pressure have played critical roles in triggering federal prosecutions. The tradition of local autonomy for law enforcement and the nation's long history of racialized policing have proved powerful and enduring.[38]

10 Lift Every Voice and Vote

The struggle to increase Black representation in government achieved some significant victories in the early 1950s. As the American Labor Party weakened, African American political activists created nonpartisan, community-based organizations in their effort to advance Black interests and candidacies.

Activists critiqued the racial gerrymandering of election districts and emphasized the right of Black communities to be represented by African American officials. They insisted that the right to vote meant the right to be represented, an idea that the federal Voting Rights Act of 1965 and its subsequent revisions would embody. At one million, the Black population in New York State was the largest in the country, but African Americans were underrepresented in city, state, and federal offices. A further hindrance to realizing greater Black representation in New York was the city's division into five boroughs, each with its own president and Democratic Party machine. The struggle for Black empowerment in New York entailed a series of separate struggles in the boroughs of Brooklyn, the Bronx, Manhattan, and Queens. Moreover, the city's growing Black middle-class neighborhoods in Queens were spatially and politically cut off from the largest Black neighborhoods in Harlem and Bedford-Stuyvesant. This political and residential landscape of discrete Black constituencies distinguished New York from cities such as Chicago and Detroit, where Black populations were more concentrated in one location. Independent Black electoral organizing faced major obstacles, including a Cold War climate of fear and conformity and a Democratic Party machine widely viewed as corrupt and linked to organized crime. Looking back at the 1950s, J. Raymond Jones, himself a former leader of Tammany Hall, concluded that "bosses, scoundrels and near criminals" ran the Democratic Party in New York City. Still, third-party Black candidacies and grassroots activism laid the groundwork for the election of several Black "firsts" in the early 1950s. But as the decade progressed, Black electoral activism, along with the postwar civil rights movement as a whole, declined.[1]

The salience of civil rights issues in the 1948 presidential election was mirrored locally in the 1949 municipal elections. The mayoral race featured a left-wing third-party challenge to the Democratic incumbent, but unlike President Harry Truman, Mayor William O'Dwyer was not associated with major civil rights initiatives, and indeed, was vulnerable on such issues as Stuyvesant Town and police brutality. With Cold War tensions escalating and the convicted Communist Party leader Ben Davis running for City Council reelection, accusations of Communism and red-baiting permeated local political discourse. The Democrats repeatedly called the American Labor Party a front for the Communist Party, a charge with much merit because the CP helped finance the ALP and shape its policy stances. But the CP also had to negotiate its goals with noncommunists in the ALP, including the formidable mayoral candidate Congressman Vito Marcantonio. Marcantonio deflected the damaging charge of Communist (and therefore Soviet) influence by emphasizing the ALP's attachment to the very indigenous and local struggle of Black civil rights. When O'Dwyer blasted the ALP as Communist controlled in a speech in Harlem, Marcantonio pounced. "Is it communism when we of the American Labor Party nominate a Negro for borough president in Brooklyn, Mrs. Ada Jackson, and in Manhattan, Ewart Guinier?" "Our fight," the charismatic congressman declared, "is for equality, for housing, rent control, for an end to Jim Crow in any manner, shape, or form . . . So you call the fight for equality communism. The mere fact that you call this communism proves that you are against it." In a similar vein, ALP candidate Manuel Medina said in a radio conversation with Ewart Guinier, the party's nominee for Manhattan borough president, "I understand, Ewart, that O'Dwyer regards the idea of a Negro being Borough President as communism." "O'Dwyer," Guinier added, "also regards our determination to bring back the five cent fare as being communism."[2]

The ALP nominated Black candidates in a variety of races in 1949 and became the first major party to nominate an African American for Manhattan borough president. Attorney Hope Stevens, who chaired Ewart Guinier's campaign committee, predicted that the race "would put an end to the lily-white standards of other political parties which have long denied the Negro people of New York representation in our city government." Guinier, a Harvard-educated immigrant, promoted a policy agenda that was pro-urban,

Ewart Guinier, American Labor Party nominee for Manhattan borough president, 1949.

prolabor, and antiracist. In addition to a vote on the Board of Estimate, which had authority over land use and the city budget in this era, the Manhattan borough president employed a staff of one thousand and issued permits and contracts to private contractors. Guinier vowed that "no firm will do business with the city of New York unless that firm has fair employment practices" and no permits would be issued to housing developers "unless they agree to rent those apartments to all regardless of race, color or creed." His platform reflected the various struggles of the New York civil rights movement: jobs for all; an end to police brutality and discrimination in housing; an inclusive, bias-free curriculum with schools "free of witch hunts"; and for Harlem, a public market and more schools, hospitals, and libraries.[3] Guinier lost, but as the candidate of a left-wing party under attack, he won an impressive 38 percent of the vote. As one news story put it, "Sooner or later, when and if a Negro candidate for public office continues attracting 100,000 votes in Manhattan as Guinier did, there's going to be a day of reckoning."[4] Marcantonio also lost, but came in a respectable second in Harlem. The election results indicated that an insurgent party, even one labeled un-American, could appeal to Blacks and other voters when the major parties were perceived as unresponsive to their interests.

The election of a Black judge to New York City's highest court in 1950 was widely hailed as a major civil rights breakthrough, and while party leaders essentially selected the nominees to this court, grassroots activists played an important role in mobilizing pressure on Tammany Hall. The Democrats had promised to nominate an African American to the Court of General Sessions, "one of the best salaried judicial positions in America," ever since the previous election. Guinier and Marcantonio repeatedly reminded Harlemites of this promise and raised it on the radio, in newspapers, and at rallies. Within the Democratic Party, Ray Jones maneuvered to get Tammany chief Carmine De Sapio's backing for his choice, Harold Stevens, and Stevens got the nomination, hailed as the "highest political achievement a Negro has reached in modern U.S. history." The highly regarded attorney won the boroughwide election and began an ascent within the New York judiciary.[5]

Harold Stevens was born on a thousand-acre farm on St. Johns Island, South Carolina, that the family lost when he was three years old. During Reconstruction, his grandfather attended the University of South Carolina, but was expelled by Governor Wade Hampton, who vowed that no Black person would ever graduate from college in his state. Harold Stevens was inspired to go to law school after learning about the lynching of a Black woman and her two brothers. He came North and worked his way through college and night law school as a painter, bricklayer, tobacco picker in Connecticut, bell hop, and resort waiter. Stevens converted to Catholicism while at Boston College Law School, and like other prominent Catholic converts of this era, he devoted his life to bringing his liberal social consciousness into the Catholic Church. During the war Stevens brought cases of discrimination before the FEPC, placing himself directly into the struggle for Black workers' rights. A. Philip Randolph and a host of dignitaries came to his swearing-in ceremony to honor this new $28,000-a-year judge.[6]

Like some other Black achievements in the 1950s, the Stevens election was hailed as an American victory in the Cold War. Randolph called it a beacon "at this time when the forces of democracy are in deadly combat with the totalitarian Russian Communist forces of the world." The *Amsterdam*

News said "the nomination of an outstanding Negro lawyer for a high judicial post is a strong argument against those who would attempt to use the Negro for their own ulterior motives in order to destroy democracy." Adam Clayton Powell, however, used this triumphalist discourse to assail the Jim Crow South. The Stevens election was a victory for civil rights in the North, he declared, in sharp contrast to "the many places in our land where democracy is only lip service. But here in Manhattan we have made democracy flesh and blood."[7]

Black activists used a third-party strategy to pressure the Democrats to nominate an African American to the state bench. In 1950 Harlem attorney Jacques Isler became "the first Negro to be nominated to the State Supreme Court." He ran on the ALP line. His fifteen-year legal career had earned him a "qualified" rating by the Bar Association—a fact that his supporters frequently pointed out to counter Democratic Party claims that there were no "qualified" Black candidates for the Supreme Court. Ewart Guinier stressed the larger import of Black representation, saying Isler's effort would "enhance our fight for an unbiased, unbossed judiciary where Negroes can expect justice." Isler lost that election, but garnered close to 100,000 votes. A year later, he attempted to get the Democratic nomination for the same post. A flier titled "An Appeal to Negroes" asked Harlemites, "Is it fair? . . . that the 68 Justices of the New York Supreme Court are all white?" . . . that 500,000 Negroes in Harlem, and 150,000 in the Bronx, are not represented in the highest court in our State?" "Lift Every Voice," the flier urged, invoking the Negro National Anthem to underscore the campaign's connection to the civil rights struggle. An ideological cross-section of Black leaders ran Isler's campaign, including Carl Lawrence of the *Amsterdam News,* the Reverend John Saunders of Convent Avenue Baptist Church, businesswoman Natalie De Loache, Charles Collins of the ALP, as well as a realtor, an Elks Club leader, an attorney, and a Republican Party leader. The Democrats failed to nominate an African American, however. Once more Isler ran on the ALP line, and lost the election.[8]

Activists seeking Black representation developed new strategies as the American Labor Party disintegrated under the enormous weight of anticommunist repression as well as the escalating suspicion of Soviet influence on American left-wing formations. They launched nonpartisan campaigns premised on racial identification, rather than ideological identification, in the hopes of fostering Black unity and challenging the white-dominated Democratic machine. This shift represented a convergence of thinking by Black activists both inside and outside the left. In the wake of Henry Wallace's 1948 defeat, the Progressive Party formed the National Committee to Elect Negroes to Public Office, with Thelma Dale, a former National Negro Congress official, as the secretary. They made the election of Black officials—regardless of party—the overriding goal. Their rationale stressed that increased African American representation in government would slow the rightward drift, revive liberalism, and strengthen respect for constitutional liberties. "Every step taken to increase Negro representation in public office is a forward step not only for the Negro people but for our entire democracy," asserted their mission statement. Guinier argued that Black representation, of whatever party, would hasten the fight for peace, weaken white supremacy, and promote democracy. W. E. B. Du Bois repeatedly sought to draw attention to the disparities in the prevailing electoral system: four million southern Blacks and six million southern whites had been disfranchised by the poll tax alone, while seven poll-tax states combined had one million fewer voters than the entire state of California. The Black left's focus on the lack of political freedom in the United States contradicted the government's claim to be the leader of the free world, but it offered racial justice as the way to make that claim meaningful.[9]

The effort to elect a Black state senator from Harlem, which had begun after the war with Charles Collins's ALP candidacy, succeeded in 1952. Activists used community mobilization, publicity, and the threat of insurgency to pressure the Democrats to nominate a Black candidate in the twenty-first senatorial district. Jacques Isler convened a seasoned group of activists, including Guinier, Carl D. Lawrence, the Reverend James Robinson, other Harlem ministers, and insurgent Democratic leaders such as Robert Blaikie and Darwin Telesford, and formed the Committee for the Election of a Negro State Senator. Isler himself was set to run, but when the Democrats nominated an African American, Julius Archibald, the committee endorsed him. Archibald's campaign embraced the civil rights and social democratic agenda that had become a hallmark of Black politics in the city. He called for rent control, state-supported day care centers "for children whose mothers must work," increased state aid to housing and slum clearance, increased welfare, and unemployment and social security benefits. He also called for "wider narcotics control" but emphasized treatment and care for juveniles.[10]

An Archibald flier reminded Harlemites of the southern voting rights struggle in order to encourage a large turnout: "This is Harlem's opportunity to show the Negroes of the disenfranchised South the value of their continued fight for the free exercise of the right to the ballot." Archibald's plea was answered and he won, becoming the first African American state senator in Albany. He was one of about fifty Blacks elected to office across the nation in 1952. In 1954 Tammany Hall refused to renominate Archibald, allegedly because he was too independent of party control. In his place, they chose Black Democrat James L. Watson, son of the late municipal court justice James S. Watson.[11]

In May 1953, on the initiative of Ewart Guinier, activists from the state senate campaign formed the Harlem Affairs Committee (HAC) to "sparkplug" a campaign for a Black borough president. A nonpartisan though left-leaning group, HAC aimed to mobilize Black voting power. Its slogan—"Good Government, Absolute Equality, Full Employment"—illustrates that a progressive platform accompanied its call for Black representation. HAC was a Black-led movement, but it was open to whites who believed in "absolute justice for people regardless of race, color or religion." As an antidote to the Democratic Party's often vague rhetoric of inclusion, HAC issued specific goals and demands. It wanted a Black borough president; a Black Supreme Court Justice; a Black council member from the twelfth assembly district—"meaning we're entitled to two councilmen"—and it wanted it "understood in advance that Harlem expects a full commissioner and four deputies from the next mayor." HAC's leader, Robert Justice, emphasized the economic benefits of winning a Black borough president. A "community's business and job importance is directly related to its political influence," he said, noting that the office "directs the spending of millions, supervises the activity of 1,000 employees, and indirectly influences the hiring of thousands in private industry."[12]

The American Labor Party nominated Andronicus Jacobs, a longshoreman involved in the struggle for racial equality on the waterfront, for borough president of Manhattan. The Republicans nominated Commissioner Elmer Carter of the State Commission against Discrimination, reportedly after clearing his selection with President Eisenhower. (At a HAC dinner in Harlem, a Republican Party leader acknowledged that HAC deserved credit for inducing the Republicans to nominate an African American.) The Liberal Party ran the veteran activist James Robinson, minister of the Presbyterian Church of the Master. After every other political party on the ballot had put forth Black candidates, pressure intensified on the Democrats. An unusually high percentage of the first African Americans elected to political office on the Democratic line in New York were Catholic. Irish Catholics wielded considerable power in the New York Democratic Party. Walter Gladwin, just elected as the first Black assembly member in the Bronx, had converted to Catholicism. Democratic assembly member Hulan Jack was a Baptist who also had converted to Catholicism. Powell called him "a political Catholic." And many believed that religion explained the selection of Judge Stevens, also a Catholic convert, over Vernon Riddick, a strong Black Protestant candidate for the Court of General Sessions.[13]

The Democrats nominated Hulan Jack but a breakaway faction in the Democratic Party nominated another Black candidate, making the election for Manhattan borough president an unprecedented contest among five Black candidates. This was a significant achievement of the postwar Black rights movement and testified to its many years of grassroots organizing. Ewart Guinier saw the election as a coming-of-age moment—a turning point in African American political history. "Negro America," he wrote, "has come to consider itself not so much a minority but part of the two-thirds of the world which is non-white." A major daily, however, sounded a note of resentment. The *New York Post* described the all-Black field as "segregation in reverse." But as Guinier noted, "They were never dismayed up to now at the lily-whiteness of the Board of Estimate."[14]

Tellingly, most of these candidates had roots in the Popular Front. The long-standing racial barriers in the two major political parties had given the left a prominent place in Black politics. "It was the thing to do," former mayor Robert Wagner recollected. "In the course of the campaign, one of the candidates, I don't know whether it was Hulan, or the Republican or Liberal, accused one of the others of being members of Communist organizations when they were younger, and no question, this fellow was a member. But they found out that all three of them had been members—it was the thing to do in Harlem at that point." Wagner added that he "didn't think any of these fellows were Communists," and probably did not know what the Communists stood for apart from being "against the Establishment."[15]

Hulan Jack won the election and became the first African American borough president of Manhattan. Born in St. Lucia to a Garveyite father who moved the family around the Caribbean and British Guyana, Jack came to New York in his youth, became a citizen, and set his sights on politics. As a state legislator from Harlem during the 1940s, he introduced many civil rights measures. Never a radical, he nonetheless participated in the Popular Front politics that were the order of the day. In 1949 Jack joined other Harlem legislators in voting against the Feinberg Act, the law that barred members of "subversive organizations" from holding civil service jobs. But three years later, when the Communist left had been more fully redefined as disloyal, Jack introduced an amendment to the penal law that imposed new constraints on the free speech rights of members of "subversive organizations." He was reportedly seeking to make the Golden Gate Ballroom in Harlem, the site of numerous political rallies and meetings in the community, off-limits to groups associated with the Communist Party. As borough president, Jack eschewed an activist profile and was widely seen as a faithful party regular. According to Anna Arnold Hedgeman, a Black Democratic Party activist, Jack believed that his election was due to Tammany Hall leaders. "During his first days at Borough Hall he had said that Negroes did not elect him and was reported to have added that he did not intend to make an 'Uncle Tom's Cabin' out of the Manhattan Borough office. This infuriated Negroes, for every other ethnic group finds ways to give its own 'a break.'" In 1960 Jack resigned after being convicted of accepting an illegal gift—a contractor had redecorated his apartment.[16]

In Brooklyn, third-party candidacies and insurgent political organizing were used to challenge white domination in the major parties. In 1949 NAACP attorney Lewis S. Flagg Jr. ran for municipal court justice on the American Labor Party line. "Emissaries" from the two major parties paid him a visit and urged him to withdraw. "They do not want a Negro elected to the bench," Flagg concluded. "They feel that if a Negro is elected as Judge, that Negroes will later demand to have Negroes as state senators, councilmen, congressmen, and district leaders in Brooklyn." The most prominent Black attorneys in Brooklyn supported Flagg, despite his association with a party accused of Communist domination.[17] He lost the election, but four years later he tried again with the aid of a citizens' committee that became the Bedford-Stuyvesant Political League (BSPL). Like the Harlem Affairs Committee, the BSPL represented a new paradigm for Black political organizing after the decline of left-wing organizations. It was founded and led for many years by the legendary Brooklyn politico Wesley McD. Holder. Holder had gotten his start in politics by managing the 1935 campaign for Kings County district attorney of Samuel Leibowitz, the lawyer who represented the so-called Scottsboro Boys, but after World War II, he devoted his energies to increasing Black representation and political clout in Brooklyn. Until its dissolution in 1965, the BSPL brought together a politically diverse group of activists dedicated to this cause. Its formation was sparked by the Democratic Party leaders' selection of a white attorney from outside a district that included Bedford-Stuyvesant to fill a vacancy on the Municipal Court, an all-white court of forty-nine jurists. The campaign to win the Democratic nomination for Flagg attracted support from virtually every prominent African American civil rights, religious, political, and civic leader in Brooklyn, including Myles A. Paige, the borough's first appointed Black jurist, Herbert T. Miller of the Carlton Avenue YMCA, ministers Milton Galamison and Boise Dent, and political leaders Maude Richardson and Clarence Wilson. Their efforts paid off, and Black Brooklynites defeated the machine. Holder credited the hard work of Anthony Tully, a Black ALP activist, for securing the victory, which after Bertram Baker's election to the state assembly in 1948 was the second Black electoral breakthrough in the borough. Like the Harlem Affairs Committee (HAC), the BSPL aimed to alter the Black community's relationship with the Democratic machine. It projected a new independent paradigm, demanding that its votes be rewarded with jobs and power. The BSPL demanded two Black district leaders, two assemblymen, one state senator, one city councilman, a county judge, and a supreme court justice.[18]

After becoming the first elected Black judge in Brooklyn, Lewis Flagg reportedly faced pressure to sever ties with the radical organizers who had helped put him in office. Flagg, a principled and committed attorney, had also represented a popular Bedford-Stuyvesant teacher who was fired for insubordination after she had refused to name names during the Board of Education's witch hunt. According to the "Uptown Lowdown" column in the *Amsterdam News,* "friends" were "urging Brooklyn's newest jurist to stay away from the Leftist crowd." During the McCarthy era, newspaper columnists sometimes served as conduits of political control and economic sanction. Flagg's quandary was doubtless faced by others in this era, since many future Brooklyn (and Manhattan, Queens, and Bronx) Black leaders had roots in the left.[19]

In the south Bronx, where the ALP had been running Black candidates for office since the war, civil rights activists were striving to build a progressive Black-Jewish electoral alliance to exert pressure on Ed Flynn, the powerful but conservative Democratic Party boss, to nominate an African American to the state assembly. In 1953, under pressure from an NAACP political action committee and the Protestant Council of Churches, the Democratic Party nominated Walter Gladwin to represent the seventh assembly district in Albany. Once represented by the ALP's Leo Isacson, the district was 45 percent Black, 40 percent Jewish, and 15 percent Puerto Rican. Gladwin supported low-income housing, more schools, the restoration of rent controls, and the abolition of the Transit Authority. He won by a landslide, becoming the first Black elected official in the borough.[20]

African Americans in the predominantly white borough of Queens did not elect one of their own until years after Harlem, Central Brooklyn, and the South Bronx, although activists began the quest for Black representation after the war when a trade unionist had run for City Council on the ALP line. But as elsewhere in the city, there was a move in the 1950s toward nonpartisan efforts with the goal of Black representation. Activists in southeastern Queens—reportedly "the fastest growing Negro community in America"—began to set their sights on a state assembly seat. In 1951, Guy Brewer, Alphonse Heningburg, Emory Hightower, and Catherine Basie formed the Non-Partisan Citizens' Committee for Reapportionment to pressure politicians to give Queens Blacks a voice in government. Heningburg called the fight for "political autonomy" for African Americans "the most important issue that has confronted this community."[21]

In 1954, Joselyn Smith, an attorney with the Jamaica NAACP, ran in the Democratic primary for state assembly on a platform that exemplified the rising income and expectations of the borough's growing Black population. He called for better schools, health facilities, and investigations of racism in home mortgage practices, taxation rates, and the licensing of building contractors. According to Hugh Mulzac, who had run in 1949 as the ALP nominee for Queens borough president, white Democratic leaders sought to mobilize an anti-Black turnout by distributing racially inflammatory bulletins to whites in the community. In any event, Smith lost the race, but took 40 percent of the vote. Finally in 1964, with the election of Kenneth Brown, Queens became the fourth New York City borough to elect an African American to the state assembly. When Brown ran for a judgeship 1967, Georgia-born Guy Brewer replaced him as state assemblyman. Brewer's Democratic club became a center of Black politics in Queens for decades and Jamaica Avenue, a major Queens thoroughfare, was later renamed Guy Brewer Boulevard. Ironically, it runs past a park named for Brewer's NAACP nemesis Roy Wilkins.[22]

In 1954, despite the undeniable achievements of Black mobilization, Black New Yorkers continued to be underrepresented at all levels of government. One million of the 14 million people in New York State were Black. Ten of the 189 judges in the city were Black, but the State Supreme Court was all white; one of fifty-eight state senators and five of 150 assembly members were Black; and there was still only one African American on the twenty-five-member City Council and only one in the forty-three-member New York congressional delegation. After the borough president campaign, HAC shifted its focus to state politics and vigorously promoted the goal of electing an African American to statewide office. Labor was demanding one of their own on the ticket; so were feminists. "Needless to say," HAC declared, "they're talking about white men and women. Nobody has mentioned statewide representation for the Negro or Puerto Rican communities yet. Isn't that some Kind of Jim Crow? . . . Let's demand a BETTER DEAL NOW." As it argued in a letter to "Mr. and Mrs. Harlem," "money and the ballot are the only things that count in our society. Both represent power, but since we have so little money as a group, about the only thing left for us is the right to help vote public officials in and out of office."[23]

The Harlem Affairs Committee stepped up pressure to include African Americans in policymaking roles in the powerful agencies of the state government. HAC tried to revive major party competition for the Black vote by pursuing Republican as well as Democratic support for their demands. They informed the liberal Republican senator Irving Ives that the "Harlems of New York" want "one of their number" on each of the state agencies for housing, banking, and insurance "for the purpose of a better deal in getting housing accommodations, mortgage loans, and all kinds of insurance protection." HAC leader Robert Justice reminded Ives that eight Black former assemblymen, all Democrats, frustrated by being "completely ignored during the past twenty years" by their party, had endorsed him for the senate. Justice even promised Ives an endorsement should he be the Republican nominee for governor. This level of alienation between African Americans and the white Democratic Party leadership in New York adds context to Adam Clayton Powell's endorsement of Republican President Eisenhower in 1956.[24]

The Democrat Averill Harriman won the 1954 gubernatorial race and the state house returned to Democratic control. By HAC's estimate, Black voters provided Harriman with his margin of victory and deserved recognition and respect. The group urged the inclusion of African Americans at all levels of state government. "Harlem elected Harriman," Harlem NAACP president Russell P. Crawford told a HAC forum. Justice and Crawford telegrammed the new governor-elect on behalf of twenty-two Harlem organizations urging the appointment of a Black secretary of state.

Several Harlem activists, including Justice, Crawford, Harlem Mortgage

Conference representative Olivia Frost, and HAC's executive assistant Ewart Guinier, met with the Harriman official in charge of appointments to lobby for firm commitments. He promised that one of the eight aides to the governor would be Black and that there would be a Black appointee to a policy-making post in the State Division of Housing. (Robert Weaver received this appointment, on his way to a cabinet post in the Johnson administration.) He also agreed to consider a list of names of "qualified Negroes" for each of twenty positions in the banking and insurance departments submitted by the Harlem Mortgage and Improvement Council. A month later the governor-elect issued a public statement that expressed the clash between the reality of group power and the illusion of colorblind individual opportunity in the United States: "I intend to name many Negroes to my administration, but I will not take the question of race into consideration."[25]

The emphasis by HAC on the issue of representation encouraged an examination of the status of women in politics and society. The topic at one of its monthly forums in 1954 was Black women in public office. "Harlem has sent 40 different Negro men to public office, . . . but no woman has ever been elected," a HAC flier announced. Black women were major participants at every level of political organizing, except the highest, and in fact outnumbered men in four Harlem assembly districts. Women were more visible in clubs, professions, civic groups, even the church, than in politics. Cora T. Walker, president of the Harlem Lawyers Association, encouraged the group to take up the issue directly: "Our women should be in elective office here. And this should be our responsibility—women and men." One male responded, "I think a woman's place is in the home." The problem with women in politics, he explained, was that a female politician would inevitably get married and have children, and then "where would you be?" A woman replied, "The same thing has been said about women in law, in medicine, in everything else and we have disproved it." Another man called such ideas "pretty advanced," and said they hadn't yet "penetrated down to the rank and file." Cora Walker suggested running a female candidate around the theme of a Black female "first" just like the successful borough presidency race. But Walker, a Republican, also stressed that education was the main way to change men's attitudes and improve women's opportunities. A male in the group disagreed, however, observing, "No in-group has ever given up anything important to an out-group without a struggle."[26]

In 1952, the Progressive Party nominated a Black woman for vice president, in part as a tribute to the achievements of women's political organizing in the 1940s. Thelma Dale, the party's associate director, had written to Paul Robeson urging that they nominate a woman, and she suggested Shirley Graham Du Bois, but Charlotta Bass from California got the nod. In 1954 the Democrats nominated Bessie Buchanan from Harlem to run for a seat in the state assembly. News accounts mistakenly described Buchanan, a former Cotton Club dancer who had joined Josephine Baker in the Stork Club battle, as the first Black woman to be nominated by the New York Democratic Party, but she was the first elected.[27] She went to Albany, but ten years passed before another Black woman, Shirley Chisholm from Brooklyn, was elected to the state assembly. Ada B. Jackson and Maude Richardson had paved the way for Chisholm, who would make an insurgent bid for the Democratic Party's presidential nomination in 1972. In 1962, NAACP attorney Constance Baker Motley became the first Black woman elected to the New York state senate. Two years later she was elected as Manhattan borough president, and two years after that, she became the first African American woman appointed to the federal judiciary.[28]

A Democrat, Robert F. Wagner Jr., was elected mayor of New York in 1954. Pledging to appoint African Americans to important posts, he won the majority of Black votes. But after his first fifty top appointments did not include a single African American, his uptown supporters mobilized and expressed their displeasure at being taken for granted. Wagner quickly appointed Anna Arnold Hedgeman as a mayoral assistant, "the first Negro in a policy making position in City Hall." Hedgeman, a little-heralded member of the first generation of national civil rights leaders, was a political ally of A. Philip Randolph. She had run the Committee for a Permanent FEPC in Washington after the war, but later had moved back to New York and devoted herself to the Democratic Party.[29]

On the eve of its dissolution, the ALP printed a booklet assessing the state of Black representation in New York. "Negro Representation NOW!" explained that while New York City was 11 percent Black, African Americans only had one-half of 1 percent of elective and appointive positions. This supposedly liberal beacon, the city with the largest Black population in the nation, was behind Chicago, Cleveland, Cincinnati, Philadelphia, and even Nashville in some measures of Black representation. Despite the significant Black political mobilization that the ALP had helped enable since the war, this activist tract aimed to stress the continuing underrepresentation of Blacks in order to make the case for greater change. The booklet's title was an implicit critique of gradualism. As a left-wing political party facing government repression, the ALP's challenge to the Cold War message of racial progress can be seen as ideologically driven. Yet it resonated with the growing sense in Black New York communities that the state's new antidiscrimination laws and the Democratic Party's ostensible embrace of civil rights were failing to produce demonstrable change. African Americans in the mid-1950s felt that progress was too slow and the racial contradictions in the nation's proclamations of freedom were too glaring.[30]

The postwar civil rights struggle demonstrated that activism made a difference in electoral politics. "Intense struggle for small gains," is how one activist many years later described the postwar era. This diminished sense of achievement, however, reflects the frustration engendered by persistent white resistance as the 1950s progressed. A third party had dramatically revealed Black voting strength and sent a strong message to the Democratic Party. With the demise of the ALP and the decline of Black registration in the Republican Party, the Democratic Party became the primary site of Black political aspirations. African American political activists adapted quickly to this new political terrain, forming community based, nonpartisan groups that helped elect African Americans to several offices that the ALP had first targeted in the 1940s. The growing conservatism and demobilization of the 1950s, however, undercut the grassroots activism and party competition that had been crucial to these electoral breakthroughs. White Democratic Party leaders continued to resist Black efforts to win their fair share of urban power, exposing a gap between the party's rhetorical embrace of civil rights liberalism and its practice of white racial privilege. Twenty-five years separated the election of New York City's first and second African Americans to Congress. In fact, it would take a lawsuit filed under the federal Voting Rights Act to end the racial gerrymandering that had long prevented Black Brooklynites from sending one of their own to Congress. In 1968, Shirley Chisholm would become the second Black New Yorker elected to the House since Powell took it by storm a quarter of a century before.

11 Resisting Resegregation

Housing and school segregation in New York City increased during the 1950s and 1960s—a period, paradoxically, when civil rights ideology was advancing throughout the United States. Federally financed urban redevelopment and suburbanization vastly increased residential segregation in New York, as well as the nation, while the manipulation of zoning lines and other policy choices by the Board of Education helped ensure that schools hewed to the racial geography. Importantly, the creation of the biggest federal welfare program in the United States—government subsidy for homeownership—preceded the northern and southern civil rights movements and the passage of antidiscrimination laws. "American apartheid," ironically, was a New Deal program.

While the spread of racial segregation in the metropolitan North has been documented, the story of Black resistance and attempts to shape the urban landscape in their own interest has been neglected. Black New Yorkers fought for better housing both inside and outside so-called ghetto areas. Rather than integration per se, they sought unrestricted access to capital and residential space—in other words, to the economic opportunities of first-class citizenship. Civil rights leaders believed that halting the spread of segregated living patterns was essential to the realization of other civil rights victories. After the landmark *Brown* school desegregation decision in 1954, Walter White announced that housing discrimination would be the primary focus of the national civil rights movement.

The fair housing laws won during the New York civil rights movement were hailed as major breakthroughs, but the state's lack of enforcement made them virtual dead letters. Activists exposed the contradiction between the government's liberal rhetoric and its laissez-faire behavior, but they faced powerful institutional resistance to residential integration. Ideological tensions polarized housing activists, but their differences were exacerbated by the fallout from a reform gone sour, as the Housing Act of 1949 came to be seen as a weapon against the poor. The Black middle class managed to gain access to new neighborhoods, but the losses in these battles set the stage for the urban rebellions of the 1960s.[1]

"Negro Removal"

Stuyvesant Town was a harbinger of the demographic effects of slum clearance and urban redevelopment. Title I of the Housing Act of 1949 authorized an unprecedented uprooting of hundreds of thousands of people from their homes; for some, moving into modern, well-maintained public housing was a step up, but many others suffered declining fortunes, moving to areas that quickly became congested. In New York, as elsewhere across the country, reformers had initially supported this massive infusion of federal funds to private developers as a means of improving the urban housing stock. But contrary to expectations, the money solidified or shored up ghetto lines by destroying poor or working-class communities in prized areas and building either housing too costly for the original residents or nonresidential structures.[2]

In 1949, the New York State Committee against Discrimination in Housing (NYSCDH) warned that urban redevelopment "can be used to build shiny new ghettos . . . or it can be used to build new neighborhoods, comfortable and available to all alike." A year later Frank S. Horne, a Black official in the Housing and Home Finance agency, warned that the Supreme Court's refusal to review Stuyvesant Town had emboldened private interests "in their refusal to play ball on a mixed basis." He told a gathering of housing advocates that "minorities legitimately fear that the program will be used to further contain them and in many instances to push them out of areas where they are now living." Horne shared the prevailing response of civil rights groups to this dilemma: win state and local antidiscrimination provisions and legislation to make up for Congress's refusal to include such provisions in the Housing Act.[3]

Radicals and liberals were divided over the best tactics to use to make urban redevelopment equitable, but as charges of racial and class discrimination grew, they parted company on whether to support the program at all. High profile organizations such as the NYSCDH and the national NAACP pressed their reform agenda on various state actors, while radicals—tenant leaders, Communists, Black nationalists, and others—organized at the grassroots to halt what they increasingly saw as resegregation. There were some exceptions to this division. The Bronx Urban League, a liberal group operating at the grassroots, became a major advocate for displaced tenants in the Bronx. But in the main, liberal housing advocates focused on making Title I less disruptive and more orderly, while criticizing the left's efforts to halt slum clearance.

For example, in 1952 and 1953 three middle-income projects in Black and Puerto Rican neighborhoods in upper Manhattan threatened to displace tens of thousands of people, at a time when the Eisenhower administration was beginning to slash public housing funds. Public housing was often promoted as the safety net for displaced slum dwellers, so federal cuts signaled a crisis in the relocation of evictees. Radicals and grassroots leaders mobilized against these projects. The American Labor Party said Title I gave "profiteers public slum clearance funds to make Manhattan into an 'exclusive' middle-class island." The liberal housing groups, for their part, called for the postponement of the projects until the city had created a central relocation agency, which it later did. Ira Robbins of the Citizens' Housing and Planning Council (CHPC) warned housing officials that Moses's stewardship was jeopardizing Title I and opening the door for Communist manipulation. The NAACP and New York Americans for Democratic Action joined the CHPC in complaining to the mayor that the ruthless operation of Title I, and the suffering and displacement that it caused, created fertile ground for "Communist dominated groups." During the civil rights era, liberals repeatedly warned elites that radicals would gain in popularity should their own more moderate proposals be rejected. In this case, the liberal groups invoked the fear of Communism in part to strengthen their own position with the city.[4]

Four neighborhood-based groups formed the United Committee to Save Our Homes and sued to halt the projects, on the grounds that they had failed to provide for tenant relocation as required under the law. Democratic city councilman Earl Brown, who, like many liberals, was a supporter of both fair housing and urban redevelopment, called the group "controlled completely by Communists . . . who are thoroughly organized to stop any and all kinds of housing." Brown saw the left as too adversarial. But the NYSCDH realized that if it abandoned the tenants, "we will have failed to assume responsibility for one of the city's most serious minority housing problems." Ultimately the NYSCDH, NAACP, Citizens' Housing and Planning Council, and Americans for Democratic Action joined the call for postponement of the projects, but Moses prevailed and the Board of Estimate approved them.[5]

The progressive dismay over race and class bias in urban redevelopment would only grow, notwithstanding the advantages that these projects brought to their middle-class residents. In 1956, the State Commission against Discrimination estimated that about 400,000 persons had been displaced in New York State urban redevelopment, about half of whom were Black or Puerto Rican. A 1961 report found that "the net result of some of these projects planned and completed under the hectic and sometimes chaotic Title I program has been the transfer of slums to adjoining areas." By coming to call urban renewal "Negro removal," many African Americans implicitly suggested that this outcome was perhaps the intention of many planners from the start. Ted Poston later identified Title I as a cause of the 1964 Harlem Riot, because it had uprooted Blacks from neighborhoods where they "had lived peacefully for generations" such as Manhattan's west side and lower east side, and sent them uptown. The disruption caused by Title I generated a broader movement that mobilized to block some future slum-clearance projects. In the meantime, gaining Black access to existing middle-income projects became the next battle.[6]

Move-ins

Activists during the New Deal and postwar civil rights movement won city and state laws against housing discrimination, including the Brown-Isaacs Law, the Wicks-Austin Law, and the 1938 Public Housing Law, which covered privately owned "limited dividend" projects. But in the 1950s, neither the state nor the city administrations actively enforced them. A 1952 *Amsterdam News* survey found that of the 23,000 apartments in publicly assisted private housing, excluding Riverton, only twenty-seven were occupied by Blacks, and twenty of these were in one development, the Queensview Houses. Only four of these twenty-two publicly assisted private developments had Black tenants, and three of these were sites of bitter conflict. Robert Moses tried to suppress a controversial report on Title I by the City Planning Commission in 1953 that found that despite the laws, "Negroes and Puerto Ricans are virtually banned from most of the city's redevelopment projects and many other tax supported dwellings."[7]

Activists used direct action, or "move-ins," in at least ten projects to initiate integration, just as they had done in Stuyvesant Town. In 1952 Edward and Carmen Strickland were ordered evicted from Knickerbocker Village, a privately owned, tax-exempt development on the lower east side, where they had moved in two years before as "guests" of a white tenant. The Knickerbocker Village Tenants Association, with support from the Civil

Rights Congress and activists in the Stuyvesant Town battle, appealed to the state for help. Housing Commissioner Herman Stichman declared the eviction lawful; granting the Stricklands a lease, he claimed, would "discriminate" against whites on the waiting list. The Stricklands lost their appeal in court, and Adam Clayton Powell denounced their eviction as an "an act of retaliation" against "their courageous fight," but city marshals removed them anyway. In the wake of their eviction, Commissioner Stichman announced that Knickerbocker Village would soon accept Black applicants. Later that year, four African American families moved in, ending eighteen years of racial exclusion. According to activists at Knickerbocker, their efforts had a wider effect: "In Hillside Homes—Bronx, Boulevard Gardens—Queens, and no doubt other limited dividend projects, Negro families have for the first time been granted leases as a direct result of the campaign waged here."[8]

A similar desegregation-by-sublet drama unfolded in the all-white Bell Park Gardens cooperative housing project, which had been built for veterans in 1949 in Bayside, Queens. The credit agency that investigated prospective cooperators made racial notations on their applications. The pastor of a nearby African American church reported that three parishioners had applied: two were quoted exaggerated prices, and one "was told flatly that he would not get to live there because his people were not wanted in that neighborhood." Bell Park Gardens rejected an NAACP request to review their applications, but a group of residents formed a Committee for Brotherhood in Bell Park Gardens to "further the pattern of inter-racial living."

In 1951 a white tenant at Bell Park Gardens subleased an apartment to a Black family, who were welcomed at a reception of over one hundred families. The board of directors abruptly changed the subleasing rules to preclude this desegregation tactic. They restricted the ability to sublet and closed the waiting list to public inspection. Milton Kaufman of the Committee for Brotherhood was three times refused permission to sublease, so in August 1952 a Black family, Mr. and Mrs. Joseph Wright and their three sons, moved into his apartment as guests. The landlord issued eviction notices to the Wrights and Kaufman, and their struggle to stay became a public issue. The Jamaica NAACP and Queens Urban League spoke out against the eviction, but Republican housing commissioner Stichman again denied the existence of racial discrimination and upheld the landlord's right to evict them.[9]

Even though the NYSCDH and other leading liberal organizations did not encourage direct action, these "move-ins" involved them as brokers. Algernon Black, who was a veteran of Popular Front organizing, tried to persuade the Mayor's Committee on Unity that the sublets were an understandable response to the state's failure to do its job. The ten "move-ins" in the past year, he argued, were all "aimed at fair housing practices." While acknowledging that they were illegal "from a strict interpretation," he insisted that they could not "from a moral point of view be completely condemned." To "take the ground out from under such tendencies," Black recommended that real estate interests and private developments "adopt a democratic tenant policy" much as many employers had adopted fair employment practices in consultation with the State Commission against Discrimination.[10]

Unsubsidized private housing developments, which were not covered by civil rights laws, soon became sites of grassroots fair housing struggles as well. The most famous battle to integrate a private apartment development was at the Metropolitan Life Insurance Company's Parkchester in the Bronx. Its 12,500 units made it the largest housing project in the world, yet its private security force was known to keep Black people off the premises of the complex entirely.[11] In 1950 a group of left-wing and liberal tenants formed the Committee to End Discrimination at Parkchester. Fair housing activists were very interested to show that racial prejudice was not inevitable, in order to counter the housing industry's common claim that white attitudes drove their segregation policies. They conducted a petition drive to demonstrate support for the admission of Black residents, just as the tenants had done in Stuyvesant Town. In July 1952 a member of the committee invited a Black couple, the DeCauters, and their two children to live in her apartment in this mini-city of nearly fifty thousand whites. Met Life promptly issued an eviction notice. The DeCauters fought the eviction for almost a year and garnered considerable community support.[12] A Popular Front–style group called the Bronx-Wide Committee for Integrated Housing, which was composed of forty-eight organizations including churches and the Bronx branches of the NAACP and the Urban League, supported the Parkchester struggle. African American residents displaced from a nearby slum clearance site also leafleted and picketed when Met Life refused to accept their applications. Oliver Eastman, the Bronx NAACP president, threatened a boycott of the world's largest insurance company until "we remove from our own life every vestige of the pernicious doctrine of white supremacy."[13]

The DeCauters lost their battle in court, and their supporters staged a large protest on the eve of eviction, hoping to win a last-minute reprieve as in Stuyvesant Town. Five hundred people attended a testimonial dinner where messages of support came from Representative Adam Clayton Powell and from federal court judge J. Waties Waring of South Carolina, whose antisegregationist rulings had made him a hero among civil rights activists. Mrs. DeCauter became a visible leader in the fair housing struggle. Insisting that the "issue of discrimination in Parkchester must be fought boldly," DeCauter and six other "mothers" from Parkchester chained themselves inside Met Life headquarters during a meeting with Vice President Frank Lowe. But racial discrimination was lawful at Parkchester—unlike Stuyvesant Town it was wholly privately owned, and Met Life successfully carried out the eviction. A news photo showed a city marshal and several police officers breaking down the barricaded door and cutting through an iron chain to evict the DeCauters, while arresting two protesters for disorderly conduct.[14]

The "incident" at Parkchester, which Hortense Gabel of the NYSCDH blamed on "irresponsible groups," nevertheless had the effect of pulling the liberal housing lobbyists into the direct action struggle. Gabel worried that the Parkchester activists "were confusing a large part of the public and winning substantial support" by "exploiting a real issue." In June 1953, she suggested that a group of moderate fair-housing advocates confer with the owners of large developments. She made the case that this "pragmatic" approach would undermine "radical action." Met Life executive Frank Lowe responded that "sooner or later" Parkchester would admit Blacks, but that they did not want to appear to be capitulating to the tenants' movement. Lowe said Met Life was "tired of being singled out" and had done more for Blacks "than any other insurance company." But he agreed to a meeting in 1954, with Gabel and representatives from "eight of the most responsible human relations agencies in New York City." Little came from this gathering, but the determination of civil rights activists to press on, despite the conservatism of the era, led to the passage in 1957 of the first fair-housing law in the United States covering private developments. True to Met Life tradition, however, Parkchester did not admit a Black tenant for five more years. By the 1960s and 1970s affirmative action–style approaches to filling vacancies in large middle-income projects would emerge as another solution to the challenge of desegregating all-white spaces.[15]

Prejudice, Private Capital, and Our Own Government

In the 1950s the fair housing movement increased its efforts to make the American dream of home ownership available to African Americans. It set

out to defeat the use of tax revenue through the Federal Housing Administration (FHA) to subsidize white outmigration and the equally formidable
power of banks to use mortgage financing as a stranglehold on Black mobility. Racial discrimination was still not illegal in the private sector, and it
flourished in the purchase and lease of homes and apartments. In 1954 testimony to the City Council in support of a bill barring discrimination in private homes financed with FHA loan guarantees, Hortense Gabel called New
York "the most segregated city in the nation and growing worse."[16]

Levittown, the all-veteran housing development on Long Island that
became a symbol of the mass marketing of suburbia and of the ordinary
worker's access to a middle-class lifestyle, was off-limits to Black Americans.
A clause in the lease for rental properties read, "The tenant agrees not to
permit the premises to be used or occupied by any person other than members of the Caucasian race." It was the largest government-aided low-cost
housing development in the country, containing ten thousand homes, a
small number of which were leased. Organized protest commenced soon after Black veterans were told that no homes would be sold to them. American Labor Party, NAACP, and Civil Rights Congress activists asked the FHA
to deny mortgage insurance for Levittown, since "Levitt is using federal aid
and assistance for an unconstitutional purpose." A group of white residents,
Black ministers, trade unionists, and activists from the Long Island branches
of all the major civil rights groups formed the Committee to End Discrimination in Levittown and vowed to defeat segregation. Their poll of Levittown
showed that 61 percent of residents favored admitting Blacks, once again illustrating the fair housing movement's contention that exclusion was not
required to make a profit.[17]

On the original leases for rental property at Levittown, Black people were
prohibited from being on the premises, even as guests. In 1950, in light of
Shelley, the FHA began to request the removal of restrictive covenants in
new deeds, and it instructed Levittown to remove racial language from its
rental properties. But while the FHA focused on removing the overt language of racial exclusion, it did not otherwise monitor racial discrimination
and continued to guarantee mortgages with covenants in older deeds. Indeed, the FHA never rejected a mortgage from Levittown for reasons of racial discrimination. In a clear signal of his commitment to his original policy,
William Levitt refused to renew the leases of two families, one who had violated the racial policy by hosting an interracial play group, and the other for
simply being sympathetic neighbors. The NAACP defended the tenants by

arguing that the Fourteenth Amendment took precedence over landlord-tenant provisions of the common law. In an amicus brief, the American Jewish Congress likened Levittown's use of the courts to enforce its racial policy to the unconstitutional use of the courts to enforce racial covenants. It also appealed to the court's responsibility to address "the dangers to our democratic way of life arising from racial residential segregation."

A Conference to End Discrimination in Levittown at Hofstra College in June 1951 drew tenants from Parkchester and Stuyvesant Town, Guy Brewer, UE Local 1227 and the Inwood, the Long Island NAACP, and Judge Delany, who gave the keynote address. The *Amsterdam News* argued that residential segregation was "a challenge to decency in American Life, a negation of the Constitution, and an affront to that large and increasing body of U.S. citizens who want to see democracy a living quality in our country." The Nassau County Supreme Court upheld Levittown's right to not renew a lease, and the appellate division affirmed the ruling in 1951. But just as in Stuyvesant Town, Parkchester, and several other projects, activists turned the eviction into a civil rights protest. The Adolph Ross family vowed to stay until "the Levitts sign their first lease with a Negro family." The night before the scheduled eviction, Brooklyn Dodger baseball player and integration activist Jackie Robinson attacked Levitt at a protest rally sponsored by the National Conference of Christians and Jews. The next day, February 19, 1952, four hundred supporters gathered at the Ross home to await city marshals, and Levitt finally backed down.[18]

In 1952 William Cotter, an African American and head of the Committee to End Discrimination in Levittown, along with his wife and children, had managed to gain occupancy of a home at Levittown, but were evicted thirteen months later as "undesirable" tenants under the Civil Practices Act. As the landlord's attorney told the judge, race fell in the category of acceptable landlord bias, beyond legal scrutiny: "If we don't like the color of your necktie, we don't have to rent to you." One hundred Levittowners filled the courtroom in support of the Cotters, who were represented by Calvin Cobb, the first Black member of the Suffolk County Bar Association, but they lost. Although a white homeowner later sold William Cotter a home at Levittown, both direct action and legal action failed to bring more meaningful change.[19]

The spread of developments such as Levittown intensified outrage at the use of tax dollars to subsidize white social mobility and acquisition of equity. At the NAACP's 1952 convention, Roy Wilkins issued a blistering attack on what he identified as the culprits: "prejudice, private capital, and our own government." The "government is using our tax money to grind us into the ghetto," he declared. The NAACP emphasized the government's culpability, and in a 1953 memorandum concluded that housing discrimination was "effectuated by *administrative* action under sanction of the *Federal Government* itself." The NAACP analysis of the political economy of housing discrimination refuted the propaganda associating race, rather than market manipulation, with relative values. The "exclusion of Negroes from large sectors of the housing supply creates an economically discriminated market" that gets less value for its housing dollar "at every level of income." The inevitable overcrowding in Black communities then "falsely identifies race as the cause of neighborhood deterioration."[20]

The effect of FHA policies combined with discrimination by banks and builders was profound. In the mid-1950s, the National Committee against Discrimination in Housing reported that 50 percent of all new construction was covered by FHA or Veterans Administration mortgages, but only 2 percent of this was available to nonwhites, most of which was in the South. "American cities," it warned, "are being ringed around by a vise of all white suburbs built with FHA and VA assistance." A New York City study revealed that of a total of 82,846 rental units with FHA insurance built between 1946 and 1952, only 893—or about 1 percent—were occupied by nonwhites. As Charles Abrams wrote in a scathing assessment of the FHA in 1955, it was the "first time in our national history that a federal agency had openly exhorted segregation." Abrams blamed the federal government for "the dissemination of racial and religious bias to homeowners," which "created a neighborhood climate often bordering on hysteria." "If FHA policy did not sanction violence, it inspired it," he argued. This critique of government maintenance of the ghetto, written the same year that Abrams assumed the chair of the New York State Commission against Discrimination (SCAD), coincided with the beginning of the southern civil rights movement. Civil rights groups sought to end FHA discrimination by passing city and state legislation. In the early 1950s the NAACP, American Jewish Congress, and other groups followed the strategy used to win SCAD: they introduced a bipartisan bill sponsored by an upstate as well as a downstate legislator to create a commission to study housing discrimination—a commission that would hopefully lead to passage of a law barring discrimination in the private sector. Algernon Black recalled years later that these efforts suffered from "the dominant McCarthy atmosphere," the power of the housing industry in the Republican controlled legislature, and the spread of propaganda associating integration with violence.[21]

Democratic Party support on the City Council however, helped lead to passage of the Sharkey-Brown-Isaacs Law in 1954. The first law of its kind in the nation, it barred discrimination in all future private multiple dwellings (three or more units) built with government guaranteed mortgages. A year later the state's new Democratic governor, Averill Harriman, signed a similar law that covered developments of ten houses or more. Drafted by the American Jewish Congress for the New York State Committee against Discrimination in Housing (NYSCDH), the new law meant that "there cannot now be another Levittown in New York State." If enforced, the law promised dramatic change. Reflecting the sense of momentum created by early civil rights milestones, Urban League president James Felt hailed it as "a natural extension of the recent Supreme Court decision ending segregated public school education."[22]

Banks, in addition to the government, white homeowners, and realtors, created and maintained the institutional foundation for white residential privilege. A bank was not prohibited from making mortgage-lending decisions based on race. The fight against redlining—a name derived from the bank's continuing practice of keeping maps on the racial composition of communities and drawing Black or mixed areas in red as bad investments—was a central component of the New York City civil rights struggle. The federal consent decree of 1948 had dissolved the Mortgage Conference of Greater New York and enjoined the member institutions from conspiring to discriminate in the future. As Charles Abrams observed, however, "There was nothing in the judgment to prevent any savings bank from acting entirely on its own in refusing to lend mortgage money to Negroes or Spanish speaking persons or refusing to lend money on real estate located in sections occupied predominantly by such people."

To break the mortgage freeze and help the city's expanding Black working class purchase homes, a group of thirteen leading Harlemites founded the first Black-owned and operated savings and loan association in New York. On January 5, 1949, Carver Federal Savings and Loan Association opened in Harlem, with assets of $225,000 pledged by eight hundred Harlemites. Carver focused on serving the neglected financial needs of Black New Yorkers and met with steady success. Fifty years later, Carver Bancorp Inc. was the largest minority-owned bank in the nation.[23]

Several times after the war, African American state legislators, usually in conjunction with a civil rights organization, introduced legislation barring discrimination in mortgage lending. In 1947 the Committee on Law and Social Action of the American Jewish Congress sponsored a bill, and in 1949 such a bill was among the first drafted by the newly formed NYSCDH. Moreover, Black leaders launched a full-scale exposé of the near total denial of mortgage loans on Harlem and Bedford-Stuyvesant properties. This fight by Black property owners to strengthen the economic foundation of their community illustrates that gaining access to white towns and neighborhoods was not the only goal of the housing struggle in New York. Harlem leaders strove to lead their community's economic renewal even as the city's financial and political institutions undermined their efforts. The Harlem Mortgage and Improvement Council conducted an investigation of lending practices in Manhattan during the postwar real estate boom that revealed that Harlem had received a pittance in home loans from 1945 to 1950—a period with the highest volume of lending in the city's history. Banks lent less than $1.5 million, or only thirteen new mortgage loans each year in Harlem, at a time when 550 loans were paid off, returning over $10 million to the banks. Bank officials could offer no "business or economic reason why loans are not made in the Harlem area," and even acknowledged that foreclosure rates were lower there than in other parts of the city. Calling this "policy of containment" "a wicked act, an economic crime against the people of Harlem," the council vowed to defeat it. Its revelations, at a time when large areas were being labeled as slums for purposes of eviction, clearance, and then redevelopment by powerful developers, give weight to their allegation of "containment."[24]

Like the goals of the Harlem Affairs Committee, a key political goal of the council was Black representation in the councils of power. Council members advocated that a Harlem representative be included on the board of directors of every major financial institution, and urged Governor Thomas E. Dewey to appoint an African American to the banking board of New York State. The group called on the City Council, which had already announced an investigation of speculators and landlords in "so-called slum sections," to include mortgage lenders. G. T. Davis, the council's president, called speculators "the chief exploiters," but viewed the systematic abandonment of Black areas by banks as the "root of the problem." In 1954 white upper Manhattan state senator Joseph Zaretzki repeatedly voted against bills authorizing the establishment of city bank branches outside the city. Since "these banks made their money in New York City and are partially responsible for the slum conditions," he demanded that they grant mortgages "between 96th Street and 165th Street." In 1954 the City Council passed a resolution calling for a state investigation of mortgage lending practices in predominantly Black areas of metropolitan New York. The Harlem Mortgage and Improvement Council launched a "crusade" to mobilize pressure on the legislature. It won the support of every major Black institution in New York—including the Baptist Ministers Conference, Harlem Tenants' Council, National Association of Negro Real Estate Brokers, Harlem Lawyers Association, NAACP, and a group called Southerners for Civil Rights in the North and South.[25]

Realtors were another culprit in segregating the metropolitan landscape. The 1948 National Association of Real Estate Boards listed "madams, bootleggers, gangsters, and Negroes" as "blights" that realtors should keep out of "respectable" neighborhoods. In fact, until 1950, the association's code of ethics required realtors to keep minorities out of new neighborhoods. And real estate textbooks across the country instructed several generations of realtors that Black people depressed property values. In 1953, an angry "Lucille D." complained in a letter to the *Amsterdam News* that realtors pulled down the for-sale sign on "new homes in Flushing, lovely ranch houses in Jersey, tidy bungalows near College Point" when a Black person arrived. "Is this New York or Mississippi?" she asked. One study of suburban New York in the 1950s identified forty-six different techniques used by Euro-American real estate agents to exclude Black families. Realtors also engaged in "blockbusting," fomenting white hostility to Black newcomers in order to encourage hasty home sales at below market prices. Then the realtor could take advantage of the limited choices of Black home buyers and resell the house for a handsome profit. In 1953, the pro-integration St. Albans Civic Improvement Association charged that "unscrupulous Long Island real estate brokers" have sent literature with anti-Black messages to white homeowners in this mixed area urging them to move to "more suitable accommodations."[26]

Government, banks, and realtors endeavored to lock African Americans into overcrowded, deteriorating racial ghettos, but Black New Yorkers, with better jobs and rising incomes, set out to improve their housing opportunities across the city and region. While class status doubtless improved one's options, it was not sufficient to defeat racial discrimination. In 1951, Stanley Nelson, a dentist living in Harlem, engaged in an extensive, fruitless search for an apartment on Riverside Drive in upper Manhattan. He was rejected with comments like, "We rent to Spanish, Puerto Ricans, Jews, and Italians, but not to Negroes," or sometimes with a door slammed in his face. Black seekers of housing faced not only institutional obstacles, but also resistance from their white neighbors. Surveys of white attitudes toward civil rights initiatives in the postwar era consistently showed greater white support for desegregated workplaces and schools than desegregated residential communities. Even among liberals there was less enthusiasm for residential desegregation. In 1951, the American Jewish Congress concluded that the battle to pass a broad fair housing law was so difficult because housing discrimination was "part of an economic structure which is hard to change piece by piece" and because it was simply "too popular." After an upstate tour, an NYSCDH activist reported that the idea of a temporary commission to investigate private housing discrimination "met with some hostility" by "some of the very people" who had supported laws targeted at public and publicly assisted housing.[27]

Violent white resistance to neighborhood integration was not as prominent in New York City as it was in Detroit or Chicago. This was due, in part, to the low level of homeownership by white workers in New York. In 1950 only 8 percent of the dwelling units in the city were detached single-family homes, compared to 17 percent in Chicago, 48 percent in Detroit, and 54 percent in Los Angeles. Nevertheless, the threat of violence enforced neighborhood borders, and occasionally exploded into open aggression. A Black couple faced "threats and insults" when they moved into a predominantly white neighborhood in Flatbush in 1949. When a Black woman on Sullivan Street in Greenwich Village complained to the police about the repeated breaking of her windows, and suggested in frustration that she might have to move, the officers said, "Maybe you should." Mr. and Mrs. Richard James bought a Bronx house despite repeated telephone threats that "somebody would get hurt."[28]

Long Island was the scene of fierce white hostility. African Americans had long lived on Long Island—they were primarily service workers who had been segregated into the least desirable sections. But the struggles to expand Black employment opportunities and the growth of the defense and aircraft industries on Long Island produced a demand for housing that threatened the all-white packaging of suburbia. In Freedom Acres in Babylon, one of the first suburban housing developments expressly marketed to Black home buyers, arsonists set two fires in backyard sheds and slipped threatening notes under the doors of new Black residents.

In 1953, the home being built by Clarence Wilson, a Brooklyn hair care products manufacturer, in Copaigue, Long Island, was twice set on fire. "The Ku Klux Klan No. 39" sent him and the Amityville NAACP threatening letters warning Blacks to stay out of the area. Then the Underwriters Association abruptly announced that no bank was able to issue a mortgage on his $17,000 ranch house. To assess the temper of his future neighbors, Wilson attended a meeting of the Deauville Gardens Community Association. He was welcomed with a barrage of insults. Wasn't he "smart enough" to notice the racial covenant in the deed when he purchased the home? a white woman asked. Other whites at the meeting warned that if African Americans moved into the area, property loss and interracial marriage would surely follow. One man reportedly boasted that "they had spent a lot of money to keep Jews out and they weren't going to let Negroes move in."

A survey by the New York City branch of the Congress of Racial Equality (CORE) found fifteen white neighbors opposed to the Wilsons' moving in, eleven not opposed, and five who refused to talk. CORE nonetheless concluded that their attitudes seemed malleable and could change after a positive personal experience with integration, in contrast to the "hysterical hostility which marked the Cicero [Illinois] situation in 1951." Meanwhile, however, Wilson had to go overseas to Lloyd's of London to secure a loan. But after losing the fire insurance on his house and finding it impossible to purchase some anywhere else, he was forced to sell. He sold the home at a loss, a decline in the value of his property that was caused by white racism rather than integration. Wilson called his rout from suburbia "a nasty development in one of the states supposed to show a liberality toward Negroes." While he lost this battle, the publicity in the case brought Wilson other offers, and pushed Long Island NAACP branches to get more involved in the housing struggle.[29]

The growth of racial segregation in the 1950s did not keep Black residential options from expanding. From 1940 to 1950 the earnings of Black workers tripled, with a substantial number meeting the income eligibility of home ownership suggested by the FHA. They gradually gained access to more residential space, although the initial homesteading of the city's Black working and middle classes proceeded on a segregated basis. A 1953 issue of the real estate journal *House and Home* acknowledged that the postwar building boom had so far ignored African Americans, "the nation's newest middle class," but predicted that the industry's desire to maintain a high level of demand would push it to address minority housing needs.[30]

Black home purchases in the neighborhoods that would anchor the city's

Black middle class over the next several decades took off in earnest in the 1950s. Southeastern Queens would become home to the largest Black middle-class community in the United States. The FHA reported a doubling of minority applications from New York City in 1953, and pledged to ease Black access to private homes, doubling to ten the number of "race relations" advisors in its employ. Former national NAACP official Madison Jones became the FHA minority affairs administrator for the New York area, creating a direct link to local civil rights leadership. The *Amsterdam News* reported an "explosion" of home buying by Blacks in Queens in the mid-1950s—in Hollis, St. Albans, Springfield Gardens, Jamaica, and South Ozone Park. They reported that it took about three years for a neighborhood to change complexion—white families with young children were the first to move, while older families stayed longer.[31]

Greater violence in "border" neighborhoods was forestalled, in part, by the fact that whites had the opportunity and inducement to move farther out in the suburbs. In the public discourse, whites were increasingly presented with two alternatives—the "safety" of segregation or the inevitable racial discord and conflict wrought by integration. Indeed many politicians invoked the fear of violence to justify their continuing opposition to fair housing legislation. Civil rights leaders, however, continually asserted that segregation caused violence. They advocated another scenario—planned, encouraged, and supported neighborhood integration. While the government never attempted to realize this scenario, some individuals did. In 1953 Neville B. Lake, a Black silkscreen worker and writer, moved with his wife and three sons into an all-white section of St. Albans, Queens. Immediately, Lake noticed "For Sale" signs pop up all over the neighborhood. He mailed letters to his white neighbors complimenting their basic acceptance of his family in the neighborhood, pointing out that in other parts of the country they would be beaten, bombed, or even killed. He urged them not to "run madly from their homes," but to stay and help build "a shining example of racial amity, instead of another of America's shameful scars which your leaving will make it." Many whites left, but others began putting "Not for Sale" signs outside their homes. Hundreds contacted Lake and praised his leadership. A year later many of these families formed the Interracial Brotherhood Council of Hollis and St. Albans to promote stable neighborhood desegregation.[32]

Black newspapers in the 1950s exploded with advertisements aimed at Black home buyers offering "inter-racial homes" that promised "a bright decent environment" to raise children. Some suburban developments were built explicitly for Black occupancy. In 1950, a Long Island builder announced he would construct Ronek Park in North Amityville, the first large-scale nondiscriminatory community of affordable homes. He planned to build from one to two thousand homes priced at $6,990 each with thirty-year mortgages and no down payment for veterans. Mirroring the demand at Levittown, the first model ranch house in Ronek Park drew eight thousand people on one Sunday alone, creating traffic problems of "unprecedented proportions" and drawing a police detail. The NAACP, American Veterans Committee, American Jewish Congress, and American Jewish Committee presented an award to the builder, Thomas Romano, in "recognition of his contribution toward breaking down discrimination in housing." This new housing was marketed to an audience heretofore excluded from the public image of the American Dream. An ad for another development, Freedom Acres near Babylon, declared triumphantly, "Yes, Mr. Wage Earner . . . now you can realize those dreams of orchards and gardens of your own with plenty of wide open spaces for the children to grow up like red-blooded Americans, instead of living dangerously on the hot streets of the city."[33]

Thus, by the mid-1950s, the Black middle class and working class gradually began to spread from Harlem, South Jamaica, and Bedford-Stuyvesant to areas that either became resegregated over time or began as predominantly or exclusively Black areas. Ten years after the struggle "to wipe out slums" commenced, however, a majority of the city's African American population still remained confined to poor and underserviced neighborhoods. Civil rights groups were increasingly caught in the bind of demanding new low-rent housing, while at the same time attacking the growing "ghettoization policy" of public housing. In 1955, 78,000 families or 300,000 people lived in seventy-four public housing projects in New York. About one-third were Black. The Eisenhower administration had slashed funds for low-rent housing and imposed income caps on residents, a change that SCAD opposed as threatening its future racial balance.[34]

Despite the law against FHA discrimination, the vast majority of new private housing was being built for and sold to whites. In 1956 the NYSCDH estimated that only about 1 percent of *new* housing in the state was available to nonwhites. Activists responded by redoubling their efforts for a comprehensive fair-housing law. The NYSCDH, Urban League, NAACP, American Jewish Congress, several Black churches, a local CORE branch, Representative Powell, and baseball great Jackie Robinson joined forces to fight for a broad fair housing law. "We had a lot of opposition to it," Mayor Wagner recalled years later. "Real estate interests, from home owners to apartment owners—you know, investors, bankers, because this was going to ruin the real estate market here, you know. And disrupt the whole structure of the New York we used to know." In 1957, the City Council passed the Sharkey-Brown-Isaacs Law barring discrimination in the sale or rental of privately owned housing, but real estate industry pressure led to its being substantially watered down—it was filled with arcane procedural requirements that were designed to make its enforcement difficult, and it was restricted to developments of ten or more homes. Nevertheless the law was hailed as a major political victory and Democrats in the city congratulated themselves for bucking powerful vested interests. "The federal government was way behind," Mayor Wagner recalled. "We were the first governmental agency, the City of New York, in the United States, to pass any such law."[35]

Activists were acutely aware of the profound consequences of housing segregation for the success of the civil rights movement as a whole. In 1950, Robert Weaver, a leader of the National Committee against Discrimination in Housing, a group spawned by the NYSCDH, foresaw the conflicting trends in federal policy. He predicted that the fight against segregation in the schools would become "academic" unless integrated neighborhoods resulted from the government's slum clearance program. In 1954, in the wake of *Brown v. Board of Education*, the Harlem Tenants' Council wrote to the state legislature, "Segregation in education, now outlawed by the Supreme Court, cannot really be eliminated until segregation in housing, too, is outlawed."

At a 1954 symposium "What of New York?" that evaluated the achievements and losses of the postwar civil rights movement, Roy Wilkins told the seven hundred people gathered at Hunter College that there had been steady progress since the Harlem riot in 1935, "except in the area of housing, particularly private housing." He cited better paying jobs, easier access to education, and "much less humiliation" in places of public accommodation, but warned that "there are still thousands of families who cannot secure decent homes of their choice and pocketbook level." Charles Abrams, a founder of the NYSCDH, became the director of SCAD in 1955, the same year it was given jurisdiction over some housing discrimination. He increasingly attacked slum clearance as a misguided reform, and asserted that "important gains" in Black access to education and employment were "being jeopardized" by the growth of housing segregation. This critical awareness of the significance of residential segregation to civil rights occurred well before the urban riots of the 1960s made it a national political issue.[36]

The Early Struggle for Integrated Schools

As the Black migration to the city swelled Harlem schools, activists fought to make integration rather than segregation the pattern for the future. As with housing, their efforts belie the myth that school segregation in the metropolitan North was an inevitable result of demographic trends. Overt racial segregation in public schools in New York State was made unconstitutional in 1938, but as the Black population in the city grew, the Board of Education facilitated the growth of racially segregated and inferior schools for Black children. Civil rights leaders exposed this governmental complicity in maintaining racially defined schools, calling into question the accuracy of the phrase de facto to describe racial segregation in New York City public schools. Although abetted by residential segregation, school segregation was also caused by a variety of public policy decisions, from the selection of sites for new schools to the drawing of district lines. Similarly, the quality of education offered to Black children was adversely affected by teacher assignment policies, the choice of textbooks, and neglect of the physical plant. African American leaders in New York fought against segregated and unequal schools years before the *Brown* decision in 1954, but their efforts culminated in the work led by Kenneth Clark from 1954 to 1957 to transform the quality of public schooling in New York City. Clark's fight for desegregation (he used this term more than the word integration) was a fight to radically change the conditions of education for Black children in New York City.

As the city's Black population expanded rapidly in the 1940s, parents and community leaders charged that the Board of Education was drawing school district lines in order to ensure racial homogeneity. Many parents noticed that as they moved closer to the borders of changing neighborhoods, district lines shifted to prevent their children from attending school with white children. They charged that the Board of Education rezoned neighborhoods to maintain racial divisions, thereby facilitating white parents' efforts to move away from mixed schools and impeding Black parents' efforts to send their children to schools that were considered white. The Bedford-Stuyvesant / Williamsburg School Council protested zoning that sent Black children to antiquated schools and kept the closer-to-home modern ones 95 percent white. Black parents in Queens made similar complaints about their frustrated efforts to send their children to newer and better equipped schools. Another study revealed that white students in northern Manhattan were bused south to avoid attending a predominantly Black school in Harlem. By such policies, the "Board of Education has been 'fighting' the new tide of melting pot communities by giving segregated schools its unofficial blessing."

State assembly member Hulan Jack twice introduced legislation prohibiting the creation or use of school districts to promote segregation. Each time opponents blocked the measure. In addition, the Mayor's Committee on Unity closely monitored the changing racial composition of schools in and around Black neighborhoods, and along with other groups, offered specific reform proposals that the city ignored.[37]

Ironically, in light of all the rhetoric about the value of "neighborhood schools" in the white antibusing movement of the 1970s, in this period some whites sought to leave the neighborhood to avoid integrated schools, suggesting that assumptions about race rather than a commitment to neighborhood was the critical motive. In a report on racial demographics in high schools, Dan Dodson of the Mayor's Committee on Unity urged the city to take active steps to prevent segregation. He pointed out that several high schools were 20 percent African American, the supposed ratio at which whites would begin to resegregate themselves by abandoning the school. The Board of Education, however, rejected his advice to enforce zoning lines as a means to forestall this so-called white flight.[38]

Dodson's study of emerging patterns of high school segregation found "a tremendous backlog of prejudice toward Negroes" among white New Yorkers. But from his surveys he concluded that the real source of concern in changing neighborhoods was the deterioration of services that usually coincided with high levels of migration: "At the point at which contact is made between Negroes and whites, where community services should function at their best in order to facilitate the integration process and relieve as many sources of friction as possible, there is too frequently such a deterioration of services that the deterioration itself aggravates or obstructs the integration process." Civil rights advocates offered many suggestions to the Board of Education on how to promote stable integrated schools, including rezoning, special programs, "intercultural" curricula, and a policy of controlled racial balance. The board, however, described the problem as "complicated" and claimed that many of the proposals for planned integration were "undemocratic."[39]

In 1950 Morris High School in the Bronx was undergoing rapid change as an attitude of "give the school to Negroes" took root among whites who were leaving Morris for Evander Childs and Taft high schools. The Bronx Urban League and Morris's principal, Jacob Bernstein, urged the city to block these racially motivated transfers and rezone the school in order to restore its previous racial balance. There was considerable support for rezoning from many parent and community groups, but they faced strong opposition from what Bernstein termed "whitist elements." Opponents of integration warned of race riots, and one white politician even obtained a doctor's note claiming his son was "psychologically unable to cope with Negroes." The integrationists, however, prevailed and Morris High School was rezoned to restore a racial balance—it went from 70 percent Black to 40 percent. Moreover, an interracial neighborhood association was formed and fights between juvenile gangs reportedly declined. Morris embarked on a modernization program that attracted students and made it a highly popular Bronx high school, exemplifying what could be accomplished with grassroots initiative and leadership.[40]

The New York civil rights movement addressed much more than the question of segregation in the schools. It fought to improve physical conditions, create multicultural curricula, hire more black teachers, appoint an African American to the Board of Education, bar racist textbooks, and remove biased teachers. In the 1940s and 1950s many complaints were made against Euro-American public school teachers for using biased speech or promoting racist ideas or theories in the performance of their jobs. In 1945, for example, Roy Wilkins called for the dismissal of a Brooklyn teacher who had been telling her students that they would have to fight in "a race war" one day. At another Brooklyn school a month later, three Black parents complained about a teacher who had made "constant racial slurs" such as "Colored people are the dumbest people on the face of the earth." Activists argued that such comments and actions made these teachers unfit to serve in the classrooms of an increasingly diverse metropolis.[41]

The most notorious case in the 1940s involved a Brooklyn elementary school teacher, May A. Quinn. She was actually the subject of two separate episodes that galvanized the city's progressive leadership. Quinn was tried by Board of Education officials in 1946 for a classroom incident that happened in 1942. Fourteen colleagues and several students complained that she had used an anti-Semitic and racist pamphlet called "The First Americans" in the classroom. She reportedly made statements that endorsed racial segregation, praised Hitler and Mussolini, and labeled Jews "a dull race," and Italians, "greasy foreigners." Leading civil rights groups called for Quinn's dismissal. Thurgood Marshall wrote the Board of Education that "the teachings of Miss Quinn as proved before your Committee can add fuel to the dangerous fires already smoldering in our city." The board, however, acquitted her of the major charges, convicting her of "neglect of duty," which brought a $650 fine and a transfer to a school closer to her home. The decision sparked a barrage of protests, administrative appeals, and parent demonstrations. The American Jewish Congress called it "a license for the teaching of hatred in New York City schools." The decision also increased demands for the appointment of an African American to the Board of Education. Assemblyman Hulan Jack sponsored a bill that grew out of the May Quinn case, to amend the penal law to cover the libel of groups of persons based on religion or color.[42]

In 1949 May Quinn was back in the news. She made more statements hostile to Blacks and Jews in the classroom, and this time received a verbal rebuke. Superintendent William Jansen expressed "keen dissatisfaction with her handling of the lesson," but cleared her of any intention "to offend the Negro people or to justify discrimination." An editorial in the liberal *New York Post* vehemently denounced Jansen's decision, drawing attention to Quinn's particular obligation as a social studies teacher. A "civics teacher has an affirmative responsibility to recognize a bigot, even if it is the face in the mirror," it wrote. Shirley Graham, the left-wing African American playwright and activist, organized a petition campaign to Mayor O'Dwyer. Quinn's classroom remarks, she wrote, "constitute a blatant apology for the un-American practice of segregation," and she urged the mayor to consider "the deep wound she must have inflicted on all the children in her class." Seventy prominent New York progressives signed the letter, including Congressman Adam Clayton Powell, Rev. B. C. Robeson, the historian J. A. Rogers, playwrights Theodore Ward and Alice Childress, E. Y. Harburg (lyricist of the *Wizard of Oz*), as well as the actors Sidney Poitier and Harry Belafonte. It was particularly ironic that Quinn retained her position on the eve of a massive antileft purge that caused hundreds of the most progressive teachers to leave the school system.[43]

In 1951 the left-wing Teachers' Union, with which the board had broken relations after its expulsion from the CIO, produced a remarkable study of textbooks currently in use in the public schools. In "Bias and Prejudice in Textbooks in Use in New York City Schools: An Indictment," the union took pains to clarify why its review did not constitute censorship. The Teachers' Union "makes a sharp distinction between censorship—which it opposes— and the elimination of material containing racist stereotypes, distortion of historical and scientific fact, and bias, whether conscious or unconscious, toward allegedly 'inferior' peoples." Prepared by the Harlem Committee of the Teachers' Union, the report reflected scholarship in U.S. history that had been ignored by the mainstream academy, and it anticipated the revisionism of the next generation of historians who came of age during the civil rights movement. United Public Workers official Ewart Guinier worked on the report. He had just managed the 1950 U.S. Senate campaign of W. E. B. Du Bois, the eminent historian whose insights in *Black Reconstruction* formed part of the intellectual underpinnings of the Teachers' Union study. In 1969, Guinier would also become the first chair of the Department of Afro-American Studies at Harvard University.

Headings in the report highlighted the themes in city textbooks: "Slavery Condoned," "Slave Revolts Ignored," "Emancipation Ridiculed," "Reconstruction Period Distorted," and "KKK Justified." One textbook, coauthored by Frank D. Whalen, a New York school superintendent, concluded that slavery brought a "happy life for the slaves. They had no cares except to do their work well." Another text widely used in high schools in the city, and coauthored by an assistant superintendent, argued that the whipping of slaves was not cruel. "White children were frequently whipped by their parents," it added. One book coauthored by a member of the Board of Examiners, which issued teaching licenses, claimed that "Some Negroes . . . thought freedom meant no more work. They caused much trouble in the South . . . begging, stealing, threatening people and creating disorder." The report quoted from a series of widely used geography textbooks coauthored by the schools superintendent himself, William Jansen. The chief educator in New York City wrote, "Because the native people of Africa, most of whom belong to the Negro race, are very backward, the greater part of the continent has come under the control of European nations since its opening up began."[44]

To compensate for the deficient materials used in city schools, the Teachers' Union created its own Black history curriculum, including "The Negro in New York, 1626–1865: A Study for Teachers." While this guide was not adopted by the board, it is possible that individual teachers used it. It began: "In New York City the Negro people constitute more than 10% of the city population. This is probably the largest Negro community of any city in the world with great and growing influence on the social and cultural life of the city and of national importance because of its leadership in the fight for civil rights throughout the country."[45]

Brown and New York City

Surprisingly, New York City was one of the first places in the nation where the 1954 *Brown v. Board of Education* U.S. Supreme Court ruling sparked a push for integration. The spark was a speech given by Kenneth Clark, psychologist and City College professor, at an Urban League dinner at the Hotel Theresa in honor of Negro History Week. Clark had recently gained national attention for his expert testimony in *Brown* on the harmful effects of segregation on Black children. "Just before I got up to speak," Clark recalled, "the Mayor came in with his entourage." Clark declared emphatically that school segregation was not just a problem in the South, but in New York City as well. He said that the education of Black children in New York City was "in a stage of decline" and challenged city leaders to question the point of distinguishing between de facto and de jure school segregation when both produced inferior education for African American children. Civil rights activists like Clark knew that comparisons between northern and southern racism tended to unnerve northern white leaders. Arthur Leavitt, president of the Board of Education, was at the dinner and he quickly disclaimed any responsibility for segregated schools. Housing segregation, he argued, was the real culprit. Clark reminded him that a majority of teachers at Black and Puerto Rican schools were inexperienced or unlicensed, a phenomenon under the board's control. The short speech was political dynamite—it reportedly "disturbed" the newly elected mayor, Robert Wagner, and precipitated a heated struggle over the obligations of the board of education to ensure racial equity and fairness in New York public schools. As the first Democrat in city hall since Mayor O'Dwyer abruptly resigned in 1949, Wagner's policies would indicate whether the Democratic Party's embrace of civil rights in 1948 would lead to genuine policy changes on the local level.[46]

After Clark's speech made headlines, activists mobilized to keep public attention on the issue. The Urban League of Greater New York organized the Intergroup Committee on Public Schools with Clark, Hubert Delany, Ella

Baker, and other Harlem leaders. Their study, "Children Apart," concluded that racially segregated schools were increasing and shortchanging Black children. "We hoped that, on the basis of obtained facts, there would be some action taken to reduce the number of existing segregated schools, and to prevent the development of future segregated schools," Clark noted, reflecting the view that social science data can prod racial reform. Pushed by *Brown,* and the flurry of publicity on the issue, Leavitt asked the nonprofit Public Education Association (PEA) to investigate Clark's allegations.[47]

Even before the study was complete, school officials began a campaign to justify the status quo. The superintendent issued a statement calling segregation in Harlem "natural" and "accidental" rather than stemming from intentional policies. Clark recalled that "some members of the Board of Superintendents were not above raising questions regarding the political loyalty or motivation of some of us who were involved." This was, after all, the McCarthy era. The initial denial of the problem by the board's white bureaucrats never eased and went a long way toward undermining Clark's efforts.[48]

A year later, the PEA report, "The Status of the Public School Education of Negro and Puerto Rican Children in New York City," confirmed every point made by the Intergroup Committee. While it did not report evidence of deliberate racial zoning by board officials, "there was evidence that many existing school boundary lines and zoning procedures did in fact facilitate segregated schools." In December 1954, the board established a commission on integration, composed of both school officials and reformers, including Clark. Its mandate was to "develop an effective integration program" for the schools, but from the start board officials dragged their feet. The commission is best understood as a concession to pressure unleashed by *Brown* combined with the mobilization of Black community leaders, rather than as a sign of the board's commitment.[49]

In a drawn-out process over the next few years, the commission established five subcommittees that each issued a series of policy recommendations. Three, concerned with raising standards within Black and Puerto Rican schools, were accepted without controversy, since as Clark felt, "they were functioning within the area of 'separate but equal.'" The other two, dealing with zoning and teacher assignment, were met with fierce resistance. At public hearings, white teachers and parents openly expressed a belief in the intellectual inferiority of Black students. Part of their resistance took the form of purposeful distortion of the proposals. Clark felt that school officials intentionally used the media to sabotage their efforts by spreading false stories that white children faced mandatory long-distance busing into Black neighborhoods. The press even reported that children in Staten Island would have to attend Harlem schools. "At no place in the report is there a suggestion that young children be 'bussed' any considerable distance," Clark pointed out; on the contrary, the board itself occasionally transported children out of district to fill underutilized schools. The zoning report merely recommended "that where present procedure can be used to facilitate integration, this should be done." In fact, until 1957 the Board of Education had been busing white children "away from a near Negro school to a more distant non-Negro school." But, as Clark noted with mounting frustration, "there were no national press alarms about this fact."[50]

The report on teacher assignment urged the board to ensure a balanced distribution of experienced teachers, an idea that many teachers' groups opposed, seeing school choice as a seniority right protected by collective bargaining. But here, too, Clark felt that their opposition was "not spontaneous." Their supervisors, he observed, had never before been so solicitous of their wishes. At public hearings, Clark "heard these otherwise decent human beings talking about Black and Puerto Rican children as if they were lepers." In the end, the board did pass these two controversial reports, but paralleling the "with all deliberate speed" ruling after *Brown,* it reserved the right to interpret the manner of their enforcement, and the person assigned to carry out this demanding task was Superintendent William Jansen.[51]

The board essentially ignored the recommendations of its committee on integration, and since it was not operating under a judicial order, there was no systematic monitoring of its so-called integration policy. Indeed, statistics show an increase in racially segregated schools in the decade after *Brown.* Between 1954 and 1960 the number of schools with a Black and Puerto Rican student population of 90 percent or more rose from zero to thirty-eight, and by 1963 to sixty-one, or 22 percent of borough schools. Thus, while the civil rights rhetoric of the Board of Education increased during the 1950s, so too did racial segregation, as the board rejected a variety of moderate proposals to create and maintain desegregated schools. According to Clark's allegations, the Board of Education participated in fanning opposition to school desegregation across the country by spreading misinformation in the national media about so-called busing.[52]

The struggle to implement the *Brown* decision in New York City sheds light on a period of demographic flux when so-called de facto segregation was not locked in and impermeable to change. Civil rights advocates proposed creative and flexible reforms, but the board's response previews the resistance it was to offer in the next decade, first to a grassroots desegregation campaign, and later to a campaign for "community control" of schools. Even more telling and just as enduring, white politicians and school leaders in New York failed to challenge the racial mythology that links African American children to educational failure and school decline.

In both housing and education in the 1950s, the government's formal adoption of some civil rights positions was at odds with a physical landscape of growing racial division. Government agencies had partnered with the most powerful industry in the nation to resegregate metropolitan America. African Americans had little means to counter this trend. Even if enforced, antidiscrimination laws seemed woefully inadequate to overcome such a massive spatial transformation. The widening gap between official rhetoric and social conditions inspired a growing Black skepticism of northern liberalism, whether from progressive writers such as James Baldwin, or nationalist street corner orators like Malcolm X. African American leaders warned repeatedly, and prophetically, that ghettoization, cloaked with growing civil rights talk, was destined to produce violent upheaval.

12 To Stand and Fight

In their push to advance in the 1950s, African American workers had few allies. Trade unionists who cared little about grassroots democracy and racial equality were gaining strength in organized labor, and the State Commission against Discrimination (SCAD) balked at challenging the union seniority systems that locked in nepotism and white privilege. But African American workers in a wide variety of occupations, including those that would be hard hit by automation and plant relocation, continued to fight for equal rights. They found support where they could. Black labor leftists struggled to remain a viable force during repressive and difficult times. The local Urban League was the most active mainstream organizational ally of Black worker struggles. And Black nationalist organizations gained new visibility in the fight for jobs. Although the Black nationalists' contentious relations with longtime activists—as well as their anti-union and anti–civil rights politics—limited their effectiveness in labor struggles, their appeals to masculine authority and race pride, and their willingness to engage in confrontational tactics, gained them admirers.

Capital and labor in the United States reached a rapprochement after a postwar strike wave that gave the unionized working class unprecedented job security, regular wage increases, medical coverage, and pensions. For all that the labor movement won for its members, however, it did not win civil rights for its members of color. The new capital-labor consensus was forged without a federal guarantee of fair employment, and the New York guarantee was barely enforced. In the 1950s, African American workers struggled against backsliding and unemployment as much as they fought for advancement. They faced an occupational structure that locked them out of skilled jobs, giving them lower wages and higher rates of unemployment. The wartime labor shortage had pulled a million Black southerners to the North and

250

West, and they were determined to make this move permanent, to build strong families and communities, and to resist attempts to remarginalize their labor.

On the Waterfront

With seven hundred miles of coastline and nine hundred piers, the Port of New York was the busiest in the world; it generated 200,000 jobs and gave 50,000 longshoremen a critical role in the daily flow of trade, including exports to Europe under the Marshall Plan. But the workers had a long list of grievances. Excessive "sling loads" made longshoring the most dangerous occupation in New York, while waterfront labor relations were plagued by rampant fraud, intimidation, and violence. In 1943 Joe Ryan, president of the corrupt International Longshoreman's Association (ILA), decreed himself president-for-life, or "King Joe" in the words of Ewart Guinier. After the war, a rank-and-file upsurge up and down the east coast transformed labor relations, rolled back the power of organized crime, and increased the regulatory role of the state. Black dockworkers were part of this struggle, but they also waged their own fight for full equality on the waterfront.

The number of African American longshoremen in New York had increased during the war to several thousand, but after the war, the workers claimed, the ILA and shipping association conspired to undercut their gains and even drive them off the waterfront. Longshoremen worked in ethnically defined gangs on a particular set of piers—pier jurisdiction was a key source of job security on the waterfront. The all-Black Local 968 in Brooklyn had pier jurisdiction for a time during the war, but now stood as the only ILA local without it. Under the leadership of Cleophus T. Jacobs, a Caribbean native and admirer of Marcus Garvey, Local 968 spent the next decade and a half struggling for two goals: pier jurisdiction and the elimination of shape-up, the daily gathering where the hiring boss unilaterally selected workers—a system that institutionalized favoritism, bribery, and racial discrimination.

By 1949, only about a hundred men in the thousand-member Local 968 had regular jobs. "Negroes aren't hired to work until all white longshoremen are shaped up," Jacobs said. The local looked everywhere for support. SCAD was no help—it found "no probable cause" to proceed after a preliminary investigation. The Mayor's Committee on Unity, mindful of its mandate to prevent racial violence, urged Mayor O'Dwyer to intervene, finding that "the situation on the waterfront represents a genuine danger to the public peace." The mayor declined, and ultimately weighed in on the other side.

Because longshoremen could not trust their union, they often relied on outside organizations for aid. Communists and other radicals, as well as "labor priests," were two major sources of assistance. Communists, for example, spearheaded a lawsuit that won unpaid overtime for longshoremen under the Fair Labor Standards Act. But in New York, African American rights groups, including the Harlem Trade Union Council (HTUC) and the Urban League, also contributed to the longshoremen's struggle. Local 968 turned to the HTUC, which had been formed in 1949 by Black labor radicals expelled from organized labor, in order to help generate publicity and support in the wider Black and labor communities.[1]

The HTUC was formed at a conference of 250 trade union leaders at the Hotel Theresa in April 1949, with Ewart Guinier as chairman and Ferdinand Smith as secretary. Local NAACP activists were rebuked by the national office for offering support. The HTUC's philosophy, according to Ben Davis, was that "the Negro working class was the most progressive and consistent force among the Negro people." They endeavored to keep the political focus on Black workers as the agents of change and to counter the middle-class outlook of civil rights leadership. As "the overwhelmingly largest section among the Negro people," Ben Davis argued, workers "alone can unite them and guarantee an uncompromising militant struggle for the immediate needs of the Negroes and for their ultimate liberation."[2]

In addition, Local 968 appealed to the national NAACP. The association expressed support for the besieged longshoremen, but opposed defending what it saw as a segregated local as well as collaborating with Communists or alleged Communists, such as Ferdinand Smith. It anxiously monitored the case, however. The dangerous world of waterfront labor relations, meanwhile, was pulling the men in another direction. Joe Ryan ominously suggested that Local 968 members physically seize possession of their former piers from the white gangs, but NAACP attorney Marian Wynn Perry strongly advised the men against it, and Cleophus Jacobs opposed it as a likely setup for a violent attack. But many of the men were impatient, and they chose to take Ryan's advice. Their leader was Jacobs's cousin, Andronicus Jacobs, who coincidentally was employed as a sandhog and had been involved in the struggle at the Brooklyn Battery Tunnel. "You will find," he told a reporter, "that Negroes don't stay in just one craft because they are not employed regularly." "These two experiences [the tunnel and the waterfront] have convinced me more than ever that there is only one way to buck this thing," he said. "That is to stand and fight."[3]

On a March morning in 1949, a nervous Marian Wynn Perry watched from a safe perch on the Brooklyn Heights promenade as several hundred men from Local 968 staged a "march on the waterfront." Andronicus Jacobs said they "went down to storm the piers and force hiring of some of our men. For a moment it looked as though there was a danger of violence. But the police came, forced us back, and let the white men into work." Perry reported back to the NAACP, "The Negro men were not able to prevent the white men from doing their work, and there was no violence."[4]

Quickly moving to another tactic, the next day a large group from Local 968 began a picket line at ILA headquarters on 14th Street in Manhattan. This protest also entailed physical risks—King Joe had recruited organizers from the state prison at Sing Sing, who deployed violence and the threat of violence to maintain ILA power on the waterfront. The HTUC tapped into the considerable progressive labor network in the city, and with their support, the longshoremen maintained the picket line for thirteen weeks. At one point, 14,000 workers marched around the clock. Reflecting a tradition in Black labor activism, the HTUC also reached out to Black church and civic leaders. Judge Myles A. Paige chaired a Brooklyn Citizens' Committee in support of Local 968 that drew many of the borough's activist clergy, like Thomas S. Harten, Gardner Taylor, and Sandy Ray, as well as the local NAACP branch. They urged Mayor O'Dwyer to grant Local 968 pier jurisdiction, but little support was forthcoming. City Councilman Ben Davis introduced a resolution calling on the state "to protect and make secure the right of Negro longshoremen to work in full equality with other workers on the piers." The ILA would later point to this resolution in court as evidence of Communist infiltration of the local.[5]

In June, about forty Black longshoremen entered Joe Ryan's office and conducted a "sit-down" strike. Many of the men had been members of Local 968 since its founding in 1917; they had considerable seniority and were determined not to be pushed off the waterfront without a fight. Their sit-in blended the moral high ground with the recognition that "force is all they understand on the waterfront." Led by Andronicus Jacobs, the men occupied their union leader's office for five hours, until Ryan's men came and broke it up. Arriving with the police, the pro-Ryan forces "snatched chairs from under the sit-downers and 'booted' the Negro unionists into the nearest corridor." Ryan screamed, "Go back downstairs with your communist pals and let them get you some jobs." The next day 2,500 members of the ILA's Marine Trades Department broke up the picket line. The men hit picketers as well as many bystanders. The police, who had just issued an order to halt the picketing, joined in the forcible dispersal of the protest, clubbing and arresting many.[6]

Ryan launched an offensive against Local 968. "Negro members of this union had gotten a better break than they perhaps deserved," he told the press. If race was not a problem, then outside agitators must be stirring up discontent. Ryan blamed the protest on the Harlem Trade Union Council, saying it was part of a Communist conspiracy aimed at Local 968. Ryan took Local 968 to court for "working with Communists," failing to discipline its members, and "falsely charging Jim Crow in the union." He also, in the words of Cleophus Jacobs, "railroaded through a motion to place our local in the hands of an administrator." The accusation of Communism jeopardized Local 968's legal standing. Although the workers were aided by labor activists in the Communist orbit, they had long-standing grievances that Communists neither invented nor aggravated. The local issued a statement declaring that they were not Communist, offering to take loyalty oaths, and repudiating "efforts of Communists to capitalize on this issue." They reiterated their demands for control over the piers near their headquarters and for the same right to jobs as other locals in the ILA.[7]

Jacobs asked Mayor O'Dwyer's brother, the progressive attorney Paul O'Dwyer, to represent Local 968, but Paul O'Dwyer, fearing that his own connections to the left would hurt their cause, asked the NAACP to take the case. He tried to assuage the NAACP's concerns about leftist involvement, writing that the local regretted having allowed "Ferdinand Smith and others" to picket. "The political question," in his view, "has just been thrown in to try to kill the Local," but the NAACP declined to represent the local, citing its all-black identity and association with the left.[8]

A state supreme court judge issued an injunction preventing Ryan from taking over the local, and Ryan agreed to desist if the local held a new election. "This is the first time in my 45 years of longshoring that I have seen Joe Ryan back down," said one man. But the rest of the local was angry that the court refused to hear their charges of discrimination. "If the courts can't settle the question of discrimination, we can," Cleophus Jacobs vowed. In the court-ordered election, Jacobs handily defeated the Ryan-backed slate, 230 to 86. The local's survival suggests that their efforts to build solidarity beyond the waterfront were essential.[9]

Discrimination on the waterfront continued, while rampant gangsterism strengthened calls for reform in the industry and union as a whole. At hearings before a crime commission appointed by Governor Thomas E. Dewey in 1953, Local 968 advanced the most democratic proposals, fusing antimafia, pro–civil rights, pro-union and proreform sentiment. While the ILA defended the shape-up and the government proposed to replace it with a state information center without protections for seniority and other worker rights, Jacobs recommended nondiscriminatory hiring halls operated by each union local, seniority protection, and a tripartite board of review to handle grievances.[10]

In 1954 the new Waterfront Commission of the New York Harbor replaced the shape-up with a government-supervised employment office, but Black workers complained that it enshrined the inequities of the old system and produced a racially segmented labor hierarchy, with the Black and Puerto Rican longshoremen on the bottom. A 1959 Urban League study found that "the abusive shape-up hiring system, which bred kickbacks and corruption, still exists" and that the seniority system "freezes and formalizes a pattern of discrimination that has existed on the waterfront for years." At the same time, the number of Black longshoremen increased, but as casual laborers, their plight highlighted the problem of unequal access to better jobs, increased pay, and union security. Local 968, meanwhile, continued to struggle for jurisdictional rights.[11]

The commission had powers to screen the labor force, ostensibly to oust felons, but it summoned Cleophus Jacobs to answer charges of being a Communist. Jacobs's attorney, I. Philip Sipser, recalled the exchange forty years later. To the question "Are you a member of the Communist Party?" Jacobs answered, "No." To the question "Are you a communist?" he replied, "I don't know what that means." Jacobs explained that his views were shaped by myriad sources and he would not discount the possibility that Communists had influenced him. But, revealing the international exposures of maritime life, Jacobs emphasized that Communism was itself diverse. "There are all kinds of communists. There are Yugoslavian communists, Russian communists, Chinese communists . . . they're all different." The board labeled Jacobs a Communist and ruled him off the port, but he successfully appealed in federal court and was reinstated.[12]

In 1959 the 1,500 longshoremen in Local 968 merged with the large Brooklyn Local 1814, headed by the powerful trade unionist Anthony Anastasia. Local 968 received "guarantees in writing" of its right to pier jurisdiction, but in reality little changed. In 1961, several workers filed complaints with SCAD that the Shipping Association, Waterfront Commission, and ILA had violated the rights of Black workers. They were supported by the new Negro American Labor Council, which had 400 of the 1,300 Black longshoremen as members. A. Philip Randolph assailed the "climate of terror, nepotism in the acquisition of jobs and exclusion because of race" on the Brooklyn piers. But mechanization—containerization—would soon reduce the need for manual labor on the docks, and the heyday of longshoring would fade.

Local 968 survived Joe Ryan's assault on wartime Black labor gains. But Black dockworkers were denied the full benefits of their unionized occupation and then suffered a second blow when their industry was transformed and their jobs disappeared. Local 968's hard-fought battle for survival and equal rights exemplified the determination of Black workers to maintain the occupational gains of the war years. The State Commission against Discrimination was of little assistance due to its controversial claim that union hiring systems fell outside its jurisdiction. Most valuable to the workers was support from labor-oriented Black rights groups, whether the Harlem Trade Union Council, the Urban League, or the Negro American Labor Council.[13]

In the 1950s, Black New Yorkers continued the grassroots struggle to desegregate metropolitan industries. The fight for jobs in the city's virtually all-white brewery industry became another long battle for justice and good jobs that had a bittersweet ending. The beer making and distributing industry in New York City employed nine to ten thousand workers in well-paying blue-collar jobs. Extremely protectionist union hiring procedures made it difficult for seasonal hires to win seniority. The seniority system was designed to promote favoritism, originally for sons of employees, but it was used in the postwar era to block racial integration.[14] Industries such as beer, soft drinks, dairy, and bakeries became major targets of Black protest in the 1950s and beyond because they generated production jobs in northern cities, African Americans were a growing market for their products, and delivery trucks with all-white crews were glaring, and vulnerable, symbols of employment bias.

In 1950 the Harlem Trade Union Committee invited six breweries and the seven brewery locals to a conference on bias in the industry.[15] Ferdinand Smith warned the unions that "we would regret being forced to resort to any other method to enforce the just rights of Negro workers," in a likely reference to a consumer boycott. The brewers balked, claiming that the

"Communist" HTUC was the obstacle to integration. Although this was a convenient excuse for the brewing industry, the red scare sidelined the HTUC. The New York Urban League stepped in and began to pressure the industry to hire more African Americans. "The hiring halls," a Union League official declared, "have a virtual monopoly on the production jobs and never send out Negro workers." According to the New York Urban League, in 1951 there were only fifty Black workers out of a total workforce of 10,000 in eleven New York breweries. Nationwide, Blacks made up just one-half of 1 percent of the industry's total workforce. The *Amsterdam News* termed this "particularly ironic since reliable studies prove that Negroes are among the largest consumers of brewery products."[16]

The United African Nationalist Movement (UANM), a Black nationalist group in Harlem led by James Lawson, also mobilized pressure on the breweries. The UANM saw itself as a rival to the Urban League as well as the brewery unions—it wanted to control the entry and flow of Black workers into the brewery industry as well as the industry's relations with the broader Harlem community. It eschewed traditional union procedures and civil rights strategies and had a reputation for using strong-arm tactics to secure jobs.[17] Other nationalist labor organizations operating outside the government's labor relations enforcement apparatus, such as the Harlem Labor Union, had been the target of such accusations from time to time. The Georgia-born Lawson first rose to prominence as a Garveyite street orator, arguing that the pursuit of racial power was the motive force of history. The UANM opposed the left's analysis of colonialism and white supremacy as well as the social welfare policies of urban liberalism; it was drawn instead to the promise of U.S. immigrant capitalism—self-reliance, patriarchy, and ethnic solidarity. Lawson had a small but dedicated following.[18]

Lawson denounced racism in the union movement, and warned that

Unless . . . a fair share of the jobs in the brewing industry is given black people forthwith, the United African Nationalist Movement will unleash a campaign against the C.I.O., for these unfair and undemocratic acts, we will bring to bear upon you the full impact of black nationalism here, in South and Central America, the Caribbean, Asia and Africa. Sirs, I promise you also, if this request is denied, "God and history will judge you," for I know that black workers and especially war veterans are not going to sit idly by and see white workers take the bread out of their children's mouths. Gentlemen, we can take just so much.[19]

The UANM called for a boycott of Rheingold beer until "black people" were given a fair share of jobs.[20] They picketed Harlem groceries, generating more pressure for change as both the Harlem grocers' association and their employees' union urged the brewers to hire Black workers. Lawson attacked New York Giants great Monte Irvin for lending "his fine name and fame" to Rheingold beer. He demanded that Irvin resign and return the "filthy" money or they would "act in any way we may decide within the law." As the boycott began to hurt beer sales, the brewers hired a few African Americans who had been referred by the Urban League.[21]

Conflict rather than common ground marked relations between the UANM and the Urban League, whose staff Lawson denounced as "the 20th Century Uncle Toms." The Urban League organized a mass meeting in Harlem on "The Negro in the Brewery Industry," which launched the Citizens' Committee for the Integration of Negroes in the Brewery Industry—a committee whose leaders included Hope Stevens, an activist attorney and businessman, and Ella Baker, president of the Harlem NAACP and a major leader of the southern civil rights movement. A dozen members of the UANM disrupted the meeting and "hurled insults" at Edward Lewis, the highly regarded New York Urban League leader. They accused the Urban League of "pussy-footing," being "in the pay of white folks," and not caring about "the Negro in Harlem." More to the point was Lawson's desire to place his members in any newly won brewery jobs. Despite their lack of unity, the nationalists and civil rights leaders each played useful roles in the brewery struggle. The Urban League stayed in the forefront of negotiations with labor and industry leaders, but the confrontational tactics of the UANM may have encouraged the brewers to work with the more moderate Urban League.[22]

Some breweries responded more favorably to the simultaneous efforts to induce them to advertise in Black newspapers and to contribute funds to Black community events. They indicated an awareness of the Black consumer market and mollified boycotts through this form of spending. In 1952 the *Amsterdam News* gave Ballantine beer an award "for outstanding contributions to democracy." Based in Newark, New Jersey, Ballantine was the first company to sponsor a Black woman in the Miss America Pageant Parade and the first, in 1951, to use African American female models in poster advertising. And Ballantine sponsored a television show featuring Brooklyn Dodger Roy Campanella, who thereby reportedly became "the first Negro to have a television show backed by a national sponsor."[23]

In 1953 a major employment breakthrough seemed at hand. The brewery locals, the Urban League, and the Citizens' Committee reached an agreement to hire at least one hundred permanent Black workers. The unions and management promised that half of the new seasonal job openings would go to Blacks, while negotiations on a plan for the thousands of white-collar positions in the industry continued. Edward Lewis called it "a milestone in breaking through a multimillion-dollar industry involving top management and organized labor coming to the League for mediation."[24]

Fierce opposition from many sides, however, destroyed the agreement. The union's attorney felt that the Brewery Workers' Joint Board had signed the agreement "under pressure from me. It was not done with a desire to really follow through."[25] The brewers had conditioned their acceptance of the plan on SCAD's approval, but SCAD soon launched a full-scale attack on the plan as an illegal "quota." The Republican-appointed SCAD used anti–affirmative action arguments to scuttle a desegregation plan that had worked well in its first month, producing forty production jobs and eighty-five less permanent jobs. Civil rights activists were outraged. The league and citizens' committee expressed "shock and dismay," and accused SCAD of refusing to admit "the difficulties inherent in the integration of new employees into this industry under present hiring procedures." According to Edward Lewis, SCAD "has abdicated its responsibility to the community by condemning the only practical solution that has been developed and by offering no alternative proposal." SCAD maintained that the union seniority system was beyond its jurisdiction. In 1954 there were only fifty African Americans among the seven thousand workers in union-covered production and distribution jobs, and fifty more in the estimated four thousand white-collar jobs.[26]

A decade later, Black brewery workers achieved a major breakthrough. With the leadership of worker Leo Rabouine, they won a victory that brought structural change to the labor system. In 1965 the Teamsters and the Negro American Labor Council negotiated an agreement that included affirmative action, changes in seniority procedures, and reform of the shape-up. And in an unprecedented innovation for a labor contract, it was agreed that complaints of racial discrimination could be brought to an outside arbitrator "whose decision shall be final and binding on all parties." Cleveland Robinson and Morris Doswell, both veterans of the postwar labor-left, played leading roles in negotiating for the brewery workers, and Hubert Delany, the former judge and civil rights veteran, was asked to be the arbitrator. This victory reflects the revival of civil rights activism during the

1960s as well as the importance of a trade union group specifically devoted to racial equality, such as the Negro American Labor Council.[27]

When the beer industry finally became a significant employer of African Americans, it relocated. This frustrating climax to years of struggle was not unique to the beer industry. Reaping the gains of the long struggle for equality in the longshore industry was foreclosed by the automation of dock work. Many industries in the northern postwar United States either relocated or automated at the historical moment that the numbers of Black employees grew, especially in skilled positions. While the causes of this are multifaceted, the historical memory in many Black communities from Pittsburgh to East St. Louis connects Black victories and advancement to plant flight and restructuring.

A Bitter Pill to Swallow

Court-ordered constraints on the right to picket discouraged the use of direct action tactics to win jobs, adding to the broader demobilization of protest in the McCarthy era. In 1950, in *Hughes v. Superior Court,* the U.S. Supreme Court ruled in a California case that picketing which advocated that a retail store hire a percentage of Black workers was not protected by the Constitution because it compelled "quota hiring." Leading liberal and civil rights groups such as the CIO, ACLU, and NAACP had filed amicus briefs that variously opposed or cautiously defended proportional hiring, but all vigorously defended the right to picket for such ends on free speech grounds.[28] Employers in postwar New York also turned to the courts to halt protests over job discrimination. In 1949 the Fay-Loevins store on 145th Street sued the NAACP for $100,000 for "unfair picketing." Both the NAACP and the Harlem Labor Union had picketed the store for four days after three Black workers were given lower positions than they had been hired for. The NAACP sign read: "Discrimination Against Negroes: Help the NAACP Beat This. Do Not Patronize This Store." The national office reproached the branch for ignoring the new NAACP policy that cases of employment discrimination be referred to SCAD. Not wanting branches to engage in activity that courts had questioned, the association condemned the picketing for drawing "unfavorable national publicity" to the NAACP.[29]

In the 1950s, SCAD's interpretation of the Ives-Quinn Law seemed to work against Black economic advancement, because it frequently ruled that both affirmative action and direct action tactics, like boycotts and picketing, were impermissible. In 1949, an era when employers escaped the law's reach with near total impunity, SCAD ruled that the Harlem Labor Union's efforts to pressure employers to hire Blacks violated the law. It accused this nationalist organization of seeking to monopolize employment in Harlem for African Americans. SCAD was crafting a "color blind" philosophy that presumed that all post-1945 labor patterns in New York State were either merit based or a result of past discrimination over which it had no power.[30]

The Republican administration's use of civil rights laws to block direct action and affirmative action doubtless reinforced Black nationalist arguments about the futility of civil rights struggles. When civil rights leader Anna Arnold Hedgeman returned to Harlem in 1952 after living for several years in Washington, D.C., she was struck by the political change. "Many former Harlem leaders had moved to Westchester or Queens. Even the Harlem NAACP was dormant." But Hedgeman did observe "streetcorner meetings calling for black unity against the outside forces of exploitation": white landlords, white store owners, "Jewish rent collectors," and white politicians. While nationalist discourse has always been part of the African American protest tradition, it was eclipsed during the civil rights upsurge of the 1940s, but regained greater visibility in the 1950s.[31]

After James Lawson, the best-known Black nationalist in Harlem in the pre–Malcolm X era was Carlos Cooks. His African Nationalist Pioneer Movement began promoting a "Buy Black" campaign in 1948 "to rid Black people of alien parasites in Black communities." The Dominican-born Cooks was a Garveyite who had met with Mississippi senator Theodore Bilbo in 1939 to discuss Bilbo's African repatriation bill. Cooks's writings fused calls for African liberation with denunciations of Uncle Toms and portrayals of Black women alternately as queens or whores. He advocated natural hairstyles and rejected the term Negro in favor of Black or African. "It is the devout policy of white supremacists to make Negroes out of every black man, woman, and child," he wrote in 1955. "The word, Negro, is a weapon and scheme of whites to disassociate Black people from the human family and their homeland Africa." Greater Black unity and consciousness, not the struggle for civil rights, was seen as the way to put Blacks in a position to emulate the entrepreneurial strategies that European immigrants had ostensibly used to advance. "New York's Harlem," he claimed, "is the only section in the city where the majority of the people who inhabit the community are not the people who own and operate the business enterprises." The nationalist challenge was to reverse "the lack of consciousness of racial economic needs, and the lack of racial unity and planning for our own advancement." Cooks also denounced communism, which he felt enticed Africans with "the bastard doctrine of miscegenation and the perverted Bolshevik Communist promises of social equality."[32]

In the struggle for jobs, Harlem nationalists were unable to galvanize an effective alternative to the traditional coalitions of trade unionists, ministers, and civil rights leaders, but they brought attention to the potential power of Blacks consuming as a bloc. Interestingly, while nationalists contended that racial feeling was the engine of human behavior, Carlos Cooks acted to construct and enforce it, rather than presuming its presence. To Cooks's distress, Black New Yorkers had insufficient group loyalty. "By refusing to patronize only Black businesses in Black communities," he warned, "they are making themselves fit candidates for just punishment." The "chronic Uncle Tom or Aunt Jemima Negro or Negress" who refuses the "peaceful appeal" to buy Black, Cooks wrote in 1955, will face the dreaded "Tactical Squad, better known as the Lead Pipe Brigade," which "moves in, destroys the merchandise, breaks a rib or two, or cracks the Negro's or Negress' head open slightly." Word-of-mouth, Cooks predicted, would do the rest.[33]

Advocacy of consumer boycotts spread in the 1950s, a testament to the ineffectual civil rights law as well as trade union racism. The journalist Carl D. Lawrence, who was active in the Harlem Affairs Committee, wrote a series of articles in 1951 in the *Amsterdam News* on the persistence of job discrimination in the post–Ives-Quinn era. Under the headline "No Negroes in Harlem Industries," Lawrence asked, "Whatever happened to the crusade for better jobs?" Expressing the growing belief in the hypocrisy of New York liberalism, Lawrence wondered "about business executives and trade union leaders who preach one thing concerning FEPC and practice another." A recent strike of four thousand bakery truck drivers had brought to light that they were all white. An unemployed Black truck driver reported that "not a single Negro driver is working for any of the big concerns and yet 400,000 Harlemites are eating bread everyday. That's an awful bitter pill to swallow."[34]

The series exposed widespread anti-Black policies in the heart of Harlem six years after passage of the law against discrimination. Meuller Dairies on 126th Street employed only white truck drivers and clerical workers. Borden's, one of the nation's largest ice cream manufacturers and milk distributors, operated two plants in Harlem, including a large pasteurizing facility on 131st Street. Neighbors reported never seeing Black workers there, and the company refused comment. A pushcart peddler told Lawrence, "They wouldn't hire a Negro as a porter. If you're looking for a job, buddy, you'd better look elsewhere because you can't work there." At the Borden plant on 143rd Street and Fifth Avenue, a "neighborhood observer" remarked: "They don't hire our people in there and you can talk about FEPC until you drop dead. They use Negroes for one thing: To buy the stuff."[35]

When the *Amsterdam News* called for a boycott to get "$100 a week" jobs for African Americans, it elicited broad support, underscoring a widespread belief that stable working-class jobs were essential to a community's well-being. Assemblyman Hulan Jack said "we can all agree to support" well-paying jobs "regardless of political differences." Lindsay White of the Harlem NAACP endorsed the "think while we buy" campaign, which also won support from the Urban League of Greater New York, Harlem YMCA, People's Civic and Welfare Association, and Consumers' Protective League. The fate of the boycott is difficult to determine, since the issue abruptly disappeared from the pages of the *Amsterdam News*, suggesting, perhaps, that advertisers were dismayed by the idea. Nevertheless, charges of racial discrimination against large manufacturers of consumer products, such as Coca Cola and Silvercup Bread, would continue to elicit calls for boycotts for the rest of the decade and beyond.[36]

Freedom Now

As organized labor was turning to the right, a group of progressive and Communist Black labor activists formed an organization called the National Negro Labor Council (NNLC) to continue the fight for racial justice in the workplace. Reflecting the convergence of the modern Black rights struggle in its ascendancy with the Communist left in its decline, the NNLC was a rare left-wing group that was formed during the height of the red scare. NNLC activists were young, products of the war as much as of earlier struggles; the Black liberation struggle would shape the rest of their lives. The National Trade Union Conference for Negro Rights in Chicago in 1950, where Paul Robeson delivered a "stirring" address to the nine hundred delegates, inspired the formation of the NNLC. At its founding convention a year later in Cincinnati, William Hood, president of the 65,000-member UAW Local 600; Coleman Young, recently ousted from the CIO; and Ernest Thompson of the United Electrical Workers were elected to lead the new organization. "After three years of restless disfranchisement," Young later wrote, "the leftist labor movement was reincarnated—smaller, peskier, and more focused than ever." The Harlem Trade Union Council became the Greater New York Negro Labor Council, led by Ewart Guinier and Victoria Garvin. Reflecting the extent of Black worker mobilization in the urban North and West in the 1940s, thirty-five branches were formed, including ones in San Francisco, Chicago, Detroit, and Newark. In its short life, the NNLC constituted a bridge between Black-labor-left formations of the 1940s and those of the 1960s, 1970s, and beyond, such as the Negro American Labor Council and the Coalition of Black Trade Unionists.[37]

The anticommunist network immediately tried to undermine the new group, and some civil rights leaders joined the opposition. On the eve of its founding convention, A. Philip Randolph, Lester Granger, and Roy Wilkins called on Black workers to stay away, on the grounds that the organization was controlled by Communists. William Hood lashed back, accusing Black anticommunists of being at "the beck and call of big white folks," but the NNLC was compromised, in the eyes of many, by its association with the Communist Party at the height of the red scare. Over a thousand people— eight hundred African Americans and three hundred women—attended the convention, which launched a petition drive for a federal FEPC and a nationwide campaign for 100,000 new jobs. The NNLC organizational objectives—as reflected in their pamphlets, speeches, and press releases—did not include advocacy for socialist goals such as public ownership of industry, nor did it give much attention to promoting a left-wing foreign policy. But it vigorously assailed corporate racism, called for public spending to create jobs, and endorsed direct-action tactics to achieve the integration of industry.[38]

A few days later, the AFL's A. Philip Randolph and the CIO's Willard Townsend released a statement calling the NNLC "another creature of the Communists" whose goal was to "disrupt the legitimate activities of bonafide American Labor Movement and Negro community groups and promote Communist propaganda." A *New York Times* headline declared, "Negro Labor Body Called a Failure." NNLC officers later learned that there had been "a battery of agents" at the convention. FBI harassment would last for the life of the organization. Records were stolen from NNLC offices and "countless people were intimidated by FBI agents in their homes, on the streets, and on the job."[39]

In the tradition of the Black labor left, the NNLC wanted to programmatically connect race and class—to infuse labor organizing with an antiracist consciousness and civil rights organizing with a class consciousness. "The struggle on the economic issues and for a job is basic to the struggle for Negro rights," Guinier stressed. In their view, the rise of a national civil rights discourse at the same moment that class struggle was being redefined as disloyal worked to submerge the economic plight of Blacks. Guinier called the economic agenda "the weakest in the fight for Negro liberation." In many ways, the NNLC was a response to the CIO's backsliding on antiracist advocacy since the purge of the left. The group targeted national giants like Sears Roebuck, and industries like airlines and the railroad, that were subject to the President's Committee on Government Contracts. The NNLC endorsed a full employment program based on a thirty-hour work week, the expansion of Social Security to cover agricultural and domestic workers, and nonsegregated public housing, schools and hospitals. Much of this agenda would be taken up by progressives in Congress in the 1960s.[40]

NNLC leaders insisted that the Black struggle be led and defined by Black people, although they welcomed the solidarity of white progressives. As William Hood declared, "The day has ended when white trade union leaders or white leaders in any organization may presume to tell Negroes on what basis they shall come together to fight for their rights." Other Black left groups adopted a similarly nationalist position. The Sojourners for Truth and Justice, an organization of Black women leaders formed in 1951 to rally support for W. E. B. Du Bois and other Black victims of McCarthyism or racial violence, was premised on what Claudia Jones described as "an elementary truth, namely, that it is the Negro people themselves who will determine what organizations they will support and what they will build, and that they will not ask permission to do so."[41]

Cultural work was an integral part of NNLC organizing. The artist Charles White illustrated NNLC literature and pamphlets with heroic renditions of Black workers. Ernest Thompson performed the Sterling Brown poem "Strong Men" at a convention. And theatrical productions at NNLC conventions dramatized contemporary happenings in the Black freedom struggle. The Cleveland convention, for example, featured a play by Chicago artist Oscar Brown Jr. about the effect of strikebreaking on a Black family. The NNLC also became an important spiritual home for Robeson during his domestic exile. Black workers, in Robeson's view, were the most progressive force in the United States and Black America. In a further sign of the NNLC's desire to locate its struggle in Black communities and because the red scare made it difficult for left-wing groups to rent halls, the group relied on the support of Black churches. Signaling the growth of the Black liberation movement, the word "freedom" became a motif in NNLC speeches, publications, and slogans. "Full freedom" was a demand alongside an FEPC; Black workers were "Negro freedom fighters." The "freedom train" was the dominant symbol and refrain, reflecting both the NNLC's campaign to break Jim Crow in the railroad industry as well as the mood of its members.[42]

The NNLC paid attention to the intersection of race and gender, or as they put it, "the compounding of two kinds of discrimination against Negro workers who are women." Improving Black women's occupational opportunities was singled out as one of the primary goals of the organization, which also provided opportunities for female leadership. Decades later, Victoria Garvin, executive director of the Greater New York Negro Labor Council and a vice president of the NNLC, said that she was "especially proud that from the 'git-go' the NNLC declared that our women were equal policymakers in our organization." Garvin attributed this stance to the fact that members came from working-class migrant communities where women's wages were crucial and women's abilities and capacities recognized. In 1953, 41.4 percent of married African American women worked for wages, while only 25.3 percent of their white counterparts did.[43]

Elaine Perry, a Black organizer with the United Electrical Workers, was "very impressed" with the NNLC. It was "the first time I had been exposed to something like that," she said, and despite widespread red-baiting of the NNLC, she stuck with it, seeing the attacks as more anti-Black than anticommunist. "Anything that benefited Black people at the time," she recalled, "was labeled by our government as red, as communist." Unfortunately for Perry, being an activist with the NNLC interfered with her ability to make more money. At Bendix, she was screened from working on projects for the Defense Department because the NNLC had been placed on the list of subversive organizations.[44]

The federal government investigated and harassed the NNLC as a Communist front organization. "Communism: A Menace to the American Negro," a pamphlet published by University Research Corporation, had, like other publications of this type, obscure origins in the anticommunist network. It stated that the NNLC was "calculated to poison harmonious white-Negro relations wherever they exist." The group's "sole object is to disrupt America by creating Negro-white friction and discord." Talk of "Negro rights" and "Negro jobs" was a calculated ruse to stir up strife in order to distract the government's attention from what "Russia does in Asia, Europe and the Far East," which, the author concluded, "they would love." Picket lines "did nothing more than antagonize employers," who "were anxious to find qualified Negroes."[45]

Anticommunist labor leaders attacked the NNLC by calling it either Communist or separatist; by stressing Black progress and American freedom; and by setting up a rival organization, the Negro Labor Committee USA (NLC-USA). Frank R. Crosswaith, "Harlem's most bitter and vocal foe of Communism" and an organizer for the International Ladies Garment Workers Union (ILGWU), headed the NLC-USA. The *Voice of America* broadcast a 1952 NLC-USA conference at the Hotel Theresa, which shed light on the racial views of organized labor. The AFL, which had nineteen unions that excluded Black members, had touted "local autonomy" in defense of Jim Crow auxiliaries in the South, echoing the states rights defense of racial segregation. James Carey, the white secretary-treasurer of the CIO, told the conference that Blacks were "individuals" who did not want "special interest or consideration." This downplaying of race, in the name of color-blindness, was echoed by the ILGWU's Charles Zimmerman, the future head of the AFL-CIO antidiscrimination committee, who said he didn't like to speak of "Negro dressmakers," only "dressmakers." Several years later, Zimmerman and the ILGWU would be accused by the NAACP of wholesale discriminatory treatment of Black garment workers. At the NAACP's 1953 convention, Herbert Hill, Alfred Baker Lewis, and others pushed through a resolution denouncing the NNLC as "communist dominated" and directing local branches to shun it. City Councilman Earl Brown, however, sounded a cautionary note. He supported exposing "the hypocrisy and fakery of the communists and their poison potions," but he feared "that too much time was spent at the Theresa berating the enemy of democracy, communism, and not enough determining ways and means of correcting democracy's defects."[46]

When the Subversive Activities Control Board (or, as Coleman Young called it, "the Negro Activities Control Board") subpoenaed the NNLC's membership list in 1956, the NNLC disbanded, denouncing the government for harassing its membership and "refusing to raise a finger against the White Citizens' Councils and other groups that are openly subverting the Constitution." Nonetheless, the NNLC experienced some success under difficult circumstances. In contrast to its portrayal by the government as a disruptive, foreign tool of Moscow, the NNLC spoke to a major domestic problem and offered a plausible plan of action. And as Black liberals so often reminded government officials, eliminating the source of Communist appeal was in the government's hands. So long as segregation remained "an Achilles' heel" in the American image abroad, Communists would be interested in supporting African Americans in their struggle against it.[47]

Civil Rights Laws and Working-Class Jobs

The wave of state fair employment laws passed after the war (from 1945 to 1950, ten FEPCs were created, eight with enforcement power) did not produce the changes that many civil rights leaders had expected. In the eyes of New York activists, the State Commission against Discrimination (SCAD) was defending the status quo rather than becoming an instrument for occupational integration. The American Jewish Congress, NAACP, ACLU, and ULGNY organized a conference in 1950 to evaluate the disappointing results of civil rights laws and consider strategies to make them more effective. "A statute that is not enforced does more harm than good in the long run, and is a setback to the cause of achieving equality of treatment for all minority groups," Will Maslow warned. This conclusion reflected a key political defeat in New York: what activists considered lawful and appropriate enforcement of the Law against Discrimination, SCAD regarded as an unlawful "quota" or preferential treatment. That the first state administration to enforce the law and shape its meaning was Republican and antiregulatory was an ironic feature of the rise of racial liberalism in New York. "This commission," SCAD declared proudly in 1955 after rejecting a union's proposed minority hiring goals, "has been consistently opposed to a quota system both as a matter of law and as a matter of policy."[48]

Affirmative action, SCAD argued, would undermine current hiring practices, which, in their view, were based on merit. In 1954, SCAD Commissioner Caroline K. Simon declared, "All persons, whatever their color or religion, should be considered for employment solely on the basis of their qualifications. We should defeat our purposes and perpetuate mythical concepts of inferiority if we should try to attain our goal through segregated quotas or other extra-legal devices." The government agency that had been created to uproot injustice from the workplace was subtly, yet effectively, promoting the notion that those individuals currently in possession of well-paying jobs were "qualified" and therefore entitled to them. In 1959, one SCAD commissioner attributed the high percentage of dismissed complaints to the lack of qualifications among complainants, many of whom "are simply unwilling or unable to recognize their own limitations."[49]

When a Democrat, Averill Harriman, was elected governor in 1955, Charles Abrams, a white fair-housing attorney, was appointed to chair SCAD. He led an effort to bolster its power to initiate complaints and conduct investigations of entire industries, but Republicans in Albany blocked it. SCAD's first twenty years were a major disappointment. During its first decade, it "adjusted," in an unspecified manner, about one-quarter of the complaints it received each year. Beginning in the late 1950s, this already low rate declined to an average of 15 percent. It dismissed the vast majority of complaints for lack of evidence. Surveys found that private employment agencies were willing to fill discriminatory job orders: an American Jewish Congress survey of Manhattan employment agencies in 1953 found that 65 percent were willing to fill such job orders, and a 1955 study found 70 percent of agencies willing to do so. Even a government agency committed open and rampant racial discrimination: a 1959 investigation found that the New York State Employment Service was coding applicants by skin color. New York State was not unique. Surveys conducted in 1963 in Los Angeles, Boston, Chicago, and Philadelphia found that 90 to 97 percent of employment agencies were willing to engage in overt racial discrimination.[50]

In earnings, labor force participation, and occupational attainment, Black workers were further behind whites in 1960 than they had been at the end of World War II. A Census Bureau study of male earnings between 1947 and 1962 found "almost no relative advance in income for the colored American." Black workers were concentrated in those semi-skilled and unskilled positions that were being eliminated by automation and technological change. In 1964 the male unemployment rate in Bedford-Stuyvesant was 17.3 percent, while citywide it was 5 percent. Black workers bore the brunt of the structural unemployment that was produced by the first postwar wave of capital flight. Moreover, employed Black workers continued to labor for subsistence-level wages, and were forced to carry extremely high rates of debt to cover basic living expenses.[51]

Many civil rights advocates recognized the failure of state civil rights laws to protect the status of Black workers. The NAACP's anticommunist labor secretary Herbert Hill wrote, "Given the significant developments in the American economy during the last twenty years together with the current status of the Negro wage earner in the states with FEPC laws, we must conclude that state FEPC laws have failed." But the postwar struggle for Black rights had not invested all hopes in antidiscrimination laws alone, even if they had been enforced. Activists had demanded full employment and fair employment. The defeat of full employment legislation, alongside growing automation and the beginnings of plant relocation, shifted the burden of delivering economic progress to antidiscrimination measures. Moreover, the labor movement after the red scare did not generate solutions to the growing crisis of Black labor. While unions produced both ardent champions of racial equality and bald advocates of white power, the AFL and CIO supported a social welfare system that benefited employed males and their dependents and resisted affirmative action.[52]

Thus, job discrimination was pervasive nationally, not regionally, when the federal Civil Rights Act was passed in 1964. It marked the end of legal segregation in the American South, but the law also addressed economic opportunity and created, at long last, a federal FEPC, the Equal Employment Opportunity Commission. The Civil Rights Act was a joint achievement of the southern and northern streams of the U.S. Black rights struggle. African American residents of northern and western states were major supporters of federal legislation, not only to break southern Jim Crow, but also because their own local and state laws had proven so ineffectual in assuring equal opportunity in their home states. Finally, in 1965, just as the Great Society was being created on the national level, legislators in Albany renamed SCAD the State Human Rights Commission and gave it the additional authority that civil rights leaders had long sought.

Black workers in the United States have struggled for access to skilled employment and economic security since emancipation. The occupational gains they made in the 1940s were a result of several intersecting factors, some ephemeral, others not: urbanization, restrictions on the entry of overseas labor, the exigencies of war, progressive CIO policies, and Black leadership that was worker centered. As Black workers challenged racialized labor segmentation and demanded wage parity, they faced a backlash with very few allies. The displacing of Popular Front progressivism with Cold War liberalism at the very moment of economic restructuring left Black workers in the private sector vulnerable, a fate shared by the rapidly increasing ranks of Puerto Ricans in the city. Municipal employment and municipal unions would continue as key locations for Black working-class and middle-class consolidation and activist leadership in New York. Black nationalism, meanwhile, gained strength in the 1950s in response to not only the increase in spatial segregation and the inadequacies of racial liberalism, but also the strong ethnic-identified culture and politics of New York. Moreover, nationalists' advocacy of consumer boycotts reflected a desire for a weapon that would reveal the untapped, collective economic power of Black people.

Despite the defeats in the postwar employment struggle, many Black workers in New York, especially those in unions, managed to permanently open doors for themselves and give their children better futures. As the first group of African Americans to live under a fair employment law, Black New Yorkers shaped future national advocacy. The northern encounter with de facto segregation and northern Blacks' demand for proportionate hiring plans accelerated the push for affirmative action and contributed to the eventual adoption of such plans by some employers and universities across the nation in the 1970s and beyond.

Epilogue: Another Kind of America

The Black rights struggle in postwar New York helped to launch a social movement that would transform the United States. Black New Yorkers pushed racial justice onto the agenda of American progressivism, creating a bridge from the New Deal to the Fair Deal and articulating claims that would be taken up by the Great Society. They helped remake the Democratic Party, positioning it to one day become an ally for the southern civil rights movement. Black New Yorkers also changed the social, political, and cultural landscape of New York City. They fought for better jobs, moved into new neighborhoods, formed their own banks, demanded equal social services and political representation, protested police abuse, and paved the way for their children to attend college. These mobilizations produced the first law in the United States since Reconstruction barring discrimination in private-sector employment and several other laws aimed at halting racial discrimination and segregation in education, housing, and public accommodations. Even though the movement was stopped midstream, leaving many of its most urgent economic and social goals unrealized, the Black World War II generation launched the modern civil rights struggle and left a rich and lasting legacy.

The story of the African American struggle for equality in New York invites a reevaluation of the narrative of the civil rights movement as a whole. The traditional portrait of the movement posits a patriotic, straightforward civil rights or integrationist spirit that evolves or devolves, depending on the writer's perspective, into calls for Black Power, increased militancy, and Black nationalism. Yet in New York, movement leaders called for broad social change, economic empowerment, group advancement, and colonial freedom from the beginning. The traditional narrative omits the move-

272

ment's full chronology and elides the critically important Black radical tradition.

The struggle for Negro rights, as Black New Yorkers called their movement, had features associated with nationalism and integrationism: its primary goal was desegregation and full equality, but its methodology was not color-blind individualism. It called instead for group-based remedies, what is now called affirmative action. Activists advocated numerical goals as a commonsense way to measure compliance with antidiscrimination laws. The movement also advocated redistributionary and regulatory measures to ensure racial justice and a democratic society. Reflecting their political roots in the New Deal era, many African American leaders thought that government had the responsibility to bring about a desegregated society. They expected the government to play a proactive, interventionist role in improving and equalizing housing, educational, health care, and employment opportunities for Black New Yorkers.

Black radicalism is rarely treated as a coherent movement or ideology. It commonly gets fragmented, with some of its goals and tactics woven into narratives of integrationism and others into accounts of Black nationalism. This is not entirely inaccurate: the red scare had destroyed much of its infrastructure and dispersed left-leaning activists into both Black liberal and Black nationalist projects and organizations. But Black radicalism deserves to be inserted into the narrative of the Black liberation movement and assessed on its own terms. It gave the equal rights struggle in New York a worldliness, a boldness, and a commitment to both ordinary folks and fundamental social change.

Many civil rights leaders in postwar New York would be active and provide leadership in the tumultuous decades ahead. For others, the end of this era ushered in the final stage of their political lives, and an overall decline in their influence. Benjamin Davis, who had been convicted under the Smith Act as a leader of the U.S. Communist Party and imprisoned in Terre Haute, Indiana, for five years, was released in 1955. At a time when American Communists were leaving the party in droves, Davis resumed his affiliation and became national secretary of the Communist Party in 1959. In 1961, in a challenge to the Cold War taboo against bringing "radicals" to university campuses, a group of Queens College students extended invitations to Ben Davis and Malcolm X. Both were considered defiant figures, feared and mistrusted by mainstream America. When Queens College canceled the event, with City University backing, students took to the streets. At Hunter College in Manhattan, hundreds of students picketed and even more boycotted classes. Like the free speech movement at the University of California, Berkeley, breaking the enforced silences of the 1950s proved to be the signal act of a new era. The worst of McCarthyism was over by the early 1960s, but actual Communists still remained targets. When he died of cancer in 1964, Davis was facing another federal prosecution; this time he was accused of failing to register as a foreign agent under the Internal Security Act. While anticommunists worked hard to destroy his reputation and bury his record of service to Harlem, his legacy is substantial. Whatever Davis's relation to the Soviet Union, he helped to forge a progressive agenda on many issues that have been at the center of urban politics, including police brutality, hate speech, housing discrimination, and multiculturalism.[1]

Soon after the Supreme Court ordered his passport returned in 1958, W. E. B. Du Bois and his partner, the writer-activist Shirley Graham Du Bois, went to Moscow for the fortieth anniversary of the Bolshevik Revolution. They spent New Year's Eve with Premier Nikita Khrushchev, the Soviet elite, and Paul Robeson. In 1961, Du Bois accepted the invitation of President Kwame Nkrumah to spend his final years in Ghana, where he intended to complete an encyclopedia Africana. As a departing act of defiance against the country that he felt no longer deserved his support, Du Bois joined the U.S. Communist Party. He died in 1963, a year before Congress passed the Civil Rights Act and breathed new life in the Fourteenth Amendment. Du Bois had devoted his life to vindicating the unfinished revolution of Reconstruction and restoring to African Americans the legal status achieved by the former slaves. But the venerable scholar-activist had finally lost faith in the possibility of attaining democracy in a nation that he saw as imperialist, avaricious, and wedded to war and white supremacy. Shirley Graham Du Bois, who had become a trusted adviser to Ghanaian president Nkrumah, devoted herself to Communist China after the military coup in Ghana in 1966.

W. E. B. Du Bois, like Paul Robeson and other leftists, had adopted the stance that Black liberation depended on stopping U.S. imperialism; and this included lending support to rivals of the U.S. government, such as the Soviet Union and China. Du Bois's socialism and admiration for the Soviet Union may have positioned him "against the grain" of civil rights leaders during the Cold War, but it foreshadowed the internationalist outlook of radical activists like Malcolm X, Angela Davis, Huey P. Newton, Kathleen Cleaver, James Forman, and Amiri Baraka. Indeed, many Black radicals of the 1960s saw themselves to the left of the Communist Party. Stopping U.S. imperialism in Vietnam, Africa, or Cuba—not solely achieving domestic civil rights gains—came to be seen as essential to Black liberation, a struggle these activists insisted was global rather than national.[2]

Paul Robeson endured a breakdown and physical decline, the causes of which remain subject to debate. Anguished by the revelations of Stalin's terrors but buoyed by the Black liberation movement, Robeson died in 1976. Despite his persecution, many of Paul Robeson's political stances have been incorporated into modern American progressivism. Yet his denunciation of U.S. corporate conduct overseas—the relentless pursuit of cheap labor and exploitation of African mineral wealth, as well as his warning that the American economy was being hijacked by the arms industry—remain as "radical" today as they were then. The end of the Cold War made possible a rediscovery of Paul Robeson on the centenary of his birth. After decades of mainstream stigma and erasure, many Americans embraced him as a brilliant and committed artist, athlete, intellectual, activist, and orator.[3]

To be sure, a left-wing Harlem perspective survived McCarthyism and, in fact, exerted a considerable influence on Black activist culture in ensuing decades. Its major expression was in *Freedomways*, a journal edited by Esther Cooper Jackson, a lifelong progressive activist and wife of Communist Party organizer James Jackson. From 1961 to 1985, *Freedomways* was a beacon of left-wing Black intellectualism, artistry, social criticism, and political debate. It expressed the Harlem radical tradition during the Black Liberation movement of the 1960s and 1970s, and brought a critique of imperialism, especially the Vietnam War, to Black political discourse. Among its contributors were W. E. B. Du Bois, Shirley Graham Du Bois, Langston Hughes, Julian Mayfield, John Henrik Clarke, Ernest Kaiser, Lorraine Hansberry, Jack O'Dell, and Ruby Dee.

McCarthyism postponed the climactic overthrow of Jim Crow. Over and over again, African American leaders and others in the late 1950s described pent-up and overdue anger, tension, and frustration. The *Brown* decision in 1954 pierced the heavy gloom and restored a sense of forward motion. Audre Lorde, a young New York writer living in Mexico with American expatriates, returned home when she learned the news: "That spring, McCarthy was censured. The Supreme Court decision on the desegregation of schools was announced in the English newspaper, and for a while all of us seemed to go crazy with hope for another kind of America." A year later, the Montgomery bus boycott imbued grassroots protest with moral fervor, removing the stigma and suspicion attached to mass activism in the McCarthy era.[4]

The revival of the civil rights movement and rise of mass protest in the early 1960s was a nationwide phenomena, and African Americans took to the streets of New York chanting "Freedom now!" Black New Yorkers were inspired by the bravery of southern protesters as well as by the exhilarating liberation from colonial rule in many African nations. In 1963 a wave of "sit-ins, kneel-ins, pray-ins, sleep-ins, hunger strikes, selective buying campaigns, boycotts and freedom marches" swept the city. "Suddenly," according to the *New York Times*, "it seems the Negro is mad at everybody." Jobs, education, and housing were the chief demands. The Urban League's Edward Lewis pointed to the failure of legislation passed in the postwar years: "Despite all the laws protecting his rights, the Negro has been for generations overcrowded, underemployed, frustrated, and poor." And City College professor Kenneth Clark stressed the illusive image of opportunity that had drawn so many southern migrants: "All these years Negroes in the North have been getting big promises and making little or no gains in jobs, education and housing."[5]

Many of the postwar civil rights activists continued to provide leadership in the 1960s, although their values and goals were deeply shaped by the political ethos of the 1940s. Ewart Guinier was part of the civil rights resurgence of the early 1960s, as a leader of the Queens Urban League. In an ironic development, the ivy league university that had discriminated against him over thirty years earlier hired him to chair its new Afro-American Studies Department. The veteran activist returned to Harvard just as Black Studies became the next battleground of the Black liberation struggle. Guinier bequeathed a political passion to his daughter, law professor Lani Guinier, who has championed electoral reform, including proportional representation—the voting system that brought political and demographic diversity to the New York City Council in the 1940s.

Hope Stevens similarly linked the early civil rights and Black liberation movements in New York City. An activist, lawyer, entrepreneur, and advisor and counselor to new Caribbean nations, Stevens exemplified his generation's commitment to public service. He practiced law for forty-five years in the same office on 125th Street, and according to the *Amsterdam News*, he "stood in the forefront of every critical struggle in Harlem." A unique combination of radical activist and prudent businessman, Stevens headed the Manhattan chapter of the National Negro Congress, was a loyal supporter of

Ben Davis, a founder of both the United Mutual Life Insurance Company and Carver Federal Savings and Loan, and the first Black president of the Uptown Chamber of Commerce. He had the transnational, diasporic affiliations that thrived in cosmopolitan and diverse Black New York. A native of the British Virgin Islands and raised in St. Kitts-Nevis, Stevens fought for self-determination for Caribbean islands and his firm represented many former British colonies.[6]

Victoria Garvin remained committed to the Black Liberation movement, but embraced the life of an expatriate, first in Ghana where she and Maya Angelou showed Malcolm X around Accra, and later in China, where she lived for many years before returning to the United States. Active through the 1990s, Garvin remained a committed "revolutionary nationalist," as well as an ardent supporter of trade unions. This early champion of women's equality and leadership also cheered the 1995 Million Man March, sponsored by the Nation of Islam.[7]

Black leftists in the labor movement pioneered paths that have remained central to the struggle for racial justice. After World War II, they insisted that affirmative action remedies were necessary to overcome institutionalized white privilege. Later, in the 1960s and 1970s, the judiciary imposed affirmative action plans on several unions that had used seniority systems and other devices to protect white workers and block Black worker equality. While this reflects the failure of radicals to prevail in the house of labor, it shows their eventual success in projecting the legitimacy of affirmative action in mainstream American liberalism. In addition, the Black-labor-left's call for multiracial, activist trade unions and their incisive critique of capital flight are still compelling answers to the rapacious force of corporate restructuring and globalization. Their stress on the importance of organizing and empowering the weakest and most oppressed segment of society is more relevant than ever as the labor force becomes predominantly female, nonwhite, and unorganized. Many issues raised by Black radicals in the early civil rights movement remain on the urban activist agenda, including affirmative action, Black history in the classroom, the unionization of Black women workers, publicly funded day care, and an end to police brutality.

Some civil rights activists who had suffered for their association with the left during the McCarthy era continued to experience repercussions in the 1960s. Algernon Black, a leader in the Ethical Culture Society and an activist at the forefront of the fair-housing movement in New York, was appointed in 1966 by Mayor John Lindsay to serve on the newly created Civilian Complaint Review Board. Opponents of the board launched an aggressive campaign against it, culminating in a ballot referendum seeking its abolition. An advertisement urged New Yorkers to call a phone number in Staten Island, "the Voice of Freedom," which related Black's "subversive" history. Algernon Black later recalled with dismay that the *New York Times* had run "a smear article" publicizing the whole thing on the Sunday before the election, in which the board was defeated.[8]

Lee Lorch, an activist in the Stuyvesant Town struggle, took a job at Penn State after being dismissed for political reasons from his position at City College. After Penn State accused him of being a Communist and fired him, Judge Hubert Delany helped him secure a position at Fisk. Lorch, who lived in Little Rock in 1957, was active in the school desegregation struggle, but his association with the Communist left brought relentless government harassment and repeated job loss, finally forcing him to move to Canada, where he retired from York University in 1985. Lorch received an honorary doctorate from City University of New York in 1990 in recognition of his academic and civil rights contributions.[9]

The Black church in New York also remained a source of social and political leadership in the 1960s. Gardner Taylor of Concord Baptist in Brooklyn fought for Black jobs at the new Downstate Medical Center in Brooklyn, for better schools and housing in Bedford-Stuyvesant, and against apartheid in South Africa. Moran Weston moved from the left-wing Negro Labor Victory Committee to become the rector of St. Philip's Episcopal Church, a prestigious Harlem congregation, where he spearheaded efforts to bring better housing and social services to the community. The Reverend Milton Galamison's community leadership had only just begun in the 1950s. In 1964 he led the biggest act of civil disobedience of the decade when thousands of parents heeded his call to boycott the racially segregated public schools. When city leaders proved unrelenting in their opposition to integration, Galamison joined the larger civil rights movement's turn toward Black power, community control, and increased militancy. He despaired at the apparent concession won in 1969 when New York decentralized elementary school governance and created thirty-two community school boards. Their lack of control over budget and teacher hiring, Galamison felt, deprived them of the power to make a meaningful difference.[10]

Indeed, before the 1960s had even begun, the frustrated efforts of Kenneth Clark to overturn de facto school segregation in New York after the *Brown* decision exposed the hypocrisy and fault lines of northern white liberalism. Looking back nearly forty years later, Clark blamed "deep-seated forms of northern racism" for the failure to realize integrated schools and cities. "I look back and I shudder at how naïve we all were in our belief in the steady progress racial minorities would make through programs of litigation and education." While he still hoped for a revival of the movement with new and innovative strategies, Clark concluded that his life had "been a series of glorious defeats."

Clark's bleak assessment of the legacy of the civil rights movement seems to fly in the face of the current media and scholarly celebration of the growth and "success" of the Black middle class. But it sheds light on a neglected feature of the movement: its goal was to open doors and improve social conditions for all African Americans, not just one segment. Clark lamented the continuing racial segregation and unequal funding of American public schools fifty years after *Brown*. But his despair could also extend to the plight of the working poor, whose share of national income has been declining for decades; the working-class youth forced to mortgage their future to attend college; and the 13 percent of African American men disenfranchised for life as a result of criminal convictions. Clark represented a cohort of Black professionals, born in the era of Jim Crow, who were raised to see themselves as part of a people to whom they were inextricably linked and to whom they owed something in return.[11]

New York City, with its history of activism, abundance of lawyers, and headquarters of many progressive organizations, continued to serve as a center of organizing, fundraising, and support for southern and other national civil rights struggles. When "local people" rose up all over the South to overthrow Jim Crow and change their lives and society, they were not alone, but part of a national web of Black activists who supported each other bodily, financially, spiritually, and politically. Robert F. Williams, the controversial North Carolina NAACP leader and advocate of armed self-defense, found many key allies in Harlem, such as Julian Mayfield, John Henrik Clarke, and Mae Mallory, who came to his aid when he fled the police and went into exile in Cuba. North Carolina–born Harlem resident Ella Baker organized or joined a myriad of support groups in New York City for the southern civil rights struggle.

The Reverend Thomas Kilgore of Friendship Baptist Church in Harlem was a primary organizer of the 1957 Prayer Pilgrimage to Washington as well as the 1963 March on Washington. Indeed, the march realized A. Philip Randolph's longtime dream and symbolically knit together the southern and northern civil rights struggles into one national movement. New York–based activists Bayard Rustin, Clarence Jones, and Stanley Levison provided invaluable support and political counsel to Martin Luther King Jr. And New York singer and activist Harry Belafonte gave numerous benefit concerts for King, the Southern Christian Leadership Conference (SCLC), and other groups.[12]

The Freedom Budget and full employment proposals put forth in 1966 by Bayard Rustin, A. Philip Randolph, and the Urban League revived the movement's projection of a broad socioeconomic agenda in Congress. The Stuyvesant Town struggle sparked the formation of the New York State Committee against Discrimination in Housing to fight for a state fair-housing law, which Albany finally enacted in the early 1960s. This coterie of activists, including Algernon Black, also created the National Committee against Discrimination in Housing, which drafted the federal Housing Act passed in the aftermath of King's assassination in 1968.[13]

The United Nations ensured that the leaders of newly independent African states would visit New York, creating occasions for Black transnational networking and increased African American participation in diplomatic protocol. One Harlem activist recalled, "Ghana's freedom inspired Black Americans more than I think people have understood. African people were speaking out for and getting their freedom." African American pride and identification with Black-governed nations was nurtured in a series of ticker tape parades in lower Manhattan's "canyon of heroes": in 1953 and 1954 for Ethiopia, Liberia, and Haiti; in 1959 for the new nation of Guinea; in 1961 for Tunisia and Sudan; and in 1965 for the Ivory Coast. New York was fertile ground for the creation of a global Black political identity. The 1960s and 1970s saw a tremendous upsurge in Black Nationalist consciousness and organizing, which built on multiple Pan-Africanist legacies, from the Garvey movement to Paul Robeson's Council on African Affairs. The United African Nationalist Movement led by James Lawson, and the African Nationalist Pioneer Movement led by Carlos Cooks, were joined by the Nation of Islam as the most visible sources of leadership. Nationalists continued the left's tradition of bringing Black American grievances to the United Nations. Activist Ora Mobley-Sweeting believes that the importance of the UN to the movement has been underappreciated. "Having the United Nations right there in New York City offered us the opportunity to approach this international body . . . it happened more often than anyone seems to admit." James Lawson, she recalled, "set up picket lines at the United Nations, speaking out about African liberation." Perhaps it was Lawson who St. Clair Drake, the distinguished sociologist, had in mind when he acidly made reference to "Harlem's fanatical black nationalists who heckle at United Nations meetings." Despite such dismissals, protests at the UN by a variety of Black radicals, including nationalists and leftists, over the murder of Congolese liberation leader and first president Patrice Lumumba helped revive Black criticism of U.S. foreign policy.[14]

Lawson and Cooks also pioneered in the growing Black consciousness movement in the city and as prominent street orators, they influenced the young Malcolm X, who was assigned to a Harlem mosque of the Nation of Islam in 1954. The political education of Malcolm X was deeply shaped by his Harlem milieu and contacts. He ultimately forged a politics that bridged Black nationalist and left-progressive ideas, crystallizing in the Organization of Afro-American Unity, the group he founded after his departure from the Nation of Islam. Malcolm X became such a regular at the UN that he was given an office there; Harlem and the UN became his home bases, his two intersecting political orbits.

Despite differences and rivalries, there was significant left-nationalist cross-fertilization in Harlem. Harlem activist Audley "Queen Mother" Moore left the Communist Party in 1950 in search of a more Black-identified movement, one that would support her quest to banish the term "Negro." Government agents tried to get her to inform, but she never would. Like most Black rank-and-file who drifted from the Communist Party, she did not become ideologically anticommunist. Like many other fighters for integration, Moore later bemoaned that desegregation had unfolded on white terms. She was deeply involved in the struggle to break the color bar in major league baseball, but came to regret the loss of Black-owned and managed ball clubs. In addition, she felt that party interracialism affected men and women differently. "All the brothers had white women, it disgusted me," she said, frustrated that white women, in her view, received race-based preferential attention from Black men. Moore fought hard to bury the appellation "Negro," a term she believed inculcated inferiority. "Being a Negro is a condition," she argued. Her most enduring contribution was her leadership in the struggle for Black reparations. She founded the first major reparations advocacy group in the United States in 1955 and for the next thirty years brought the issue to the attention of younger activists. On a flight to Tanzania, Moore sought to persuade the young man seated next to her, Charles Ogletree, of the justness of reparations for slavery and segregation. Ogletree, a professor at Harvard Law School, is the co-chair of the Reparations Coordinating Committee, which in 2002 is preparing class action lawsuits against state and federal governments for the injuries caused by slavery and racial segregation.[15]

In contrast to Moore, Harold Cruse was a Black nationalist who enacted a much sharper, even vitriolic, break from a left-wing past. Cruse's highly influential *The Crisis of the Negro Intellectual: A Historical Analysis of the Failure of Black Leadership*, published in 1967, assailed Black radical activists and intellectuals in New York City for what Cruse saw as their failure to seek racial group power and their pathetic pursuit of assimilation, white patronage, and white models of success. According to Cruse, the Black middle class, including even the literary intelligentsia, was the engine of Black communal economic advancement. But, he argued, this class had failed miserably in its task of building Black-owned cultural institutions and businesses. The chief political failing of the Harlem intelligentsia, he claimed, was their flirtation with leftism and then headlong plunge into integrationism.

On the contrary, history suggests that Black economic advancement has been linked to the fortunes of the working-class majority rather than the talented tenth. The Black majority's status has depended on the configuration of broader social forces, rather than the potential employing power of an institutionally marginalized Black middle class. Nevertheless, the *political* affinities and alliances of the middle class have been a decisive factor in Black advancement. A socially conscious and politically progressive middle class strengthened the postwar African American rights struggle. This cohort of leaders espoused a race and class ideology that embraced workers' interests as an extension of their own, rather than an ideology that privileged their own class advancement.

In the late 1950s and early 1960s, conflict erupted in the anticommunist civil rights–labor alliance. A. Philip Randolph and NAACP Labor Secretary Herbert Hill, who both had endorsed the ouster of the left from organized labor, found that racism remained alive and well in the AFL-CIO. In 1959 a group of AFL-CIO trade unionists formed the Negro American Labor Council (NALC) to coordinate the fight for racial justice in the workplace and in organized labor. The NALC provided important assistance to Black longshoremen and brewery workers in New York. When the NALC assailed racism in the AFL-CIO, however, the federation denounced it, and its leader Randolph, as racists. Randolph, in turn, castigated the "moral decay of American labor," and then, in a stunning rebuke to its own vice president, the executive council of the AFL-CIO censured A. Philip Randolph. In the end, Randolph and the AFL-CIO mended fences, but the NALC dissolved after Randolph withdrew support, fearing Communist infiltration.[16]

In 1962 Herbert Hill waged a highly contentious battle against the racism and lack of democracy inside the International Ladies Garment Workers Union. Hill and the ILGWU had once been on the same side; they fought vigorously to counter leftists in Harlem, in the NAACP, and in the labor movement. The ILGWU was the biggest union in the city and half of its members were Black and Latino, but every single union official was white, including the entire executive board and every local manager, even those who headed segregated all-Black and Latino locals. The ILGWU defended its ban on internal caucuses and extremely restrictive office-holding qualifications on the grounds that they were designed to prevent Communist infiltration. Italian- and Jewish-American garment workers monopolized the skilled, higher-paying job categories, while workers of color labored in sweatshop conditions for the minimum wage. Hill mobilized the NALC, civil rights groups, and the state and federal government to win some changes, but the case exemplified the continuing racism in the labor movement. It also underscored the vital importance of having Black and Latino union leaders to defend the interests of nonwhite union members. The trade unions in New York in which Black workers have maintained high levels of membership and some leadership gains are often in industries that cannot relocate, such as subways and hospitals, and/or are in the public sector, which owing to the history of private-sector discrimination has employed larger numbers of African Americans.[17]

Black electoral gains have come in New York at a snail's pace. It was only in 1994 with the election of Carl McCall as New York State controller that an African American was elected to statewide office, a goal first set in 1950 by the Harlem Affairs Committee. State electoral laws and rules have blunted the use of third parties and insurgency to enable fuller access to political leadership. Thus the struggle has proceeded primarily within the two major parties. Guy Brewer, a political activist and NAACP dissident, was the second African American elected to the state legislature from Queens; he served for ten years and built a formidable political club that still schools Queens politicians. Bessie Buchanan, a former Cotton Club dancer and star of the Broadway hit "Shuffle Along" who challenged discrimination at the Stork Club with Josephine Baker, became the first African American woman elected to Albany in 1954. She fought for fair housing and won passage of a law that removed racial designations from state forms, including marriage licenses. Her husband, Charles Buchanan, was the treasurer and manager of the famed Savoy Ballroom for thirty years and chair of the United Mutual Life Insurance Company, the only Black-operated mutual insurance company in the state.[18]

In the 1960s, African American women made greater gains in winning elective office. The 1964 Harlem state senate race featured two prominent lawyers who offered contrasting strategies for Black advancement. Constance Baker Motley, an NAACP attorney with a distinguished record of civil rights advocacy in federal court, ran on a strong civil rights platform. Her Republican opponent was Cora T. Walker, a civic leader and former president of the Harlem Lawyers Association. Walker emphasized self-help, criticized the welfare system, and said that Harlem schools should be improved rather than busing their students to other neighborhoods. "Our sense of values is cock-eyed," she declared. Motley won easily, but Walker's views have increased in popularity. In 1966 President Lyndon B. Johnson appointed Motley to U.S. District Court, and she became the first African American woman appointed to the federal bench. Republicans fought bitterly against her confirmation.[19]

In 1968, Shirley Chisholm won election to Congress as the first Black representative from Brooklyn, and incredibly, only the second in the city since Powell in 1944. A Brooklyn College graduate from an immigrant (Barbados) family, her mentor was Wesley McD. Holder, founder of the insurgent Bedford-Stuyvesant Political League. As a state senator, Chisholm won passage of a law that extended unemployment and Social Security laws to agricultural and domestic workers. With this she achieved a major Black political goal first articulated in the 1930s when these occupations had been excluded from New Deal legislation in order to appease racist southern politicians. A feminist, Chisholm was an advocate of legal abortion and the Equal Rights Amendment, and in 1972 made history when she ran for the Democratic Party's presidential nomination.[20]

Adam Clayton Powell reached the zenith of his power in the 1960s. As chairman of the House Labor and Education Committee under a liberal Democratic president, Powell was uniquely positioned to help realize his longtime legislative agenda. President Lyndon Johnson and Powell shared a devotion to the legacy of Franklin Roosevelt, but both saw the New Deal as only the first step in providing a safety net to all Americans. Powell was in many respects a coauthor of the Great Society; he shepherded a score of laws through his committee, from food stamps to Head Start to federal aid to desegregated education—a law that finally implemented the Marcantonio and Powell amendments that had been such a thorn in Democrats' side for so many years. The Great Society measures of the 1960s aided many Americans who had not been reached by the New Deal, including African Americans. Defeated in 1970 by Charles Rangel, Powell's last few years were marked by allegations of improprieties and an unprecedented Congressional attempt to oust him. A federal court overruled this Congressional abuse of power, but not before Powell's constituents spurned Congress with their votes and put him back in the House themselves.

The northern civil rights movement made an important contribution to the rise of defendants' rights in the postwar criminal legal system. A grassroots social movement to end the infamous "third degree," to bar evidence from unlawful search and seizure, to treat juveniles differently, and to give poor people the right to counsel preceded the landmark Supreme Court rulings of the early 1960s that extended the Bill of Rights to state, rather than exclusively federal, criminal courts. New York was at the forefront of this crucial but neglected component of the civil rights movement. The contemporary rollback in defendants' rights, the massive rise in the incarceration of people of color, and the virtual evisceration of the Fourth Amendment in Black and Latino communities is part of a broad assault on the gains of the civil rights era, including the attacks on affirmative action and Black voting rights.

The racial history of the post-*Plessy* United States calls into question the conventional notion that segregation and discrimination in the North was de facto—the result of market forces and the personal choices of whites rather than laws or public policy. The category of de facto segregation tends to relieve the state of responsibility for producing, and thus remedying, racial inequality. But is de facto segregation an adequate way of describing such phenomena as a government-insured mortgage granted to someone who openly refused to sell to Black buyers; the intentional failure to enforce state and federal fair housing laws; or the use of Black tax dollars to construct apartments that were leased to whites only? Similarly, the New York State Employment Service filled racially identified job orders for at least twenty years after a state law barring job discrimination was passed. Was that de facto segregation? The efforts by the New York Board of Education to maintain racial homogeneity in public schools after *Brown* further illustrates the deceptiveness of the term de facto segregation.

The defeats of the postwar struggle for Negro rights had a profound effect on the next generation. The continued racial oppression of the Black population in the urban North produced urban upheaval and violence in the 1960s, just as Congress passed major civil rights laws. New York State had passed antidiscrimination laws years before Congress had, but they were not solving the growing crisis of Black unemployment or reversing the spread of residential segregation. A riot in Harlem in the summer of 1964 followed one in Philadelphia, and prefigured the much greater convulsion in Los Angeles a year later. Defeats in housing, police reform, and employment struggles in the postwar years set the stage for the escalation of conflict in the 1960s and beyond. The continued restrictions on Black residential mobility and access to capital, despite advancements in the law, increased Black cynicism about the possibility of realizing the highly touted American Dream. Poor, predominantly Black neighborhoods have received inferior city and state resources and services in health care, education, recreation, sanitation, and housing. Police misconduct thrives in segregated neighborhoods. The context for nearly all of the riots in the 1960s was a police shooting, or an incident exposing deep police-community conflict, in conjunction with a sharp recent decline in factory or other stable employment for young unskilled males.

But the story of the early civil rights movement forces us to acknowledge that "the urban crisis" of the 1960s and 1970s was not inevitable or unpreventable. Numerous and creative proposals to avert it had been put forth on many occasions by Black New York leaders, and there are lessons to be learned from their analysis of northern metropolitan racism. Many labor leaders, especially those in the National Negro Labor Council, called plant relocation and the deindustrialization of the urban core an attack on the gains of Black migrant workers. There was strong support in the postwar Black rights movement for trade unions. The unionization of Black workers empowered Black workers and strengthened their families and communities. In contrast to most liberal leaders who came to accept an American welfare state that distributed medical, pension, and housing benefits in ways that reinforced race, occupational, and gender inequities, African American rights groups such as the Urban League and the NAACP advocated a single, universal package of social and economic supports. In contrast to the anti-urban direction of postwar American planning and development, Black leaders encouraged pro-urban policies. They sought to improve and modernize the urban housing stock and remove race-based restrictions on Black residential mobility. They supported mass transit, a state university system, and public clinics and hospitals in Black neighborhoods. Finally, civil rights leaders became convinced that strengthening the rights of a person in police custody and reforming police practices are essential to guaranteeing the citizenship rights of African Americans, indeed of all Americans.

The massive Black migration of the 1940s transformed the racial geography of the nation and raised the question of whether segregation would intensify and spread in the North and West. Civil rights leaders in New York City mobilized Black New Yorkers and pushed this question onto the city's political agenda. The New York civil rights struggle arose from the migrant generation's desire to find protection from racial subordination and violence, claim the fruits of their labor, and vindicate their rights as first-class citizens. The migration and northern movement that it spawned also contributed to the transformation of the South. Black New Yorkers helped to change national politics and created solidarity networks that were crucial when southern African Americans rose up against Jim Crow and needed sustenance, attorneys, arms, and money.

Abbreviations

The following abbreviations are used in the notes. Unless otherwise noted, all archives are located in New York City.

Adams Papers	Wilhemina Adams Papers, Schomburg Center for Research in Black Culture
American Jewish Congress Papers	Papers of the Library of the American Jewish Congress
American Labor Party Papers	American Labor Party Papers, Rutgers University, New Brunswick, N.J.
Bass Papers	Charlotta Bass Papers, Southern California Library for Social Studies and Research, Los Angeles
Bell Papers	Daniel Bell Papers, Tamiment Library, New York University
Black Papers	Algernon Black Papers, Rare Book and Manuscript Library, Columbia University
Bolin Papers	Jane Bolin Papers, Schomburg Center for Research in Black Culture
Civil Rights Congress Papers	Civil Rights Congress Papers, Schomburg Center for Research in Black Culture
CORE Papers	Papers of the Congress of Racial Equality, Columbia University (microfilm)
Davis Papers	Benjamin J. Davis Papers, Schomburg Center for Research in Black Culture
Galamison Papers	Milton Galamison Papers, Schomburg Center for Research in Black Culture

Garvin Papers	Victoria Garvin Papers, Schomburg Center for Research in Black Culture
Guinier Papers	Ewart Guinier Papers, Schomburg Center for Research in Black Culture
ILA Papers	International Longshoreman's Association Papers, Tamiment Library, New York University
Isaacs Papers	Stanley Isaacs Papers, Manuscript Collection, New York Public Library
Lee Papers	Canada Lee Papers, Schomburg Center for Research in Black Culture
Marcantonio Papers	Vito Marcantonio Papers, Manuscript Division, New York Public Library
Mayor's Committee on Unity Papers	Mayor's Committee on Unity Papers, Municipal Archives
Mills Papers	Saul Mills Papers, Tamiment Library, New York University
Moses Papers	Robert Moses Papers, Rare Book and Manuscript Division, New York Public Library
NAACP Papers	Papers of the National Association for the Advancement of Colored People (NAACP), Library of Congress, Washington, D.C.
National Negro Congress Papers	National Negro Congress Papers, Schomburg Center for Research in Black Culture
Negro Labor Committee Papers	Papers of the Negro Labor Committee, Schomburg Center for Research in Black Culture
New York State AFL-CIO Papers	Papers of the New York State AFL-CIO, Tamiment Library, New York University
N.Y. Board of Education Papers	Papers of the Board of Education of the City of New York, Rare Book and Manuscript Library, Teachers College, Columbia University
O'Neal Papers	Frederick O'Neal Papers, Schomburg Center for Research in Black Culture
O'Dwyer Papers	William O'Dwyer Papers, Municipal Archives
Randolph Papers	A. Philip Randolph Papers, Schomburg Center for Research in Black Culture (microfilm)
Robeson Collection	Paul Robeson Collection, Schomburg Center for Research in Black Culture
Stevens Papers	Harold Stevens Papers, Schomburg Center for Research in Black Culture

Notes

Prologue

1. *New York Age,* January 5, 1946, and June 9, 1945.
2. *Malcolm X Speaks,* George Breitman ed. (New York: Grove Weidenfeld, 1965), 31.
3. John H. Johnson, transcript of radio address over WNYC, "The Democratic Ideal in New York City," February 6, 1945, Mayor's Committee on Unity Papers, box 1613; Howard Selsam, *The Negro People in the United States: Facts for All Americans* (New York: Jefferson School, 1953); Hugh Bradley, "Next Steps in the Struggle for Negro Freedom" (New York: New Century Publishers, 1953), 30, in "CP (US) and Negroes" vertical file, Tamiment Library, New York University, New York.
4. Robert S. Weaver, *Negro Labor: A National Problem* (Port Washington, N.Y.: Kennikat Press, 1946), 15; National Negro Congress, "Statement on Problems of Negro Workers in the State of New York," n.d. (ca. 1940), "National Negro Congress," vertical file, Tamiment Library; Nat Brandt, *Harlem at War: The Black Experience in World War II* (Syracuse, N.Y.: Syracuse University Press, 1996), 73.
5. Cheryl Lynn Greenberg, *Or Does It Explode? Black Harlem in the Great Depression* (New York: Oxford University Press, 1991), 203; Brandt, 80; Weaver, 152; Merl E. Reed, *Seedtime for The Modern Civil Rights Movement: The President's Committee on Fair Employment Practice, 1941–1946* (Baton Rouge: Louisiana State University Press, 1991).
6. As David Levering Lewis has pointed out, Du Bois's "The African Roots of War" preceded Lenin's analysis of imperialism. For Black agency in forging the CP position on the Negro question, see Winston James, *Holding Aloft the Banner of Ethiopia: Caribbean Radicalism in Early Twentieth Century America* (New York: Verso, 1998); and Mark Solomon, *The Cry Was Unity: Communists and African Americans,*

1917–1936 (Jackson: University Press of Mississippi, 1998). On Communists and the antiracist struggle, see Mark Naison, *Communists in Harlem during the Depression* (Urbana: University of Illinois Press, 1983); Robin D. G. Kelley, *Hammer and Hoe: Alabama Communists during the Great Depression* (Chapel Hill: University of North Carolina Press, 1990); and Gerald Horne, *W. E. B. Du Bois and the Afro-American Response to the Cold War, 1944–1963* (Albany: State University of New York Press, 1986).

7. Works on the Black left suggest that the 1940s and 1950s were much more than a story of decline. See Gerald Horne, *Black Liberation/Red Scare: Ben Davis and the Communist Party* (Newark: University of Delaware Press, 1994); and Penny M. Von Eschen, *Race against Empire: Black Americans and Anticolonialism, 1937–1957* (Ithaca, N.Y.: Cornell University Press, 1997).

8. Coleman Young and Lonnie Wheeler, *Hard Stuff: The Autobiography of Coleman Young* (New York: Viking Press, 1994), 128–129; Powell quoted in Edwin Lewinson, *Black Politics in New York City* (New York: Twayne Publishers, 1974), 118.

9. National Negro Congress, *Negro Workers after the War* (New York, April 1945) in "National Negro Congress" vertical file, Tamiment Library.

10. See Hugh Mulzac, *A Star to Steer By* (New York: International Publishers, 1963).

11. The NLVC became a rival of the local March on Washington Movement (MOWM), which rejected any participation by Communists. Scholars have concluded, however, that by 1943 the MOWM was fairly inactive. A labor columnist for the *Amsterdam News* lamented that they could not unite: "As I see it, a consolidation of ideals, efforts, time and finances could be effected between the two groups to give the race the utmost in accomplishment. If the two organizations could merge, iron out whatever may be their differences and present a unified front, our causes would be advanced by many a year." *Amsterdam News*, July 18, 1942.

12. See the National Negro Congress Papers, part 4: *The Negro Labor Victory Committee, 1942–1945*, 9 reels.

13. Memorandum, "1945 Negro Freedom Rally," n.d., National Negro Congress Papers, reel 34; *People's Voice*, June 23, 1945; "Negro Labor Victory Committee," n.d., clipping file, Schomburg Center.

14. See Barbara Dianne Savage, *Broadcasting Freedom: Radio, War and the Politics of Race, 1938–1948* (Chapel Hill: University of North Carolina Press, 1999); WEAF, Paul Robeson speech, January 2, 1944, Radio Transcripts, box 3, Schomburg Center.

15. For an analysis of the riot and its local as well as national causes, see Dominic J. Capeci, *The Harlem Riot of 1943* (Philadelphia: Temple University Press, 1977) and Brandt; Dorothy Funn, minutes from the Citizens Emergency Conference on Interracial Unity, September 25, 1943, Hunter College, National Negro Congress Papers, part 4, reel 5.

16. For the MCU see Gerald Benjamin, *Race Relations and the New York City Commission on Human Rights* (Ithaca, N.Y.: Cornell University Press, 1974).

17. Brandt, 217; *New York Age*, January 27, 1945; "Fact Sheet for June 25: First An-

niversary of the Korean War, Tenth Anniversary of the Wartime FEPC," 1951, Randolph Papers, reel 17; Edwin Lewinson, *Black Politics in New York City* (New York: Twayne Publishers, 1974), 71; Brandt, 178; Robert E. Weems, *Desegregating the Dollar: African American Consumerism in the Twentieth Century* (New York: New York University Press, 1998).

18. *New York Age*, October 9, 1948.
19. Regarding civil rights advocacy for universal government programs, see Dona Cooper Hamilton and Charles V. Hamilton, *The Dual Agenda: The African American Struggle for Civil and Economic Equality* (New York: Columbia University Press, 1997).
20. See Nelson Peery, *Black Fire: The Making of an American Revolutionary* (New York: The New Press, 1994) for a vivid picture of Black soldiers' resistance to Jim Crow and racism in Army training camps, as well as overseas.
21. Lester Granger to the Editor, March 19, 1945, Mayor's Committee on Unity Papers, scrapbook in box 1608.
22. Darlene Clark Hine, "Staupers, Mabel Keaton," in Hine, ed., *Encyclopedia of Black Women in America* (New York: Facts on File, 1997), 115–118; Mabel K. Staupers, *No Time for Prejudice: A Story of the Integration of Negroes in Nursing in the United States* (New York: Macmillan, 1961), 117–121.
23. Andrews over WMCA, National Urban League sponsored broadcast, March 18, 1943, and Harris over WNYC, "Looking Forward," March 19, 1944, Radio Transcripts, box 3, Schomburg Center.
24. A. Philip Randolph, "The Negro's Struggle for Power," n.d. (mid-1940s), Randolph Papers, reel 30.
25. Stephen S. Wise to Stanley Isaacs, June 10, 1946, Isaacs Papers, box 13; Greenberg, 203.
26. Weaver, 306; Philip A. Klinkner and Rogers M. Smith, *The Unsteady March: The Rise and Decline of Racial Equality in America* (Chicago: University of Chicago Press, 1999), 166; Donald R. McCoy and Richard T. Ruetten, *Quest and Response: Minority Rights and the Truman Administration* (Lawrence: University Press of Kansas, 1973), 17.
27. Peter J. Kellogg, "Civil Rights Consciousness in the 1940s," *Historian* 42 (November 1979): 18–41; *New York Age*, June 9, 1945; *People's Voice*, March 31, 1945; *New York Age*, March 30, 1946, and May 12, 1945.

1. Jobs for All

1. Will Maslow, "The Law and Race Relations," *Annals of the American Academy of Political and Social Sciences* (March 1946): 79; Maslow quoted in Louis Ruchames, *Race, Jobs and Politics: The Story of the FEPC* (New York: Columbia University Press, 1953), 165; Robert S. Weaver, *Negro Labor: A National Problem* (Port Washington, N.Y.: Kennikat Press, 1946), 308.
2. The 1938 state constitution prohibited the violation of an individual's "civil rights" because of race, color, creed, or religion, and the right to equal opportunity in employment was explicitly defined as a civil right. Maslow, 77.
3. Metropolitan Council on Fair Employment Practices, Press Release, February 4,

1945, National Negro Congress Papers, reel 45; Algernon Black, transcript of radio address over WMCA, February 15, 1945, Black Papers, box 4; John H. Johnson, transcript of radio address, "The Democratic Ideal in New York City," February 6, 1945, Mayor's Committee on Unity Papers, box 1613.

4. *New York Herald Tribune,* February 21, 1945; Dorothy Funn to Joint New York State Senate and Assembly hearings, n.d., National and Hulan Jack address to Assembly, n.d., Negro Congress Papers, reel 45.

5. *New York Herald-Tribune,* February 2 and February 21, 1945; United Neighborhood Houses, Memorandum, February 19, 1945, Isaacs Papers, box 12.

6. Moses in *New York Journal American,* February 21, 1945; Morroe Berger, "The New York State Law against Discrimination: Operation and Administration," *Cornell Law Quarterly* 35 (1950): 751.

7. Berger, 751. The Law against Discrimination declared that "the opportunity to obtain employment without discrimination" was a civil right. It created the five-member State Commission against Discrimination, which had the power to call hearings, issue subpoenas, compel testimony, and issue legally enforceable cease and desist orders. A party found to be in violation could be required to hire, reinstate, or upgrade a worker, or to perform some other "affirmative action" that "in the judgment of the Commission, will effectuate the purposes" of the law.

8. Dorothy Funn, "Report of Legislative Bureau, National Negro Congress," February 21, 1946, National Negro Congress Papers, part 2, reel 30; A. Philip Randolph, "Address at Madison Square Garden Rally," February 28, 1946, Randolph Papers, reel 28; *People's Voice,* March 2 and March 9, 1946; *New York Age,* March 9, 1946.

9. Algernon Black, transcript of radio address, "Democracy and Racism" May 31, 1945, Black Papers, box 4.

10. Canada Lee, "What the Negro Wants and Hopes for in the Postwar World," May 7, 1945, Vassar College, Canada Lee Papers, box 5; Joshua B. Freeman, *Working-Class New York: Life and Labor since World War II* (New York: The New Press, 2000), 61, 67.

11. Earl Brown, "Harlem, 1945," O'Dwyer Papers, box 37; *New York Age,* October 13 and October 20, 1945; *People's Voice,* August 2, 1947.

12. Uptown Chamber of Commerce, "Tentative Program for a New York Committee," November 28, 1944, Negro Labor Committee Papers, reel 14.

13. National Negro Congress, *Negro Workers after the War* (New York: NNC, 1945); National Negro Congress, vertical file, Tamiment Library, New York University, New York.

14. National Negro Congress, "Proceedings of the Conference on Postwar Employment," January 13, 1945, National Negro Congress, vertical file, Tamiment Library. In 1947 the New York State Communist Party chairman called seniority modification "a striking practical application of our position that the Negro question is a *special* question, and the special oppression of the Negro people must be met with special demands." Robert Thompson, "Notes on the Negro

Question," *Clarity* (1947): 3–10, in "CPUSA and Negroes," vertical file, Tamiment Library.

15. Collins, Metropolitan Area Labor Conference on Reconversion and Related Problems, minutes, March 24–25, 1945, National Negro Congress Papers, part 4: *The Negro Labor Victory Committee, 1942–1945,* reel 1.

16. Weaver, 304; Robert H. Zieger in *The CIO, 1935–1955* (Chapel Hill: University of North Carolina Press, 1995), 159–160.

17. *Daily Worker,* April 10, 1945; *People's Voice,* December 29, 1945; *New York Age,* January 5, 1946; *People's Voice,* January 19, 1946.

18. Wiley Simmions, Educational Director, Local 450 UE-CIO, to Mayor William O'Dwyer, O'Dwyer Papers, box 37; *People's Voice,* March 23 and June 15, 1946.

19. *People's Voice,* January 26, 1946; Proceedings of the Conference on Postwar Employment, New York City, January 13, 1945, National Negro Congress Papers, part 4, reel 2.

20. *People's Voice,* September 22, 1945; *New York Age,* September 29, 1945, "Call for an Emergency Jobs Conference," September 18, 1945, National Negro Congress Papers, part 2, reel 45; *New York Age,* February 1, 1947.

21. *People's Voice,* September 7 and September 14, 1946; *New York Age,* September 21, 1946.

22. Thelma Dale, "The Status of Negro Women in the United States of America," February 3, 1947, National Negro Congress Papers, part 2, reel 34.

23. Weaver, 311.

24. *People's Voice,* June 1, 1946.

25. *New York Age,* March 15, 1947.

26. Earl Brown, "Harlem," n.d., O'Dwyer Papers, box 36.

27. The title of the conference reveals the left's approach to race: race is foregrounded, but in an interracial context. The party opposed all-Black formations; later many Black leftists pushed for Black-led, predominantly Black organizations.

28. Charles A. Collins, "Summary of Provisional Officers Report," National Negro Congress Papers, part 2, reel 36.

29. Freeman, 69.

30. *Arguing the World,* a documentary film by Joseph Dorman (New York: Riverside Film Productions, 1997).

31. *New York Times,* February 7, 1990 (obituary); Interview with Ewart Guinier by James Jennings, May 19, 1980, Guinier Papers.

32. *People's Voice,* October 6, 1945.

33. Ibid., March 8, 1947 (three articles) and April 5, 1947; Florence Herzog to Senator William Langer, May 27, 1947, American Labor Party Papers, box 5; *People's Voice,* April 19, 1947.

34. Florence Herzog to Senator William Langer, May 27, 1947, American Labor Party Papers, box 5; *People's Voice,* May 17, May 21, May 31, June 7, and June 21, 1947; *New York Age,* June 14 and July 5, 1947.

35. Herbert Aptheker, ed., *A Documentary History of the Negro People in the United States,* vol. 5 (New York: Carol Publishing Group, 1993), 245.

36. Elaine Perry interview, March 26, 1979, in "Oral History of the American Left," Tamiment Library; *People's Voice*, November 30, 1946; *New York Age*, February 14, 1948; Freeman, 70.

37. Central Trades and Labor Council, transcripts of hearings at the Hotel Pennsylvania, March 23 and April 23, 1946, Papers of the Board of Education of the City of New York, Subject Files Related to Hearings, box 23, folder 7, Rare Book and Manuscript Library, Teachers College, Columbia University; *New York Age*, February 16, 1946; *People's Voice*, May 4, 1946; *Amsterdam News*, editorial, September 7, 1946; *New York Age*, May 11, 1946; *People's Voice*, December 29, 1945.

38. National Maritime Union, "Resolutions," October 1947, Marcantonio Papers, box 52.

39. Victoria Garvin, speech, February 14, 1996, University of the District of Columbia, reprinted in "Celebrating Women's History Month with Vicki Garvin," Garvin Papers, box 1.

40. *The SSEU Fights Jim Crow* (New York, May 1949), in vertical file "TUF UOPWA Local 19 (SSEU)," Tamiment Library.

41. *New York Age*, January 11, 1947.

42. Jules Tygiel, *Baseball's Great Experiment: Jackie Robinson and His Legacy* (1983; New York: Oxford University Press, 1997), 54.

43. From reelection pamphlet for Ben Davis, 1945, National Negro Congress Papers, part 4, reel 2.

44. *People's Voice*, April 14, 1945; Tygiel, 54.

45. *People's Voice*, May 5, May 19, June 9 and July 21, 1945.

46. *People's Voice*, August 11, 1945; Tygiel, 56–57.

47. *People's Voice*, August 18, 1945; *New York Age*, August 25, 1945; *People's Voice*, August 25, 1945; *New York Age*, September 22, 1945.

48. Tygiel, 69, 85.

49. According to one of its founders, the UNAVA was instrumental in getting millions of dollars in terminal leave pay distributed to Black veterans in the South. Former members helped organize the Deacons of Defense, an armed southern Black liberation group in 1955. See interview with Howard Johnson, conducted for the film *Seeing Red*, in the "Oral History of the American Left," Tamiment Library.

50. *People's Voice*, July 19 and July 26, 1947; *New York Age*, August 16 and August 23, 1947.

51. *People's Voice*, August 23, 1947.

52. Ibid., September 27, October 18, and November 1, 1947, and January 10, 1948.

2. Black Mobilization and Civil Rights Politics

1. See for example, Donald R. McCoy and Richard T. Ruetten, *Quest and Response: Minority Rights and the Truman Administration* (Lawrence: University Press of Kansas, 1973); William C. Berman, *The Politics of Civil Rights in the Truman Administra-*

tion (Columbus: Ohio State University Press, 1970); Philip Klinkner and Rogers M. Smith, *The Unsteady March: The Rise and Decline of Racial Equality in America* (Chicago: University of Chicago Press, 1999); and Mary L. Dudziak, *Cold War Civil Rights: Race and the Image of American Democracy* (Princeton, N.J.: Princeton University Press, 2000).

2. "History of Elected Officials in New York," *Freedom* (September 1953); *Amsterdam News,* January 31, 1934; Sarah Delany and A. Elizabeth Delany, *Having Our Say: The Delany Sisters' First One Hundred* Years (New York: Kodansha International, 1993); *New York Post,* April 3, 1945.

3. Program, "Judicial Friends, Fourth Annual Rivers, Toney, Watson Dinner," December 13, 1984, Queens, New York, Bolin Papers, box 3; Jesse H. Walker, "Seven Negro Judges Show Way Race Has Progressed," *New York Age,* October 29, 1949.

4. Jane M. Bolin, speech at the Schomburg Center, May 7, 1957, Bolin Papers, box 3; Jane M. Bolin to Justine Wise Polier, October 24, 1978, Bolin Papers, box 1. See also "For a Remarkable Judge, a Reluctant Retirement," *New York Times,* December 8, 1978 (in the "Style" section).

5. *Smith v. Allwright* 321 U.S. 649 (1944); Thomas Brooks, *Walls Come Tumbling Down: A History of the Civil Rights Movement, 1940–1970* (Englewood Cliffs, N.J.: Prentice Hall, 1974), 17.

6. "A Message to the Republican and Democratic Parties from the Negroes of America," June 17, 1944, Negro Labor Committee Papers, reel 4.

7. Works on Powell include Will Haygood, *King of the Cats: The Life and Times of Adam Clayton Powell Jr.* (Boston: Houghton Mifflin, 1993); and Charles V. Hamilton, *Adam Clayton Powell Jr.: The Political Biography of an American Dilemma* (New York: Collier Books, 1992).

8. *People's Voice,* November 2, 1946; *Daily Worker,* January 22, 1945; *New York Age,* June 30, 1945.

9. *People's Voice,* December 14 and December 28, 1946.

10. For a treatment of Davis's career as a Communist Party leader, see Gerald Horne, *Black Liberation/Red Scare: Ben Davis and the Communist Party* (Newark: University of Delaware Press, 1993).

11. See Kenneth Greenberg, "Benjamin Jefferson Davis, Jr. in the City Council: Harlem's Reaction to Communism in the 1940s," master's thesis, Columbia University, 1970; Campaign Committee, "Full Record of Councilman Benjamin Davis in the City Council," June 21, 1949, in "Ben Davis" vertical file, Tamiment Library, New York University, New York.

12. *People's Voice,* May 12, 1945; *New York Age,* May 12, 1945; John C. Walter, *The Harlem Fox: J. Raymond Jones and Tammany Hall, 1920–1970* (Albany: State University of New York Press, 1989); Greenberg, 34–35.

13. Claudia Jones, "On the Right to Self-Determination for Negro People in the Black Belt," *Political Affairs* 25 (January 1946): 67, 73; For various perspectives, see William Z. Foster et al., *The Communist Position on the Negro Question* (New York: New Century Publishers, 1947).

14. Jones, 69. The resolution saw the "struggle for equal rights in the South as a movement toward full nationhood." See Foster et al., 11–13. In 1968 a member of the Republic of New Afrika urged the National Lawyers' Guild Convention to support a separate Black state. Guild president and former CP member Victor Rabinowitz called the speech "demagogic and racist" and believes the mostly white guild passed the resolution to assuage "their guilt." Rabinowitz also "thought the Party's advocacy, in the early fifties, of a separate 'black nation' . . . was nonsense." Victor Rabinowitz, *Unrepentant Leftist: A Lawyer's Memoir* (Chicago: University of Illinois Press, 1996), 188–189, 81.

15. Greenberg, 38. See also Edwin Lewinson, *Black Politics in New York City* (New York: Twayne Publishers, 1974), 78; *New York Age*, July 28 and August 4, 1945; Horne, 150; A. Philip Randolph to L. D. Reddick, August 20, 1945, in "McLaurin," clipping file, Schomburg Center; *New York Times*, August 8, 1963.

16. "An Open Letter to the Honorable Benjamin J. Davis" from Benjamin F. McLaurin, October 13, 1945, in "McLaurin" clipping file; *People's Voice*, April 24, 1948; Greenberg, 52.

17. *New York Age*, June 23 and November 3, 1945; Greenberg, 59; *Amsterdam News*, November 3, 1945; *People's Voice*, August 11, 1945; *New York Age*, October 6 and October 20, 1945.

18. *New York Herald Tribune*, August 24, 1964 (obituary); Greenberg, 62; *People's Voice*, February 9, 1946.

19. *People's Voice*, August 17 and October 26, 1946; *Amsterdam News*, November 4, 1950.

20. *New York Age*, June 1 and June 22, 1946; *People's Voice*, June 15 and July 13, 1946.

21. Charles A. Collins, "Summary of Provisional Officer's Report," n.d., National Negro Congress Papers, part 2, reel 36; *New York Age*, July 13 and July 20, 1946; *People's Voice*, July 13, July 20, July 27, August 17, and August 31, 1946.

22. *People's Voice*, July 27, 1946; *New York Age*, August 17, 1946; *People's Voice*, September 7, October 5, September 14, and October 12, 1946; *New York Age*, November 16 and November 30, 1946.

23. *People's Voice*, July 13, August 3, and August 17, 1946; *New York Age*, August 3, 1946.

24. *People's Voice*, June 29, August 3, November 2, September 28, and November 16, 1946.

25. *Daily Worker*, October 26, 1947; *People's Voice*, October 5, March 23, and August 17, 1946.

26. *New York Age*, August 31, 1946; *People's Voice*, August 31, September 7, and November 2, 1946; *Amsterdam News*, November 16, 1946; Interview with Bertram Baker in Carlos E. Russell, "Black Brooklyn Oral History," Ph.D. diss., Union College, 15–17; Robert Thompson, "Notes on the Negro Question," January 13, 1947, *Clarity* (n.d.) in "CP (US) and Negroes" vertical file, Tamiment Library.

27. *People's Voice*, July 5, 1947; *New York Age*, October 11, 1947; Handbill, Brooklyn NAACP, 1948, NAACP Papers, II, C, 118; *People's Voice*, November 1, October 11,

and November 15, 1947; *Daily Worker,* October 26, 1947, and August 9, 1948; *New York Age,* October 30, 1948.

28. Gerald Meyer, *Vito Marcantonio: Radical Politician, 1902–1954* (Albany: State University of New York Press, 1989), 35–36.

29. *New York Times,* June 17, 1947; Keep P.R. Committee of Jamaica, "Do You Want to get Rid of P.R.?" handbill, n.d., NAACP Papers, II, C, 121,; *People's Voice,* April 12, October 11, and November 1, 1947; NAACP Press Release, "New York Branches Urge PR Retention," NAACP Papers, II, C, 133.

30. Miscellaneous notes, American Labor Party Papers, box 23.

31. Duberman, 325; Carter, 370; Meyer, 31, 38. Baker served in Albany for over twenty years. He was president of the New York State Tennis Association and executive secretary of the American Tennis Association. *Amsterdam News,* June 11, 1949; Harold X. Connolly, *A Ghetto Grows in Brooklyn* (New York: New York University Press, 1977), 166.

32. "ALP Facts: Negro-Americans in New York City," 1949, American Labor Party Papers, box 12.

33. Harold A. Stevens, Speech at Fordham University, 1955, Stevens Papers, box 15; William Berman, *The Politics of Civil Rights in the Truman Administration* (Columbus: Ohio State University Press, 1970).

34. Meyer, 60–61; Hamilton, 226–235.

35. "Impeach Senator Bilbo," pamphlet, Communist Political Association, Chicago, in "Theodore Bilbo," vertical file, Tamiment Library; President's Committee on Civil Rights, *To Secure These Rights* (Washington D.C.: Government Printing Office, 1947), 38; *People's Voice,* March 17, May 15, September 8, and August 25, 1945.

36. New York Civil Rights Congress, "Speaker's Material on Theodore G. Bilbo," November 8, 1946, and CRC, "Action Bulletin," December 9, 1946, in Civil Rights Congress Papers, Los Angeles chapter, box 8, Southern California Library for Social Studies, Los Angeles; "Canada Lee, 1907–1952," in L. Mpho Mabunda, ed., *Contemporary Black Biography,* vol. 8 (Detroit: Gale Research, 1995). In 1939 Bilbo introduced a bill that "called upon the Federal government to provide a billion dollars to finance the cost of deporting 12 million Negro citizens to Liberia." Carlos Cooks, a New York Garveyite, supported this initiative and went to Washington to meet with Bilbo.

37. *People's Voice,* July 14 and August 11, 1945; *New York Age,* July 6, December 21, and November 2, 1946; *New York Age,* November 1, 1947.

38. See Brenda Gayle Plummer, *Rising Wind: Black Americans and U.S. Foreign Affairs* (Chapel Hill: University of North Carolina Press, 1996); and Penny Von Eschen, *Race against Empire: Black Americans and Anticolonialism* (Ithaca, N.Y.: Cornell University Press, 1997).

39. Plummer, 170–171; Civil Rights Congress, *We Charge Genocide* (New York: CRC, 1951).

40. Kenneth R. Janken, "From Colonial Liberation to Cold War Liberalism: Walter White, the NAACP, and Foreign Affairs, 1941–1955," *Ethnic and Racial Studies* 21,

no. 6 (November 1998): 1074–1095; National Association for the Advancement of Colored People, under the Editorial Supervision of W. E. Burghardt Du Bois, *An Appeal to the World: A Statement on the Denial of Human Rights to Minorities in the Case of Citizens of Negro Descent in the United States of America and an Appeal to the United Nations for Redress* (New York: NAACP, 1947).

41. President's Committee on Civil Rights.

3. Lynching, Northern Style

1. NYU NAACP ad hoc Committee for Justice in the Christianii Case, "Why the Killing of Enus L. Christianii?" (1952), American Labor Party Papers, box 23.
2. Christopher Waldrep, "War of Words: The Controversy over the Definition of Lynching, 1899–1940," *Journal of Southern History* 66 (February 2000): 84; Michael Denning, *The Cultural Front: The Laboring of American Culture* (New York: Verso, 1996), 399; *New York Age*, July 27, 1946.
3. Carl T. Rowan, *Breaking Barriers: A Memoir* (Boston: Little, Brown, 1991), 64.
4. Stanley Faulkner to Thurgood Marshall, March 13, 1946; Committee for Justice in the Ferguson Case to "Friend," February 10, 1946; *People v. Richard A. Ferguson,* February 5, 1946; and Franklin H. Williams to Thurgood Marshall, March 19, 1946, all in NAACP Papers, II, B, 152.
5. Harry Raymond, "Dixie Comes to New York: Story of the Freeport GI Slayings," pamphlet, in vertical file "Communist Party U.S. and Negroes," Tamiment Library, New York University; Committee for Justice in the Ferguson Case to "Friend," February 10, 1946, NAACP Papers, II, B, 152; Franklin H. Williams, "Report on the Freeport Long Island Case," March 4, 1946, NAACP Papers, II, B, 152.
6. Report of the Activities of the New York Committee for Justice in Freeport, n.d., NAACP Papers, II, B, 152 and *Nassau Daily Review Star,* February 12, 1946, from a scrapbook in the possession of Stanley Faulkner, New York City.
7. Ibid.
8. Interview with Stanley Faulkner by author, May 15, 1994, New York City; Franklin H. Williams to Walter White, March 8, 1946, NAACP Papers, II, B, 152—this memo lists the affiliations of all the executive committee members, with check marks penciled next to seven names, including Communist Party leader Ben Davis; Roy Wilkins to Thurgood Marshall, February 14, 1946, NAACP Papers, II, B, 152.
9. Stanley Faulkner, "In the Matter of the Petition of Adele G. Smith, Ruth Hughes and Richard Sanders to the Governor of the State of New York," April 10, 1946, quote from the draft of March 13, 1946, NAACP Papers, II, B, 152; Arthur Garfield Hayes, Osmond K. Fraenkel, Paul O'Dwyer, Will Maslow, and Franklin H. Williams, "Memorandum in Support of Petition by Stanley Faulkner," April 10, 1946, NAACP Papers, II, B, 152.
10. *People's Voice,* March 2, 1946; Franklin H. Williams to Walter White, March 8, 1946, NAACP Papers, II, B, 152.

11. *People's Voice,* March 9, 1946; *New York Age,* March 16, 1946; Franklin H. Williams to Miss Baker, March 5, 1946, NAACP Papers, II, B, 152; Charles Lohman of the Communist Party of New York State to Madison Jones, March 2, 1946, NAACP Papers, II, B, 152. For the Columbia attack, see Gail Williams O'Brien, *The Color of the Law: Race, Violence and Justice in the Post–World War II South* (Chapel Hill: University of North Carolina Press, 1999).

12. *People's Voice,* March 16, 1946; *Daily Worker,* March 28, 1946; *New York Age,* April 20, 1946; Dorothy Langston, Report of Activities of the New York Committee for Justice in Freeport, n.d., NAACP Papers, II, B, 152; copy of the citation in the National Negro Congress Papers, part 2, reel 23.

13. *New York Age,* July 13, 1946, and Stanley Faulkner, Memorandum in Support of Petition, July 17, 1946, in possession of Stanley Faulkner, New York City. *People's Voice,* July 27, 1946; *Newsday,* July 24, 1946, in scrapbook in possession of Stanley Faulkner; *New York Age,* July 27, 1946.

14. *Amsterdam News,* October 30, 1948. In the early 1990s Faulkner petitioned Governor Mario Cuomo for a special prosecutor in another New York State town where charges of racism had been leveled at local law enforcement after a Black youth was racially attacked at a movie theater. Interview with Stanley Faulkner; *New York Age,* May 11, 1946, and July 6, 1946.

15. *People's Voice,* July 27, August 3, and August 8, 1946; *New York Times,* June 1, 1999; *New York Age,* August 3, 1946; Herbert Aptheker, ed., *A Documentary History of The Negro People of the United States,* vol. 5 (New York: Carol Publishing, 1993), 37.

16. *People's Voice,* July 27, August 3, and August 10, 1946; *New York Age,* August 3, 1946.

17. *People's Voice,* September 14, 1946; *New York Age,* August 24, 1946; Charles J. Evans, Chairman, Communist Party of Jamaica, Resolution, August 7, 1946, O'Dwyer Papers, box 37; *People's Voice,* August 10 and September 28, 1946.

18. *New York Age,* August 24 and September 28, 1946; *PM,* August 28, 1946; William C. Berman, *The Politics of Civil Rights in the Truman Administration* (Columbus: Ohio State University Press, 1970), 47. In the Georgia case a federal grand jury of twenty-one whites and two African Americans heard one hundred witnesses but failed to produce an indictment. Forty-five years later a white male witness to the shootings, who had been ten years old at the time, contacted the FBI and the case was reopened. He claims that the Klan was responsible, but there have been no arrests. George Dorsey's nephew doubts there ever will be: "There might be a book wrote about it, but justice? No, justice will never be done." *New York Times,* June 1, 1999.

19. Donald R. McCoy and Richard T. Ruetten, *Quest and Response: Minority Rights and the Truman Administration* (Lawrence: University Press of Kansas, 1973), 47–53; Penny M. Von Eschen, *Race against Empire: Black Americans and Anticolonialism, 1937–1957* (Ithaca, N.Y.: Cornell University Press, 1997), 110–112. For White's style see Kenneth R. Janken, "From Colonial Liberation to Cold War Liberalism: Walter White, the NAACP, and Foreign Affairs, 1941–1955," *Ethnic and Racial*

Studies 21 (November 1998); National Emergency Committee to President Truman, August 6, 1946, NAACP Papers, II, A, 319 (microfilm, part 7a, reel 35).

20. Walter White to Paul Robeson, September 10, 1946; Gloster Current to Walter White, September 24, 1946; and Charles Shorter to Gloster Current, September 26, 1946, all in NAACP Papers, II, A, 319 (microfilm, part 7a, reel 35).

21. Duberman, 307; *People's Voice,* August 10, September 7, and September 14, 1946; *Philadelphia Tribune,* September 24, 1946, and *Chicago Defender,* September 28, 1946, in Aptheker, 142–144; Drew Pearson, "Washington Merry-Go-Round," n.d., NAACP Papers, II, A, 319 (microfilm, part 7a, reel 35). An NAACP leader later said that Robeson's performance vindicated their critique of the American Crusade against Lynching. Robeson's discussion of "Nuremberg, China and Greece" was off the subject and represented the left's attempt to "foist their opinions on other matters on the unsuspecting public." Gloster Current to Walter White, September 24, 1946, in NAACP Papers, II, A, 319 (microfilm, part 7a, reel 35).

22. Truman wrote to a friend in Missouri, "When a mayor and city Marshal can take a Negro Sergeant off a bus in South Carolina, beat him up and put out one of his eyes, and nothing is done about it by the state authorities, something is radically wrong with the system." David McCullough, *Truman* (New York: Simon and Schuster, 1992), 589.

23. *People's Voice,* October 28, 1946; *New York Age,* October 5, 1946; President's Committee on Civil Rights, *To Secure These Rights: The Report of the President's Committee on Civil Rights* (Washington, D.C.: Government Printing Office, 1947); Dudziak, 79–80.

24. Langston Hughes, *Fight for Freedom: The Story of the NAACP* (New York: W. W. Norton, 1962), 98. Algernon Black, "The Role of the Police," September 10, 1974, Black Papers, box 7.

25. *Gideon v. Wainwright* 372 U.S. 335 (1963). See Harry J. Abraham, *Freedom and the Court: Civil Rights and Liberties in the United States,* 5th ed. (New York: Oxford University Press, 1988).

26. *People's Voice,* October 20, November 17, and November 24, 1945; *People's Voice,* December 15, 1945; *New York Age,* September 1, 1945; *People's Voice,* August 18, 1945; *New York Age,* June 8, 1946.

27. Civil Rights Congress, "Cases of Police Brutality in New York City," August 12, 1946; Ben Davis to Mayor William O'Dwyer, July 30, 1946, both in O'Dwyer Papers, box 37.

28. Walter White to files, August 5, 1946, NAACP Papers, II, B, 117; Arthur Wallander, untitled statement, August 7, 1946, O'Dwyer Papers, box 37.

29. Marshall, "Lynching Northern Style: Police Brutality," Davis Papers, box 5.

30. *People's Voice,* October 25, 1947; *PM,* October 22, 1947; Marshall, "Lynching Northern Style"; *Daily Worker,* October 28, 1947; *People's Voice,* November 1, 1947.

31. Marshall, "Lynching Northern Style"; *People's Voice,* November 22, 1947, and *New York Age,* November 22, 1947; Guy R. Brewer to John H. Johnson, Decem-

ber 8, 1947, and Benjamin J. Davis to John H. Johnson, December 9, 1947, NAACP Papers, II, B, 117; Memorandum on Procedures Developed by the Committee to Review Cases of Police Brutality, n.d., Mayor's Committee on Unity Papers, box 1615; Citizens' Committee to End Police Brutality, Press Release, February 14, 1948, NAACP Papers, II, B, 117; *Daily Worker,* May 10, 1948.

32. Dan W. Dodson, "Intergroup Relations in New York City," March 10, 1948, Mayor's Committee on Unity Papers, box 1620; Arthur W. Wallander to Dan W. Dodson, March 8, 1948, Mayor's Committee on Unity Papers, box 1615; Minutes of the Mayor's Committee on Unity, June 15, 1948, Mayor's Committee on Unity Papers, box 1608.

33. *People's Voice,* March 6 and March 20, 1948; *New York Age,* March 27 and July 17, 1948; Minutes of State Conference, May 22, 1948, NAACP Papers, II, C, 133.

34. *Amsterdam News,* March 5, 1949; Henry J. Abraham, *Freedom and the Court* (New York: Oxford University Press, 1988), 144; *Amsterdam News,* March 5, 1949.

35. Brooklyn Branch, NAACP, "Petition to Hon. Thomas E. Dewey, Governor of the State of New York," April 22, 1949, American Labor Party Papers, box 9.

36. *Amsterdam News,* May 7, 1949; Thirteenth Annual New York State Conference of NAACP Branches, minutes, May 28, 1949, NAACP Papers, II, C, 133.

37. *Amsterdam News,* February 10, 1951, October 27, 1951, and April 26, 1952.

38. Flier, "NAACP-NY" clipping file, Schomburg Center for Research in Black Culture, New York; Conference flier, NAACP Papers, II, C, 118; *Amsterdam News,* July 16, 1949; Brooklyn NAACP, "Spotlight on Public Affairs," June 1949, NAACP Papers, II, C, 118; Gloster Current, Memorandum to files, June 8, 1949, NAACP Papers, II, C, 118.

39. *Amsterdam News,* August 13, 1949; Robert L. Carter to John M. Murtagh, September 19, 1949, NAACP Papers, II, B, 114; Joint Committee of NYC Branches to All Branches in NYC Area, September 29, 1949, NAACP Papers, II, B, 117; *Amsterdam News,* October 15, 1949. Guy R. Brewer, chairman of the Long Island Conference on Civil Rights, Address, March 26, 1950, NAACP Papers, II, C, 121.

4. Desegregating the Metropolis

1. Marian Wynn Perry, Memorandum to Files, February 11, 1947, NAACP Papers, II, B, 67.

2. American Jewish Committee and the Anti-Defamation League of B'nai B'rith, "Joint Memorandum," April, 1952, Mayor's Committee on Unity Papers, box 1613; *People's Voice,* January 13, 1945; *People's Voice,* August 25, 1945, and *New York Age,* August 18, 1945; *New York Age,* July 19, 1947, and *People's Voice,* June 7 and July 19, 1947; Thurgood Marshall to Clifford E. Minton, December 15, 1948, NAACP Papers, II, B, 62.

3. Langston Hughes, "New York and Us," August 31, 1946, in Christopher C. De Santis, ed., *Langston Hughes and the Chicago Defender: Essays on Race, Politics and Culture, 1942–62* (Urbana: University of Illinois Press, 1995); "The Types of Segregation and Jim-Crowism," January 24, 1947, Mayor's Committee on Unity

Papers, box 1618; Mary L. Dudziak, "Josephine Baker, Racial Protest and the Cold War," *Journal of American History* 81 (September 1994): 548; *New York Age,* August 11, 1945, and *People's Voice,* August 11, 1945.

4. *People's Voice,* December 8, 1945, and May 18, 1946; *New York Age,* May 29, 1948; *People's Voice,* July 7 and October 6, 1945; *New York Age,* November 1, 1947.

5. "The Story of the Committee on Civil Rights in East Manhattan, March 1949–April 1951: An Informal Survey," April 20, 1951, Mayor's Committee on Unity Papers, box 1616; Committee on Civil Rights in East Manhattan, Inc., "Recruiting Information for CCREM's Housing Survey," n.d., Mayor's Committee on Unity Papers, box 1613; Olivia Frost, "Significant Values Inherent in the Restaurant Audit," copy of speech delivered at Freedom House, April 26, 1951, Mayor's Committee on Unity Papers, box 1616.

6. *New York Age,* August 31, 1946; *People's Voice,* July 27 and August 31, 1946; Theodore Stanford, "Committee of Racial Equality Carries Forth the Good Fight," *Pittsburgh Courier,* September 25, 1948. James Peck wrote two accounts of the struggle, "Bilboism in New Jersey" and "Alabama in New Jersey," whose titles reflect the eras in which they were written. See, respectively, *The Crisis,* January 1948, in Mayor's Committee on Unity Papers, box 1620, and Peck, *Freedom Ride* (New York: Simon and Schuster, 1962).

7. This account relies on Peck, "Alabama in New Jersey" as well as newspaper accounts such as *People's Voice,* August 2, 1947. The leading law enforcement officials who forcibly broke up the demonstrations were found to be on a mob payroll. After the Kefauver hearings in 1951, the police chiefs of Fort Lee and Cliffside Park and the Bergen County prosecutor were indicted.

8. Peck, "Bilboism in New Jersey"; *New York Age,* August 16, 1947. Attorney Hiram Elfenbein succeeded in getting the thirty-five arrests dropped or the convictions reversed on appeal.

9. Peck, "Alabama in New Jersey," 34–37; Congress of Racial Equality, *CORE-lator* (June–July 1953), Congress of Racial Equality Papers, reel 13; *Amsterdam News,* August 29, 1953.

10. *Morgan v. Commonwealth of Virginia* 328 U.S. 373 (1946). Ironically, CORE, because it anticipated violence, would not permit women to participate in its 1947 "Freedom Ride" through the upper south to test *Morgan,* much to the disappointment of Ella Baker who longed to go. See Joanne Grant, *Ella Baker: Freedom Bound* (New York: Wiley, 1998).

11. *People's Voice,* January 11, 1947.

12. Ibid., August 2, 1947; NAACP Press Release, July 25, 1947, NAACP Papers, II, B, 191; Berta Mae Watkins to Franklin H. Williams, December 15, 1947, NAACP Papers, II, B, 191; *People's Voice,* February 21, 1948.

13. *Amsterdam News,* September 4, 1948.

14. Schuyler Warren to Milton D. Stewart, June 16, 1949, Mayor's Committee on Unity Papers, box 1605; Minutes of a meeting, September 14, 1949, Mayor's Committee on Unity Papers, box 1608; MCU Press Release, October 20, 1949, Mayor's Committee on Unity Papers, box 1605; *Amsterdam News,* July 8, 1950,

and April 14, 1951; Howard Selsam, "The Negro People in the United States: Facts for All Americans" (Jefferson School of Social Science, 1953) in "CP (U.S.) and Negroes," vertical file, Tamiment Library, New York University, New York. Number three on the 1947 MCU list of "The Types of Segregation and Jim-Crowism Which Are Most Irritating to the Negro Minority" was the difficulty in hailing a taxi and "the refusal of accommodations such as taxicab service to Negro neighborhoods." See "Types of Segregation and Jim-Crowism," January 24, 1947, Mayor's Committee on Unity Papers, box 1618.

15. *Amsterdam News,* September 29 and October 6, 1951; American Jewish Congress, Memorandum, October 8, 1951, Mayor's Committee on Unity Papers, box 1613.

16. Nina Mjagkij, "History of the Black YMCA in America," Ph.D. diss., University of Cincinnati, 1990, 260; *New York Age,* August 24, 1946; Minutes of meeting, February 28, 1950, Mayor's Committee on Unity Papers, box 1608; *People's Voice,* May 11, 1946.

17. *Amsterdam News,* December 15, 1951; Harold X. Connolly, *A Ghetto Grows in Brooklyn* (New York: New York University, 1977), 147; *Amsterdam News,* June 19, 1954.

18. *Amsterdam News,* November 7, November 14, and December 5, 1953.

19. WMCA, *New World A'Coming,* June 4, 1944, transcript, in Radio Transcript Collections, box 4, Schomburg Center for Research in Black Culture, New York.

20. *New York Age,* March 10, 1945; *People's Voice,* May 4 and July 13, 1946, and October 18, 1947.

21. MCU, Memorandum, September 1948, Mayor's Committee on Unity Papers, box 1613.

22. Mrs. Walton Pryor to Dear Reverend, October 31, 1947, Mayor's Committee on Unity Papers, box 1613; Minutes of meeting, February 9, 1948, Mayor's Committee on Unity Papers, box 1613; *People's Voice,* November 22, 1947; Minutes of Meeting, January 15, 1948, Mayor's Committee on Unity Papers, box 1618; *New York Age,* November 15, 1947, and January 10 and January 24, 1948; Leopold Philipp to Charles Evans Hughes, December 19, 1947, Mayor's Committee on Unity Papers, box 1613.

23. MCU, Memorandum, September 1948, Mayor's Committee on Unity Papers, box 1613; *Pittsburgh Courier,* March 20, 1948; *Amsterdam News,* January 7 and November 25, 1950.

24. Algernon Black, "CWCCH-Consumer Problems SubCommittee," Black Papers, box 9; Press Release, Consumers' Protective Committee, January 15, 1953, Mayor's Committee on Unity Papers, box 1613; *Amsterdam News,* January 8, 1949; *New York Times,* November 8, 1955.

25. *Amsterdam News,* November 28, 1953; Kerner Commission, *Report of the National Advisory Commission on Civil Disorders* (New York: Bantam Books, 1968), 274–275.

26. See "Summary of Material" from Conference, March 16, 1947, Murray Hill Hotel, New York City, National Negro Congress Papers, part 2, reel 34.

27. Canada Lee, "Radio and the Negro People" (speech), 1949, Lee Papers, box 5;

Robert E. Weems Jr., *Desegregating the Dollar: African American Consumerism in the Twentieth Century* (New York: New York University Press, 1998), 42.

28. *Amsterdam News,* May 20, 1950; Minutes of Meeting of Joint Executive Committee of New York Branches, October 13, 1947, NAACP Papers, II, C, 133; *People's Voice,* October 25, 1947.

5. Dead Letter Legislation

1. Paul D. Moreno, *From Direct Action to Affirmative Action: Fair Employment Law and Policy in America, 1933–1972* (Baton Rouge: Louisiana State University Press, 1997), 121, 159. For the early years of SCAD, see Jay Anders Higbee, *Development and Administration of the New York State Law against Discrimination* (University: University of Alabama Press, 1966).

2. See Stuart Svonkin, *Jews against Prejudice: American Jews and the Fight for Civil Liberties* (New York: Columbia University Press, 1997).

3. *New York Age,* November 10, 1945; City-Wide Citizens' Committee on Harlem to Governor Thomas E. Dewey, August 31, 1945, Black Papers, box 7.

4. *New York Age,* February 1, 1947; State Commission against Discrimination, Press Release, January 8, 1947, NAACP Papers, II, B, 108; *New York Age,* January 11, 1947; *People's Voice,* January 18, 1947.

5. *People's Voice,* April 5, 1947; Will Maslow to Henry C. Turner, February 17, 1947, Mayor's Committee on Unity Papers, box 1619.

6. *People's Voice,* September 15, 1945; Statement by Walter White, January 22, 1948, NAACP Papers, II, A, 457; *People's Voice,* July 13, 1946.

7. Press Release, June 4, 1946, NAACP Papers, II, B, 107; Herman D. Bloch, *The Circle of Discrimination: An Economic and Social Study of The Black Man in New York* (New York: New York University Press, 1969), 58–59.

8. Marian Wynn Perry, "Memorandum to Files," March 4, 1948, NAACP Papers, II, B, 107.

9. Ibid.; Press Release, September 2, 1948, in NAACP Papers, II, B, 107; *Amsterdam News,* September 19 and October 24, 1953.

10. The workers who are building the Third Water Tunnel hail from the West Indies and Ireland. Begun in 1970, it is the largest public works project in the nation's history, and the most dangerous. As of 1997, twenty-four workers had died. Thomas Kelly, "A Man a Mile," *Esquire,* October 1997, 54–59.

11. Committee against Discrimination of Local 147, "Statement in Support of the Appeal to the International Executive Committee of the International Hod Carriers' Building and Common Laborers Union of America," n.d., NAACP Papers, II, B, 108.

12. NAACP Press Release, November 11, 1948, NAACP Papers, II, B, 107; Sandhog Union Discrimination Committee, Untitled Statement, n.d., NAACP Papers, II, B, 108.

13. Marian Wynn Perry to Walter White, December 10, 1948, NAACP Papers, II, B, 108.

14. Ed Cross Oral History, March 20, 1980, in *New Yorkers at Work,* Tamiment Library, New York University, New York; Marian Wynn Perry to William O'Dwyer, January 13, 1949, and Walter White to William O'Dwyer, February 14, 1949, NAACP Papers, II, B, 108; Robert A. Caro, *The Power Broker: Robert Moses and the Fall of New York* (New York: Alfred A. Knopf, 1974), 736; Robert Moses to Marian Wynn Perry, April 20, 1949, NAACP Papers, II, B, 108.

15. In a 1949 election in Local 147, a dissident white candidate ran on the slogan: "Black and White unite and fight for the building of a tunnel to Staten Island!" Marian Wynn Perry to Stanley Isaacs, April 29, 1949; Press Release, October 28, 1949; and "To All Members of Local 147," July 12, 1949, all in NAACP Papers, II, B, 108. See also Cross Oral History.

16. "Draft Report of Committee to Support the Ives-Quinn Law to Our Three Sponsoring Agencies," January 13, 1949, NAACP Papers, II, B, 106; Moreno, 117–119.

17. Moreno, 117–119.

18. Newbold Morris to Thomas E. Dewey, January 25, 1949, NAACP Papers, II, B, 106; Newbold Morris to Walter White, February 25, 1949, NAACP Papers, II, B, 109.

19. Shad Polier, quoted in *Congress Weekly,* November 29, 1945, Black Papers, Box 8; *People's Voice,* February 24 and February 3, 1945; *New York Age,* May 18, 1946.

20. Memorandum, July 11, 1946, Isaacs Papers, box 14; *New York Age,* January 19, June 15, and June 22, 1946, and January 4, 1947.

21. "Proceedings of the Conference against Discrimination," Hotel New Yorker, September 23, 1946, Isaacs Papers, box 14; Representatives at State Conference, September 23, 1946, NAACP Papers, II, A, 119.

22. Louise McDonald to Dear Friend, February 24, 1947, NAACP Papers, II, A, 119; *New York Age,* March 1, 1947; ULGNY and Harlem Committee against Discrimination, "There Is a Need for a State University," October 20, 1947, NAACP Papers, II, A, 119.

23. Draft copy of Fair Educational Practices Act for New York State, December 10, 1947; Shad Polier to Stanley Isaacs, December 12, 1947; and Stanley Isaacs to Hubert T. Delany, December 15, 1947; all in Isaacs Papers, box 14.

24. *New York Times,* January 2, 1948; David S. Berkowitz, *Inequality of Opportunity in Higher Education: A Study of Minority Group and Related Barriers to College Admission* (Albany, N.Y.: Williams Press, 1948), available at Schomburg Center for Research in Black Culture, New York.

25. Will Maslow to New York State Committee for Equality in Education, June 29, 1948, American Jewish Congress Papers, Education file.

26. Stephen S. Wise to Chancellor William J. Wallin, March 26, 1949, American Jewish Congress Papers, Education file; Will Maslow, "Civil Rights Laws in the North," June 28, 1950, CLSA Materials file.

27. Maslow; Minutes of meeting of New York Council on Civil Liberties and Civil Rights, January 25, 1951, Mayor's Committee on Unity Papers, box 1616.

28. *Amsterdam News,* February 19, 1949; Harlem Committee against Discrimination

in Education, "Will You Help Save the New York State University?" February 21, 1949, Mayor's Committee on Unity Papers, box 1604; James Egert Allen to Branch Executives, March 10, 1949, NAACP Papers, II, C, 133; J. K. Weiss to Walter White, March 29, 1949, NAACP Papers, II, A, 120.

6. An Unnatural Division of People

1. New York State Committee on Discrimination in Housing, "Housing Segregation and Discrimination in New York State," 1949, Black Papers, box 8; Lewis W. Gillenson, "Harlem . . . New York's Tinder Box," *Look* (November 14, 1949) in Mayor's Committee on Unity Papers, box 1605.
2. *Buchanan v. Warley* 245 U.S. 60; Conrad J. Lynn, *Black Justice Exposed!* (Philadelphia: Civil Liberties Department, IBPO Elks of the World, 1947), 14 (pamphlet on microfilm at the Schomburg Center for Research in Black Culture, New York); Robert C. Weaver, "Hemmed In: The ABC's of Race Restrictive Covenants," 1945, National Negro Congress Papers, part 2, reel 17.
3. "The Reminiscences of Charles Abrams," April 1964, Oral History Research Office, Columbia University, New York, 11–12; Kenneth T. Jackson, *Crabgrass Frontier: The Suburbanization of the United States* (New York: Oxford University Press, 1985), 213; Douglas S. Massey and Nancy A. Denton, *American Apartheid: Segregation and the Making of the Underclass* (Cambridge, Mass.: Harvard University Press, 1993), 52.
4. New York State Committee on Discrimination in Housing, "Housing Discrimination and Segregation in New York State."
5. *PM*, May 4, 1948; New York State Committee on Discrimination in Housing, "Housing Discrimination and Segregation in New York State"; "The Reminiscences of Algernon Black," Oral History Research Office, Columbia University.
6. WMCA, *New World A'Coming*, program no. 5, 1944, audiotape, Schomburg Center; *People's Voice*, October 13, 1945; "The Types of Segregation and Jim-Crowism Which Are Most Irritating to the Negro Minority," Mayor's Committee on Unity Papers, box 1618; Gillenson; Algernon Black, "Brotherhood and Segregation," transcript of radio address, February 27, 1949, Black Papers, box 5.
7. *People's Voice*, July 13, August 10, and August 17, 1946; Charles Abrams, *Forbidden Neighbors* (New York: Harper, 1955), 174–175.
8. NAACP Press Release, August 8, 1946, NAACP Papers, II, B, 78; Ted Poston, "Harlem," *New York Post Magazine*, July 26, 1964, 23.
9. *People's Voice*, March 20, 1948; Abrams, 175.
10. *People's Voice*, December 22, 1945; *Daily Worker*, January 29, 1945; Algernon Black, "Segregated Housing: Racial Covenants and Zoning," n.d., Black Papers, box 8; *People's Voice*, December 20, 1947.
11. Flier, National Negro Congress Papers, part 2, reel 23.
12. *New York Age*, May 18, July 20 and June 1, 1946; Shapiro quoted in fragment, n.d., Scrapbook, Isaacs Papers, box 50; *People's Voice*, September 7, 1946.
13. Weaver; Lynn, 13.

14. *New York Age,* June 8, 1946. Canada Lee invited Kemp to *On Whitman Avenue,* but he declined. *New York Age,* June 29 and August 10, 1946; *People's Voice,* September 7, 1946; Memorandum, n.d., NAACP Papers, II, B, 133; Howard Selsam, "The Negro People in the United States: Facts for All Americans," pamphlet by the Jefferson School of Social Sciences, 1953, in "CP (U.S.) and Negroes" vertical file, Tamiment Library, New York University, New York.

15. "NAACP Restrictive Covenant Fight Strongly Supported," Press Release, November 8, 1946, NAACP Papers, II, B, 133; Commission on Law and Social Action, Report of Activities, November 1–15, 1946, AJC-CLSA Folder, American Jewish Congress Papers; "Brief of Defendant Samuel Richardson in Support of Motion to Dismiss the Complaint," *Kemp v. Rubin,* Supreme Court of the State of New York, NAACP Papers, II, B, 133; Commission on Law and Social Action of the American Jewish Congress, "Queens Restrictive Covenant Attacked in New York Court," *Law and Social Action,* November 1946, NAACP Papers, II, B, 133.

16. *New York Age,* February 22, 1947; *New York Times,* February 14, 1947; Press Service of the NAACP, "NAACP Claims Restrictive Covenants Violate United Nations Charter," February 14, 1947, NAACP Papers, II, B, 133; Minutes of Meeting, January 9, 1948, Mayor's Committee on Unity Papers, box 1620; "NAACP Wins N.Y. Covenant Case," Press Release, July 22, 1948, NAACP Papers, II, B, 79.

17. Desmond King, *Separate and Unequal: Black Americans and the U.S. Federal Government* (New York: Oxford University Press, 1995), 191, 193; NCDH, "1952," Memorandum, n.d., Black Papers, box 9; King, 196, 198.

18. Arthur Simon, a pastor of a lower east side Lutheran church, wrote an account of the Stuyvesant Town campaign. See *Stuyvesant Town, USA: Pattern for Two Americas* (New York: New York University Press, 1970).

19. Robert Moses to H. A. Overstreet, August 30, 1943, box 134, Robert Moses Papers, Rare Book and Manuscript Division, New York Public Library.

20. Charles Abrams, "The Walls of Stuyvesant Town," *Nation,* March 24, 1945, in Black Papers, box 8.

21. Robert Moses to Frederick H. Ecker, July 24, 1943, and Memorandum, dictated over the telephone by Judge Samuel Seabury, August 11, 1943, both in Moses Papers, box 20.

22. Algernon Black, "Battle for Stuyvesant Town," n.d.; City-Wide Citizens' Committee on Harlem to the Board of Estimate, June 3, 1943; Newbold Morris to the Board of Estimate, June 3, 1943; Black, "Battle for Stuyvesant Town," all in Black Papers, box 8.

23. Robert Moses to Frederick H. Ecker, February 25, 1944, Moses Papers, box 21; Minutes, "Informal Meeting on Riverton Project," October 25, 1944, Black Papers, box 8.

24. City-Wide Citizens' Committee on Harlem, Press Release, January 10, 1945, Black Papers, box 8; *People's Voice,* March 1, 1947.

25. Black, "Battle For Stuyvesant Town"; Black, "Battle of Stuyvesant Town—Renewed," n.d., Black Papers, box 9; Simon, 57–59; Abrams quoted in New York

Post, August 25, 1947; Citizens' Housing Council of New York, *Housing News,* February–March 1945, in NAACP Papers, II, B, 73.

26. Charles Abrams, "A Housing Program for New York City," October 10, 1945, Black Papers, box 8; Algernon Black to Mayor William O'Dwyer, January 4, 1946, Black Papers, box 8; *New York Age,* May 17, 1947; Citizens' Housing Council, Press Release, February 13, 1948, NAACP Papers, II, B, 74.

27. *People's Voice,* August 9, 1947; Simon, 62–63.

28. *People's Voice,* August 9, 1947; *New York Age,* August 9, 1947; Simon, 140.

29. William Z. Foster, et al., *The Communist Position on the Negro Question* (New York: New Century Publishers, 1947); Robert Thompson, "Basic Aspects of the Negro People's Struggle," *Clarity* (January 1947), 10 in "CPUSA and Negroes" vertical file, Tamiment Library.

30. Simon, 70; *Amsterdam News,* April 2 and April 16, 1949, and December 11, 1948; Interview with Fred Zeserson, New York City, April 4, 1997; Interview with Lee Lorch, Toronto, Canada, April 20, 1999.

31. Town and Village Tenants' Committee to End Discrimination in Stuyvesant Town, "What's Wrong with This Picture?" pamphlet in author's possession.

32. Simon, 71–72; Thurgood Marshall to "Dear Friend," November 5, 1948, NAACP Papers, II, B, 131; "List of Individuals and Organizations Joining as *Amici Curiae,*" n.d, NAACP Papers, II, B, 131; Abrams, 335.

33. Simon, 65; *New York Times,* July 20, 1949; Shad Polier and Charles Abrams to the Editor, *New York Times,* July 20, 1949; *Amsterdam News,* July 30, 1949.

34. Griffin Fariello, *Red Scare: Memories of the American Inquisition* (New York: Avon Books, 1995), 489–492; Simon, 77.

35. *People's Voice,* August 30, 1947; the United Office and Professional Workers' of America challenged Met Life's insurance discrimination before the state insurance department. See Ewart Guinier, transcript of speech to the IWO, ca. 1953, Guinier Papers, box 9.

36. Simon, 85; *Amsterdam News,* November 5, 1949; Ewart Guinier, transcript of radio broadcast, WMCA, October 5, 1949, Guinier Papers, box 6; Speech by Vito Marcantonio, October 25, 1949, Marcantonio Papers; Gerald Meyer, *Vito Marcantonio: Radical Politician, 1902–1954* (Albany: State University of New York Press, 1989), 212.

37. Sara Harris, *Father Divine: Holy Husband* (New York: Doubleday, 1953), 178; Akiba Sullivan Harper, ed., *The Return of Simple* (New York: Hill and Wang, 1994), 71; Philip S. Foner, ed., *Paul Robeson Speaks: Writings, Speeches, Interviews* (London: Quartet Books, 1978), 221.

38. Algernon Black, NYSCDH Memorandum, n.d., Black Papers, box 8.

39. The three cases were *McLaurin v. Oklahoma State Regents* 339 U.S. 637 (1950), *Sweatt v. Painter* 339 U.S. 629 (1950), and *Henderson v. United States et al.* 339 U.S. 816 (1950).

40. *Daily Compass,* February 18 and March 2, 1951.

41. Simon, 81–92; *Amsterdam News,* June 24, 1950; Town and Village Tenants' Committee to End Discrimination in Stuyvesant Town, "A Landlord vs. The People,"

pamphlet in author's possession; Algernon Black, "Stuyvesant Town," January 29, 1975, Black Papers, box 9.

42. New York Branch NAACP, "Resolutions Adopted at Membership Meeting," June 13, 1950, NAACP Papers, II, C, 126; Simon, 85–93.

43. Esther Smith, Executive Secretary, Town and Village Tenants' Committee to End Discrimination in Stuyvesant Town, "Emergency Memorandum," January 10, 1952, American Labor Party Papers, box 30; Simon, 95–97.

44. Simon, 97–98; National Executive Board, "Report on District 65," April 12, 1951, Papers of District 65, box 50, Tamiment Library; *Amsterdam News,* January 19, 1952; Simon, 98, 99; Hortense Gabel, "Executive Director's Action Report," January 31, 1952, Black Papers, box 9; Algernon Black, "Tenants against Discrimination in Stuyvesant Town," January 28, 1975, Black Papers, box 9.

45. *Amsterdam News,* February 2, 1952.

46. Simon, 106; Black, "Tenants against Discrimination."

47. *Amsterdam News,* January 26, 1952; Simon, 106–110.

7. Anticommunism and Civil Rights

1. The literature on this subject is voluminous. See Ellen Schrecker, *Many Are the Crimes: McCarthyism in America* (New York: Little, Brown, 1998).

2. Stanley Isaacs to the Editor, *New Republic,* May 2, 1946, Isaacs Papers, box 13.

3. *New York Age,* January 27, 1945, and March 30, 1946; Statement by Ewart Guinier, international secretary-treasurer of the UPWA-CIO, for the hearings of the Mundt-Nixon Bill by the Senate Judiciary Committee, May 29, 1948, Guinier Papers, box 6; *Amsterdam News,* December 18, 1954.

4. *People's Voice,* April 26, 1947 and March 29, 1947.

5. Schrecker, 292; *Amsterdam News,* November 12, 1949; Schrecker, 285.

6. "NAACP Votes to Defend Loyalty Purge Victims," November 11, 1947, NAACP Papers, II, B, 90; *Amsterdam News,* November 13, 1948; and September 3, 1949; *The Public Record,* November 1947, in Guinier Papers, box 9.

7. *Amsterdam News,* November 13 and 20, 1948, February 12 and September 24, 1949, and May 19, 1951.

8. Duberman, 325–327; The Reminiscences of Thomas I. Emerson, January 1955, volume 5, part 2, Columbia Oral History Collection, Columbia University, New York; *New York Times,* March 20, 1948; *New York Age,* June 19, 1948; *Amsterdam News,* October 30 and November 6, 1948; Henry A. Wallace, "Ten Extra Years," address to the National Convention of Alpha Phi Alpha fraternity, Tulsa Oklahoma, December 28, 1947, American Labor Party Papers, box 7.

9. Text of radio address by Henry A. Wallace over NBC, September 13, 1948, American Labor Party Papers, box 7.

10. William C. Berman, *The Politics of Civil Rights in the Truman Administration* (Columbus: Ohio State University Press, 1970), 97; "Testimony of A. Philip Randolph. Prepared for Delivery before the Senate Armed Services Committee," March 31, 1948, Randolph Papers, reel 28.

11. "Some people talked me up as the mentor of Humphrey on civil rights. We talked a lot about civil rights and human rights." Johnson in David Brauer, *Nellie Stone Johnson: The Life of an Activist* (St. Paul, Minn.: Ruminator Books, 2000), 138; Donald R. McCoy and Richard T. Ruetten, *Quest and Response: Minority Rights and the Truman Administration* (Lawrence: University Press of Kansas, 1973), 113; United Public Workers of America, CIO, *The Public Record*, May 1948 and September 1948, Guinier Papers, box 9.

12. McCoy and Ruetten, 134; Walters, 106; McCoy and Ruetten, 142–143; *New York Age*, August 28, 1948; *Amsterdam News*, November 6, 1948; Paul Robeson Jr. to author, April 14, 2000, New York; Paul Robeson, transcript of speech over WNBC, October 14, 1949, American Labor Party Papers, box 10; Anna Arnold Hedgeman, *The Trumpet Sounds: A Memoir of Negro Leadership* (New York: Holt, Rhinehart and Winston, 1964).

13. Clifford quoted in Martin Bauml Duberman, *Paul Robeson: A Biography* (New York: Alfred A. Knopf, 1988), 324.

14. Henry A. Wallace, address in Chicago, April 10, 1948, American Labor Party Papers, box 8; Duberman, 328–330.

15. McCoy and Ruetten, 138, 143; Berman, 128–130.

16. *Amsterdam News*, December 4, 1948.

17. Robert H. Zieger, *The CIO, 1935–1955* (Chapel Hill: University of North Carolina Press, 1995), 253–255, and Joshua B. Freeman, *Working Class New York: Life and Labor since World War II* (New York: The New Press, 2000), 72–95.

18. Central Trades and Labor Council, transcripts of hearings at the Hotel Pennsylvania, March 23 and April 23, 1946, NY Board of Education Papers, Subject Files Related to Hearings, box 23, folder 7.

19. *Amsterdam News*, April 24 and May 15, 1954; see *Maisenberg v. United States* 356 U.S. 147 (1958) and *Nowak v. United States* 356 U.S. 660 (1958).

20. *Amsterdam News*, July 9, 1949, and Harris, 138.

21. Transcript of Interview with George Carney, March 19, 1967, box 10, Guinier Papers; Transcript of hearings, Greater New York CIO Industrial Council before CIO Executive Board, October 14–15, 1948, Washington, D.C., Mills Papers, box 4, folder 4; CIO typescript, "The Expulsion of the UPWA from the CIO," January 9, 1950, Bell Papers, box 7.

22. Mark H. Maier, *City Unions: Managing Discontent in New York City* (New Brunswick, N.J.: Rutgers University Press, 1987), 58; *Daily Worker*, May 24, 1950; *Amsterdam News*, February 5, 1949; May 27, June 17, and September 23, 1950; May 19, 1951; and April 25, 1953.

23. "Statement of Local 1, UPW-CIO on the Banning of Local Observances of National Negro History Week by the Welfare Department," February 8, 1950, American Labor Party Papers, box 10.

24. Daniel Horowitz, *Betty Friedan and the Making of the Feminine Mystique: The American Left, the Cold War, and Modern Feminism* (Amherst: University of Massachusetts Press, 1998), 135; Elaine Perry, interview, March 26, 1979, in the *Oral History of the American Left*, Tamiment Library, New York University, New York.

25. "Report by Victoria Garvin," n.d. (ca. 1950), Garvin Papers, box 1; *Amsterdam News,* October 2, 1948 and September 23, 1950; Officer's Report, May 27–28, 1950, Papers of Local 65, box 50, Tamiment Library; Jack Paley, Report, 1950, Papers of Local 65, box 50; *Amsterdam News,* June 20, July 11, July 25, and August 1, 1953.

26. Hugh Mulzac, *A Star to Steer By* (New York: International Publishers, 1963).

27. Ibid., 250–253; *New York Times,* obituary, February 1, 1971; *Amsterdam News,* March 15, 1952; Schrecker, 269.

28. Captain Hugh N. Mulzac to C. B. Powell, September 30, 1951, American Labor Party Papers, box 19.

29. See Herbert Hill, "The Problem of Race in American Labor History," *Reviews in American History* 24 (June 1996): 189–208. See also Zieger, 372–377.

30. Gerald Horne, *Black Liberation/Red Scare: Ben Davis and the Communist Party* (Cranberry, N.J.: Associated University Presses, 1994), 168.

31. Schrecker, 97–98; *New York Times,* February 16 and February 17, 1949.

32. Horne, 227–243; Ted Poston in the *New York Post,* November 2, 1949, in Davis Papers, box 5.

33. Radio transcript, WMCA, November 7, 1949, American Labor Party Papers, box 10.

34. *New York Age,* October 15, 1949; *Amsterdam News,* November 5, 1949 (endorsing Earl Brown); Greenberg, 90; Poston, *New York Post,* November 9, 1949; Ben Davis campaign poster, 1949, Davis Papers, box 5; Benjamin J. Davis, *Communist Councilman from Harlem* (New York: International Publishers, 1969), 233; Edwin R. Lewinson, *Black Politics in New York City* (New York: Twayne, 1974), 79.

35. Claudia Jones, "Ben Davis: Fighter for Freedom," National Committee to Defend Negro Leadership, 1954, 37; "The Negro People vs. The Smith Act," n.a., n.d., Robeson Papers, reel 7.

36. Duberman, 337.

37. Ibid., 343; David Levering Lewis, "Paul Robeson and the USSR," in Jeffrey C. Stewart, ed., *Paul Robeson: Artist and Citizen* (New Brunswick, N.J.: Rutgers University Press, 1998), 225; Penny Von Eschen, *Race against Empire* (Ithaca, N.Y.: Cornell University Press, 1997), 126; see also Brenda Gayle Plummer, *Rising Wind: Black Americans and U.S. Foreign Affairs, 1935–1960* (Chapel Hill: University of North Carolina Press, 1996), 195–196.

38. Duberman, 344–345; Wilkins, unsigned editorial in the *Crisis,* May 1949; Duberman, 347–348.

39. David Levering Lewis, *W. E. B. Du Bois: The Fight for Equality and the American Century* (New York: Henry Holt, 2000), 539–540; Max Yergan, "The American Negro and Mr. Robeson," *New York Herald-Tribune,* April 23, 1949.

40. Arnold Rampersad, *Jackie Robinson: A Biography* (New York: Alfred Knopf, 1997), 213–216; Wilson Record, *The Negro and the Communist Party* (Chapel Hill: University of North Carolina Press, 1951), 303; Jackie R. Robinson, *I Never Had It Made: The Autobiography of Jackie Robinson* (New York: Putnam, 1972), 98.

41. Herbert Shapiro, *White Violence and Black Response: From Reconstruction to Montgomery* (Amherst: University of Massachusetts Press), 378–391.

42. Robert Alan, "Paul Robeson: The Lost Shepherd," *Crisis* 58, no. 11 (November 1951); Von Eschen, 126–127. Paul Robeson Jr. states that evidence from government files in his possession point to a broad effort by the INS, IRS, Justice and State Departments, and CIA to undermine and hurt his father. See Paul Robeson Jr., "The Counterfeit 'Paul Robeson,'" *Amsterdam News*, February 16, 2000, and "The Paul Robeson Files," *Nation*, December 20, 1999, 9.

43. Walter White, "The Strange Case of Paul Robeson," *Ebony* (February 1951), 78–84; Kenneth R. Janken, "Walter White, the NAACP, and Foreign Affairs, 1941–55," *Ethnic and Racial Studies* 21, no. 6 (November 1998): 1075.

44. *New York Times*, March 14, 1950; *Daily Worker*, March 15, March 17, and March 20, 1950. See also Ewart Guinier, "The Paul Robeson That I Knew," *Black Scholar* (March 1978): 45.

45. Duberman, 361; Von Eschen, 126.

46. Louis T. Wright to W. E. B. Du Bois, September 13, 1948, in Herbert Aptheker, ed., *The Correspondence of W. E. B. Du Bois, vol. 3: Selections, 1944–1963* (Amherst: University of Massachusetts Press, 1978), 245; Plummer, 188–190.

47. Gerald Horne, *Black and Red: W. E. B. Du Bois and the Afro-American Response to the Cold War, 1944–1963* (Albany: State University of New York Press, 1986), 141; "Statement by Dr. William E. B. Du Bois, ALP Candidate for U.S. Senate," Hotel Theresa, New York, September 24, 1950, Guinier Papers, box 10; "Statement by Bishop W. J. Walls," October 3, 1950, American Labor Party Papers, box 9; W. E. B. Du Bois, "The Trial," in David Levering Lewis, ed., *W. E. B. Du Bois: A Reader* (New York: Henry Holt, 1995), 774–785.

48. Aptheker, 306–331; Elizabeth Lawson, "The Gentleman from Mississippi: Our First Negro Senator" (New York, March 1960), Pamphlet Collection, Reference Center for Marxist Studies, New York.

49. Reverdy C. Ransom to National Council of the Arts, Sciences and Professions, October 26, 1951, and Resolution, General Alumni Association of Fisk University in Aptheker, 317, 315; Langston Hughes, "The Accusers' Names Nobody Will Remember, But History Records Du Bois," October 6, 1951, in Christopher C. De Santis, ed., *Langston Hughes and the Chicago Defender* (Urbana: University of Illinois Press, 1995), 187; Hubert T. Delany to Du Bois, November 27, 1951, in Aptheker, 320.

50. Charles P. Henry, *Ralph Bunche: Model Negro or American Other?* (New York: New York University Press, 1999), 180; Plummer, 195–196.

51. *Harlem Quarterly* 1, no. 1 (Winter 1949–1950): 21–26.

8. The Paradoxical Effects of the Cold War

1. Guy Brewer, "Report of Legislative Committee, Jamaica Branch, NAACP," February 21, 1949, NAACP Papers, II, C, 121, emphasis in original; "Portion of a Legislative Committee Report, Jamaica Branch," March 12, 1949, NAACP Papers, II, C, 121.

2. Donald R. McCoy and Richard T. Ruetten, *Quest and Response: Minority Rights and the Truman Administration* (Lawrence: University Press of Kansas, 1973), 179; Thomas Brooks, *Walls Come Tumbling Down: A History of the Civil Rights Movement, 1940–1970* (Englewood Cliffs, N.J.: Prentice Hall, 1974), 77–78; *Amsterdam News,* January 14 and January 7, 1950.

3. FBI file on the NAACP, 61–3176, Schomburg Center for Research in Black Culture, New York; *Amsterdam News,* January 21, 1950; Interview with Ewart Guinier by James Jennings, May 19, 1980, audiotape, Guinier Papers.

4. Lindsay H. White to Louis T. Wright, February 7, 1950, NAACP Papers, II, C, 126; Roy Wilkins to Lindsay H. White, April 10, 1950, NAACP Papers, II, C, 126; *Afro-American,* January 21, 1950, in Guinier Papers, box 7.

5. Lindsay H. White to Louis T. Wright, February 7, 1950, NAACP Papers, II, C, 126; *Amsterdam News,* February 18 and March 18, 1950.

6. Resolution adopted by the Forty-first Convention, Boston, June 23, 1950, NAACP Papers, II, C, 121; Kenneth O'Reilly, *"Racial Matters": The FBI's Secret Files on Black America* (New York: The Free Press, 1989), 22; *New York Times,* June 24, 1950; Interview with Lee Lorch by author, Toronto, Canada, April 1999.

7. Alfred Baker Lewis to A. Philip Randolph, February 6, 1950, Randolph Papers, reel 1; Herbert Hill, *The Communist Party—Enemy of Negro Equality* (New York: NAACP, August 1951), in "Herbert Hill" vertical file, Tamiment Library, New York University, New York.

8. Alfred Baker Lewis to Winifred Gittens, n.d., Negro Labor Committee Papers, reel 4; Alfred Baker Lewis, "Memorandum," n.d., Negro Labor Committee Papers, reel 4; *Amsterdam News,* May 6, 1950; Gloster Current to Walter White, June 30, 1950, NAACP Papers, II, C, 126; Madison Jones to Gloster Current, December 21, 1950, NAACP Papers, II, C, 126.

9. Gloster Current to Roy Wilkins, October 28, 1949, NAACP Papers, II, C, 126; Lucille Black to Walter White, February 27, 1953, NAACP Papers, II, C, 120; Donald Jones to Gloster Current, January 31, 1952, NAACP Papers, II, C, 126; Current to Rabbi Katz, October 14, 1953, NAACP Papers, II, C, 120; Schrecker, 393. For repression of branch independence and activism in the South, see Ben Green, *Before His Time: The Untold Story of Harry T. Moore, America's First Civil Rights Martyr* (New York: Free Press, 1999).

10. Lucille Black to Roy Wilkins, June 9, 1950, NAACP Papers, II, C, 121.

11. Lawrence R. Bailey to Fellow Members of the Jamaica Branch, n.d., NAACP Papers, II, C, 121.

12. James H. Robinson to Roy Wilkins, November 18, 1957, NAACP Papers, III, C, 102; "New York NAACP Branch Refunds Membership Fee of Communist," November 14, 1957, NAACP Papers, III, C, 102.

13. O'Reilly, 424.

14. A. Philip Randolph to Robert Church, April 12, 1949, Randolph Papers, reel 16; Theodore E. Brown to Randolph, February 3, 1950, Randolph Papers, reel 16; Joanne Grant, *Ella Baker: Freedom Bound* (New York: Wiley, 1998); and Conrad Lynn, *There Is a Fountain: The Autobiography of a Civil Rights Lawyer* (Westport: L. Hill, 1979).

15. Interview with Ewart Guinier by James Jennings, May 19, 1980, audiotape, Guinier Papers.

16. Wilson Record, *The Negro and the Communist Party* (Chapel Hill: University of North Carolina Press, 1951), 275, 273, 315; William A. Nolan, *Communism versus the Negro* (Chicago: Henry Regnery Company, 1951), 181, 197.

17. Program Services Section, Ideological Advisory Unit, "Ideological Specials #22, 24, 25," August 21, August 22, and August 24, 1951, box 6, Radio Transcripts Collection, Manuscripts, Archives, and Rare Book Division, Schomburg Center. In 1970, Wilson Record self-identified as a white Texan in a grant proposal to study the alienation of white sociologists by the rise of Black Studies. See Record, "Black Studies and White Sociologists," 1970, Typescript Collection, Schomburg Center.

18. Daniel Webster Wynn, *The NAACP versus Negro Revolutionary Protest* (New York: Exposition Press, 1955).

19. Ellen Schrecker, 228, 76; Delacy W. Sanford, "Congressional Investigations of Black Communists, 1919–1967," Ph.D. diss., State University of New York, Stony Brook, 1973, 119; Manning Johnson, *Color, Communism, and Common Sense* (New York: Alliance, 1958), 23, 61.

20. Saul Moskoff to William Jansen, November 30, 1951, and Subject Files Related to Hearings, William Jansen to Saul Moskoff, March 21, 1955, N.Y. Board of Education Papers, box 16; *New York Post,* September 6, 1958; "The Reminiscences of William Jansen," May–June 1963, Oral History Research Office, Columbia University, New York.

21. Teachers' Union, "Statement Requesting Reinstatement of Eight Teachers," May 9, 1950, Subject Files Related to Hearings box 22. See also Paul Buhle, "Albert Shanker: No Flowers," *New Politics* 6 (Summer 1997).

22. See Subject Files Related to Hearings; Dorothy Funn to Max Yergan, February 22, 1947, National Negro Congress Papers, reel 36.

23. In 1956 HUAC subpoenaed George B. Murphy, someone Funn had named. Murphy, the grand secretary of the I.B.P.O. Elks of the World, refused to cooperate and suggested that the committee investigate White Citizens' Councils instead. See Sanford, 160.

24. U.S. Congress, House Committee on Un-American Activities, 83d Congress, 1st sess., May 4, 1953 (Washington, D.C.: Government Printing Office, 1953); Telephone interview with Thelma Dale by author, January 2000; George Schuyler, "Views and Reviews," *Pittsburgh Courier,* May 16, 1953.

25. U.S. Congress, House Committee on Un-American Activities, 83d Congress, 1st sess., May 4, 1953, 165.

26. "Facts on the Blacklist in Radio and Television" (Mimeographed, ca. 1950), Radical Collection, Special Collections, Michigan State University Library, Lansing, Mich. For Scott, see *Scandalize My Name: Stories from the Blacklist,* a documentary film by Alexandra M. Isles (New York: Chalice Well Productions, 1998).

27. "Profile: Canada Lee," *New Yorker,* February 1945, O'Neal Papers, scrapbook, box 2; James J. Podesta, "Canada Lee, 1907–1952," in L. Mpho Mabunda, ed.,

Contemporary Black Biography, vol. 8 (Detroit: Gale Research, 1995), 156–160; "Statement of Canada Lee," n.d., box 5, Lee Papers; Canada Lee to editor (unknown), June 15, 1949, Lee Papers; Canada Lee to Walter White, April 1, 1952, box 3, Lee Papers; *New York Times,* obituary, May 10, 1952.

28. Arnold Rampersad, *The Life of Langston Hughes,* vol. 2 (New York: Oxford University Press, 1988), 209–222; Hughes, "Why Ill Winds and Dark Clouds Don't Scare Negroes Much," October 22, 1953, in Christopher De Santis, *Langston Hughes and the Chicago Defender* (Urbana: University of Illinois Press, 1995), 190.

29. *Scandalize My Name; St. Louis American,* May 12, 1949, scrapbook, O'Neal Papers, box 2; "Did you see a Negro on Television last night?" CCNP Flier, O'Neal Papers, box 2; Coordinating Council for Negro Performers, Press Release, June 16, 1954, O'Neal Papers, box 2.

30. CCNP Newsletter, November 1957, Dick Campbell, ed., O'Neal Papers, box 2.

31. *Amsterdam News,* May 22, 1952; *Daily Worker,* February 22, 1952; *New York Post,* September 13, 1955.

32. *New York Times,* editorial, September 18, 1955; FBI File Number 62–97280, June 29, 1954, in author's possession.

33. "The Reminiscences of Algernon Black," 175–219, Oral History Project, Columbia University, New York. Twenty years later, Black expressed ambivalence at having signed the statement, viewing it as a sacrifice of principle.

34. Ibid., 226.

35. See Penny M. Von Eschen, *Race against Empire: Black Americans and Anticolonialism, 1937–1957* (Ithaca, N.Y.: Cornell University Press, 1997).

36. James H. Robinson, *Tomorrow Is Today* (Philadelphia: Christian Education Press, 1954), 23; *Amsterdam News,* December 27, 1952.

37. *Amsterdam News,* January 23, 1953; *Freedom,* September 1951; Ewart Guinier, speech to the Harlem Affairs Committee, 1953, Guinier Papers, box 11; *Amsterdam News,* January 17 and January 31, 1953. In 1964 Reverend Robinson testified before HUAC. See U.S. Congress, House Committee on Un-American Activities, "Testimony of Reverend James H. Robinson," Hearing, 88th Congress, 2d sess., May 5, 1964 (Washington, D.C.: Government Printing Office, 1964).

38. Robinson, 30–53.

39. Robinson noted that he was never compensated for any of his consulting, writing, or travels for the United States.

40. James H. Robinson, ed., *Love of This Land: Progress of the Negro in the United States* (Philadelphia: Christian Education Press, 1956), x (available at the Schomburg Center).

41. Hugh Bradley, *Next Steps in the Struggle for Negro Freedom* (New York: New Century Publishers, November 1953), 21–25 (available at Reference Center for Marxist Studies, New York); Benjamin J. Davis, "The Negro People and the Struggle for Peace and Freedom," report to the 15th convention of the Communist Party, December 1950, New York, "Communist Party (U.S.) and Negroes" vertical file, Taminent Library.

42. E. Franklin Frazier, ed., *The Integration of the Negro in American Society* (Washington D.C.: Howard University Press, 1951), iii.

43. Hortense Gabel to Albert Mayer, January 13, 1953, Black Papers, box 9; *New York Times,* March 20, 1953.

44. McCoy and Ruetten, 266; William C. Berman, *The Politics of Civil Rights in the Truman Administration* (Columbus: Ohio State University Press, 1970), 173; For the beneficial effect of the Cold War, see Mary L. Dudziak, *Cold War Civil Rights: Race and the Image of American Democracy* (Princeton, N.J.: Princeton University Press, 2000). For a look at how anticommunism bolstered white supremacy in the South, see Michael K. Honey, *Southern Labor and Black Civil Rights: Organizing Memphis Workers* (Urbana: University of Illinois Press, 1993), 245–277.

45. The AJC and NAACP, *Civil Rights in the U.S. in 1950: A Balance Sheet of Group Relations* February 28, 1951, Mayor's Committee on Unity Papers, box 1613; *Amsterdam News,* March 10, 1951.

46. McCoy and Ruetten, 180; *Amsterdam News,* January 13, 1951; A. Philip Randolph, "Fight for FEPC Might Breakdown One-Party System of the South," March 6, 1948, Randolph Papers, reel 28; A. Philip Randolph to Robert Church, April 12, 1949, Randolph Papers, reel 16.

47. *Amsterdam News,* September 23, 1950.

48. Ibid., February 3 and July 28, 1951.

49. Ibid., February 9, 1952; Lewison, 119–120; Wil Haygood, *King of the Cats: The Life and Times of Adam Clayton Powell Jr.* (New York: Houghton Mifflin, 1993), 203–204; *Amsterdam News,* June 4, 1955.

50. *New York Post,* October 22, 1951; Ralph Blumenthal, *Stork Club: America's Most Famous Nightspot and the Lost World of Café Society* (New York: Little, Brown, 2000), 162–163.

51. Blumenthal, 164.

52. *People's World,* July 18 and 19, 1951, Civil Rights Congress Papers, Los Angeles chapter, Southern California Library for Social Studies, Los Angeles, box 8.

53. *New York Post,* October 22, 1951; Neal Gabler, "A Head for an Eye," in *Walter Winchell: Gossip, Power and the Culture of Celebrity* (London: Picador Books, 1995).

54. *New York Post,* October 22, 1951; Blumenthal, 164–165, 174.

55. *New York Post,* October 22, 1951; *Amsterdam News,* October 27, 1951.

56. Walter White to Members of the Committee on Administration, November 7, 1951, NAACP Papers, II, C, 126; Mary L. Dudziak, "Josephine Baker, Racial Protest, and the Cold War," *Journal of American History* 81 (September 1994): 550.

57. MCU, "Stork Club Controversy," December 20, 1951, Mayor's Committee on Unity Papers, box 1605; *New York Post,* December 5 and December 27, 1951, and January 2, 1952; *Amsterdam News,* January 5, 1952; Blumenthal, 170–174.

58. Dudziak, 566–570; *Amsterdam News,* January 5, 1952; Blumenthal, 174; NAACP, Memorandum, March 10, 1952, NAACP Papers, II, A, 120; Minutes of the Brooklyn Human Rights Conference, April 28, 1955, Mayor's Committee on Unity Papers, box 1615.

59. Coleman Young and Lonnie Wheeler, *Hard Stuff: The Autobiography of Coleman Young* (New York: Viking, 1994), 128–129.

9. Racial Violence in the Free World

1. Herbert Shapiro, *White Violence and Black Response* (Amherst: University of Massachusetts Press, 1988), 370; William Patterson, *We Charge Genocide: The Crime of Government against the Negro People; A Petition to the United Nations* (New York: Civil Rights Congress, 1951).

2. *Amsterdam News,* December 16, 1950.

3. Ibid. Brown ejected an American Labor Party delegation from his office, claiming, "They've got absolutely no interest in the Derrick case. All they want to do is agitate for Stalin and Russia." Ibid., January 20, 1951.

4. Roy Wilkins complained about the presence of alleged Communists on the Derrick Committee, citing "the long records of Left Wing activism" of three of the vice presidents. Wilkins to Gloster Current, February 27, 1951, NAACP Papers, II, C, 126.

5. James H. Robinson to Arthur W. Wallander, December 26, 1950, NAACP Papers, II, C, 126; *New York Times,* January 9, 1951; *Daily Worker,* January 8 and January 9, 1951; *Daily Compass,* January 5, 1951.

6. *Amsterdam News,* February 10, February 17, February 24, December 21, and March 3, 1951, February 21, 1953, and June 30, 1951; and Adam Clayton Powell Jr., *Adam by Adam: The Autobiography of Adam Clayton Powell* (New York: Dial Press, 1971).

7. *Amsterdam News,* June 2, 1951; *Daily Worker,* January 9, 1951.

8. *Daily Worker,* May 28, 1951, and *Amsterdam News,* June 2, 1951.

9. *Daily Worker,* May 28, 1951.

10. *Jewish Life,* July 1951; *Amsterdam News,* June 2 and editorial, June 9, 1951.

11. *Amsterdam News,* June 9, 1951.

12. *New York Times,* June 23 and June 29, 1951.

13. Herbert H. Hill to Gloster Current, July 18, 1951, and Herbert H. Hill to Henry Moon, July 23, 1951, NAACP Papers, II, C, 118.

14. *Amsterdam News,* July 28, 1951; *Daily Worker,* September 11, 1951; *Amsterdam News,* December 1, 1951, and March 29, 1952; *Daily Worker,* September 15, 1952; *New York Times,* May 5, 1954.

15. See Billy Rowe's obituary in the *New York Times,* September 23, 1997.

16. *Amsterdam News,* March 29, 1952; *Daily Worker,* January 4, 1952; *Amsterdam News,* May 9, 1953, and June 28, 1952; *New York Post,* n.d., in a scrapbook, "Police Brutality," Schomburg Center for Research in Black Culture, New York; *Amsterdam News,* December 15, 1951; *New York Times,* February 19, 1953.

17. See Gerald Horne, *Communist Front? The Civil Rights Congress, 1946–1956* (Rutherford, N.J.: Fairleigh Dickinson University Press, 1988).

18. Lorraine Hansberry in *Freedom,* October 1951; American Labor Party, Press Release, April 24, 1951, American Labor Party Papers, box 19.

19. "Free the Ingram Family Now!" flier, and Maude White Katz to Mrs. Geni Guinier, Guinier Papers, box 1; *People's Voice*, March 27 and April 17, 1948; *New York Age*, June 5, 1948.

20. Mary L. Dudziak, *Cold War Civil Rights: Race and the Image of American Democracy* (Princeton, N.J.: Princeton University Press, 2000), 64–65; Patterson, 27; Aptheker, 30–52.

21. Kenneth R. Janken, "Walter White, NAACP, and Foreign Affairs, 1941–1955," *Ethnic and Racial Studies* 21 (November 1998): 1087–1089.

22. In an effort to impugn the NAACP's Cold War strategy, Ewart Guinier noted that "when Walter White called for a work stoppage in protest of the Moore murders, the CIO said he was talking like a Communist." "Red-baiting by the top leaders of the NAACP," he concluded, "has neither brought progress in our fight for civil rights nor brought them immunity from attack." Jobs Action Conference, Greater New York Negro Labor Council, Hotel Theresa, March 8, 1952, Guinier Papers, box 9.

23. *Amsterdam News*, January 5, January 12, and January 16, 1952. In *Before His Time: The Untold Story of Harry T. Moore, America's First Civil Rights Martyr* (New York: Free Press, 1999), the author Ben Green argues that the mastermind of the killings was most likely KKK leader Joseph Neville Cox, who committed suicide the day after he was questioned by the FBI.

24. *Amsterdam News*, January 5, 1952; Charlotta Bass speech in New York, n.d., Bass Papers, additions, box 1.

25. *Amsterdam News*, October 4, 1952.

26. NYU NAACP ad hoc Committee for Justice in the Christianii Case, "Why the Killing of Enus L. Christianii (NYU Graduate Student)?" (1952), American Labor Party Papers, box 23.

27. Walter White, Statement submitted to the House Judiciary Subcommittee, March 20, 1953, NAACP Papers, II, A, 456; *Amsterdam News*, February 21, 1953. For background on the Justice Department in the 1940s, see *To Secure These Rights* and Gail Williams O'Brien, *The Color of the Law: Race, Violence and Justice in the Post–World War II South* (Chapel Hill: University of North Carolina Press, 1999); *Amsterdam News*, March 7, 1953.

28. *New York Times*, February 17 and March 3, 1953; *Amsterdam News*, February 21 and February 28, 1953.

29. *Amsterdam News*, September 13, 1952.

30. Ibid., March 7, 1953; transcript of telephone call from Adam Clayton Powell Jr. to Roy Wilkins, February 19, 1953, NAACP Papers, II, A, 456; *Amsterdam News*, February 28, 1953.

31. *New York Times*, February 17, 1953; Herbert Wright to Youth Councils, College Chapters, and Affiliated Organizations of the NAACP, n.d., NAACP Papers, II, A, 456.

32. Ella Baker to Mayor Vincent R. Impellitteri, February 16, 1953, NAACP Papers, II, A, 456; *New York Post*, February 19, 1953; Press Release, "Civic Groups Demand Action against Secret Rights Pact," February 19, 1953, NAACP Papers, II, A, 456; *Amsterdam News*, February 28, 1953.

33. *Amsterdam News,* May 16, 1953; "Civic Groups Demand Action against Secret Rights Pact."

34. *New York Times,* February 28, 1953; *Amsterdam News,* March 7, 1953.

35. *Amsterdam News,* March 21, 1953; Walter White, Statement, n.d., NAACP Papers, II, A, 456; *Amsterdam News,* March 21, June 6, June 13, and June 27, 1953.

36. *New York Telegram and Sun,* July 6, 1954, and *New York Times,* July 7, 1954, in NAACP Papers, II, A, 456; *Amsterdam News,* March 28, 1953; *New York Times,* May 23, 1953; and *Amsterdam News,* May 30, 1953.

37. *Amsterdam News,* May 30, 1953.

38. Walter White, Statement Submitted to the House Judiciary Subcommittee, March 20, 1953, NAACP Papers, II, A, 456.

10. Lift Every Voice and Vote

1. John C. Walter, *The Harlem Fox: J. Raymond Jones and Tammany, 1920–1970* (Albany: State University of New York Press, 1989), 137.

2. Speech by Vito Marcantonio, October 25, 1949, Marcantonio Papers; Radio interview over WMCA, November 2, 1949, transcript, American Labor Party Papers, box 11.

3. Independent Citizens' Committee for the Election of Ewart Guinier, Press Release, October 21, 1949, Ewart Guinier to Hope Stevens, September 26, 1949, American Labor Party Papers, box 11.

4. *Amsterdam News,* November 12, 1949.

5. Ibid., May 13, June 3, and November 11, 1950; Lewinson, 86.

6. Ted Poston, "The Making of a Judge," *New York Post,* August 15, 1955. For portraits of other Catholic converts and an analysis of their worldviews, see James T. Fisher, *The Catholic Counterculture in America, 1933–1962* (Chapel Hill: University of North Carolina Press, 1989).

7. *Amsterdam News,* July 15, 1950.

8. "Biographical Sketch of Jacques Isler," n.d., American Labor Party Papers, box 17; Guinier, "Informal Memorandum for Discussion," September 7, 1950, American Labor Party Papers, box 9; Flier, "An Appeal to Negroes," and Non-Partisan Conference, Press Release, September 6, 1951, American Labor Party Papers, box 17.

9. National Committee to Elect Negroes to Public Office, Draft Statement, n.d., American Labor Party Papers, box 23; Telephone interview with Thelma Dale Perkins by the author, January 2000.

10. Ewart Guinier, *National Guardian,* July 28, 1953, Guinier Papers, box 7; *Daily Worker,* July 1, 1952; Open letter by the Committee to Elect a Negro State Senator, August 13, 1952, Guinier Papers, box 7; American Labor Party, New York County, *Bulletin,* July 1952, in Guinier Papers, box 7; Campaign leaflet for Julius Archibald, in Guinier Papers, box 7; *Amsterdam News,* January 17, 1953.

11. Flier in Guinier Papers, box 7; *Amsterdam News,* August 23 and November 8, 1952, and July 10 and August 14, 1954.

12. Eugenia Guinier to Mollie Herman, September 13, 1953, in possession of Lani

Guinier; *Amsterdam News*, August 1, 1953; Jacques Isler, "Open Letter," May 6, 1953, Guinier Papers, box 7; Harlem Affairs Committee, "Open Letter," August 10, 1953, Guinier Papers, box 7; Robert Justice to "Harlemites Interested in Political Progress," June 12, 1953, Guinier Papers, box 7.

13. Harlem Affairs Committee, "Open Letter," August 10, 1953, Guinier Papers, box 7; Eugenia Guinier to Mollie Herman, September 13, 1953; *Amsterdam News*, August 1 and August 22, 1953; *New York Times*, July 28, 1953; Robert F. Wagner Oral History, Oral History Research Office, Columbia University, May 4, 1978, 838. After the election, Powell and the Baptist Ministers Conference announced plans to form the United Protestant Political Action Movement. See *Amsterdam News*, January 30, 1954.

14. The *New York Post* editorial quoted in Ewart Guinier, "The Fight for First Class Citizenship," September 28, 1953, *National Guardian*, Guinier Papers, box 17.

15. Wagner Oral History, May 4, 1978, 838.

16. *Amsterdam News*, April 2, 1949, and January 26, 1952; Notes by Guinier, n.d., Guinier Papers, box 7; *Amsterdam News*, August 8, 1953; Anna Arnold Hedgeman, *The Trumpet Sounds: A Memoir of Negro Leadership* (New York: Holt, Rinehart and Winston, 1964), 121. Jack won a seat in the assembly in 1968, but resigned two years later after conviction for another incident of political corruption—that time he served three months in jail. In 1980 Jack worked as a political consultant in the presidential campaign of Lyndon LaRouche, the global conspiracy theorist. He died in 1986. See Virgil S. Powell, *Notable Black Americans* (Cedar Rapids, Iowa: WMT Stations, 1971); Hulan Jack, *Fifty Years a Democrat: The Autobiography of Hulan Jack* (New York: New Benjamin Franklin House, 1982).

17. *Amsterdam News*, October 29 and September 24, 1949.

18. "Citizens Committee," open letter, March 2, 1953, Correspondence, 1953–1987, Galamison Papers, box 1; *Amsterdam News*, May 16, September 12, and December 5, 1953, and January 2, 1954; Shirley Chisholm, *Unbought and Unbossed* (Boston: Houghton Mifflin, 1970), 34–35; Interview with Wesley McD. Holder in Carlos Russell, "Black Brooklyn Oral History," Ph.D. diss., Union College, 129–134.

19. *Amsterdam News*, March 13, 1954; Russell, "Introduction," 4.

20. *Amsterdam News*, August 1 and November 14, 1953; Lewinson, 87.

21. *Amsterdam News*, June 23 and October 20, 1951.

22. *Amsterdam News*, August 7, 1954; Lewinson, 105.

23. *Amsterdam News*, July 10, 1954; HAC flier, December 5, 1954, Guinier Papers, box 7; Harlem Affairs Committee to Mr. and Mrs. Harlem, n.d., Guinier Papers, box 7; *Amsterdam News*, editorial, August 28, 1954, adopting HAC's call for statewide representation.

24. Robert Justice to Senator Irving Ives, August 26, 1954, Guinier Papers, box 10.

25. *Amsterdam News*, September 4, 1954; New York NAACP and HAC, Press Release, December 13, 1954, Guinier Papers, box 10; *Amsterdam News*, December 11, 1954, and January 11, 1955.

26. Flier and handwritten notes with speakers designated by sex, February 21, 1954, Guinier Papers, box 7.

27. Guinier penciled in a correction to an *Amsterdam News* article of October 2, 1954. Ruth Whitehead Whaley was the first nominee, in 1945. See Guinier Papers, box 7.

28. Thelma Dale to Paul Robeson, February 26, 1952, reel 8, Robeson Collection; *Amsterdam News,* October 2, 1954; Chisholm, 53.

29. *Amsterdam News,* January 2 and January 23, 1954; Hedgeman, 120.

30. Elaine Ross, *Negro Representation NOW!* (New York: New York State Committee of the ALP, 1955), American Labor Party Papers, box 51.

11. Resisting Resegregation

1. Walter White in the *Amsterdam News,* May 29, 1954. For housing segregation see Arnold R. Hirsch, *Making the Second Ghetto: Race and Housing in Chicago, 1940–1960* (New York: Cambridge University Press, 1983); Kenneth T. Jackson, *Crabgrass Frontier: The Suburbanization of the United States* (New York: Oxford University Press, 1985); Douglas S. Massey and Nancy A. Denton, *American Apartheid: Segregation and the Making of the Underclass* (Cambridge, Mass.: Harvard University Press, 1993); Thomas J. Sugrue, *The Origins of the Urban Crisis: Race and Inequality in Postwar Detroit* (Princeton, N.J.: Princeton University Press, 1996).

2. Robert Caro wrote the classic critique of urban renewal, *The Power Broker: Robert Moses and the Fall of New York* (New York: Knopf, 1974). See also Joel Schwartz, *The New York Approach: Robert Moses, Urban Liberals, and Redevelopment of the Inner City* (Columbus: Ohio State University Press, 1993).

3. NYSCDH Pamphlet, "Rebuilding Our Cities for Everybody," Conference, Hotel Martinique, December 2, 1949, Black Papers, box 8; Black, "Urban Redevelopment," n.d., Black Papers, box 8; Horne quoted in "Minutes of the Conference on Democracy in Housing," June 15, 1950, Hotel New Yorker, NAACP Papers, II, B, 79.

4. In 1953 the federal government issued a new rule compelling residents in federally assisted housing projects in New York to sign a statement disclaiming membership in any of 203 "subversive groups." *Amsterdam News,* January 3 and February 21, 1953.

5. American Labor Party bulletin, July 1952, Guinier Papers, box 7; Schwartz, 194–197; *Amsterdam News,* December 10 and March 22, 1952; Hortense Gabel, "Executive Director Action Report," June 19, 1952, Black Papers, box 9; Gabel, "Executive Director Action Report," December 10, 1952, Black Papers, box 9.

6. Caro, 965–978; Algernon Black, "The Housing Act of 1949," January 28, 1975, Black Papers, box 9; SCAD Press Release, "Discrimination in the North," n.d. (ca. 1956), New York State AFL-CIO Papers, box A-4; "1961 Report to the Commission on Civil Rights from the State Advisory Committee," clipping file, "Civil Rights—New York," Schomburg Center for Research in Black Culture, New York; Ted Poston, "Harlem," *New York Post Magazine,* July 26, 1964.

7. *Amsterdam News,* March 22, 1952; Ted Poston, *New York Post,* December 5, 1953; "Analysis of Racial Impact of New Middle Income Housing," n.a., n.d., Guinier Papers, box 11; *Amsterdam News,* July 3, 1954.

8. Knickerbocker Village Tenants Association, "Facts on Anti-Negro Discrimination in Knickerbocker Village," March 1952, Civil Rights Congress Papers, part 2, reel 37; KVTA, "The Strickland Story—Background and Developments," n.d., American Labor Party Papers, box 32; *Amsterdam News,* April 26, 1952, and May 9 and June 13, 1953.

9. *Amsterdam News,* March 15, 1952; Sylvia De Shore, "Statement by Committee for Brotherhood of Bell Park Gardens, Bayside, N.Y.," n.d., Black Papers, box 9; *Amsterdam News,* November 22, 1952, and January 31, 1953.

10. Algernon Black, "Statement to Be Read at Mayor's Committee on Unity Meeting," January 9, 1953, Mayor's Committee on Unity Papers, box 1605.

11. James Egert Allen, teacher and state NAACP leader, met with Met Life president Frederick Ecker in his "palatial offices" in 1941. Allen said that as a policyholder in Met Life, a mutual corporation, "I consider myself to be a part owner." Thinking of all the Black policyholders whose "hard-earned dollars" had helped build the company, Allen canceled his life-insurance policy, "a small price to pay" to protest corporate injustice. James Egert Allen, *Black History Past and Present* (New York: Exposition Press, 1971), 82–84.

12. *Amsterdam News,* May 20, 1950, and October 25, 1952.

13. *Amsterdam News,* February 14 and February 28, 1953, July 24, 1954, and March 28, 1953.

14. *Daily Worker,* March 1, 1953; *Amsterdam News,* May 2 and May 30, 1953.

15. Hortense Gabel to Algernon Black, Robert C. Weaver, Stanley Isaacs, and Ira Robbins, June 8, 1953, Black Papers, box 9; *Amsterdam News,* March 20, 1954; Simon, 105.

16. Mayor's Committee on Unity, "Conference of Brooklyn Council for Social Planning," April 29, 1954, Mayor's Committee on Unity Papers, box 1615.

17. *New York Herald Tribune,* March 12, 1949, Mayor's Committee on Unity Papers, box 1604; *Amsterdam News,* April 2, April 23, and June 11, 1949; Maggie Garb, "Levittown Revisited: A Portrait of a Community in Conflict," research paper in possession of the author.

18. *Daily Worker,* June 17, 1951; *Amsterdam News,* December 9, 1950; American Jewish Congress, "Brief *Amicus* in *Novick et al. v. Levitt and Sons, Inc.*" AJC-CLSA Briefs, 1951, American Jewish Congress Papers; *Amsterdam News,* January 6, 1951; Algernon Black, "1951," n.d., Black Papers, box 9; *Amsterdam News,* February 23, 1952.

19. *Amsterdam News,* July 18, August 15, and December 5, 1953, and September 29, 1951. In 1960, not a single Black family lived in Levittown according to Jackson, 241.

20. Roy Wilkins, audiotape of address to the 1952 NAACP Convention, Moving Image and Recorded Sound Division, Schomburg Center; NAACP Legal Defense

and Educational Fund, Inc., "Racial Discrimination in Housing," 1953, NAACP Papers, II, B, 76, emphasis in original.

21. NCDH, Press Release, April 1955, Adams Papers, box 5; *Amsterdam News*, October 13, 1951, and January 19, 1952; Algernon Black to New York State Democratic Platform Committee, September 16, 1954, Black Papers, box 9; *Amsterdam News*, February 13, 1954; Black, Memorandum, January 31, 1975, Black Papers, box 9.

22. Committee on Law and Social Action, *CLSA Reports*, April 5, 1955, Mayor's Committee on Unity Papers, box 1615; *Amsterdam News*, July 17, 1954.

23. Martin K. Hunt and Jacqueline E. Hunt, *History of Black Business: The Coming of America's Largest Black-Owned Businesses* (Chicago: Knowledge Express, 1998), 177–186.

24. Committee on Law and Social Action, *Law and Social Action*, March–April 1947, American Jewish Congress Papers; Algernon Black, "Brotherhood and Segregation," February 27, 1949, Black Papers, box 5; *Amsterdam News*, November 21, 1953.

25. *Amsterdam News*, April 7, 1951; November 14, November 21, November 28, December 5, and December 26, 1953, and March 6, February 13, and October 30, 1954.

26. *New York Age*, January 31, 1948; *Amsterdam News*, May 23, 1953; Massey and Denton, 50; *Amsterdam News*, May 30, 1953.

27. *Amsterdam News*, July 28, 1951; American Jewish Congress, "Discrimination in Housing," December 5, 1951; Committee on Law and Social Action, Executive Committee, "Minutes," December 13, 1951, AJC-CLSA materials, July–December 1951, American Jewish Congress Papers; Edwin Newman, "Upstate Swing," confidential memo, Fall 1949, Black Papers, box 8.

28. Joshua B. Freeman, *Working Class New York: Life and Labor since World War II* (New York: New Press, 2000), 30; *Amsterdam News*, October 22, 1949; Civil Rights Congress, "Information Sheet," February 28, 1950, Civil Rights Congress Papers, part 2, reel 37; *Amsterdam News*, June 5, 1954.

29. *Amsterdam News*, February 7, November 28, and December 5, 1953, and January 30, 1954; *Daily Worker*, January 25, 1954; Congress of Racial Equality, *CORE-later*, January–February and March–April 1954, CORE Papers, reel 13.

30. *House and Home*, April 1953, Black Papers, box 9.

31. Robert Frederick Burk, *The Eisenhower Administration and Black Civil Rights* (Knoxville: University of Tennessee Press, 1984), 116; *Amsterdam News*, June 15, 1957.

32. *Amsterdam News*, September 18, 1954.

33. Ibid., January 28, February 4, and April 1, 1950, and August 4, 1951.

34. Ibid., April 21, 1951; *Daily Worker*, March 23, 1954; Frank R. Crosswaith, "New York City: Progress against Discrimination in Housing," *American City* (May 1955); State Commission against Discrimination, "Discrimination in the North," April 12, 1956, New York State AFL-CIO Papers, box A-4.

35. NYSCDH, "New York Needs a Fair Housing Practices Law," December 1956,

New York State AFL-CIO Papers, box A-4; The *CORE-later,* Fall 1957, CORE Papers, reel 13; Interview with Mayor Robert F. Wagner, Oral History Research Office, Columbia University, August 9, 1978, 908–909.

36. *Daily Worker,* June 22, 1950; Harlem Tenants' Council, "Legislative Demands, 1954," n.d., Guinier Papers, box 7; State Commission against Discrimination, "Discrimination in the North," April 12, 1956, New York State AFL-CIO Papers, box A-4.

37. *People's Voice,* October 19, 1946; *Daily Worker,* April 11, 1945; *New York Age,* February 9, 1946; *People's Voice* (series), June 7, June 28, and July 5, 1947; *People's Voice,* March 2, 1946, and January 18, 1947.

38. Dan W. Dodson, "A Progress Report on Integration of Negroes in Secondary Schools in New York City," June 3, 1946, O'Dwyer Papers, box 43.

39. Dan W. Dodson, "Integration in High Schools," December 27, 1946, Mayor's Committee on Unity Papers, box 1605.

40. Edward S. Lewis, "The Urban League, A Dynamic Instrument in Social Change: A Study of the Changing Role of the New York Urban League, 1910–1960," Ph.D. diss, New York University, 1961, 185; *Amsterdam News,* April 15, 1950; *People's Voice,* June 28, 1947.

41. Roy Wilkins to May Dillon, May 16, 1945, NAACP Papers, II, C, 117; *People's Voice,* June 16, 1946, and *New York Age,* June 9, 1945.

42. *New York Age,* November 3, 1945; Committee on Law and Social Action, *Law and Social Action,* March 1946, American Jewish Congress Papers; Thurgood Marshall and Marian Wynn Perry, "Memorandum to the Trial Committee of the Board of Education," January 16, 1946, NAACP Papers, II, B, 145; *New York Age,* March 9, 1946; *New York Herald Tribune,* March 1, 1946; CLSA, *Law and Social Action,* March 1946, American Jewish Congress Papers.

43. *New York Post,* December 21, 1949, Mayor's Committee on Unity Papers, box 1608; "Statement by Dr. Jansen on the Case of Miss May Quinn," December 16, 1949, NAACP Papers, II, B, 145; Shirley Graham (and others) to Hon. William O'Dwyer, March 9, 1950, American Labor Party Papers, box 16.

44. Teachers' Union, "Bias and Prejudice in Textbooks in Use in New York City Schools," n.d. (ca. 1951), Guinier Papers, box 6.

45. Teachers' Union, "The Negro in New York, 1626–1865: A Study for Teachers," n.d., American Labor Party Papers, box 52.

46. For Clark's account of these events, see Kenneth Clark, "Segregation and Desegregation in Our Schools," in Algernon Black, Kenneth Clark, and James R. Dumpson, *Ethical Frontiers: The City's Children and the Challenge of Racial Discrimination* (New York: Ethical Culture Society, 1958), available at the New York Public Library.

47. *Amsterdam News,* February 27, May 1, June 26, and October 16, 1954; Clark, 15.

48. *Amsterdam News,* July 3, 1954; Clark, 15.

49. Lewis, 279–287.

50. Clark, 17–18.

51. Ibid., 21–22.

52. For segregation in the 1950s, see Harold X. Connolly, *A Ghetto Grows in Brooklyn* (New York: New York University Press, 1977), 151, 214–215, 220, and for the 1964 boycotts, see Clarence Taylor, *Knocking at Our Own Door: Milton A. Galamison and the Struggle to Integrate New York City Schools* (New York: Columbia University Press, 1997).

12. To Stand and Fight

1. *Amsterdam News,* June 18, 1949; Milton D. Stewart, "Notes for Discussion with the Mayor," March 25, 1949, Mayor's Committee on Unity Papers, box 1608. For a recent treatment of longshoremen in New York, see Bruce Nelson, *Divided We Stand: American Workers and the Struggle for Black Equality* (Princeton, N.J.: Princeton University Press, 2001), 79–89.
2. *Amsterdam News,* April 9 and October 15, 1949; *Daily Worker* (Harlem edition), April 24, 1949; Gloster Current to Roy Wilkins, October 28, 1949, NAACP Papers, II, C, 126.
3. Jacobs in *Daily Compass,* August 15 and August 17, 1949; ILA Papers, box 5; Marian Wynn Perry to Clarence Mitchell, Memorandum, March 3, 1949, NAACP Papers, II, B, 89.
4. Marian Wynn Perry to Clarence Mitchell, Memorandum, March 3, 1949, NAACP Papers, II, B, 89; Jacobs in *Daily Compass,* August 15, 1949, International Longshoremen's Association Papers, box 5; Federated Press Release, June 21, 1949, ILA Papers, box 5.
5. Ewart Guinier, Speech to the NNLC Convention, October 28, 1951, Guinier Papers, box 6; *Amsterdam News,* March 12 and April 2, 1949; *Daily Compass,* August 15, 1949.
6. *New York Times,* June 8 and June 9, 1949; *New York Herald-Tribune,* June 8, 1949; *Amsterdam News,* June 11, 1949.
7. *Amsterdam News,* June 11 and June 18, 1949; Marian Wynn Perry to Herbert Hill, June 14, 1949, NAACP Papers, II, B, 89; Clarence Mitchell to Roy Wilkins, June 20, 1949, NAACP Papers, II, B, 89; Cleophus Jacobs to "Sirs and Brothers," July 25, 1949, NAACP Papers, II, B, 89; *Amsterdam News,* June 18, 1949.
8. Memorandum from Marian Wynn Perry to Thurgood Marshall and Clarence Mitchell, July 15, 1949, and Marian Wynn Perry, Memorandum to Files, July 29, 1949, both in NAACP Papers, II, B, 89.
9. *Daily Compass,* February 7, 1950.
10. *Amsterdam News,* June 13, 1953; Interview with I. Philip Sipser by author, New York City, July 22, 1997.
11. *Amsterdam News,* January 23, May 22, June 5, October 30, and December 4, 1954; *New York Times,* September 15, 1959; Urban League of Greater New York, "An Indictment of the 'Shape-Up' Hiring System . . ." June 1959, ILA Papers, box 3.
12. Interview with Sipser.
13. Vernon Jensen, *Strife on the Waterfront: The Port of New York since 1945* (Ithaca,

N.Y.: Cornell University Press, 1974), 232; Interview with Sipser; Herman Bloch, *The Circle of Discrimination* (New York: New York University Press, 1969), 115–120; *New York Times*, October 3, 1961.

14. Interview with Sipser. Sipser was the attorney for the brewery workers union that operated this seniority system.

15. These seven included both AFL and CIO locals. Later in the 1950s they merged into two locals and all came under the jurisdiction of the AFL Brotherhood of Teamsters.

16. *Amsterdam News*, June 10, 1950; United African Nationalist Movement, Press Release, December 21, 1951, Mayor's Committee on Unity Papers, box 1616; *Amsterdam News*, August 12, 1950. These statistics reportedly did not include menial laborers and "contact men for Negro areas."

17. "Everybody distrusted Lawson. They thought he was a crook. I think he was a crook." Interview with Sipser.

18. *The Connection*, July 27–August 9, 1985, available at the Schomburg Center for Research in Black Culture, New York; *New York Times*, obituary, July 14, 1985; *New York Age*, July 30, 1949. Lawson hosted the first annual Marcus Garvey Day in Harlem in 1949.

19. *People's Voice*, November 23, 1946; *Amsterdam News*, April 19, 1952; United African Nationalist Movement, Press Release, October 15 and December 21, 1951, Mayor's Committee on Unity Papers, box 1616.

20. "Black" contrasted with the prevailing use of Negro and was usually put in quotation marks in the *Amsterdam News*.

21. *Amsterdam News*, April 26 and March 8, 1952.

22. *Amsterdam News*, April 26, June 28, and July 5, 1952.

23. *Amsterdam News*, April 30, 1966.

24. Edward S. Lewis, "The Urban League, a Dynamic Instrument in Social Change: A Study of the Changing Role of the New York Urban League, 1910–1960," Ph.D. diss., New York University, 1961, 266–269; *Amsterdam News*, February 7, 1952, and March 7, 1953.

25. Interview with Sipser.

26. *Amsterdam News*, March 14, March 28, April 25, October 31, and March 20, 1953, and April 10 and December 11, 1954.

27. Interview with Sipser, July 22, 1997; John Hoh, "One Union's Formula to End Hiring Bias," unpublished paper in possession of Philip Sipser; "Agreement made this 10th day of February, 1965 . . ." and "Stipulation and agreement . . ." in possession of Philip Sipser (copies in author's possession).

28. Moreno, 84–106; Winston Charles McDowell, "The Ideology Of Black Entrepreneurship and Its Impact on the Development of Black Harlem, 1930–1955," Ph.D. diss., University of Minnesota, 1996, 118, 195.

29. *Amsterdam News*, October 15, 1949; Gloster Current to Roy Wilkins, October 28, 1949, NAACP Papers, II, C, 126.

30. Moreno, 127–128.

31. Anna Arnold Hedgeman, *The Trumpet Sounds: A Memoir of Negro Leadership* (New York: Holt, Rinehart and Winston, 1964), 108.

32. *Amsterdam News,* December 16, 1950; Carlos Cooks, "Strange, Isn't It?" in Robert Harris, ed., *Garveyism and Marxism* (Harlem, N.Y.: United Brothers Communications Systems, 1978), 19.

33. Carlos Cooks, "Hair Conking: Buy Black," in Robert Harris, Nyota Harris, and Grandassa Harris, eds., *Carlos Cooks and Black Nationalism from Garvey to Malcolm* (Dover, Mass.: Majority Press, 1992), 68–69.

34. *Amsterdam News,* July 14 and July 28, 1951.

35. Ibid., July 21 and July 28, 1951.

36. Ibid., August 4 and August 11, 1951.

37. Ernest Thompson's daughter wrote a thesis on the NNLC while she was a student of Herbert Aptheker's at Bryn Mawr. See Mindy Thompson, *The National Negro Labor Council: A History,* Occasional Paper no. 27 (New York: American Institute for Marxist Studies, 1978), Guinier quoted on p. 8. The NNLC published a beautifully illustrated pamphlet on the history of Black railroad labor, *Let Freedom Ride the Rails*—see Robeson Collection, reel 8; Coleman Young and Lonnie Wheeler, *Hard Stuff: The Autobiography of Coleman Young* (New York: Viking, 1994), 113.

38. Ewart Guinier, "Cooperation Not Permission," December 1951, Guinier Papers, box 17; Address by William R. Hood, October 27, 1951, in "National Negro Labor Council," vertical file, Tamiment Library, New York University, New York; *New York Times,* October 29, 1951.

39. Negro Labor News Service, Release, November 12, 1951, Negro Labor Committee Papers, reel 4; *New York Times,* November 12, 1951.

40. Minutes of the United Public Workers, International Executive Board meeting, February 15–16, 1952, Guinier Papers, box 6; Ewart Guinier, "A New Wind Is Blowing" (speech), January 29, 1952, Guinier Papers, box 6; Herman D. Bloch, *The Circle of Discrimination: A Study of the Black Man in New York* (New York: New York University Press, 1969), 72–73; "G.E. Spearheads Operation Dixie," Robeson Collection, reel 8.

41. Claudia Jones, "Negro Women in the Fight for Peace and Freedom," in Negro History Week booklet, 1952, "CPUSA and Negroes" vertical file, Tamiment Library.

42. Minutes of the Jobs Action Conference, March 8, 1952, Guinier Papers, box 6, GNYNLC folder; Thompson, 30–40.

43. "Resolution on Job Opportunities for Negro Women," NNLC Third Annual Convention, Chicago, December 4, 1953, Robeson Collection, reel 7; Victoria Garvin, speech at the NNLC Reunion, Detroit, June 4, 1993, Garvin Papers, box 1; Garvin, "Some Pertinent Facts on the Economic Status of Negro Women in the U.S.," n.d. (early 1950s), Garvin Papers, box 1.

44. Elaine Perry interview, March 26, 1979, *Oral History of the American Left,* Tamiment Library.

45. "Communism: A Menace to the American Negro," Chicago: University Research Corp., n.a., n.d., Guinier Papers, box 6.
46. John Howard Seabrook, "Black and White Unite: The Career of Frank R. Crosswaith," Ph.D. diss., Rutgers University, 1980, 270; Negro Labor Committee USA, "A Program to Obtain Democracy for All," March 2, 1952, Negro Labor Committee Papers, reel 3; *Amsterdam News,* June 9, 1951, and February 21, 1953; *Daily Worker,* September 30, 1953; *Amsterdam News,* March 1 and March 8, 1952.
47. Young and Wheeler, 121, 142; NNLC, "Brownell Adds to Our Country's Shame," Garvin Papers, box 1.
48. The NAACP and AJC, *Balance Sheet of Group Relations,* 1950, Mayor's Committee on Unity Papers, box 1613; Moreno, 128.
49. *Amsterdam News,* May 15, 1954; Jay Anders Higbee, *Development and Administration of the New York State Law against Discrimination* (University: University of Alabama Press, 1966), 126.
50. Higbee, 165; *CLSA Reports,* April 6, 1953, Mayor's Committee on Unity Papers, box 1614; Berger, 178; *New York Times,* May 8, 1959; Berger, 187.
51. William H. Harris, *The Harder We Run: Black Workers since the Civil War* (New York: Oxford University Press, 1982), 131; Bloch, 75–76, 72–73; Hope R. Stevens, "Aspects of the Economic Structure of the Harlem Community" (1963), in *Harlem USA,* ed. John Henrik Clarke (Brooklyn: A&B Books, 1971), 183–202.
52. Moreno, 156.

Epilogue

1. Gerald Horne, *Black Liberation/Red Scare: Ben Davis and the Communist Party* (Newark: University of Delaware Press, 1994), 258; "Hunter Acts Wisely," *Manhattan East,* November 11, 1961, "Civil Rights-NY" clipping file, Schomburg Center for Research in Black Culture, New York.
2. David Levering Lewis, "Paul Robeson and the USSR," in Jeffrey C. Stewart, ed., *Paul Robeson: Artist and Citizen* (New Brunswick, N.J.: Rutgers University Press, 1998); David Levering Lewis, *W. E. B. Du Bois: The Struggle for Racial Equality and the American Century* (New York: Henry Holt, 2000); Gerald Horne, *Race Woman: The Lives of Shirley Graham Du Bois* (New York: New York University Press, 2000).
3. Lewis, "Paul Robeson and the USSR," 228.
4. Audre Lorde, *Zami: A New Spelling of My Name* (Freedom, Calif.: Crossing Press, 1982), 172.
5. *New York Times,* August 12, 1963.
6. Ibid., February 7, 1990, and June 25, 1982 (obituaries); *Amsterdam News,* July 17 and July 3, 1982.
7. Victoria Garvin, speech, February 14, 1996, University of the District of Columbia, reprinted in "Celebrating Women's History Month with Vicki Garvin," Garvin Papers, box 1.

8. "The Reminiscences of Algernon Black," 226, Columbia Oral History Project, Columbia University, New York; for Black's account of the CCRB, see Algernon Black, *The People and the Police* (New York: McGraw Hill, 1968).

9. Griffin Fariello, *Red Scare: Memories of the American Inquisition* (New York: Avon Books, 1995), 489–492.

10. See Clarence Taylor, *Knocking at Our Own Door: Milton A. Galamison and the Struggle to Integrate New York City's Schools* (New York: Columbia University Press, 1997).

11. Kenneth B. Clark, "Racial Progress and Retreat: A Personal Memoir," in Herbert Hill and James E. Jones, eds., *Race in America: The Struggle for Equality* (Madison: University of Wisconsin Press, 1993), 18.

12. Timothy Tyson, *Radio Free Dixie: Robert F. Williams and the Roots of Black Power* (Chapel Hill: University of North Carolina Press, 2000); Joanne Grant, *Ella Baker: Freedom Bound* (New York: Wiley, 1998); *New York Times,* February 10, 1998 (obituary).

13. See Charles V. Hamilton and Dona Hamilton, *The Dual Agenda: The African American Struggle for Civil and Economic Equality* (New York: Columbia University Press, 1997).

14. Schomburg Center for Research in Black Culture, *The Black New Yorkers: 400 Years of African American History* (New York: Wiley & Sons, 2000), 292; St. Clair Drake, "Hide My Face? On Pan-Africanism and Negritude," in Herbert Hill, ed., *Soon One Morning: New Writing by American Negroes, 1940–1962* (New York: Alfred Knopf, 1963), 102; Ora Mobley-Sweeting with Ezekial C. Mobley Jr., "Nobody Gave Me Permission: Memoirs of a Harlem Activist," (ca. 1996) unpublished manuscript, Schomburg Center.

15. Audley Moore interview, *Oral History of the American Left,* December 23, 1981, Tamiment Library, New York University; Charles Ogletree, Speech to the National Reparations Convention, Chicago, March 24, 2002.

16. Paula Pfeffer, *A. Philip Randolph: Pioneer of the Civil Rights Movement* (Baton Rouge: Louisiana State University Press, 1990).

17. Herbert Hill, "The ILGWU Today—The Decay of a Labor Union," August 18, 1962, pamphlet, Northwestern University Library, Special Collections; Herbert Hill, "Black Workers, Organized Labor, and Title VII," in Herbert Hill and James E. Jones, eds., *Race in America: The Struggle for Equality* (Madison: University of Wisconsin Press, 1993), 291–301.

18. *New York Times,* November 6, 1978, September 11, 1980, and December 14, 1984.

19. Negro Heritage Library, *Profiles of Negro Womanhood,* vol. 2 (New York: Educational Heritage, 1966), 281–286.

20. Shirley Chisholm, *Unbought and Unbossed* (Boston: Houghton Mifflin, 1970).

Acknowledgments

I have benefited enormously from many teachers, colleagues, archivists, students, friends, and family in the years that I spent researching and writing this book. In college my friend Elpidio Villarreal convinced me to major in U.S. history rather than "third world studies" (which actually did not exist as a major), and made me promise to take anything offered by Eric Foner. So for that reason I found myself in "America in the Era of Jacksonian Democracy," and embarked on an undergraduate and graduate study of African American history. I was part of a cohort of graduate students who came to Columbia to train with Eric, and he inspired us to aspire to the highest standards of both scholarship and citizenship. I am extremely grateful for his brilliant teaching, generous and incisive comments on many stages of this work, unfailing support, and all-around expert advice. I also want to thank Elizabeth Blackmar, Alan Brinkley, Joshua Freeman, Ira Katznelson, and Daryl Scott, whose insightful criticisms and advice sharpened my thinking and strengthened this book. As a historian of working-class New York, Josh offered invaluable feedback. I was also fortunate to be surrounded by brilliant graduate students who read and critiqued my work. I want to thank, in particular, Cyrus Veeser, for his generosity, sense of humor, and steadfast solidarity. And I couldn't have made it out of the 1940s without Penny Von Eschen. Her support and advice encouraged me down the long road from dissertation to manuscript.

Gerald Horne's scholarship sparked my interest in many of the issues in this book. His wise counsel, encouragement, and penetrating insights were invaluable.

Research for this book was funded by the Ford Foundation through the Schomburg Center for Research in Black Culture's Scholars-in-Residence Program. At the Schomburg, I was immersed in a like-minded scholarly community that aided this project immensely. Colin Palmer offered generous and insightful feedback, and his dining-room salons in Yonkers sparked stimulating intellectual and political exchange. Kathryne Lindberg, Lydia Lindsay, Ivor Miller, and Shawn Michelle Smith gave my work close readings and offered very insightful suggestions. Thanks especially to Kathryne and Lydia for pushing my thinking in many areas. At public presentations at the Schomburg, I also benefited enormously from comments and conversations with many New Yorkers. Winston James and Robin D. G. Kelley read portions of the manuscript and gave very helpful advice. Robin later read it all and his support helped make the publication possible. Many, many thanks to Howard Dodson, Diana Lachatanere, Mary F. Yearwood, James B. Murray, Andre Elizee, Steven Fullwood, Michael Roudette, Troy Belle, Alison Quammie, Paula Williams, Aisha Al-Adawiya, Betty Odabashian, and Lela Sewell-Williams at the Schomburg, who helped me gain access to the materials I needed to complete this project. Thanks to Sharon Howard for her friendship and support, and to Bill Rhoden who was so encouraging. Thanks also to Peter for his sense of humor and peerless research skills.

I have gained many insights from other scholars of New York African American history, especially Clarence Taylor and Wendell Pritchett. Thanks to Robert Self, a scholar of postwar California, for helpful advice and support. I am extremely grateful to Lani Guinier for her generosity and warmth in sharing stories and memories of her father. Thanks to Thomas Borstelmann, whose comments forced me to sharpen my approach to the Cold War, and to Patricia Sullivan for generous and helpful comments. Chicago is where I finished this book, and I want to thank my wonderful friends and colleagues in African American Studies at Northwestern—Sandra Richards, Mary Pattillo and Michael Hanchard. Thanks to members of the history department for helpful comments, especially Nancy MacLean, and the students in my graduate history seminar, who offered very helpful suggestions—Ebony Utley, Deborah Cane, and especially Erik Gellman, who also did a masterful job of proofreading. And thank you to Tommie Shelby for broadening my understanding of Black nationalism.

I am grateful to Barbara Ransby for her efforts at fostering a sense of community for progressive folks in Chicago. The use of Lynette Jackson's Barnard office one summer was a lifesaver. I treasure her friendship, impassioned political judgments, and deep solidarity. In graduate school a stream of Columbia to Yale folks kept telling me I "had to meet Adam Green," a graduate student at Yale working on postwar Black Chicago. Now a friend and colleague, Adam's deep appreciation for history's connection to the present has moved and motivated me. Thanks to Bennett Johnson for his insights and great stories, and to the students in the Northwestern Reparations Committee.

Thanks to everyone at Harvard University Press who aided in the publication of this book, especially David Lobenstine and my editor, Joyce Seltzer. I am extremely grateful for the attention and support that Joyce gave this project; her advice and comments strengthened the book enormously. And thanks to Julie Carlson, the manuscript editor, who did an outstanding job. I am very grateful for the care that she gave to the book. Many thanks as well to everyone who worked on the book's production and publicity, especially Mary Ellen Geer and Rose Ann Miller. Finally, I am indebted to Richard Iton, whose generous assistance helped get me through the final stage of proofreading.

Thanks to Bernardo Masoko for all his support, and to Josefina Tavares, whose friendship and generosity helped get me through a difficult stage. Bill Toles's encouragement, advice, and ready ear meant a lot. His frequent "When's the book coming out?" kept the fire under me. Dean Bowman's voice was the soundtrack during my final revisions. Thank you, Dean. Thanks to Bruni Burres for being part of my 106th Street family. Thanks to Annie Costanzo, whose love, support, and political and intellectual influence were crucial to this project. My biggest thanks go to Elaine Charnov, who defines the meaning of friendship. Her unfailing support and devotion have rescued and sustained me more times than I can say, and her loyalty, integrity, and faith have been deeply inspiring.

Finally, I want to thank my parents, Ann M. Matteis and James G. Biondi, for their faith in me, love, encouragement, and support through the long years of this project. For their love and support as well, thanks to Richard, Jane, Paul, Sarah, Jed, Brien, Amy, Vanessa, Vicky, Sue, Molly, Zach, Jack, Grace, and Sam; and to Verstella and James A. Biondi.

Illustration Credits

Index

Abrams, Charles, 116, 123, 124–125, 129, 232, 233, 240, 269
Abtey, Jacques, 189
Abyssinian Baptist Church, 57
Acheson, Dean, 161, 181
Addisleigh Park, 120
Addison, Chester, 50
Affirmative action, 22, 24, 105–111, 135, 229, 259, 260, 261, 268, 270, 273, 277
AFL: and Collins, 49; and National Emergency Committee against Mob Violence, 68; and CIO, 152; and National Emergency FEPC Mobilization, 166; and quota systems, 260; and National Negro Labor Council, 264; and segregation, 267; and affirmative action, 270. *See also* Labor movement
AFL-CIO, 282
AFL Trade Unions Council, 31
Africa, 164, 181, 184, 276, 280
African Blood Brotherhood, 4
African diaspora, 57–58
African Nationalist Pioneer Movement, 261
Alan, Robert: "Paul Robeson: The Lost Shepherd," 158
Alexander, Edith, 91
Alexander, Fritz W., 124

Allen, James Egert, 63, 68, 80
All Harlem Legislative Conference, 42
American Airlines, 87
American Civil Liberties Union, 63, 124, 159, 268
American Council on Race Relations, 12, 67
American Crusade to End Lynching, 68
American Federation of Musicians, 94
American Jewish Committee, 239
American Jewish Congress: and NAACP, 15; Committee on Law and Social Action, 15, 106, 107, 109, 124, 234; and civil rights, 16; and work, 18; and Ferguson incident, 63; and National Emergency Committee against Mob Violence, 68; and travel, 87; and Ives-Quinn law, 105; and education, 107, 244; and housing, 117, 118, 124, 131, 133, 231, 232, 233, 236, 239; and anticommunism, 170–171; and Cold War, 184–185; and Quinn, 244; and law enforcement, 268, 269. *See also* Jews
American Labor Party (ALP): and employment, 30; creation of, 38; and Rivers, 40; and Collins, 48; and Black candidates, 50, 52; and Jackson, 51; and Wilson-Pakula Law, 52; and Democratic Party,

341